*There's Only One United*

# *There's Only One United*

## The Official Centenary History of Manchester United

by

Geoffrey Green

HODDER AND STOUGHTON

LONDON SYDNEY AUCKLAND TORONTO

British Library Cataloguing in Publication Data

Green, Geoffrey
There's only one United.
1. Manchester United Football Club – History
I. Title
796.33'463'0942733 GV943.6.M3

ISBN 0-340-22895-4

 *First printed 1978. Third impression 1978.*  *Photoset and printed in Great Britain for Hodder and Stoughton Limited, Mill Lane, Dunton Green, Sevenoaks, Kent, by Lowe & Brydone Printers Limited, Thetford, Norfolk.*
*Hodder and Stoughton Editorial Office: 47 Bedford Square, London, WC1E 3DP.*

# *Acknowledgments*

The author would like to acknowledge the following newspapers for the use of their material: *The Guardian, Manchester Evening News, The Times, The Sunday Telegraph, The Sunday Express, The Daily Mail*; and also Peter Corrigan, *The Observer* and Welsh Brewers Ltd. for *100 Years of Welsh Soccer* (1976); Maurice Golesworthy and Pelham Books for *We are the Champions* (1972); the Naldrett Press for his own *Official History of the F.A. Cup* (1949, revised); Arthur Hopcraft and William Collins for *The Football Man* (1967); David Meek and Stanley Paul for the *Manchester United Annuals,* (1960 etc.); David Miller and Stanley Paul for *Father of Football – Matt Busby* 1970; Frank Taylor and William Heinemann for *The Day a Team Died* (1960); and Dr. Percy Young and William Heinemann for *Manchester United* (1960).

The author is also grateful to Tony Pullein and the Manchester United administration staff for supplying information for the appendices.

# Introduction

## by Sir Stanley Rous, C.B.E. Honorary President F.I.F.A.

I KNOW OF NO one who writes about football better able to tell the story of Manchester United – its joys and sorrows – than Geoffrey Green. He is not as old as the club, which was founded in 1878, but for thirty years has known intimately the directors, managers, secretarial staff and the players of the club.

Geoffrey Green reveals the history of the club from its early association with the railway wagon works at Newton Heath to its present prosperous and envied position in the world of football; from its near liquidation in the early years to its financial ability to pay huge transfer fees for players and to own a luxurious modern stadium.

When the Club was impoverished two men saved it from extinction, J. H. Davies and James Gibson. Their aim was to obtain players, a first priority, whose skill would bring success in League and Cup competitions and add to the growing numbers of supporters not only at Old Trafford, their home since 1910, but at away matches in other cities. Directors such as Harold Hardman, J. A. Gibson, L. C. Edwards (now Chairman) and Matt Busby followed. They were good 'pickers' of players and teams included such men whom I often met on international match duty, as John Carey, Allenby, Chilton, Jack Rowley, Henry Cockburn, Bobby Charlton and others.

Later the 'Busby Babes' continued the success in the domestic competitions and in Europe. At the height of their glory, in 1956, when the Union of European Football Associations (U.E.F.A.) had been formed and the United were invited to compete in the newly-formed Champions' Club competition they were at first frustrated because the year before, Chelsea, F.C. had been forbidden by the Football League to take part. I well remember Mr. Hardman and Matt Busby coming to see me, as at that time I was the Secretary of the Football AssocitION and a member of U.E.F.A. We found that an English League club could not be prevented legally from taking part in a European competition.

Geoffrey Green has written in his most sympathetic manner the sad story of the Munich disaster, when tragedy struck the club a cruel blow. Players like Duncan Edwards, who would surely have been Captain of England for many years, and seven others lost their lives. They seemed irreplaceable, but the courage of those who survived inspired the officials and supporters of the club to restore its prestige, when their immediate grief was lessened by the healing hand of time.

The years when Matt Busby returned to the club from his long convalescence are especially exciting, and tell of winning the F.A. Cup and other trophies at regular intervals.

This book has been written by the author in his inimitable style, to record the history of a hundred years of the Manchester United F.C. It reveals in detail its growth from obscurity to its present eminence by describing the men who made it into one of the foremost clubs in this country. Long may its torch shine brightly. Long may those connected with it maintain their pride in it and do everything to preserve its reputation.

I hope that whatever the club does, it will do well, and find enjoyment doing it.

*April 1978* Stanley Rous

# *Preface*

# Manchester United Centenary

Like Proteus, easily avoiding his would-be captors, a book is apt to change shape in the very process of being written. This is probably true of the present volume. It started under the pretentious guise of being a history of a hundred years of a famous football club. But since a club – and indeed football itself – is all about people, and because so many books, as profuse as daisies in a field, already abound about the modern characters who helped to make Manchester United a byword in the land, this present effort is perhaps more of a mixture of an anthology, a scrapbook, and a miscellany than anything else. It is as such that it now appears.

The stages in its development are perhaps instructive. One morning the telephone rang at home. It was February 1977. The voice belonged to Sir Matt Busby, the creator of modern United's fame, saying that the Board of Directors would like me to write of their club's Centenary, to be celebrated in 1978: was I interested?

The reaction was immediate. It would be a privilege, an honour and a labour of love.

But once, having put down the receiver, my heart sank. The responsibility of it, the research involved at a distance, the feeling that, after all, there were others more closely involved with the club and nearer the scene of action – to say nothing of the amount of midnight oil to be burned – all suddenly weighed down on me. As near as a touch I almost rang back to say I felt unable and unqualified to undertake the duty. Then I recalled what Sir Matt himself had said to me once when I asked him what he felt he had contributed to football and to the growth of Manchester United. 'The time to judge me is when I am at the bottom,' he replied. 'At least I have never run away from a challenge . . .'

Then, too, I remembered how fate had withheld me from the tragic aeroplane crash at Munich in 1958 when the manager of *The Times,* almost at the eleventh hour, had ordered me to cancel my air tickets to Belgrade and go instead to report a World Cup qualifying match at Cardiff between Wales and Israel. Life indeed, is largely a matter of luck and timing and but for that strange throw of the dice I should now probably be roaming the Elysian Fields with the many friends I lost that day. It was almost as a duty to them that my hand was suddenly stayed and my telephone remained silent.

History tends to repeat itself and historians (such as they are) to repeat each other. The danger here, of course, is for errors in the matter of fact to be perpetuated until the truth emerges finally. But then, as a university professor once remarked, 'There is *your* truth, there is *my* truth and there is *the* truth.' Where indeed does it lie?

In the main, however, facts are incontrovertible and as such are sacred, as C. P. Scott, famous editor of the *Manchester Guardian,* once remarked. They have their uses, too. Like a lamp-post, they can either illuminate the way or provide support for the late-night reveller.

If I happen to pop up here and there in the story – much perhaps to the annoyance of some – this seems unavoidable. My connections with United over the past thirty years have been close. I am one of those supposedly neutral journalists whose heart has always beaten faster for them than anyone else.

Having decided to face the challenge, I set forth to spend some time in Manchester to start my excavation of the past, staying in mid-July last year with my old friend Dickie Highland-Longdon, for many years Chairman of the Northern Nomads Football Club, winners of the F.A. Amateur Cup in the early 1900s.

Life, as I have indicated, is largely luck and timing and as it happened the eyes of the country were largely fixed on Manchester that July. I was in the right place at the right time. To begin with, England beat Australia by nine wickets in the second Test Match at Old Trafford cricket ground. That was something to cheer for a change.

On the dark side of the coin, however, there came the dramatic dismissal by Manchester United of their controversial manager Tommy Docherty, for reasons of personal misbehaviour, a mere two months after he had taken United to Wembley to win the F.A. Cup against Liverpool, the League and European champions. At his departure, United speedily settled upon a replacement in Dave Sexton, who had only a short time previously resigned from Queens Park Rangers and had almost thrown in his lot with Arsenal as coach. Such is the way fate deals the cards as I found myself near the eye of the storm.

Yet it was the distant past, lying buried in the lava of time, that really concerned me. Since all Manchester United's early records of their development in the nineteenth century – from their formation in 1878 – had been destroyed by a German air-raid which reduced the Old Trafford ground to virtual rubble early in the Second World War, the whole truth of those romantic beginnings represented peering into a cracked mirror in a darkened room.

But with much kind help from various quarters – not least from Leslie Olive, the United secretary – the surviving minute books dating back to 1903 were put at my entire disposal and each interesting fact was clutched like a hot water bottle on a cold winter's night.

Thus United's past has unfolded jerkily to avalanche into the present. The day of settlement has arrived and I can only hope that it is somewhere close to truth and reality.

One afternoon near the end of that Manchester visit I wandered into the summer sunshine of Old Trafford to sit alone on the concrete terraces. In a few weeks' time a new season was due to begin. All around me that vast stadium, its row upon row of red seats gleaming in the sunlight, resembled a handsome tabernacle, a powerful magnetic place of worship for crowds 50 and 60,000 strong. Feathery plumes of water, activated by concealed undersoil jets, sprayed the green pitch in preparation for the future.

It was silent and peaceful as the mighty ground stood empty and expectant, like an operating theatre awaiting the coming operation. Soon enough it would be filled with a roaring multitude as the warm juice of emotion poured over it for each approaching new challenge.

I sat there silent in a kind of wonder at this towering oak tree, trying to imagine the tiny acorn from which it grew a hundred years ago and from time to time recalling some of the great players who had dazzled my younger eyes over the departed three decades of magic and sorrow – players like Di Stefano, Puskas, Gento and Kopa of Real Madrid; Stanley Matthews, Tom Finney, Jimmy Greaves, Danny Blanchflower, John Charles; and not least, United's own great cavalcade of Johnny Carey, Duncan Edwards, Eddie Colman, Dennis Viollet, Tommy Taylor, Roger Byrne, Bobby Charlton, Denis Law, George Best, Pat Crerand and the rest.

It was moving to think that all this had grown from the humble beginnings of a century ago when the Dining Room Committee of the Carriage & Wagon Works of the Lancashire & Yorkshire Railway (L.Y.R.) first formed their football team under the name of Newton Heath (L.Y.R.), playing their matches on a muddy patch of a ground at North Road, Newton Heath. The mind boggled at the thought.

But time itself, though open ended, must have a beginning somewhere. In terms of football, at least, the late Professor H. A. Giles, of Cambridge University, found evidence of its seeds in China, allotting the game to the third and fourth centuries B.C. From the medieval Florentine game of calcio, which is still played in the Piazza Della Signoria, in Florence, on the first Sunday in May and on June 24, the feast of St. John the Baptist, we can follow the thread through the sixteenth-century Shrove Tuesday mob football, played in Derby between the young men of the parishes of All Saints and St. Peter's, up to the first signs of an organised game in the mid-1800s. It was then that many now famous football clubs emerged from Sunday Schools in an age of muscular Christianity, when teachers went through the land with a Bible in one hand and a football in the other.

Such are some of the antecedents of games which in this mid-twentieth century have become clothed in a dark violence. Yet with the present has come another trend – the marriage of music with certain sports.

Certainly it has long been a duty of the local priest to mark in song, calypso fashion, the advancing score of a Basque pelota match; bullfighters, who light candles in the little chapel of every *plaza de toros* before entering the ring, weave their passionate craft in the sun to the background of a harsh fanfare of trumpets. Welsh Rugby, backed by a stirring choir of 60,000 at Cardiff Arms Park, has for long had its traditional 'Cwm Rhondda' and 'Land of my fathers'.

But other sports – perhaps by the very nature of their character – have lagged behind in this field. Not until the early 1950s did cricket in these islands hear even a blue note. It came with the sudden invasion of jubilant West Indians with their lively calypsos (those dear old friends of mine Ramadhin and Valentine) who raised shocked eyebrows and caused a flutter in the Long Room during a Test Match at Lord's.

We have also yet to hear 'Put my money on a bobtailed nag' chanted at Epsom or Ascot. We await too, the 'Swing, swing, together' of the Eton Boating Song raised along the towpath from Putney to Mortlake during the Boat Race. Nor has the chorus of Arnie's Army yet bellowed 'The wearing o' the green' as Palmer putts the last hole with Watson, Nicklaus and Player. One day, however, all this may come.

Meanwhile modern soccer has got with the pop scene. Before the war there was little or no singing from the terraces. Newcastle may have had its 'Blaydon Races', Portsmouth 'The Pompey Chimes', sung to the notes of Big Ben, and West Ham United their 'I'm forever blowing bubbles', a relic of the popular tune of the early 1920s when the club helped to christen Wembley's first Cup Final.

North of the border, too, one half of Glasgow has long chanted 'Follow, follow, we will follow Rangers'; the other (Celtic) half, 'Sure it's a grand old team to play for, it's a grand old team to know'. And when I took an American to the Cup Final, where organised community singing was born, he remarked astonished, 'Why do you English always mix religion with sport?' as the last strains of King George V's favourite hymn 'Abide with me' died away.

All this, however, is pleasantly old-hat compared for instance with the hot feeling, the reverence and the wit heard in the voice of the great swaying choir on the Liverpool Kop. They live at Anfield. They do not merely exist or 'Walk alone' there.

This rich contemporary vocal response from the crowd has coincided with a folksong revival, so I am told by a correspondent, Mr Stanley Kelly, who produced a long-playing record of the Kop sound, at present shyly entitled 'O Liverpool We Love You' from the eponymous song.

When Scouse, the Liverpool vernacular, says, 'Ah, dat was when Jesus wuz playing full back fer Israel', it means that it happened a long time ago. Yet it is all happening now and it will continue to happen so long as the Old Trafford Stretford End chants, 'We are the Champions' and 'There's only ONE United . . .'

Indeed, it did all happen a long time ago. But what manner of men were they, are they, who fashioned the shape and policy of Manchester United over these one hundred years? What were the problems they had to face, and still do face? To gain a balanced impression of their contributions, both the ancient and modern elements have to be taken into account, for sometimes in achieving a picture of past events new features are seized upon and the overlap of the past is ignored.

The appeal of history is imaginative. The impulse is to feel the reality of life in the past, to be familiar with 'the chronicle of wasted time' and to hear lost voices and see lost looks as the photographs of yesterday stare down at us unwavering.

As G. M. Trevelyan wrote in his *English Social History*: 'Consider all that lies in that one word *past*! What a pathetic, sacred, in every sense poetic, meaning is implied in it . . . History after all is the true poetry. And reality, if rightly interpreted, is grander than fiction.'

Meanwhile, whether or not my interpretation is anywhere near the mark, I am indebted to a great many people for assisting me in this task in a number of ways, too various to mention. Though it may be invidious to name only some of them, I would like to thank the following in particular: Leslie Olive for his willingness to put the resources of Manchester United at my disposal on all occasions; Dave Smith, chairman of the Manchester United Supporters' Club, for a wealth of detailed information; David Meek and Owen French of the *Manchester Evening News* for much valued annuals and research into his newspaper's archives; Dr. Percy Young for his earlier history of Manchester United (Heinemann, 1960); David Miller with his *Father of Football. The Story of Sir Matt Busby* (Stanley Paul, 1970); Frank Taylor's *The Day a Team Died* (Stanley Paul, 1960); and Sir Matt Busby, Jimmy Murphy, Johnny Carey, Bobby Charlton, Pat Crerand and Denis Law (who also made me innumerable cups of coffee!) for sparing their precious time to talk to me on a tape-recorder and so bring a human element to the story.

I would like, also, to express my appreciation of the support I have had from the Manchester United Board of Directors. It was their idea that this book should be written and having asked me to undertake it, they gave me complete backing and freedom of action. If the outcome falls short of their expectations the fault is mine, not theirs.

In approaching this wide subject I have tried, rightly or wrongly, to tell the story virtually back to front. In those terms the first half covers the period from the start of the Second World War to the present; the later half runs from United's stumbling beginnings until World War II.

I have done this because United's universal fame has been established primarily with the younger generation over the past thirty years: the early growing pains belong to the grey beards and to our fathers and grandfathers. In other words, I have put the chicken before the egg.

In those hundred years life has changed dramatically. What began in the age of the penny postage stamp, and the invention of the telephone and the steam engine is now the age of jet air travel, colour television, the computer and conquest of the moon. We are dealing with two quite separate worlds of contrasting values and widely different tempos of existence.

Ten years ago, Arthur Hopcraft, then a correspondent of *The Observer,* wrote as an introduction to his book *The Football Man* (Collins):

No player, manager, director or fan who understands football, either through his intellect or his nerve ends, ever repeats that piece of nonsense, 'After all, it's only a game'. It has not been only a game for eighty years: not since the working classes saw in it an escape route out of drudgery and claimed it as their own. What happens on the football field matters, not in the way that food matters but as poetry does to some people and alcohol to others; it engages the personality. It has conflict and beauty, and when these two qualities are present together in something offered for public appraisal they represent much of what I understand to be art.

This is what I have attempted to capture.

*Geoffrey Green*

LONDON, DECEMBER 1977

# Contents

# *Illustrations*

ACKNOWLEDGMENTS
1 Manchester Evening News
2 Keystone Press Agency
3 *Sunday Express* (Manchester)
4 BEA
5 *Times Newspapers Limited*

# *Part One*

# 1

# *1940–1948:*

# *The Sleeping Giant Stirs*

BEFORE THE SECOND World War Manchester United were just another provincial club with a minimal national following, and no major success to boost their name since the accession to the throne of King George V in 1911.

Throughout the 1930s theirs was a parochial existence eked out in an era of mass unemployment, trouble in the coal mines, Jarrow marchers, trade recession on a world scale, the Wall Street crash, the Spanish Civil War and a world blithely closing its eyes to the gathering forces of Fascism and Communism as the thunder clouds of an approaching conflict mounted on the far horizon. It was a lost decade where a few warning voices were ignored.

During those ten years the club had bobbed like a cork on the troubled football waters of relegation and promotion and financial hardship. While Arsenal had dominated the 1930s under the astute leadership of Herbert Chapman, United had finished bottom of the League Championship in 1931; spent five years in the Second Division before promotion in 1936; were relegated again immediately after only one year; then returned to the First Division at once for season 1938-39 when they ended in fourteenth place before the lights went out in Europe for six years of war and hardship.

In that restless, uncertain period of eight years, in fact, they were relegated twice and promoted twice, as if uncertain of their rightful place in the world. They swung back and forth like a lace curtain caught in the wind before an open window.

Only those living in Lancashire and the environs of Manchester itself knew or cared much about United at that time. They were the poor relations living in the shadow of their neighbours Manchester City just across the way at Moss Side, a thriving club who had captured the F.A. Cup in 1934 (after losing the final only twelve months earlier) and then won the league title in 1937. They played some fine attacking football under the creative influence of a certain

Scotsman, Matt Busby, for whom destiny, had he but known it, was keeping a special place just down the road. City, indeed, in their delicate sky-blue shirts, were high in the heavens at that time. United, decked in red, represented a lantern warning of dangerous pitfalls in the rocky road ahead.

It is at this point that we begin to gather up the first threads of the remarkable story of modern Manchester United, as they grew to be the colossus of the late 1940s, the '50s, '60s and '70s. For three decades now they have become the John Gielgud and Laurence Olivier of the English football stage while Old Trafford, their home, has itself taken on the presence and aura of a Drury Lane or Covent Garden as a theatre where only the highest quality of entertainment is to be served up and savoured.

There are many paths to Parnassus and few are lucky enough to find their way to the top. By some strange, ironic twist, however, it was the action of the enemy that in a sense put United's feet on the road which had eluded them for so long.

On the night of March 11, 1941, a German air-raid saw the Luftwaffe attack the industrial target of Trafford Park in Manchester. In the process, some of their heavy bombs were off-loaded on Old Trafford nearby, reducing the main stand to a burnt-out shell, turning some of the terraces into rubble and leaving a deep scar in the middle of the pitch as part of their visiting card to the city.

Thus was a fine ground of an earlier vintage put out of action – once the scene of the replayed Cup Final of 1911 between Bradford City and Newcastle United; of the Khaki Cup Final of 1915 between Sheffield United and Chelsea; the setting for an England v. Scotland match on April 17, 1926, for the fiftieth official meeting of the two countries; and where in 1939 as a young reporter at the start of my journalistic career I had been part of a 76,962 crowd for an F.A. Cup Semi-Final between Wolverhampton Wanderers and Grimsby Town, an attendance that still stands as a record for Old Trafford.

Built originally in 1910 at a cost of £60,000 – a vast sum in those days when the pound was worth a pound and workers considered themselves fortunate enough to earn a sovereign a week – here was a disaster equivalent to the collapse of the temple when Samson's locks were shorn; the more so since in March 1940, the club itself was weighed down by a debt of some £75,000 in terms of a mortgage, overdraft, and sundry creditors.

It was at that point that the reigning chairman, Mr. James Gibson, again advanced further funds from his own pocket, free of interest, against any expenditure beyond the overdraft limit, thereby underlining the inescapable fact that but for his generous patronage at various crises, United might well have departed into limbo.

The 1930s, in fact, had seen the club constantly under threat of being engulfed by money troubles. There was talk of closing down in one of the darkest periods of United's life. At that point the future looked grim until Gibson, the philanthropist and lifelong friend of the club, stepped in to assume financial control and pilot the ship through its troubled waters.

James Gibson, indeed, is worthy of a memorial as one of United's saviours in their long fighting history of ups and downs, a fact perhaps not fully appreciated by some of the heirs of the heritage, as that generous man now looks down upon the present from his gilt-framed portrait within the club's offices.

That damage to Old Trafford was a grievous blow and the record of the fact in the minutes of a board meeting held on August 21, 1941, stands as a typical example of British understatement:

> It was reported that consequent upon enemy action on the night of 11/12 March last, the grandstand and buildings had been extensively damaged and that arrangments had been made with the Stretford Corporation to salvage the damaged steel from the site and carry out demolishing operations as required: that form V.O.W.I. had been duly filed in respect of this and of previous damage incurred on December 22 1940 and same had been duly acknowledged.

Thus in simple matter-of-fact language the previous thirty years were swept away and the path cleared for a new future. Little did those Luftwaffe pilots know what they had set in motion!

Claims for war damage to property took many a tedious and tortuous turn in those times. Claims had to be filed, forms filled in and all the while correspondence back and forth between the relevant official departments piled up. Like the mills of God, the bureaucratic machine ground slow and exceeding small.

Fortunately Gibson and his Manchester colleagues had a friend at court in the person of Mr. Ellis Smith, Member of Parliament for Stoke-on-Trent, living in Eccles, who had been a United supporter since his earliest days. He took up the cudgels on behalf of the club in the struggle for government help in their plight.

Some ten years later, following the death of James Gibson, his widow wrote to Ellis Smith concerning the restoration of the ground: 'It will,' she said, 'be a great day when the Manchester United ground is covered everywhere. It was a very great wish and ambition of my late husband to have this done and I am sure it would have given him great pleasure for it to have been carried out in his lifetime. But, of course, that wretched war altered so many things, but there is no doubt it will come to pass as all things . . .'

A realist with a philosophical slant on life, she has been proved right. In the fulness of time Old Trafford has come to be roofed in on all sides with shelter for all, though perhaps the sight of tall iron spiked railings around the extremities of the playing area would not be so pleasing to those of a gentler age. But that is another story.

Meanwhile the struggle for indemnity proceeded on its tedious way. On November 17, 1944, the War Damage Commission wrote to the directors that 'the Old Trafford property is not considered as a total loss'. However, on August 21, 1945, a licence for £4,800 was granted for the demolition of the grandstand after consultation with the engineering firm responsible. Though no reconstruction work could be started in the meantime, the next painful step forward came on November 10, 1947, when Mr. Ellis Smith demanded of the Minister of Works in the House how many damaged First Division grounds had been refurbished.

Following considerable pressure from the floor of Parliament, it was revealed that ten clubs had been granted licences of repairs. As a result Manchester United were permitted to spend £17,478, a sum considerably in advance of the next highest figure of £5,000 given to Goodison Park, Everton. Even so, a deputation from Manchester United – never ones to do things by halves or to be side-tracked by officialdom – on December 9, 1947, presented their case for greater generosity to Mr. Charles Key himself, then the Minister of Works.

The following day Walter Crickmer, Manchester United's long-serving secretary, wrote to Ellis Smith: 'I gave the directors a report on your activities on our behalf and while, as can be expected, they were disappointed that no more could be done I think they were very satisfied with the splendid efforts you had made. We are now going into the matter very thoroughly to see what steps we can take to carry out our object of re-opening the ground at the earliest opportunity.'

Page 140 of Percy Young's definitive book, *Manchester United* (Heinemann, 1960), continues the story:

> In January 1948, Ellis Smith approached the Minister of Works to ask if stands 'of a light alloy similar to that used for the roof of the cinema at Rye' could not be erected at Old Trafford. They could not. On 11 February, the persistent Member took up a point from a speech delivered by the Chancellor of the Exchequer that day in which it was

said 'the government desired to encourage all forms of entertainment'. The directors of Manchester United, he said, 'would like to finish the building of the ground so that it would hold 120,000 people'. That was the long-term policy which had been in being since the move to Old Trafford was first made. For the time being, however, the club would be content if they could build a small stand of 'tubular and scrap metal' in place of that demolished in the war. On March 19 Walter Crickmer again wrote to Ellis Smith: 'While we are pleased for any small mercies received these days, I think the big song made is out of all proportion to the very trivial licence we are going to be granted, and it certainly seems to have misled everybody, who appears to have got the impression that we are coming back to Old Trafford to a completely re-instated ground, which as you know is far removed from the truth. It is no use, Ellis, I cannot see First League Football being staged here without a stand, although driven into a corner we may have to put up with anything. If so, I dread the consequences. One would have thought in our present glory our friends at Court might have arranged to stretch a point and allow us to do something really substantial if only as a compliment to this great industrial centre, whose people have certainly made a magnificent effort in the export drive.'

Throughout this period Manchester City had shown their good neighbourliness by sharing their Maine Road ground with United for League matches and F.A. Cup ties. None the less there was a price to the arrangement. A minute of June 17, 1947, gives the figure settled between the respective chairmen. For that 1947–48 season United were to pay City a sum of £5,000 in four instalments of £1,250 each, on October 1, 1947, and January 1, April 1, and June 30, 1948. It was much to City's advantage, since apart from the hire they were gaining their share of the huge gates a successful United side were now attracting to Moss Side. In the season 1948–49, for instance, to quote two particular examples, there was a crowd of 82,950 at Maine Road to see United draw 1–1 with Arsenal in a League game; and later an attendance of over 81,000 gathered for the visit of non-League Yeovil Town in the F.A. Cup.

At the end of 1948, however, Manchester City helped United obliquely in their struggle for official help to rebuild Old Trafford by serving a formal notice on their brothers and neighbours to quit Maine Road. This was the thin edge of the wedge, resulting a month later in the Ministry of Works permitting a further stage of restoration.

In spite of all the slow progress, however, United finally took the plunge by returning to their natural home in August 1949 where on the 24th of that month the curtain at last went up on the incomplete Old Trafford stage for the first time since before the war. United celebrated the occasion with a 3–0 win over Bolton Wanderers with a side which read: Crompton; Carey, Aston; Warner, Lynn, Cockburn; Delaney, Downie, Rowley, Pearson and Mitten.

It had been a wait of ten long years. But United were already hardened to difficulties and misfortune. There was a deep resilience about the whole club built up over the years. They knew that Rome was not built in a day. They were prepared to wait, work and pull together both on and off the field. There was heart and football in the very bricks and mortar of Old Trafford and in the spirit of the men who guided their fortunes. All this was to be demonstrated later in an even deeper, more cruel crisis in the decade ahead.

If the restoration of Old Trafford was an important factor in those lost years, of far greater significance was the appointment of a single man to the United staff, someone who in the passage of time proved to be a man of singular gifts, influence and integrity, capable of reshaping the whole pattern of the future.

The event was recorded at a board meeting held in Mr. Gibson's office on February 15, 1945. The minute of the proceedings reads simply enough, that the chairman had met Mr. Matt Busby who had heard of a 'post-war vacancy for a team manager at Old Trafford'. He had already received offers of a number of similar appointments elsewhere but 'would prefer the Manchester area for family reasons'. Being impressed with Busby's 'ideas and honesty of purpose', Gibson soon carried his co-directors with him in confirming the new addition, a brilliant footballer in his day and captain of Scotland in a career cut short by the war. It was agreed unanimously that Busby 'be appointed manager for a period of five years, his duties to commence a month after his demobilisation from the services'.

The die was cast. No club before – except in the case of Arsenal and Herbert Chapman – or since, ever made a wiser decision. Unforeseen at that moment, United were destined to be launched on a triumphant course that was to propel them to the top of the ladder and bring them such fame, wealth and passionate support as was not dreamed of before. Ahead lay all the great days, but, meanwhile, let Busby tell his own story of those beginnings:

'My father and three uncles were all killed in the First World War. All the men in the family were gone and at the age of sixteen, at the side of my mother, I left school. Since all her sisters had already departed to a new world across the Atlantic, it was decided that we, too, should follow suit and go to America.

'In the meantime, while waiting for our quota to come through for emigrating – such was the rush that it was taking up to nine months – I had started to work in the pits as a kid. My God! was that tough. Words can't describe it. Anyway, I was playing a bit of football then in my spare moments. A pal of mine, Frank Rogers, used to turn out for Denny Hibernians and in due course moved on to Manchester City. Then I was asked to join Denny Hibs from my local village side. That was in Stirlingshire.

'I don't think I'd appeared for them more than half a dozen times or so, when the head of Denny Hibs, a man called McNeil, told me that a certain Mr. Hodge, from Manchester City, would like to talk with me. We only met for a minute or two when the matter of coming to play in Manchester cropped up. To which I replied that it was impossible since I was going to America with my mother.

'Anyway, to cut a long story short, I did travel to Manchester and played in a Central League trial game against Burnley. Then I went home. But I suppose I must have done reasonably well because City were up to see me again the following week. After my game they took me into Willy Maley's restaurant – the Bank Restaurant; he was the old Celtic manager – and really went to work on me. The theme was to leave the pits and enjoy myself at Manchester City for a season and then go to America. The travel quota had still not come through so nothing was being lost.

'You see, I had no father to turn to, no one really to offer me advice. Anyway, silver-tongued oratory proved successful. They signed me at £5 a week in the playing season and £4 in the summer, and hardly had I done that than the chief Celtic scout approached me to go to Glasgow. I had to say that he was too late. But when I told my mother my news she was heartbroken.

'However, I advised her to go on ahead to the States and I would follow soon. But she cancelled the application for a quota and never did go there on a permanent basis. I, of course, was left with a guilty feeling of holding her back and keeping the family split up. Yet she did go once a wee bit later to see her sisters and sisters-in-law, who by then were scattered all over the place – one in Pittsburgh, another in New Jersey and so on. But the great satisfaction of it all for me was when she returned, she said to me: "Matt, I'm glad we never went to that mad country . . ."

'Well then, I settled down to play for Manchester City for a few years at the side of many great players – men like Bray, my other wing half, Tilson, Herd, McMullan, Eric Brook and others. In 1933 we lost the Cup Final to Everton, but a year later, with virtually the same side, we returned to Wembley to beat Portsmouth 2–1 as thunder and lightning crashed over the stadium, with Stanley Rous the referee.

'Feeling in need of a change, I eventually moved to Liverpool in February 1936 and stayed with them until the war broke out when I joined the Army Physical Training Corps with many other footballers and sportsmen.

'As the war moved towards its end, Liverpool kindly offered me a five-year contract to return to Anfield on demobilisation as a first team coach. However, meanwhile in charge of an Army football side full of fine players like Tommy Lawton, Joe Mercer, Arthur Rowe, Britton, Mullen and others, sent out to Italy to entertain the troops behind the advanced lines, I ran across Jimmy Murphy against whom I had played often before the war when he was with West Bromwich Albion and a wing half for Wales.

'Just prior to that, too, when I was an instructor at Sandhurst Military Academy, I had had a letter from Louis Rocca, the famous old Manchester United scout, telling me of the managerial vacancy at Old Trafford and that Mr. Gibson, the chairman, would like to see me. That meeting duly came about and in February 1945, I was offered the post upon my demobilisation.

'It was with this under my belt that I took my army team out to Italy as a form of relaxation for the fighting men. And it was at Bari in south-east Italy that I met Murphy again. He was running all the sporting activities at a rest camp and so impressed was I with his work that I told him of my impending job at United and that I hoped he would join me if and when he was free.

'So, in due course, it came to pass. I was demobbed in September 1945 and a month later in October, I took up the reins officially at Old Trafford – or what remained of it. A year later, in 1946, Jimmy Murphy joined me as my right-hand man, and one way or another we have remained together ever since.'

All the threads by now were drawn together for a famous partnership that scaled the heights and plumbed the depths over a quarter of a century with never a rift in the lute. A Scotsman and a Welshman in harness, their Celtic strains melded and though fundamentally different in character – 'I was always the hard basket,' says Murphy – they proved the perfect foil for each other.

Busby had now taken on a mammoth task that would have deterred most men. For seven years, since before the war when Scott Duncan had departed to Ipswich Town of the Southern League, United had struggled on with no manager, their broken strings held together by a dedicated Board of Directors under the venerable and venerated Mr. James Gibson and by the efficient loyalty of Walter Crickmer, the secretary. In addition, there was no ground and an overdraft of £15,000 was a further burden. It was from such a dark and arid base that Busby began to build a mountain from a molehill.

From the very start he knew the sort of team he wanted. Himself a creative wing half in his day, the *Manchester Guardian* in 1934 had once published a perceptive appreciation of his qualities as a player which have remained with him always, as natural as breathing in and breathing out. As the late Sir Neville Cardus, the poet laureate of cricket in his time, once wrote: 'Style is the man . . .'

> At best Busby has no superior as an attacking half back. It is his bewildering footcraft which most delights the crowds. His crouching style may not be pretty but the control is perfect, the effect akin to conjuring. His dribble is a thing of swerves, feints and deceptions. Few opponents are not hoodwinked by his phantom pass. Even the real one is nearly always masked. It skids off to the right when one could swear it was destined for the centre. Busby scorns the obvious. His passes not only look good, they sound good. There is that same healthy thwack of leather that means a scurry in the outfield in a cricket match.
>
> Busby is not so sound in defence. A lack of speed he cloaks in shrewd positional play, so that he intercepts more often than he tackles, but it is a flaw in his armour. Some would find another in the spirit of adventure which will not be repressed even in front of his own goal. . . Sometimes he does dare-devil things that make the directors feel old before their time. But who would have him different? He laughs equally at his blunders and his triumphs, which of course is the privilege as well as the proof of a great player. He would be a certain choice for that select eleven of Footballers Who Obviously Love Football – and that is the highest praise of all.

*The Guardian* had put their finger on the spot. But Busby not only loved football. He loved people, too, and this he showed from the beginning.

He has said: 'I always wanted – let me get the right word for it – creative football. I wanted method. I wanted to manage the team as I felt players wanted to be managed. To begin with I wanted a more humane approach than there was when I was playing. Sometimes lads were just left on their own. The first team hardly recognised the lads underneath. There never seemed to be enough interest taken in players. The manager was at his desk and you saw him once a week. From the start I tried to make the smallest member think he was part of the club.'

More than any other manager, Busby put his faith in the youth policy in football which has been so important in the development of the game since the war. He had a clear mental picture of the kind of football he wanted, and he created a side to match it. This was the brilliantly gifted, but intensely methodical team of the 1950s, almost wholly composed of young, home-trained players. But that is to cross in advance one of the bridges ahead.

As it was he started at grass roots with the forces at his command. 'Actually I was very lucky with the players left to me,' he remembers. 'Quite a number of them were still away in uniform when I arrived, but from before the war there still remained on the books the likes of Johnny Carey, Allenby Chilton, Stan Pearson, Jack Rowley and Charlie Mitten. These duly formed a basis of my first team. But there were also younger boys such as John Aston, Johnny Morris and Joe Walton who had come through the M.U.J.A.C.s – Manchester United Junior Athletic Club – while little Henry Cockburn had joined from Goslings, a local works team. Every one of these duly became internationals: Carey, in fact, first played for the Republic of Ireland before appearing in the United first team!

'While United had ended fourteenth in the First Division just before the war, theirs was by far the youngest side in the league at the time and their expectations for the future had been promising. In addition, the reserves had won the Central League Championship, while the A team had headed the Manchester League, and to complete the picture the two junior M.U.J.A.C. combinations had topped their league and won nearly all their friendly games against opposition two or three years their seniors. So, in truth, there was plenty of material here to work on, especially in the youth policy begun by Walter Crickmer in 1938 and continued until 1941 when pressure of war requirements put a stop to it.'

To be strictly accurate, then, those who have said in the past that Busby inherited nothing in the way of a playing staff were wide of the mark. Ability was on top to a degree, but the new captain on the bridge was quick to show his instinctive skill in welding them into a composite whole and finding their best places on the field.

His real genius, in fact, lay in the switching of players' positions. Having bought Jimmy Delaney from Celtic for £4,000 at outside right in his first season in the chair, Busby thereby quickly showed his flair for taking a gamble, since the balding Scottish international had a suspect damaged shoulder and was advancing in years for a winger.

But the real master stroke came in converting both Carey and Aston from inside forward to full back, two ball players who were to take their skills to the rear of defence and open the door to a new and unconventional trend in full back play. With the powerful, raw-boned Chilton as the defensive centre half, and either

Old Trafford the morning after the blitz of March 11, 1941.

European Cup semi-final, Madrid 1957: Wood picks the ball off Di Stefano's head in the match against Real Madrid at the Bernabeu Stadium. Edwards (left), Whelan, Byrne and Jackie Blanchflower watch anxiously. Real Madrid won 3-1.

Drawing 2-2 with Real Madrid in the return game at Old Trafford: Kopa tackled by Byrne scores his team's first goal as keeper Wood comes off his line.

Jackie Blanchflower deputising in goal for the injured Wood, cannot stop Aston Villa's McParland scoring his team's winning goal in the Cup Final at Wembley, 1957.

Anderson or Warner and Cockburn ball winning, destructive wing halves, the new idea was to use Carey and Aston as artistic creators from the rear, a tactic which confused many an opposing side. Talking of the aforementioned Delaney, indeed, Carey the Irishman, with his dry Irish wit, soft brogue, and pipe, has since said that when he himself wanted a breather he would work the ball up the right wing and give it to Delaney. 'That done, I could take a rest for five minutes while "Baldie" waltzed round the place for a time!'

At the end of Busby's first season in command United ended fourth in 1945–46 in the war-time Northern League, then in its dying embers before the return of full-scale League football in 1946–47. The side at his command then read: Crompton; Hamlett, Chilton; Aston, Whalley, Cockburn; Delaney, Pearson, Rowley, Buckle and Wrigglesworth.

The following season of 1946–47 saw the return to full-scale League and Cup competition at national level and to join the fray there came the release from the services of Carey, Morris, Mitten and others. It was then that Busby, the sculptor, really began to shape a work of art to his heart's desire.

With Jimmy Murphy now at his side to build up and educate the youth of the club, the future began to take shape with Crompton in goal; Carey and Aston switched from inside forward to full back; a half back line of Anderson or Warner, Chilton and Cockburn; and a penetrating attack of Delaney, Morris, Rowley, Pearson and Mitten. The tide had begun to run sweetly in the right direction.

Four times in the opening five seasons after the war United ended as runners-up as a prelude to winning the Championship in 1951/52. It had been a long wait since the previous occasion, forty years back in 1911, soon after the death of Edward VII. If ever coming events cast their shadows before them this was it.

In 1947 United were second to Liverpool; in 1948 they ended behind only Arsenal but completed a fine season by lifting the F.A. Cup for the first time since 1909; in 1949 Portsmouth beat them to the title; in 1950 they slumped – a word used only in comparative terms – to fourth position; but in 1951 they were back in contention only a few points behind an articulate Tottenham Hotspur side. Such was United's consistent build-up to their Championship title of 1952. They had been knocking imperiously at the door and at last it was opened unto them.

But that is to overstep our mark again. The signpost of this chapter takes us only to 1948. It is time to stop at the inn and luxuriate in the memories of that magical run to the Cup Final of 1948 when Carey led his team up the steps to the Royal Box to receive the trophy. As he was chaired later, before the lap of honour, the sun danced on the silver bauble while he held it aloft as if to confirm that a 100,000 crowd had just seen what was to be the best and most consistently articulate ninety minutes of a Cup Final played since the war.

Their run to Wembley that year, it must be remembered, was achieved without a single Cup tie being played on their own ground, since Old Trafford itself still struggled to get back into some sort of shape after its war damage of seven years earlier.

Bearing this in mind, the extent of United's feat assumes an added significance. Every one of their wins was achieved by a margin of not less than two goals; nor were they once held to a single draw along the way, as they won 6–4 at Villa Park; 3–0 against Liverpool at neutral Goodison Park; 2–0 against Charlton Athletic, the holders, at neutral Huddersfield; 4–1 against talented Preston North End at Maine Road; 3–1 against Derby County, the winners of 1946, in the semi-final at Hillsborough where Stan Pearson scored a brilliant hat trick; and finally 4–2 against Blackpool at Wembley. That added up to six wins in six matches, with a tally of twenty-two goals against eight. It showed where United's accent lay – in attack.

But it is the beginning and the ending of this run that still lives in the windmills of memory. If the Final, as I have commented, has perhaps been unsurpassed over-all since the war, United's tie in the third round, which set them on their way, remains one of the best contests – as a match pure and simple, full of drama and courage – between English club sides in my experience. I still relive that day.

The sunny morning of January found me heading towards the third-round Cup tie to be played at Villa Park, that large edifice of red brick which still brings a whiff of Victorian prosperity, respectability and power, from the time when England blossomed and there was no major war, when no catastrophe threatened from without and when men, safe behind the shield of the Navy, thought of life in terms of peace and security.

Here was a Cup tie of enormous appeal, where every prospect pleased in anticipation. The very thought of it acted like a magnet. Villa Park that day had become my Camelot. The reason was simple.

At Christmas time I had written in *The Times* that the two clubs I most fancied to reach Wembley for the Cup Final in April were Aston Villa and Manchester United. The season then had run some four months, and was about halfway gone. But already Villa were showing signs of some of their former authority and were lying sixth or seventh in the First Division. Manchester United, on the other hand, stood about fourteenth. Yet I had seen them give Arsenal – destined to be the champions that year – a stiff match at Highbury earlier on, in September. I was much taken at the time with their style, ideas and polish. There was some indefinable, poetic quality about them that took my fancy. And now, around Christmas, they had begun to catch a tide of success as they crept slowly up the table. When I named United with Villa, those famous Cup fighters, I was merely playing a hunch. More than that, in fact, I was emboldened enough to back it in cash. Getting some early ante-post betting at the generous odds of twenty-five to one, I put a fiver on them for the Cup. Even a colleague on the sports pages, the racing correspondent, a gambling man, followed my outside tip.

Imagine my feelings, then, when the draw for the Cup third round was made. Out of the velvet bag came those little numbered boxwood balls, side by side. When they were identified by Sir Stanley Rous, the F.A. Secretary, they set the stage for what was to prove an heroic event – Aston Villa v. Manchester United! My Cup Final was fated to take place at the start and not the finish. So for me there could only be one place to be that day. Villa Park was written on my heart.

Villa Park itself was full to the topmost layer. This was Cup day, and a 65,000 crowd – mostly out on the open terraces, and already half-drenched – was not going to have its fun and excitement spoiled by anything. The atmosphere was electric. When the teams appeared briefly, one after the other, to have group photographs taken, the roar that greeted them in turn seemed to open the clouds even more as the rain slanted down pitilessly.

Once photographed – Manchester United in royal blue shirts, not to clash with the traditional claret and blue of the Villa – both sides disappeared again down the dark tunnel under the main stand. Down in their secret chambers below one could imagine the delivery of last-minute instructions; one could almost smell the embrocation in each dressing room as the tension tightened a notch or two.

At last battle was joined, and the clash of arms still re-echoes across the years for those lucky enough to have been there. Many times since I have been asked it that was the greatest match that I've seen. It is a difficult question to answer.

Certainly for dramatic content and depth of plot that Villa-United Cup tie lives with the best. Maybe it lacked the extraordinary magic created by the artistry of the Hungarians and

Brazilians at their height. But yes. Perhaps as a match of high drama, swaying one way then another and heightened by the storm of rain, it takes some beating. Yet, of course, I was younger, fresher then and involved emotionally. Distance, too, probably lends enchantment to the view. If so, then I am happy enough to let it be so, since it is still capable of stirring the ashes of a memorable day.

But let me say this. The 65,000 inside Villa Park that January day certainly had their money's worth. Ten goals in all and deep human qualities flowered before our eyes, and if the skies wept they proved to be tears of joy. Here was an afternoon to remember; a grey, damp winter's day touched by magic. It was a match of superlatives, in which football science was later challenged by undying courage. Yet where to begin the story?

First, perhaps, by saying that we shall always remember the football Manchester United played before half time, after an opening gambit had brought Aston Villa a goal direct from the kick-off. Not a Manchester man had touched the ball and the Villa were ahead in thirteen-and-a-half seconds by the stop watch. The chances had been delicately poised, but here, surely, was a touch to disturb the balance of the game. Certainly not many teams would have lived with Aston Villa after such a beginning. Yet at half time Manchester United led by five goals to one, and it was their superb forward line that had won them their position. Delaney, Morris, Rowley, Pearson and Mitten thought as one man and moved as one at top speed. Their approach passing was brilliant and imaginative. Here was the sort of football one dreams about and Aston Villa were cut to ribbons.

If that first half had been breathtaking, what came after stirred the blood. Inch by inch and goal by goal Aston Villa arose to fight back until, with only nine minutes left, all but one of the Manchester goals had been wiped off. Earlier, the hopes of Aston Villa had been a dying flame; now there was a raging fire. Manchester, however, to their eternal credit, withstood the challenge at the last and settled the issue two minutes from the end with one final attack. In such a match every man was a hero, but surely one must mention Carey and Morris for Manchester and Dorsett and Brown for Villa.

Manchester United were the artists and they deserved the victory. Five of their goals were clean-cut, but if one of them – the third – had a touch of luck about it when a fierce free kick by Rowley ricocheted to Pearson in an open space, this was balanced by an exact replica that later came to Aston Villa. Manchester's attacking football, one repeats, was supreme in that first half. It was mathematical, swift and exact. Aston Villa could not match such brilliance, but what gave them a chance was an unquenched spirit and a wise change of tactics after the interval.

Using their greater weight and height on a battlefield now churned up under a persistent drizzle, they tackled like demons, kept the ball in the air with wide passing and snatched what the gods had to offer. Manchester attacked along the ground to the end, but slowly the rhythm was knocked out of their game by the fire of their opponents and finally they were shaken to their very roots. The crisis, however, was survived and justice done, but in such a game it was cruel that there had to be a loser.

At once Aston Villa set the vast throng roaring. The kick-off, a quick dribble and pass by Brown to Smith and there was the ball in the Manchester net, shot home swiftly by Edwards from Smith's low centre. Here, in seconds, could have been the knock-out blow, but Manchester brushed it off as if it had been no more than a fly that had settled for a moment. Within six minutes they were level when, following a corner kick by Delaney, Mitten beat Potts on a sixpenny piece and Rowley headed his lobbed pass beyond Jones. At the end of seventeen minutes Delaney, taking a glorious pass from Morris, was tackled in the nick of time by Moss at the expense of a corner and from his kick Morris completed the cycle by heading home as clean as a whistle.

Manchester were now in the lead and from that moment their forwards were irresistible. Delaney and Mitten were being set free by the exquisite passing of their insides. Morris in particular was a delight. After half an hour came Manchester's third goal – the lucky one – and two minutes later a fourth, as Morris met another centre from Mitten with his head. Just before half time Delaney completed a dextrous move between himself, Morris and Pearson and Aston Villa at this point could do little but stand and gape.

But the second half gave us something quite different. There was consolation for the Villa within a minute when Crompton, under pressure, let a corner kick by Edwards slip over the line. It was raining hard now and the ground began to wear a black look. Aston Villa's strength was slowly telling. With twenty minutes to go they were back in the match with a chance when Dorsett's free kick was diverted to Smith. That was 5–3 and Manchester were being hurled back by sheer will-power. Dorsett and Lowe were on the attack; Brown an inspiration. Nine minutes from the end Chilton in the goal area impeded Ford, who by now was a positive menace. Dorsett shot the penalty home like a thunderbolt and the excitement had reached bursting point: 5–4.

But Manchester held on and in the dying minutes Rowley, Delaney and Mitten produced a move of earlier vintage. Jones turned Mitten's shot bravely over the bar and from the corner kick Pearson put Manchester beyond reach with a sixth goal.

There we had it, a dramatic start and a dramatic final curtain to a wonderful game. As I headed away from Villa Park towards the station – Snow Hill in those days – amidst that long tide of throbbing people. I felt quite limp and emotionally drained. It was still raining, and the water made a gurgling sound as it ran in the street gutters. Yet we were all on fire. At that moment I would have been happy enough to be nailed down in a box and buried ten foot deep.

And amidst all the crowded excitement I carried home with me to London, there lingered the sight of Johnny Carey, Manchester's captain. When Villa delivered that lightning rapier thrust in the opening seconds the first United player to get a touch of the ball was Jack Crompton, the goalkeeper, as he fished it out of his net. While he was doing so Carey put his hands on his hips, looked around at his fellows and gave them a wide, courageous Irish smile. It was as if to say, 'Now my lads, let's show 'em . . .' There, indeed, was a much needed tonic. There was captaincy. It was a smile that was to take Manchester United up Wembley's Royal Box three months later to receive the Cup itself from the hands of King George VI.

Teams:
Aston Villa: Jones; Potts, Parkes; Dorsett, Moss, Lowe; Edwards, Martin, Ford, Brown, L. Smith.

Manchester United: Crompton; Carey, Aston; Anderson, Chilton, Cockburn; Delaney, Morris, Rowley, Pearson, Mitten.

Inexorably, almost inevitably it seemed, United moved towards the one place, Wembley, where their brand of football was worthy of being set before Royalty and before the nation.

The morning of April 26, 1948, dawned fine and sunny. It was as if that smile of Johnny Carey was still shining all over the world. Certainly it had helped to illuminate Manchester United themselves, for here they were on that April day poised to face Blackpool in the Cup Final without having played a single tie on their own ground. As the luck would have it United, having won gloriously at Aston Villa, were drawn at 'home' successively in the fourth, fifth and sixth rounds. But Manchester City, too, had equal good fortune. They were drawn at Maine Road for the third, fourth and fifth rounds, which forced United to look for alternative accommodation. Not until the sixth round, with City already knocked out, were they able to return to Maine Road, their temporary home from home, to dispose of Preston North End 4–1. The semi-final next saw them silence talented Derby County – with Raich Carter and Billy Steel, the dynamic Scotsman, at inside forward – 3–1 at neutral Hillsborough.

So here they were at Wembley, refugees and gypsies on the run, having over-stepped every obstacle in their path. It is worth looking at their goalscoring over that run just to underline the penetrative power stored in that forward line of Delaney, Morris, Jack Rowley, Pearson and Mitten. To repeat it: 6–4, 3–0, 2–0, 4–1, 3–1, an aggregate of eighteen goals against six in five Cup ties, all on foreign soil. It makes the mind boggle in these days of highly scientific defensive planning!

Blackpool, too, were full of goals. With the two Stans, Matthews and Mortensen, in their attack – the 'terrible twins' – they had cut their way past Leeds United 4–0 at home; Chester 4–0 at home; Colchester United 5–0, at home; Fulham 2–0, at Craven Cottage; and Tottenham Hotspur 3–1 after extra time in the semi-final, at Villa Park.

Theirs had been far the easier trip until they ran into Spurs. There, indeed, was a dramatic climax. With only a minute to go Tottenham led 1–0 and virtually had both feet through the twin towers of Wembley. But with the last seconds draining away, Matthews wheedled his way free down the right and there was Mortensen to flash in the equaliser in the nick of time! In the extra half hour Mortensen completed his hat trick and the conjurors had produced their rabbit at the last breath. Unlucky Spurs!

With eighteen goals against six on United's side and eighteen to one on the Blackpool card, all the signs pointed to an attacking final. The question was: could Manchester hold Matthews and Mortensen? Blackpool themselves had caused something of a surprise by splitting up the devastating right-wing triangle composed of 'the terrible twins' and Harry Johnston, at wing half behind them. Morty was moved to centre forward, but for those in the know this was a clear indication of their intentions. It was the signal that they had decided to play on the uncertainty of the United centre half, the tall, angular Allenby Chilton. And how nearly the plan worked!

As anyone interested now knows United lifted the Cup that day 4–2, only their second victory ever in the competition, and their first since the season 1908–9. A long interval. Yet it was worth waiting for. Now they showed their character as well as their skill. With the end drawing near Blackpool led 2–1, and it looked as if Stanley Matthews was at last about to collect his first winning Cup Final medal.

But then came the whirlwind. With only twenty minutes left Blackpool were in the lead by two goals to one, and once again it seemed that there was to be an addition to the long list of favourites who would fail at the supreme test. Blackpool, after surrendering an early lead through a defensive misunderstanding, had regained it before half time, and with the game having run three parts of its course they still held a position of command. It was a position they had gained not because of any superior quality in their football, pure as it had been, but by snatching their chances. Manchester, in fact, had perhaps enjoyed the greater share of the attack. They held a long lead in the matter of goal kicks and corners forced on both wings, but the mechanism had not clicked near goal. Their putts on the green, so to speak, had failed to drop.

There we were, then, at the last phase, with Blackpool looking for all the world like winners and the curve of Manchester's hopes at its lowest point of the afternoon. For a period after half time the fire and precision went out of the Manchester game; they lost touch, and inspiration eluded them.

With twenty minutes to go, however, Morris prepared to take a free kick gained to the right of the Blackpool penalty area. As he advanced to the kick a gentle breeze, had we only sensed it, had alreay begun to stir. A moment later the ball lay snug at the bottom of the Blackpool net, headed there like a flash by Rowley, who had timed his advance perfectly between Hayward and Shimwell. Manchester United were level.

Even then Blackpool had one more chance to recover the prize that only a short time ago seemed to be theirs. Chilton, who spent a thoroughly anxious and uncomfortable afternoon, took one more unnecessary liberty with Mortensen, lost the ball and there was Mortensen streaking through the open Manchester defence. It looked any odds on a goal, and Mortensen's shot was hard and true for the far corner. But Crompton saved brilliantly at full length. That, if anything, was surely the turning point, for within seconds Manchester had their noses in front for the first time, with a piercing thrust at the other end by Pearson. There was no stopping them. The gentle breeze had now become a strong and friendly wind, and Manchester sailed home with an astonishing outburst of brilliance.

Whether Mortensen would have been a greater danger at inside right must always remain a matter of opinion, but the fact remains that his tactical switch to centre forward nearly won Blackp[illegible] match. It was clear they were going to hammer Chilton, an[illegible] they did with a fair measure of success from the beginning. Actua[illegible] the Blackpool forwards, with Munro doing the work of two men a[illegible] a midfield link, moved the ball about beautifully on the ground amongst themselves, far more than one had expected, but the opening approach, especially before half time, was usually left to Matthews, and the final thrust to Mortensen. Certainly Mortensen, with his great speed and opportunism, was a danger from first to last – he snatched his usual goal, to score in every round of the competition – but the game flowed away from Matthews in the later stages after he had left Aston facing the wrong way many times in the first half. But Aston stood the test coolly enough and came out of his duel with credit.

The Manchester forwards, apart from that phase soon after half time when they lost their rhythm, were usually moving together as a single unit and, if things could not go right for them for a long time near goal, they certainly came with a glorious burst at the end. Within the superior frame of the Manchester teamwork came the power, intelligence and thrust of Rowley, Pearson and Morris, and this was the deciding factor. They saw to it that Delaney, against the inexperienced Crosland, was used as much as possible. Crosland was not disgraced, but Blackpool were never quite sure where to find Delaney next. Both pairs of wing half backs, especially Cockburn and Johnston, played their parts splendidly, but the most polished and studied defender on the field was Carey, who finally subdued a lively winger in Rickett.

The presentation to the King and the opening ceremonies over, it was Blackpool who set the standard at the beginning. After only a quarter of an hour Manchester had their first real shock, when Mortensen, gathering a long pass down the middle, swept past Chilton. Mortensen was just clear when a despairing tackle by the centre half from behind brought him down. The referee, who controlled the game excellently, decided it was inside the area, and Shimwell duly shot the penalty past Crompton. Manchester, unmoved, began to settle down to a beautiful smooth approach, and at the end of half an hour, after a constant stream of corners, they were level. Carey found Delaney on the right and, as Hayward and Robinson left the winger's forward lob to each other, Rowley slipped between them to flick the ball sideways and roll it into an empty net. It was sheer tragedy for Blackpool, but within five minutes they were ahead again. This time a free kick by Matthews, square and cleverly placed, reached Kelly, and there was

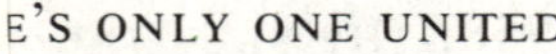

o pounce on the forward pass and beat
ot.
interval. For the first quarter of an hour of
ol slowly but surely began to take a grip of
ned to be draining away from Manchester.
or all their studied attack earlier. With but
kpool, it seemed, were now nearly home.
Morris's vital free kick and the beginning
ind.

Rowley's superb header, as one has said, snatched the equaliser. Ten minutes from the end Pearson, in a quick, closely-linked approach with Morris, aimed for bull, hit the target and Manchester were ahead. A few moments later Anderson shot past a bewildered Robinson from fully thirty yards and Blackpool were left flat footed. It was a stirring climax indeed to a clean and glorious game in which both sides had brought the best out of each other.

The teams which duly mounted the steps to receive the winning and losing medals in the Royal Box, where sat the King and Queen, were, first:

Manchester United: Crompton; Carey, Aston; Anderson, Chilton, Cockburn; Delaney, Morris, Rowley, Pearson, Mitten.

Then:

Blackpool: Robinson; Shimwell, Crosland; Johnston, Hayward, Kelly; Matthews, Munro, Mortensen, Dick, Rickett.

Having seen every Cup Final since 1946 – and quite a few before, back to my first at Wembley as a boy in 1926 – I subscribe to the view that the 1948 affair was probably the best all-round climax to the competition in terms of quality over the whole ninety minutes since the war. There was, of course, the highly personalised and dramatic 'Matthews Final' of 1953, but there the real sting was in the tail.

Usually Cup Finals prove to be something of a disappointment. The world and his wife trundle up Olympic Way full of the joy of spring, full of expectation, exuding a feeling of carnival. There is a Bank-Holiday air about it all. But too often the match itself is spoiled by teams who are afraid of defeat and draw in their horns defensively.

Manchester United and Blackpool, however, set a new standard that sunny afternoon. They pointed a lesson to the whole of football by their insistence upon attack, and the sheer enjoyment of it. They showed that all-out defence is negation; that attack is life, and because of that they took us by the hand into a land where the outlines were sharper and the colours a bit brighter.

Afterwards, as always, came the talking points. Was that a penalty for Blackpool at the start? The Movietone News film in slow motion seemed to show Chilton hook up Mortensen *outside* the United penalty area. But Morty's speed took him into a headlong tumble over the line which led to what, in that split second, seemed a correct decision by the referee.

As for the 'terrible twins' they had different views on the turning point of the game. Matthews blamed the Blackpool defence for letting Morris take that free kick so quickly, which gave Rowley the opening to head United back into the match at 2–2 with only twenty minutes left. 'Somebody should have stood over the ball as a delaying tactic until the others took covering positions.' Gamesmanship? But, of course.

As for Mortensen, he said, 'If only I had shot high into the crowd when I was clean through at 2–2 near the end, we wouldn't have lost. Jack Crompton made that marvellous save; the ball sped from one end of the field to the other; Stan Pearson scored and it was all over . . .' My last image of a fine struggle lay in the Movietone film of the occasion. There, high up on the Wembley terraces, was the picture of a small boy sitting on his father's shoulders, his head adorned with a Blackpool supporter's paper hat, his face crumpled in a flood of tears as his favourites went down to defeat. In that moment the eye of the camera provided a poignant human document. It said more than any words.

Reality, however, always intrudes on sentiment and emotion. A football club by definition is a business, a company which has to try to balance profit and loss. And football after the war was to become a vast entertainment industry. Having been in the red for so long it was clearly uplifting to the directors to find their stock on the rise. Attractive football and success on the field was reflected in the balance sheets of 1946, 1947, and 1948 when the profits of the club rose dramatically from £10,215 15s. 1d. to £13, 393 2s. 1d. and then £22, 329 13s. 0d. as the weight of debt was off-loaded.

By 1948, too, the players whom Busby had inherited had clearly been reshaped to his liking. That Cup Final side represented seven changes, including positional switches, from the one he had taken over so that in every sense he could feel with justification that it was of his own making.

In the background, too, with the dedicated support of Jimmy Murphy and Bert Whalley, the up-and-coming young players were being groomed for the future. It was a policy that was eventually to pay the most handsome dividends. The earlier M.U.J.A.C. sides had comprised youngsters between the ages of fifteen and a half and sixteen and a half for the B-combination and sixteen and a half to seventeen and a half for the A-team. The Colts covered the next age group of seventeen and a half to eighteen and a half years; and the official A-side (the club's third) eighteen and a half to twenty. That was the broad framework on which the United 'factory' was based, though here and there in the future certain exceptional players – the prodigies – broke through the ranks quickly to reach the top.

In essence it was an unending production line, but a conveyor belt with a difference. It was not robots who emerged from the pipeline but young men who were encouraged to retain their individual personalities.

Busby and Murphy, indeed, were disciplined artists at heart, reminding one of the sculptor who once showed a friend a vast, square slab of stone in his studio. Upon being asked what he intended to shape out of it, he replied, 'An elephant'. 'But how on earth do you make an elephant from that mass?' enquired the friend. 'Simple,' replied the sculptor. 'I just knock off the bits that don't look like an elephant.'

That was what Busby was busy doing – knocking off the bits that didn't look like a Manchester United footballer.

# 2

# *1949–1958*

# *A Dream Becomes Reality*

HAVING EMERGED FROM a dark cave of war, football, sustained only by a skeleton game, faced the sternest test of its long history at the end of 1945.

Although public interest was sky high in its search for all forms of entertainment, there was no ample reservoir of youth to be called upon liberally. Conscription to military service still remained in operation and employment under the Essential Works Order had first to be answered.

Thus the majority of clubs were forced to temporise, uncertain of their needs and hampered by the inflation of the transfer fees of the day. The transfer figures of a quarter of a century ago certainly look puny compared with the present, but at the time they were very real and hurtful. The immediate future of the game, indeed, carried a large question mark.

If we are to regard the period 1946 to 1959 as a decade in general terms and review some of the trends of that period, then it can now be seen how important they were in helping to shape the future. In fact, it is perhaps no exaggeration to say that those years were among the most eventful in the whole history of British football.

Consider what the 1950s brought forth. There was England's staggering 1–0 defeat by America in the World Cup of 1950 with the sound of that historic goal that re-echoed around the world. Next followed Hungary's glorious 6–3 triumph at Wembley in 1953 (reinforced by England's 7–1 rout in Budapest in May 1954) which led to an urgent reappraisal at the highest levels of our existing standards of play. This in turn led to a long-needed amendment in training methods and tactics.

Almost as a natural consequence, there next came a change of fashion in kit and playing equipment, heavily influenced by the Continent and South America. Mini-shorts and ballet-type footwear became the vogue, taking the place of constricting knee-length trousers and heavy boots, fit more for soldiers footslogging in the mud of Flanders than for footballers.

These were mere details of change. Of a far wider and deeper significance was the arrival of floodlighting in the mid-1950s and with that the birth of European club competition which opened up a whole new horizon. Meanwhile, just below the surface, the slow fuse of a time bomb was burning, as players began to agitate for increased wages and a fresh status. Behind all this shifting scenery and the roar of the crowd lay this struggle of the individual, which was to explode dramatically at the end of the decade.

In 1946 there had been the vague threat of a strike by the Players' Union under the chairmanship of Mr. Jimmy Guthrie, who in 1939 had captained Portsmouth to victory in the F.A. Cup at a time when the basic wages were £8 in the playing season and £6 in the close period of summer. By the late 1940s and throughout the 1950s there now followed a gradual advance, painfully and laboriously gained step by step, which finally led in 1961–62 to the abolition of the maximum wage and a new deal for the player. Once more a strike threat was the weapon used.

The following table of basic wages per week shows the progress made throughout the period under review:

| Year | Playing Season | Close Season |
|---|---|---|
| 1946–47 | £10 | £8 |
| 1947–48 | £12 | £10 |
| 1951–52 | £14 | £10 |
| 1954–55 | £15 | £12 |
| 1957–58 | £17 | £14 |
| 1958–59 | £20 | £17 |

To pick one's way through the maze of the struggle is to work gingerly through a minefield. But one incident during this phase, played a significant part in the coming passage of events. It was the flight in 1949–50 of certain players – amongst them N. Franklin and G. Mountford (both of Stoke City), C. Mitten (Manchester United) and W. Higgins (Everton) – from their League clubs to Bogota, in Columbia, a South American country not then under the wing of the International Federation (F.I.F.A.). Offered salaries, bonuses and other perks far in advance of anything to be earned in the United Kingdom, these men saw in their mind's eyes a land far away, flowing with milk and honey. Sadly, it all proved to be a mirage so that, disillusioned, they duly returned home to be disciplined by the Football Association. Abortive the journey might have been, but those men were pioneers in the contemporary movement of players to the larger rewards to be earned overseas.

It was in all this changing pattern of affairs that Manchester United themselves expanded and prospered to become a major power in the land. The dream at the end of the 1940s became a reality of the 1950s.

Having already demonstrated his skill of judgment, his authority and humanity in man management, it was only to be expected that in the restless and demanding waters of the game Busby's services would be sought by others.

In April 1949 Tottenham Hotspur approached him with the offer of managership at a reputed salary of some £3,000 a year. He turned it down. 'There was a contact made by Spurs,' he recalls. 'But I was happy at United and I had started a job I wanted to complete. There was even an offer made to me by Mr. Bob Smith, the chairman, to go to Manchester City. "But I'm under contract to Old Trafford," I told him.' There was also an offer to become manager of the Italian national team at a huge salary. Yet in Busby's code of ethics contracts were made to be honoured. They were not just scraps of paper to be discarded at will.

What Busby had set out to do at Old Trafford was to build a new football world based on humane relationships, loyalty and integrity. He wanted a team to play the game in every sense of the word: on the field, in the way he himself felt the poetry of football; off it, with a sense of pride in belonging to United.

Hand in hand with this went the policy of youth, which he left in the able care of his first lieutenant, Jimmy Murphy. 'Right from the start,' says Busby, 'I was keen and determined to develop our policy of grooming youth to our method and standards. Some might have called it brain washing. It was nothing of the sort. It was just a matter of bringing them up with the right values and instincts.'

Soon the word got around that United's youth were the best in the land. That and the magnetic appeal of the first team soon enough had the effect of young players *wanting* to join Old Trafford. Bobby Charlton, for one, has said, 'When I was young I felt that if I could make it at United I could make it anywhere. It was as simple as that. It was a challenge and I never lived to regret it.'

Murphy paints in his part of the picture. 'When the war broke out I joined up and in due course went to the Far East for a spell and then to the desert with the 8th Army for four and a half years, so I saw most of the worst of it. When "Jerry" was driven out of North

Africa I landed up in Italy, taking over from Stan Cullis in a rest camp at Bari. It was there I met Matt again and he asked me to join him at Old Trafford to look after the kids. This I did in 1946.

'The ground was a bombed-out shell; we had no money; there was some sort of a pokey little dive of an office where Walter Crickmer, as club secretary, operated; then Matt got hold of a Nissen hut which the lads used for changing. The practice pitch was a mile or so away, while the business of the directors was carried on largely at Mr. Gibson's – the chairman's – office at his cold storage firm in Cornbrook. It was in this topsy-turvy set-up that we got on with things and began to gather the youngsters into our hands.

'Matt and I, of course, had our contacts around the place and the most number of scouts we had then were four or five, with the indefatigable little Joe Armstrong a key figure.'

The way was hard at the beginning as Busby, Murphy and Armstrong travelled thousands of miles up and down the countryside watching school teams, youth and works teams. Most of the tip-offs came from schoolmasters who were supporters and friends of United. Those who have remarked that Busby did not really need an extensive scouting system were right in a sense. He had built up good will. But those who said that United were fundamentally a Catholic club and that their best agents were priests up and down the country were not strictly accurate.

'Not at all,' said Murphy. 'We had no religious bias. If a boy showed promise he was for us, whether he was a Muslim, a Hindu, an Arab, or even an atheist. What we looked for was basic skill, an innate instinct which, hopefully, we could help to develop; and beyond that a genuine desire to *want* to play for United.'

In those terms the welfare of the boys was of paramount importance. A hand-picked team of motherly landladies were chosen to house and look after them in their spare time, making them feel at ease in new surroundings. In addition, too, they were sent home to their parents for weekends whenever possible, while every encouragement was given to the fledglings to study for an alternative career.

In this way did the system Busby set out to establish in due course bring forth its abundance. He did not look only to his stars in the front line: he set out to create a layer of teams in the background, each moving up the scale in their time. It is a system developed extensively and scientifically on the Continent.

Busby, of course, always had the final responsibility of when to bring the young ones into the firing line at the front. This he began to do after the Championship had been won in 1952 with Carey still

The "Busby Babes' " last League match in England, five days before the Munich plane crash. Airborne, left to right, Evans of Arsenal, Viollet and Taylor of United.

Matt Busby briefs some of his team in Belgrade before the Red Star match in February 1958.

Byrne, the United captain, exchanges the customary pennants with the Red Star captain. The game was drawn 3-3 .

as captain, though that great all-rounder was already beginning to think of hanging up his boots.

Having achieved the new blend he sought, the club next won the Championship in the successive years of 1956 and 1957 so that the fresh-faced young men drafted in to win the glory were quickly labelled as the 'Red Devils' and the 'Busby Babes', two clichés which soon found a wide popular appeal. In truth, they might just as well have been called 'Murphy's Marvels' or 'Whalley's Wonders' since it was they who had spent the vital, formative years grooming this new wave for the master, Busby. Not that there was any jealousy anywhere within the camp. United they were, and united they all stood, concerned collectively only with the success and welfare of the club as a whole.

Murphy has added more brush strokes to his personal canvas of the years. A warm-hearted, emotional man – he cried, literally, when speaking of Duncan Edwards as a boy and had to leave the room in search of a handkerchief – he said:

'You must remember this, Matt and I were new to this kind of job. We were both raw as pigeons. But having been put in charge of youth, one thing I always looked for was quality; always looked for the best. We still had very little money. If it hadn't been for Mr. Gibson, the chairman, we'd have been out of the Football League altogether. It was only his personal generosity and love for the club over the years that kept our heads above water. He saved the club.

'You know how time passes in football. Sir Harold Wilson, when he was Prime Minister, once remarked that "a week is a long time in politics". Well, that applies very much to our game. At any rate, soon enough we started to hit the jackpot. Matt and I always had a drink on Friday evening after we had chosen our respective teams, and on one of those occasions he said to me quietly: "You know, Jimmy, we're doing a good job here".

'As you know, the reserves were my responsibility – quite apart from the youngsters – and in my first year we had won the Central League by nine clear points and Matt was as happy as a Christmas tree. On the Monday, after our final fixture on the Saturday, he and his wife, Jean, came round to our home. "Full marks, you've done a great piece of work, Jimmy," he enthused. "Congratulations." To which I replied, "Maybe, Matt. But there's not one player there for you, or for us."

'So in the march of time those men were phased out quietly, and we started a new wave from the bottom. The game is all about experience and judgment. You can't buy judgment. And what a new wave it proved! All those kids who were later dubbed the "Busby Babes" were reared there on the spot – fellows like Duncan Edwards, Bobby Charlton, Eddie Colman, David Pegg and others. It was wonderfully rewarding and exciting to see them develop into great players who brought fame to the club and to themselves. It was like watching little apples grow.'

While all this metamorphosis was under way, the directors had been steering the ship out of troubled waters. Nothing succeeds like success and it was the success of Busby's teams under the full glare of national publicity that made the vital difference. Wherever they played the crowds flocked to see United.

Sadly and ironically, just as the directors were beginning to see the wood for the trees, two of their company passed away. First in 1950 – when the dedicated Louis Rocca, who had worked so faithfully for the club finding players over so many years, also died – it was Matthew Newton who departed, a man who had played his part in steering the United vessel through the rapids. In that same year, too, Mr. James Gibson fell ill.

It was on June 20, 1950 that Gibson signed his last minute as chairman, his place being taken henceforth by Mr. Harold Hardman as acting chairman. Gibson meanwhile continued to keep in touch with affairs from a distance and it must have lightened his heart before his death on September 11, 1951 to know that at last Old Trafford had become debt free earlier that same year.

It was the passing of an epoch during which the clouds of extinction finally rolled away through his influence. At the next board meeting a week later on September 18, the directors put their deep appreciation of his twenty years of work on record:

> Mr Hardman recalled that some 20 years ago Mr. Gibson at great personal risk took over the responsibility of the Club at a most critical period of its history, and how by his unbounded enthusiasm, personal help and guidance he had been the driving force and to a large degree responsible for restoring the Company to the stable and high position it now occupies as one of the leading Football League Clubs in the country.

Mr. Hardman was duly elected to succeed as chairman and in the following year of 1952 a further step was taken forward when the Cliff ground, the practice area, which had previously been under lease from the Clowes Estate, finally became the absolute property of the club.

It had been the unswerving broad ideas of the directors over the years, boosted by Busby's success on the field, that had at last seen them over the hill. It was a triumph of civic pride as the dream moved towards fulfilment.

Little remains static for long in football. After all, the welfare of a club depends upon the health and success of its players in competition and it was there beneath the surface that Busby and his faithful lieutenants were constantly at work on the master statue of Manchester United, knocking off the pieces that did not look right and adding those that did.

One who was entirely right for the style of the team – he had already proved it abundantly – but did not fit off field in his attitude was Johnny Morris. A curly-haired, talented little sprite, a brilliant ball player, he began to set himself up precociously in questioning some of Busby's theories. A storm brewed and burst. Old Trafford, so to speak, was not big enough for both of them and Morris duly went, sadly, to Derby County in March 1949 for a sum of £25,000, a record fee at that time, after first having turned down a move to Liverpool. In his place as a creative inside forward Busby at once signed his biggest cheque till then by procuring Downie from Bradford Park Avenue for £20,000. The manager's action was confirmed in a minute of March 9, 1949. In that same year, too, Ray Wood was signed as a goalkeeper from Darlington for £5,000 as an insurance for the future.

By 1949/50 Cockburn, Pearson and Aston had already been picked for England in the prestigious ancient fixture against Scotland and the staff had been augmented by yet another goalkeeper in Reg Allen, from Queens Park Rangers, as further defensive cover. Yet by the end of that season one more sharp tooth was lost from the dazzling forward line that earlier had devoured so many opponents with its deadly fangs. Following a close-season tour of America, Mitten, the flying outside left, whose great hobby was the backing of greyhounds, announced that he was going to try his luck in Bogota, Columbia. Like the others who went with him at the time – Neil Franklin, of Stoke, and company – he lived to regret it.

However, as so often, when one door closes another opens and it now swung wide for Roger Byrne, first acquired in 1948, who found a place in the 1952 Championship side as either the outside left or at left back. Here again Busby showed his sleight of hand in being able to switch players from one position or another. While Byrne alternated with Bond on the left wing, he also doubled with Aston when the full back moved now and then to centre forward in place of the injured Jack Rowley. Rowley himself, too, would occasionally appear at outside left. It was all something of a three card trick.

In November 1950, yet another member of that pulverising 1948 forward line departed – the probing Jimmy Delaney, who returned to his native Scotland having fulfilled exactly what Busby had wanted of him from the start. But his departure, too, soon opened the way for a new face, that of Johnny Berry, a tricky right winger from Birmingham City. When United had lost at home to Birmingham in the 1950/51 season the man who did all the damage was Berry. It was upon him that Busby's shrewd eye alighted. After a long hunt Busby, like a Canadian mounted policeman, got his man for the outlay of £25,000, a sum quickly repaid when Berry played a major role in the winning of the League Championship of 1951–52.

Not for forty-one years had the title come to Old Trafford, though to anyone with half any eye it had been on the cards ever since the war. The five previous seasons had seen United finish second, second, second, fourth, and second in the League and in 1948 win the Cup. Justice was not only done, but seen to be done: yet just in time, for the calendar was turning fast for four of the side who had been with the club since before the war.

## 1951–52, A Summary[1]

Time was running out for some of their star players, four of whom had figured in the League before that war, but with the introduction of John Berry and Roger Byrne in 1951 United went on to win the title by a margin of four points over Spurs and Arsenal, who finished second and third respectively.

After Portsmouth had fallen away from an early lead it was Arsenal who ran United closest for the top honour, and when these two clubs met at Old Trafford for the final game of the season Arsenal still had a remote chance of winning the elusive League and Cup 'double'.

It really was a long-shot however, for they needed to beat United by seven goals to snatch the Championship on goal average, but, unfortunately for them, the game served to show the irresistible power of a United side founded upon a great half back line – Carey, Chilton and Cockburn. Arsenal were disjointed through injuries and reduced to ten men after twenty-four minutes

[1] From *We are the Champions* by Maurice Golesworthy (Pelham Books, 1972).

but even this could not detract from the skill of the home side who delighted a crowd numbered over 53,000 with a 6–1 triumph (Rowley 3, Pearson 2, and Byrne).

A week later Arsenal were beaten 1–0 at Wembley by Newcastle United in the Cup Final – a case of so near yet so far from the elusive double.

No man in the United side at this period was more deserving of praise than the captain Johnny Carey, a model captain and among the most complete and versatile footballers in history. He played in every position for United except outside left, once actually being chosen in goal on the morning of a match at Sunderland because of the sudden illness of the regular, Jack Crompton!

He also played in seven different places for Ireland at international level and once had the unique honour of captaining a Rest of Europe XI against the British Isles at Hampden Park in May 1947 in a celebration match to mark the return of the United Kingdom to the International Federation, a distinction gained because Eire were under the aegis of F.I.F.A. at that time and not of the Home Countries.

Cool and calculating, Carey was one of the pre-war players in the side together with Allenby Chilton (who eventually succeeded Carey as the United captain) Stan Pearson, the inside left, and centre forward Jack Rowley.

'Gunner' Rowley scored thirty goals that season (including seven in the first three matches), the best figures of his 208 goal league career, while Chilton, previously underrated, was at the peak of his power although late in his career. Pearson provided the brains of an attack which collected more goals than any Championship title winners since their neighbours, City, had done when winning the prize in 1936–37.

Team: Allen; McNulty, Aston (or Byrne); Carey, Chilton, Cockburn; Berry, Downie, Rowley (or Aston), Pearson, Bond (or Byrne or Rowley).

Reg Allen (goalkeeper): The first goalkeeper to command a five-figure transfer fee; United paid Queens Park Rangers £11,000 for him in 1950 after twelve years on the London club's books. Born in Marylebone, he was a reliable keeper of class, but illness ended his career after only sixty-five League games for United.

Tom McNulty (right back): A local discovery born in Salford, he made twenty-four appearances in the Championship side but never really established himself at Old Trafford before going to Liverpool in 1954.

Roger Byrne (left back or outside left): Full of confidence and one of the fastest full backs of his day, he later captained United to the Championships of 1956 and 1957 as well as to the Cup Final. That was in 1956/57 when United lost 2–1 to Aston Villa. He actually played outside left in the last six games of 1951–52, scoring seven goals! Born in Manchester, he gained thirty-three England caps and made 276 league appearances for the club before being killed in the Munich air crash of 1958.

John Carey (right half): One of the all-time greats of football. Cost United only £200 when signed from Dublin club, St. James's Gate, in 1937. Played in almost every position on the field, including goal, during sixteen years with the United before going to Blackburn Rovers as manager in 1953. This quiet Irishman always made the game look easy; he used his brains and was never ruffled. Captained Rest of Europe team v. Britain in 1947. 'Player of the Year' in 1949 and 'Sportsman of the Year' in 1950. Capped twenty-nine times by Eire and seven times by Northern Ireland. 306 League games for United. Born Dublin.

Allenby Chilton (centre half): Born in South Hylton. Went to Old Trafford from Seaham in 1938 and made League debut in 1939. One of United's most regular first-team men during the first eight seasons after the war. Had been wounded at Normandy but made a good recovery. Cup winners' medal 1948 and was United's only ever-present in the 1951–52 Championship season. Had helped Charlton Athletic win the War-time League South Cup at Wembley in 1944. Succeeded Carey as captain and took his total League appearances to 353 before becoming player-manager of Grimsby Town in 1955. Two England caps.

Henry Cockburn (left half): Lack of height and weight was no handicap to this determined wing half who always played a hard game and usually won the ball in the air. F. A. Cup winners' medal 1948. 243 League appearances. Went to Bury in 1955. Born Ashton. Thirteen England caps.

John Berry (outside right): Cost United £25,000 when signed from Birmingham City in August 1951. Only a little 'un (5ft 5ins) but this nippy winger played havoc with the opposition. Had made 247 League appearances when injuries sustained in the Munich disaster ended his career. Four England caps. Born Aldershot.

John Downie (inside forward): Transferred from Bradford P.A. for £20,000 in March 1949, this Scot (born Lanark) made an important contribution to the Championship-winning campaign, his best while at Old Trafford. 110 appearances. Went to Luton Town for £10,000 in 1953.

Jack Rowley (centre forward): Born in Wolverhampton, a powerful centre forward who always sought the most direct route to goal and took some stopping. He began with the Wolves but never appeared in their League side before joining Bournemouth in 1936. Moved to Old Trafford in October 1937 and scored over 200 League and Cup goals before transferring to Plymouth Argyle as player-manager in February 1955. In six appearances for England his forceful style won him a place in every forward position except outside right. Winner of a Cup medal in 1948, he made 391 league appearances for United, including a number on the wing.

Johnny Aston (left back or centre forward): Born locally, he joined United during the war and made his League debut in 1946. Originally an inside forward he was switched to wing half then to full back, where he earned his reputation with seventeen England caps gained at back. A wholly loyal United servant, he moved to centre forward when Rowley was injured in 1950–51 and continued there for a spell while Rowley returned to action on the left wing. Illness shortened his career, whereupon he retired to Ashton-under-Lyne in 1954. With a Cup winners' medal in 1948, he made 253 League appearances for United.

Stan Pearson (inside left): Stylish, intelligent player and consistent goalscorer, he made his bow for United in 1938–39. A clever ballplayer, noted for his sweeping passes, he won a Cup winners' medal in 1948, eight England caps and made 304 League appearances (125 goals) for United before going to Bury in February 1954. Born in Salford.

Ernie Bond (outside left): Born in Preston and spotted playing for Leyland Motors, he first played for United in this championship season of 1951–52. His stay, however, was brief. After only nineteen League appearances he went to Carlisle United early the following season.

The retirement of Carey in 1953 proved to be a major landmark. It was a wrench but his had been a long and distinguished act of service for the club since joining from Southern Ireland in 1936. So valued was he, indeed, that the directors took the unusual step of inviting him to one of their board meetings on May 19 of that year to express their appreciation of all he had done. The minute of the occasion reads: 'The Directors expressed their deepest regret at his decision to end his playing career and unanimously agreed to put on record their great appreciation of his long and loyal service. By his outstanding personality as a true sportsman, the honours he had won as an international and in club matches, he had covered his career with glory and set a shining example to all who follow him.'

On learning that Carey would be interested in an appointment with the club it was unanimously agreed to offer him an engagement as coach at a remuneration of £1,000 a year and the matter was duly left in the hands of Busby to act accordingly. In the event Blackburn Rovers pounced with the better offer of a managership which Carey accepted but with some diffidence and misgivings because his heart still belonged to United.

Thus, after eighteen seasons, the knot was cut, and his going had about it the departure of some honoured Roman senator from the Forum. Busby himself also felt the break deeply. Both religious men of the same faith and of similar outlook on loyalty, service and integrity, they were more like brothers than manager and player. They shared, too, the same feel for football, seeing in it 'a game hurtling with conflict yet passionate and beautiful in its art'.

Here, indeed, was a man who had been one of the outstanding footballers of his times, an architect of constructive defence and almost as great in his ways as Matthews, the destroyer of defence. At first glance, with his thinning hair and thoughtful expression, he looked older than his true age. But there was no doubting his maturity. From the moment he led out his side, you got the impression that he was bringing out a pack of schoolboys who were to be put through their paces under his supervision. Not that he was overbearing. On the contrary. Yet there was something in his measured, stately tread that engendered an instant feeling of respect and authority.

But Carey never encouraged any exploitation of his personality. For him the game was one thing; personal triumphs at best were an irrelevancy. And in defining his art there is some temptation to use only negatives. He was not audacious (though he did possess an audacity of thought). He was not a showman. He was not magnetic in an obvious, vulgar sense. Yet there was nothing negative about his craftsmanship. If he rightly won his place among the great as a full back, he must also rank as perhaps the finest all-round player who ever took the field. Once the fabulous 'Nudger' Needham, of Sheffield United, was spoken of with bated breath at the turn of the century. There was a player who alone was able to subdue the immortal Steve Bloomer and gain for himself the title of supreme all-rounder by playing for England in every defensive position but goal.

Yet Carey I'll wager to be just as great, if not greater. After all, ten different positions in the immaculate Manchester side and seven for Ireland was a fair enough recommendation of anyone's ability.

Many other memories remain of Carey, the artist. His exact anticipation; the smooth, unhurried positional play that carried him to the right place at the right moment with no more show than if he were taking a quiet stroll on a summer's evening; his exquisite balance and control, especially on a 'sticky dog'; the way he measured his clearances, with the ball always used to the best advantage of the colleague in front of him. And if sometimes he broke the accepted canons of a full back by beating his opponent in the dribble near the danger zone, well, never mind, it was something that could be excused in him, because he was above the lesser mortals. For, in effect, he was a full back who combined the constructive ability of wing half with the footwork and intelligence of an inside forward, and as such he mastered the arts and graces of the game.

Carey, always the most generous of men and of opponents, had earned his plaudits to the end. So had his 1952 side with the title, which, after four decades, had made a long-awaited return to Old Trafford. The occasion was even considered worthy of a leading article in the serious-minded *Guardian*:

> After an interval of forty-one years, Manchester United have regained the championship of the Football League. The title has never been better earned. Not only has the team, in the five seasons before this one, finished second four times and fourth once in the League and won the F.A. Cup; it has been captained, managed and directed in a way that is a lesson to many others. J. Carey, the captain in this period, had been a model footballer – technically efficient, thanks to hard work; a fighter to the last, without ever forgetting that he is a sportsman; a steadier of the younger and inexperienced, an inspirer of the older and tiring, and at all times the most modest of men, though he has won every football honour open to him.
>
> M. Busby, the manager, has shown himself as great a coach as he was a player, with an uncannily brilliant eye for young local players' possibilities, whether in their usual or in other positions; a believer, in the certainty of good football's eventual reward, and a kindly, yet, when necessary, firm father of his family of players.
>
> Between them they have built up a club spirit which is too rare in these days, a spirit which enables men to bear cheerfully personal and team disappointments and to ignore personal opportunities to shine for the good of the whole.
>
> Moreover, by eschewing the dangerous policy of going into the transfer market whenever a weakness develops and giving their chances instead to the many local citizens on the club's books they have made it likely that this club spirit will persist, since the club today is a

> Manchester one not in name only but in fact as far as most of its players are concerned.
>
> Manager and captain could never have brought about this happy state of affairs had they not had through these years such full authority and support from the Board of Directors as must be the envy of many other officials in all parts of the country.

Yet there were those who realised that many of that side were reaching a collective autumn. Six months after winning that title the red light shone clear warning as United were bracketed with Manchester City at the foot of the Championship table. There came a restless stirring among the shareholders. But Busby ironed out their worried brows by saying, 'There is no deep cause for worry although we have slumped for the moment. We have £200,000 worth of skill in our youth and reserve sides.' It was not an idle boast. He and Murphy knew the cards they held and Busby decided to play them in a friendly match at Kilmarnock. Into the team came the pick of the youngsters – Jackie Blanchflower, Whitefoot, Colman, McGuinness, Edwards and Pegg. It was a daring stroke calculated to make or break.

The new wave did not fail. They answered the call with all the alacrity of a war horse at the sound of a bugle. The re-shaped young side won 3–0 at Kilmarnock, drew at Huddersfield and then with Arsenal and Busby knew almost at a stroke that his gamble had paid off. The directors, with every faith in their man, had backed him to the hilt and supported him also in acquiring the dashing centre forward Tommy Taylor from Second Division Barnsley. It was Taylor's arrival and his impact on affairs that were largely responsible for United raising themselves from bottom place to eighth position by the end of that season. The tide, slowly but almost imperceptibly, had turned.

So at a stroke a great side that was about to go over the hill was replaced. Those who stepped down, however, were not coldly abandoned after all their fine service. Delaney earlier had already returned to Scotland, and now Pearson and Cockburn were allowed to go on generous terms to Bury, while those warriors Chilton and Rowley departed to Grimsby and Plymouth respectively as player-managers. As always, United treated those who had served them as human beings and not as mere numbers to be discarded in some bingo game.

Meanwhile the new young players had to fight for their places. Competition was extensive and keen as Busby shuffled his resources in search of the ideal blend. By then, too, he had bought outsiders like Berry at outside right, Taylor, the centre forward, and Wood in goal to become, as it were, his prefects in a classroom preparing for scholarships. There was also another shrewd and telling move at this stage, the marriage of a new full back partnership of Foulkes and Byrne. If not in the same class as the great Carey and Aston before them in technique and as creative artists from the rear, none the less they brought tenacity. Byrne, with his speed which he had used earlier to effect as a left winger, now proved an outstanding success and within a year had gained a regular place in the England side to appear in the World Cup of 1954 in Switzerland, winning thirty-three consecutive caps for his country until fate overtook him at Munich.

The real key to the future, however, lay in the fact that the United youth side had made the F.A. Youth Cup virtually their private property throughout this period. For five consecutive seasons, from 1953 to 1957, they won that competition. Here was the deep reservoir that fed those years and took United to unimagined heights.

Finishing eighth in the First Division in 1953 (after being bottom at one stage of the season), fourth in 1954, and fifth in 1955, the explosion was at hand in 1956 with a side which read: Wood; Foulkes, Byrne; Colman, Jones, Edwards; Berry, Whelan (or J. Blanchflower), Taylor, Viollet, Pegg. Of these only Berry and Byrne remained of the title side of four years earlier and now Edwards, Colman, Viollet and Pegg had moved up through the ranks from the junior to the senior school. And to think that there was still the young Bobby Charlton to burst upon the scene!

Although surprisingly they won only one F.A. Cup tie in those three years, 1954, 1955 and 1956 – the biggest upset being a 4–0 defeat by Bristol Rovers in 1956 – that very same season United ran away with the League Championship to win the title by a record margin for the twentieth century of eleven points. Quite apart from their regular annual triumph in the F.A. Youth Cup, the Reserves also won the Central League so that the club virtually had swept the board. No one could hold a candle to them at this stage; and they were still in the process of development.

This they confirmed the very next year when they even went a step further by winning the League title again and reaching the F.A. Cup Final, when almost certainly they would have been the first club to achieve the double in the twentieth century but for a decisive injury to Wood in goal early in the match, perpetrated by McParland, the Aston Villa outside left. With Blanchflower as the stand-in goalkeeper and reduced to ten men for most of the match, they lost bravely 2–1. Beyond this, too, they reached the semi-final in their first entry to the European Cup before bowing to the richly talented Real Madrid side. That venture is described later in Chapter 4.

The 1957 season, in fact, saw them scaling Everest and getting within sight of its peak; the exciting prospect of winning three major trophies, a feat never previously approached by an English club. They rode a tricycle only to slip sadly twice near the end.

## 1955–56, A Summary[1]

Here was one of the youngest sides – average age, twenty-two years – to win the League title. All but three of the United's team were the club's own developments and such was the power and mobility of this combination that they won the Championship with a margin of eleven points, thus equalling the record created by Preston in 1888–89 and equalled by Sunderland (1892–93) and Aston Villa (1896–97).

The team had changed almost completely from that which had won the League's blue riband four years earlier, only John Berry and Roger Byrne retaining their places, and there was still a good deal of team shuffling at the start before a settled combination was obtained. When the right blend was found in December they really set the First Division alight, suffering only two defeats in the second half of the season, being undefeated in their last fourteen games.

The victory that put United on the right road was the 2–1 win over Sunderland on December 3, Doherty and Viollet scoring the goals that sent United to the top of the table, a point ahead of Blackpool.

It was against Blackpool on April 7 that United made sure of the Championship with two games still to play. Blackpool took the lead at Old Trafford and it looked as if United might suffer their first home defeat of the season when they were still behind at the interval, but in the second half the young ones tore into action and got two goals, Tommy Taylor netting the winner after being off the field for a spell with a cut head.

Team: Wood; Foulkes, Byrne; Colman, Jones, Edwards; (from) Berry, Whelan, Doherty, Taylor, Viollet, Blanchflower, Pegg. Greaves replaced the injured Foulkes late in the season.

[1] From *We are the Champions* by Maurice Golesworthy (Pelham Books, 1972).

Ray Wood (goalkeeper): One of only three players in this team who cost United a fee. They paid £5,000 for him in 1949 when he came from Darlington. Spent most of his first four years at Old Trafford in the Reserves before gaining a regular place in the League side in 1953–54. Two League medals, one Cup runners-up medal and three England caps. Survived the Munich disaster. 188 League games. Born Hebburn-on-Tyne.

Bill Foulkes (right back): A dedicated professional who later achieved a club record total of 567 League appearances before retiring in 1970. Three League Championship medals and three F.A. Cup Final appearances crowned by a win in 1963. Worked on the pit face before being noted playing in his home town, St. Helens, for Whiston B.C. Switched to centre half later in his career and won a European Cup medal in 1968. One England cap. A Munich survivor.

Roger Byrne (left back): See under 1951–52.

Eddie Colman (right half): Captained United's successful youth side before graduating to the League team in October 1955. With a deceptive body swerve he was soon heralded as one of the club's finest prospects. Won two League medals and played in the 1957 F.A. Cup Final. Died at Munich.

Mark Jones (centre half): Born in Barnsley, he made his League debut in 1950 when only seventeen. Good in the air and an efficient 'stopper', he was ever present in 1955–56 season. Died at Munich.

Duncan Edwards (left half): Powerfully built but quick off the mark, a unique future was promised for this young man who was already rated as one of the all-time masters at wing half when he perished at Munich. He was the complete player, able to play in defence or attack, and the scorer of many goals from the edge of the penalty area. Only seventeen when he gained a regular League place in 1953 and the youngest to gain an England cap. 151 League appearances; eighteen England caps; two League medals and a losing Cup Final appearance in 1957, he died in the Munich tragedy.

John Berry (outside right): See under 1951–52.

Liam (Billy) Nolan (inside right): Acquired from Home Farm, Dublin, in 1953, an entertaining ball-player who could read a game intelligently. Made his debut in 1955. Seventy-nine appearances, forty-three League goals; four Eire caps, two League medals and losing Cup Final appearance in 1957. Died at Munich.

Tommy Taylor (centre forward): Signed from Barnsley for £29,999 in 1953, he was a determined attacker who had been with Barnsley since the age of seventeen in July 1949. Began as an inside forward, but United switched him to centre forward. Dangerous in the air and always on the move, he played 163 League games and scored 112 goals for United before dying at Munich. Two League medals; F.A. Cup runners-up medal and nineteen England caps.

Dennis Viollet (inside left): A player who could snap up half chances, he developed in United's youth team and made League debut in 1953. Some thought him too frail, but he had great footballing ability and was noted for his accurate distribution. Two League medals with United, and, after going to Stoke City in January 1962 for £25,000 he was leading scorer for that club when they won their way back to the First Division. Born Manchester. Made 441 League appearances (218 goals), including 259 and 159 respectively for United. Cup Finalists' medal 1958. Two caps.

David Pegg (outside left): Another victim of the Munich air disaster. This popular, smiling player turned professional with United in 1953 at the age of seventeen and made initial League appearance the same season. Two League medals and a Cup Finalists' medal. 127 League games. Born in Doncaster.

Jackie Blanchflower (inside left): Born in Belfast. Younger brother of Danny Blanchflower who helped Spurs win the 'double' in 1960–61. Joined United 1949 and came to the fore in 1953–54 as a wing half. Played mostly at inside left in this Championship season, but when he won his second medal in the next season it was at centre half where he was recalled to take over from injured Mark Jones. Two Irish caps. Cup Finalist, 1957. Injured at Munich.

John Doherty (inside forward): A local lad who first appeared in 1952–53 but had to wait three seasons for his next chance. However, despite making sixteen appearances in the 1955–56 campaign, he was unable to establish himself in the side. Born in Manchester.

## 1956–1957, A Summary

No club at this time could fully match the talent at Old Trafford with the exception perhaps of Wolverhampton Wanderers, their great rivals under Stan Cullis. But for Munich the next year there is no knowing how far United might have gone. Here was virtually the same team that had won the League the previous season. One important newcomer was Bobby Charlton who made thirteen appearances at inside left, one at centre forward and ended with ten goals to show his potential as a lethal finisher. He scored twice in his first appearance at Old Trafford against Charlton Athletic and rubbed salt in the Londoners' wounds by claiming a hat trick against them in the away game at the Valley. He was too athletic for Charlton!

Winning the League for the second season running, United also reached the Cup Final this year, the semi-final of the European Cup, won the F.A. Charity Shield, and the F.A. Youth Cup for the fifth successive year.

With the championship title confirmed by Easter Saturday, United beat Burnley 2–0 on the Monday with seven reserves. On the same day their Reserve side, including nine youth team players, won 3–1 at Burnley in the Central League.

Competition in the First Division was keener this season than a year earlier, but United still kept ahead. The combination of a secure defence and an exciting young attack saw them gather in a total of sixty-four points to win the League, the highest total for twenty-six years. Winning by eight points, they kept a strong Tottenham Hotspur at bay.

Team: Wood; Foulkes, Byrne; Colman, Jones, Edwards; Berry, Whelan, Taylor, Viollet, Pegg.

This was the side that appeared in the Cup Final that season except that Jones and Viollet were both injured and were replaced by Jackie Blanchflower and Bobby Charlton.

Words are not toys. They should be treated with care. So it is with much care and some uncertainty that one approaches the question of who first spotted the potential of the various young players who were drawn to United like moths attracted to a flame. Some would say one and others another. To seek the kudos is a human trait but to apportion the praise is to skate on thin ice. Suffice it to say that many prying eyes were involved and that in the last analysis it was a team effort.

Busby himself was doubtless the central computer to whom all the data would be fed. But being a man who delegated authority to those whose judgment he trusted, he left it to his team of Murphy, Armstrong, Whalley and one or two others to do the basic work of sifting the good apples from the bad. In this general process, too, there were outsiders to consider – schoolmasters and the like who saw in Manchester United a good home and a worthwhile stepping stone to a sporting career for promising youngsters.

There are a myriad stories to be told in this cat-and-mouse game of catching the young. United, however, have always stressed that they never stooped to underhand material persuasion in getting the players they wanted. Following instinct, with no evidence to the contrary available, their word has to be believed. To take three major cases in point.

Young Duncan Edwards, for one, strongly built and rich in promise, soon became the pot of honey to attract a swarm of clubs. Born at Dudley in Worcestershire, it was natural to assume that nearby Wolverhampton Wanderers would become his landing place. But it was to prove otherwise.

Busby's ears were first pricked about Edwards by Joe Mercer, at that time the first professional coach assigned to the English Schools' XI. It was his fulsome recommendation that set the wheels in motion. Murphy, Armstrong and Whalley were given the scent and soon enough the young giant was in their net to the deep chagrin of Wolves. The reason was simple enough. It was the burning passion of Edwards to play for United, whom he idolised.

What an unqualified prize he was! Here was a man amongst boys who would surely have reached undreamed of heights in the world game but for destiny and Munich. As Bobby Charlton once said, 'Playing against men in works teams as we did when I first joined United as a kid – often we had to wait for the factory whistle to blow before the chaps came out to change from their overalls – I felt I could hold my own with anyone. That was part of the marvellous training we once had at Old Trafford in our youth, something which, I believe, the youngsters of today lack. Anyway, I always fancied my chance with anyone – with one exception. That was Duncan Edwards. He was the one chap who always made me feel inferior.'

Murphy, his Rhondda accent thick with Welsh emotion, his eyes glistening with tears, still talks of Edwards like his own lost son. 'He was the Kohinoor diamond amongst our crown jewels. Even when he had won his first full England cap and was still eligible to play for our youth team, he used to love turning out at a lower level. And most important, he never changed. He remained an unspoiled boy to the end, his head the same size as it had been from the start. He just loved to play anywhere and with anyone.

'The tales I could tell of him and of the great goals he scored when they were most needed! There was an occasion, playing for the England Under-23 side against Scotland across the border. Switched from wing half during the match to centre forward when a player left the field through injury, Duncan proceeded to put the ball in the Scottish net four times. That was typical of him. On one

Flames and smoke pour from the wrecked plane at Munich in which eight players and three club officials died.

**Playing their first match since the Munich disaster, United beat Sheffield Wednesday 3-0 in their fifth round F.A. Cup tie at Old Trafford. This was the first goal, scored direct from a corner by Brennan.**

Denis Law signs for United, watched by Gigi Peronace, Jimmy Murphy and Matt Busby.

occasion, too, in our youth team here, when we happened to be losing at half time, I'd go into the dressing room for a word of advice and a chat and Duncan would say to me, "Don't worry, son. I'll get a goal or two for you this half." And he invariably did – from wing half, too. That's what I loved about that kid. He always called me "Son"!' That reflected the kind of relationship Murphy established with the young players, an exchange of affection spiced with discipline and respect.

Bobby Charlton was another case in point. First recommended to United by a headmaster from a different school (Jack Charlton's in fact), a certain Mr. Hemingway – who in his fashion helped to write a page for sporting history probably as lasting as any masterpiece produced by the famous American author of the same name – it was assumed that he would probably join forces with Newcastle United. Born at Ashington, a nearby mining village in Northumberland, with a famous football uncle in Jackie Milburn, the Newcastle and England centre forward, St. James's Park was Charlton's obvious home.

Yet on a cold winter's day in Jarrow, when Jarrow were playing Hebburn in a youth game, his life turned a corner. 'After the match,' he recalls, 'someone said that the Manchester United scout had been watching and I later learned that he had spoken to my mother. It was proved to be little Joe Armstrong and he was the first in a queue for me which later grew enormously after I had played and scored a couple of goals for the England schoolboys at Wembley.

'Well, the fact was that because Manchester were the first to come to me and were prepared to back their judgment before I'd reached the England schools' side, and because Joe Armstrong was the personality he was, I felt a sympathetic respect for the club. Beyond that, too, I remember listening to the 1948 Cup Final on the radio and wanting United to win when nearly everyone else wanted Blackpool and Stanley Matthews to pull it off.

'Even then, subconsciously, I must have been smitten by whatever bug bites you here at Old Trafford. By then, also, the cream of youth was here and I wanted to match myself against them, fellows like Duncan Edwards (who came to United in 1952), Whitefoot, Dennis Viollet and others. Duncan, in fact, became a great pal. He looked after me like a father. He was a lovely person, naive in many ways: not crafty. He just loved life and football, at which he was more gifted than any other player I have ever seen. Yes, that's why I joined United. I just wanted to. It was as simple as that.'

So, the Pied Pipers of Old Trafford prospered with their magic allure for youth. Once asked what were the qualities he sought in a United player Busby replied, 'Skill, flair and character. And the greatest of these is character.' It was these qualities that drew him to Tommy Taylor, already established in a League club.

Jimmy Murphy continues the saga. 'Several of us had run the rule over him and I was finally dispatched to settle the affair. Several times did I drive over to Barnsley and talk to Tommy out on the Yorkshire moors. But he remained adamant. "No, Mr. Murphy," he would say, "I like Barnsley and I have all my pals here." I could see I was flogging a dead horse. But Barnsley at that moment were being relegated to the Third Division and I thought I'd make one more effort.

'We sat in my car out on the moors,' he recalls. 'I said, "You don't want to go down to the Third, Tommy, surely? I'm offering you a great future". He fell silent for a while, deep in thought. Finally he agreed, then added, "But there's one thing I want". Immediately I thought to myself, "Oi, oi! He's after money". But I said to him, "Go on, Tommy, son, put your cards on the table. This is the last time I shall worry you". Do you know what he wanted? A couple of complimentary tickets at Old Trafford for his mother and father every time he played! "They like to watch me perform," he added. "Son," I replied, "we'll let you have a stand full of tickets if you so want!"

'That's how Taylor came to join us. Matt and I duly drove over to Barnsley together and after endless cups of tea with the Barnsley chairman, Mr. – later Sir – Joe Richards, it was settled. The figure actually agreed was £30,000 but Matt, being the psychologist, didn't want the player weighed down with such a price tag, so that it was reduced to £29,999. But I believe Matt tipped the tea lady who had been serving us faithfully with a £1 note so that in fact Tommy *did* cost us £30,000!'

A calm influence in the background in all these affairs of those years was the United chairman, Mr. Harold Hardman. Himself a footballer in his day, an amateur outside left who gained four full international caps for England at the turn of the century, he had been a member of the Everton side that won the Cup at the old Crystal Palace in 1906. A quiet, sparse man, dedicated and of deep character, he lived simply. A shrewd solicitor with offices in the centre of the city, his appetite and needs were small.

Dick Highland-Longdon, once chairman and now president of the amateur Northern Nomads, a club of which Hardman himself was once a playing member in the old days, has told of lunches they used to have in the town. 'Harold was always the same. Unfailingly he would have a bun and a coffee. Afterwards a few of his cronies would join us and we'd play dominoes until it was time to return to the office. Simple and disciplined, the pattern never changed. Almost always, too, whatever the weather, Harold would walk to and from work from his home some four or five miles distant.'

Murphy, too, recalls once returning to Old Trafford from an away match. 'It was raining and there standing at a bus stop was Mr. Hardman, wearing a pack-a-mac and his inevitable trilby hat. I greeted him with the words, "Good evening, Mr. Chairman. It's raining, you know. Why don't you flag a taxi cab?" "I don't need it," he replied. "The bus is good enough. Anyway, if it doesn't come soon I'll probably walk home." That was the sort of man he was and everyone respected him.'

Small and thin of stature, his heart, however, was that of a lion. But for his advanced age he, too, would have been on the aeroplane at Munich. As it was, he was one of those left the burden of that terrible disaster. The emotional strain on him can only be imagined as he and his fellow directors faced the sad duty of attending the funerals and memorial services of so many close friends. He bore the strain remarkably for one of his age, with the added knowledge and determination that somehow or other Manchester United must again rise from the ashes. His message in the United programme of February 19, 1958, said it all:

> Although we mourn our dead and grieve for our wounded, we believe that great days are not done for us. The sympathy and encouragement of the football world and particularly of our supporters will justify and inspire us. The road back may be long and hard but with the memory of those who died at Munich, of their stirring achievements and wonderful sportsmanship ever with us, Manchester United will rise again.

Almost at once those brave words found an unbelievable response as United, with a patchwork side put together with tape and string, won their way against all odds to their second successive Cup Final. Only a season earlier Roger Byrne, the captain, had said after the unlucky defeat by Aston Villa, 'Never mind. We'll be back next year.' Little did he or anyone else know what the cruel fates had in store.

That extraordinary reawakening and upsurge of spirit as United swept to Wembley again so soon after Munich, was carried along on a tide of national emotion. First, existing on reserves and even third team players out of position, they beat Sheffield Wednesday in a fifth round F.A. Cup tie originally postponed to allow them breathing space to get together some sort of a team. Next came West Bromwich Albion who were accounted for 1–0 in the very last minute of a replay, following a 2–2 draw at the Hawthorns and a dramatic surging run by Bobby Charlton who made the winning goal for Webster.

In the semi-final – already bolstered by the acquisition of the clever little Ernie Taylor, who had already gained Cup winners' medals with Newcastle United and then Blackpool as Stanley Matthews' partner; and of Crowther, the left half from Aston Villa – United accounted for Fulham 5–3 in an exciting replay at Highbury after an opening 2–2 draw at Villa Park.

United, remarkably, were on the last lap at Wembley once more and not even the powerful new floodlights erected at Old Trafford at long last in 1957 could shed a clearer beam on the truth than that all England wanted Manchester to win the Cup for the sake of their departed comrades.

But it was not to be. The last stride to the summit was a stride too much and two goals by Nat Lofthouse – the second when he charged Gregg over his goal-line – gave the trophy to Bolton Wanderers.

Since we have now reached 1958 and the end of this particular phase of the story perhaps one could conclude with an account of the match when those marvellous 'Red Devils', so soon to be destroyed, were last seen on these shores in all their glory.

Sometimes an event is branded indelibly on the minds of those present. Such an example occurred on February 1, 1958. The occasion was a League match between Arsenal and Manchester United at Highbury. The final score that Saturday read: Arsenal 4, Manchester United 5. In itself the match was a classic, but it is as an epitaph, above all else, that it now stands. Within a week five of the side who helped fashion that victory were numbered among the United players who died in Munich. That Highbury match was to be the last played on British soil by a young Manchester side which arguably contained more potential than any other to play for the club.

The Manchester side on that day read as follows: Gregg; Foulkes, Byrne; Colman, Jones, Edwards; Morgans, Charlton, Taylor, Viollet, Scanlon. With Jackie Blanchflower, the centre half, Berry and Pegg, the wingers, and the inside forward Billy Whelan, all being rested, this was the side that held Red Star to a 3–3 draw in Belgrade in the European Cup the following Wednesday.

At Highbury, Manchester United gained a quick ascendancy. After only ten minutes they snatched the lead through their powerful wing half Duncan Edwards. A neatly laid-off pass from Viollet found Edwards a few yards outside the penalty box. In this position he was irresistible. His shot was driven too powerfully for Kelsey to handle and United were one up. The goal was typical of Edwards' shooting power. He had scored in much the same way against Scotland at Wembley; a similar goal also won the match against the German World Cup holders, captained by Fritz Walter, at the Olympic Stadium in Berlin.

Next, on the half hour, United were two up with a goal that was a model for the quick counter-attack. At one moment Gregg was saving superbly under the United crossbar; seconds later, straight from the clearance, Scanlon sprinted seventy yards down the left flank and Bobby Charlton crashed in the centre with all the explosive power that was to become his hallmark. The goal prompted the *Guardian* correspondent into what was perhaps a rather belated acknowledment of Charlton's genius. 'R. Charlton,' he noted, 'has grown from a limited left-sided player of little pace into a brilliant inside forward.'

United's magnificent performance was, of course, a team effort, but the contribution of their wing halves stood out above all else. There can have been few pairs of wing halves with more contrasting styles and appearances as Edwards and Colman, but both shared a belief in the old dictum that attack is the best form of defence. Each complemented the other to perfection; the one the aggressive dreadnought, the other the pocket Napoleon, they prompted and prodded the forwards into unceasing action. As the rhythms and directions of the attack were changed in midfield, the attack itself blossomed in response. Morgans, Charlton, Taylor, Viollet and Scanlon moved like one man.

A third goal was to come before half time. Scanlon crossed from one wing, Morgans returned the ball from the other and Tommy Taylor slotted the ball past Kelsey in the centre to complete a goal of symmetrical precision. At half time the rest of the game looked to be a formality. Up to that point the Manchester side, reigning Champions and Cup Finalists of the previous season and European Cup semi-finalists, had revelled in all-out attack.

The second half did indeed look to be a formality, but football was then a good deal less predictable than it is now. For it was an era when even the players with the technique and know-how of 'putting up the shutters' invariably lacked the inclination to do so when the alternative was to move on yet again with attack. The unexpected was in store. With half an hour left, phase two of the game exploded on the crowded scene. In a dazzling space of two and a half minutes, Arsenal were level. One moment United were freewheeling to victory, the next they were hauled back to level-pegging.

The goals tumbled out against a solid wall of noise. The breathless recovery was started by Herd, when he volleyed in a clever lob by Bowen. Gregg could only have heard that one. In another minute the score was 2–3, as Groves headed down Nutt's centre for Bloomfield to score. The cheers were still ringing as the match became all-square. Nutt's cross was low and precise and there was Bloomfield, diving forward to glance the ball into the net off his eyebrows. Highbury was a big top spinning madly; the stands nearly took off in the pandemonium.

Having turned the game on its head, Arsenal burst every blood-vessel to push home their initiative. At that point Bowen had become an inspiration at wing half; Tapscott, Herd and Groves threatened danger every time the stylish Bloomfield threaded the ball through to them with pin-point passes.

Where others would have sagged and died, United, however, as so often over the years, refused to wilt at the crisis. They trimmed their sails, steadied the boat with a firm hand on the tiller and rode out the storm. Step by step over the last twenty minutes they took charge again like champions. By sheer force of character and will-power they superimposed their skill to dominate events once more.

A flowing passage between Charlton and Scanlon saw Viollet, an exceptional player before the Munich crash, head the ball sharply past Kelsey to give United a 4–3 lead. Yet another sinuous attack by Colman and Morgans sent in Taylor to score a remarkable goal from an acute angle. Even then Arsenal refused to admit defeat. Tapscott, always a great competitive spirit, burst clean through United's middle to score from a clever opening by Bowen and Herd, and a see-saw match of nine goals finally drew to a close with the score at 4–5.

By the end the thermometer was doing a war-dance. Spectators and players alike were breathless as the teams left the field arm in arm. They knew instinctively that they had created something for pride and memory. Yet, in the event, the match was to become an obituary.

It was the last time most spectators were to see the great Duncan Edwards. He had made his debut for United at the age of fifteen; at eighteen he was the youngest player to win an international cap. He was a player of immense stature; the embodiment of all that was best in professional football. Jimmy Murphy, assistant manager at

Old Trafford, felt that he was 'the one player who, had he survived, would have made the rebuilding of the United side so much easier'. Murphy also pertinently asked where England would have played Bobby Moore had Edwards come away from Munich unscathed. Beside Edwards four others were killed: Tommy Taylor, a remarkable centre forward who, with his unselfish running off the ball anticipated the likes of Hurst at a time when the battering-ram rôle of the centre forward was only just beginning to lose ground; defenders Roger Byrne and Mark Jones, and the midfield player Eddie 'Snake-hips' Colman, of whom Harry Gregg said, 'When he waggled his hips, he made the stanchions in the grandstand sway.'

The teams that day were:

Arsenal: Kelsey; Charlton (S), Evans; Ward, Fotheringham, Bowen; Groves, Tapscott, Herd, Bloomfield, Nutt.

Manchester United: Gregg; Foulkes, Byrne; Colman, Jones, Edwards; Morgans, Charlton (R), Taylor, Viollet, Scanlon.

Let that game stand as an epitaph for a side the gods loved too much.

# 3

# *Munich, February 6, 1958: A Nation Mourns*

AS TOLD IN the Preface, the fates spared me the horror of the Munich air disaster on Thursday, February 6, 1958, the tragic day a team died in the snow, slush and ice of a German aerodrome runway on their way home from a European Cup tie in Belgrade.

Nor was I alone in this reprieve. Two others of us live on free from a bitter afternoon of 'terrible beauty', to borrow the words of the Irish poet W. B. Yeats. One was Jimmy Murphy, United's assistant manager and Busby's strong right-hand man; the other a leading Yugoslav journalist, Miro Radojcic, a political writer but temperamentally a lover of sport, who has been based in London for the past ten years as a representative of his newspaper. Their different stories are worth the telling as the gods shielded our collective destinies.

Murphy at that time was also the manager of the Welsh national team. On Wednesday, February 5, Wales were due to play Israel in a World Cup qualifying match at Ninian Park, Cardiff – the very game my own feet were directed to by the manager of *The Times*. On that same afternoon United were to face Red Star in Belgrade in the second leg of their quarter-final tie in the European Cup.

Murphy had said to Busby at the time that his heart was really with the club, that he could excuse himself from the Welsh commitment, and that, as usual, he would far rather go to Belgrade with the boys. But Busby had demurred, 'No, Jimmy. Your duty is with Wales on this occasion.' So it was that while he went to Cardiff, Bert Whalley, United's respected and well-loved coach, took the seat in the aeroplane next to Busby, which Murphy himself always occupied. Whalley was killed instantly in the crash.

Radojcic's story is equally ironic as he, too, now lives on borrowed time. Residing in Belgrade at the time, he had seen that European Cup tie and later spent several hours interviewing the United players as they relaxed at the Skadarija Bar into the dark hours, making particular friends with Tommy Taylor and Duncan Edwards. Ironically, the name of that inn, being translated, means 'Way of Life'.

When, finally, the United players retired to their beds for an early take-off next morning, Radojcic sat on alone over his beer and slivovic thinking what delightful new acquaintances he had made and cogitating on the article he would write on them next day in his paper *Politika.*

As the left hand of dawn began to creep into the sky of February 6, a sudden thought struck him. Why not fly with them back to Manchester and perhaps find a new angle to a human story? Gathering up the remains of himself he returned to his flat, threw a few necessities into an overnight bag and took a taxi to the airport where, as a well-known local personality, he was sure he could talk his way on to the United aeroplane.

Having got there, however, and joined up with United, it was discovered that he had left his passport at home. Asking that the aeroplane be delayed a while until his return, he dashed off in another taxi, collected the offending document and returned post haste, only to find that the aeroplane meanwhile had departed. On such delicate tendrils are lives suspended.

Recently he paid a flying a visit to his home town of Belgrade and brought me back a photostat copy of the whole front-page story he wrote later that day following news of the crash. A portion of it is reproduced here.

Having dinner with him one night last winter at the Yugoslav club in London I got Miro to translate his piece into my tape-recorder. At one point, to his own embarrassment, he became choked with tears as he read:

> Death is but an instant. But then the whole of life in a sense is but an instant . . . The memory that lingers on is of the banquet given after the match to both teams that night at the Majestic Hotel in Belgrade. When the lights were doused and the waiters entered with candles flaming on the bowls of iced sweetmeats the whole United side applauded and, led by Roger Byrne, the captain, rose to sing, 'Let us meet again'. Then followed the simple, warm-hearted words of Matt Busby and Walter Crickmer as they said, 'Come to us. The doors of Old Trafford will always be open to you.'
>
> And after that lovely, crazy night as I parted from 'Old International', the football writer of the *Manchester Guardian,* he said to me: 'Why didn't you score just one more goal? Then we could have met a third time . . .'

Ever since that day the Yugoslavs in general and Red Star in particular have felt an emotional bond with United which it would be hard to destroy. Here is something to illustrate that very genuine link, no matter however hard and sometimes cruel their meetings may have been on the field of play (I remember, in particular, a tough battle with Partizan, Belgrade, in a European Cup semi-final of 1966).

Once, in the spring of 1965, England were in Belgrade to play Yugoslavia. At one of their training sessions on a local school pitch, Bernard Joy, of the London *Evening Standard,* himself a former Arsenal player, and myself, found ourselves having to entertain a swarm of Yugoslav schoolchildren while the England players were getting changed into their strip. Suddenly, an elderly man pushed his way through the crowd. His face was heavily-bronzed and deeply lined, like some old crab-apple. He bore with him a framed, colour group photograph of that Manchester United Munich team. Each player who perished he had marked with a cross in ink on his red shirt. He had a few words of English and he made it clear to us that he had seen and admired the United of that day. As he spoke tears made two small rivulets down the scars of his face. We were embarrassed and touched.

Later in the afternoon, he sought me out again. It transpired that he was the groundsman, both of the school fields and of a huge new stadium, belonging to Red Star, which was being built near by. He proudly produced a photograph of himself kneeling beside a model of the new Red Star temple-to-be, wrote his name and address on the back and together with a Red Star lapel badge, plus a packet of ten Yugoslavian cigarettes, asked me to present the little package to Matt Busby on my return to England. 'I had the honour and the much pleasure to meet him when Manchester United came here then . . .,' he said haltingly. Sir Matt was very moved when I gave him these small, but precious gifts later in his office at Old Trafford and, knowing him, I'm sure that he found time to drop the old man a letter.

The people of Belgrade, indeed, still feel themselves emotionally involved with Manchester United. Early in the 1971 season, I received a telephone call saying that Red Star were anxious to invite United over there to take part in a celebration match to mark the switching on of the floodlights ('the best in Europe', they claim) of that new stadium of theirs, which can now hold something like a 110,000-capacity crowd. I was asked to smooth the way with Manchester in the matter. In the event, they were unable to fit in a suitable date so that in the end Red Star played host to Benfica, of Portugal.

But the thought was there.

Everyone will have their own memories of that dark February day twenty years ago when the world seemed suddenly to shift on its axis and disintegrate. For myself, having returned to London overnight from Cardiff, I went to a cinema that Thursday afternoon.

On emerging around teatime, the first thing I saw on the street was an evening paper billposter screaming out the dreadful news in the heaviest type. I ran home like a hare just in time to hear the telephone ringing. It was the office. For two hours they had been trying to make contact. Then the B.B.C. rang. At that stage precise information on the casualties was scarce and confused. No one knew anything for certain apart from the stark fact that United's aeroplane had crashed on take-off at Munich Riem Airport.

Sometime after midnight I finally got home having written two pieces for the paper in the office and done four broadcasts at the B.B.C. all virtually in the dark of uncertain knowledge. One of those broadcasts was in company with Walter Winterbottom, himself a former United player and at that time manager of the England side due to take part only four months later in the World Cup of 1958, in Sweden. Little was he to know at that moment that his team had lost three key figures, one in each department of its make-up: Roger Byrne at full back, Duncan Edwards at half back and Tommy Taylor at centre forward. For myself, on returning home, I went to bed and wept at the loss of so many friends.

When Jimmy Murphy got back to Manchester and Old Trafford from Cardiff he had no inkling of what had happened. There were only three or four of the staff on duty, but a strained, unreal atmosphere seemed to hang in the air. Going into one of the offices he ran into a secretary who appeared white, dazed and scarcely able to speak. Then her tears began to fall; she stammered out the news and the enormity of the disaster struck him. Taking a bottle of whisky from a sideboard he quickly retired to his own office and wept.

By nightfall there were few people in Britain unmoved by the extent and nature of the tragedy. Manchester itself became a dead city as the blinds were drawn in every house as if somehow to keep out the truth and reality of it all.

H. E. Bates, the novelist, later epitomised the universal feeling in a tribute published in the *F.A. Year Book* of 1958–59:

At six o'clock, out of pure curiosity, I turned on my television set. As the news came on, the screen seemed to go black. The normally urbane voice of the announcer seemed to turn into a sledge hammer. My eyes went deathly cold and I sat listening with a frozen brain to that cruel and shocking list of casualties that was now to give the word Munich an even sadder meaning than it had acquired on a day before the war, after a British Prime Minister had come home to London waving a pitiful piece of paper and most of us knew that new calamities of war were inevitable.

In the end fate reaped a deadly harvest of eight United players (five of whom had played in the 3–3 draw the previous day), eight journalists, three Manchester club officials, two members of the aircrew (one the co-pilot) and two other passengers – a total of twenty-three from a full complement of forty-three who had set out on the flight.

*The Departed:*

*Players*

Roger Byrne (left back)
Geoff Bent (reserve left back)
Eddie Colman (right half)
Mark Jones (centre half)
Duncan Edwards (left half)
David Pegg (outside left)
Tommy Taylor (centre forward)
Liam ('Bill') Whelan (inside right)

*Journalists*

Alf Clarke (*Manchester Evening Chronicle*)
Don Davies (*Manchester Guardian*)
George Follows (*Daily Herald*)
Tom Jackson (*Manchester Evening News*)
Archie Ledbrooke (*Daily Mirror*)
Henry Rose (*Daily Express*)
Frank Swift (*News of the World*)
Eric Thompson (*Daily Mail*)

*Officials*

Walter Crickmer (Man. United secretary)
Tom Curry (Man. United trainer)
Bert Whalley (Man. United team coach)

*Crew*

Captain K. G. Rayment (co-pilot)
Mr. W. T. Cable (steward)

*Others*

Mr. B. P. Miklos (travel agent)
Mr. Willie Satinoff (Man. United supporter)

*The Survivors:*

Matt Busby (Man. United manager)

| *Players* | *Press* |
|---|---|
| John Berry (outside right) | E. Ellyard (*Daily Mail* photographer) |
| Jackie Blanchflower (centre half) | Peter Howard (*Daily Mail* photographer) |
| Bobby Charlton (inside left) | Frank Taylor (*News Chronicle* sports writer) |
| Billy Foulkes (right back) | *Others* |
| Harry Gregg (goalkeeper) | Mrs. Vera Lukić and baby |
| Ken Morgans (outside right) | Mrs. B. P. Miklos |
| Albert Scanlon (outside left) | Mr. N. Tomasevic |
| Dennis Viollet (inside left) | |
| Ray Wood (goalkeeper) | |

Without question that was the darkest day in British sport, more solemn and far reaching even than the Burnden Park crowd disaster when thirty-three people were crushed to death and suffocated during an F.A. Cup tie between Bolton Wanderers and Stoke City in 1946; more traumatic even than the Ibrox Park disaster later in Glasgow when over sixty people died in a pile-up on the exit steps of the stadium during the final minutes of a match between those traditional rivals Rangers and Celtic.

The significant difference lay in the fact that while those other tragedies, shocking though they were, seemed almost faceless and anonymous (except to the families involved), those young Manchester United players had appeared many times on the television screens of every front parlour the length and breadth of the country. To millions they had become identified in their many exploits almost as personal friends. Some years earlier, in 1949, a similar kind of accident had happened in Italy when the great Torino team – seven or eight of them then current members of the Italian national side – crashed into Superga Hill in their aeroplane on the way back to Turin from Spain. On that occasion, too, some half a dozen journalists travelling with the party had perished with most of the players. Like the plaque that has stood in the Old Trafford press box these past twenty years commemorating the deaths of those eight Munich air disaster pressmen, there stands in the Comunale Stadium in Turin a similar memorial to their Italian brothers. And over the portals of both grounds also are enshrined the names of the players who were taken before their time.

Yet the Superga disaster had by no means the same world-wide impact as Munich. This was brought home to me a summer or so later when on holiday in Spain. I was approached by a young

Spanish boy. Anxious to earn a few pesetas, he offered to conduct me to the local bull-ring and a church or two. The afternoon sun was high and the heat simmered like an iron as he took on the role of experienced guide.

During our conversation he suddenly produced a grubby cigarette card from his trouser pocket. I could see it held the face of a footballer. Realising I was from England, he asked if I knew of the player. I took the card into my hand. It was Tommy Taylor. I nodded my head, whereupon with dramatic use of his little hand he illustrated how the plane had crashed. Then, to my utter astonishment, he told how his village school had gone into mourning and had been closed for a week. I remember wondering at the time whether one of our own little schools back home would have reacted similarly had a Spanish football team perished likewise. I doubted it.

Two years after Munich, my good friend and colleague Frank Taylor – then of the *News Chronicle* and the only correspondent to survive the holocaust – knowing well of my attachment to Manchester United, their players, staff and press corps and of my wish to have been with them on that occasion as on so many others – sent me an inscribed copy of the moving book he wrote – *The Day a Team Died* (Stanley Paul & Co., 1960).

Unashamedly and with his permission I now quote certain extracts, hoping meanwhile not to open old wounds unduly and stir sad memories. But the fact is that Munich is now firmly stitched into the fabric of the Manchester United story. Indeed, I would go further. I believe it to be the continuing emotional charisma that surrounds the club and has taken its name round the world. As such it cannot be brushed conveniently under the carpet.

After two abortive attempts at take-off on a runway thick with slush and snow – both abandoned before the point of no return — the Elizabethan charter aircraft carrying the United party, coded ZULU UNIFORM – 609 (G-ALZU), taxied back to the terminal buildings for a check-up by the technical ground crew.

The passengers alighted to wait in the airport lounge. In less than quarter of an hour all were aboard again, the authorities satisfied that all was well. The time was 14.59 hours and the third take-off about to be attempted. It was just four and a half minutes to disaster.

Frank Taylor wrote of the drama thus:

> Inside the passengers' cabin we relaxed, expectantly rubbing hands, clearing the tables in front of us ready for the meal soon to be served.

The last radio message from the control tower was the signal for the motors to burst into thunderous life. Louder . . . louder . . . louder, until they reached the familiar high-pitched whine. The seconds were ticking away. We raced down the runway, picking up speed, 70 knots . . . now 80 . . . 100 . . . right on up to 117 knots. Peter Howard thought he heard the starboard engine note drop, like a car changing gear. Harry Gregg had the same impression. If that engine did suddenly drop its revs I didn't notice it in my seat on the other side of the plane. I was too busy watching that port wheel; the huge wave of slush thrown back as we ploughed along at high speed The ship was steady enough, but we ought to be airborne by now. Surely we had passed the point on the runway where we had stopped on the two previous runs. Had that wheel gone up yet?

I shouted to Dennis Viollet in the seat in front of me: 'Can you see whether that wheel has gone up yet, Dennis?'

No reply. I don't think he heard me above the roar of the engines. The plane was still hurtling along, and it was quite impossible to see through that infernal spume whether we had left the ground, although I felt certain we must be beyond the point of no return.

I turned half right to look over my shoulder at the way ahead as the machine tore on. I felt a sudden surge of alarm, as, directly ahead, there was a wooden fence . . . *the perimeter fence.* In that freezing moment I felt a sickening blow behind the left ear . . .

He continued: The City of Manchester didn't believe the news when it first broke. It was just a catchpenny newspaper stunt; it couldn't have happened, not to Manchester's Red Devils. Whoever heard of such a thing happening to a famous football team? Why, they would be flying into Ringway at 6.30 as arranged. It was probably just a little bump to their aeroplane or something like that, and the newspapers were just making a song and dance about it.

The first indication that anything was wrong came in the Stop Press of the early afternoon editions of the *Manchester Evening Chronicle* and the *Manchester Evening News.*

The news-boys dashed along the streets shouting: 'Manchester United plane held up in Munich snowstorm.'

Almost as soon as those editions hit the streets, the rotary presses were spewing out fresh editions with a new, more dreadful story: 'Manchester United players in plane crash.'

Crowds clustered round the newspaper sellers. The B.B.C. broke into their programmes as the housewives were tuning in for 'Mrs. Dale's Diary'.

A chill hysteria gripped Manchester. Men and women wept openly and unashamedly on the streets. Many of them had never seen a football match, but this was an accident that touched them all. In the newspaper offices they had never known a day or night like it before – not since the war anyway.

> As the story stuttered over the teleprinters, editors hastily summoned their conferences. At Old Trafford, Manchester United's ground, the staff were stunned by the news and then made plans to see what help could be offered to the players' and officials' relatives.

Many were the heroic, painful stories of those survivors, who bit by bit were pieced together by the devotion and skill of Professor Maurer and his team of doctors and surgeons at the Rechts der Isar Hospital in Munich. Foremost among them, of course, was Busby. The wall of his chest crushed, endangering his lungs, and a smashed right foot, saw him fight a long battle for survival which only his personal courage, determination and spiritual faith helped him to survive. So ill was he that for a long time the loss of his players and close colleagues was kept from him – especially the passing of the unique young Duncan Edwards, who for some sixteen days had fought for life in a coma. In the end, however, the gods loved him too much.

Of Busby, Frank Taylor wrote:

> Of all the many miracles of Munich, I think maybe the greatest of all was the way Matt Busby, Commander of the British Empire, dragged himself up from the floor and came back to the game of football.
>
> He was taken into Munich's Rechts der Isar Hospital with his life ebbing away, his life's work in ruins, and many of his closest and dearest friends killed. The Germans, of course, did not know at first that he was a famous figure in British sport. To them he was just another patient, and a badly injured one at that. He could speak no word of German; his fame and contacts were of no use to him now. Only the man Busby mattered. Only his own physical strength and tremendous will-power, allied to the skill of the doctors, could save him. He spoke the universal language all could understand by his flaming courage in adversity; his silent acceptance of the pain; his tremendous mental stamina when the full appalling details of the crash were revealed to him.
>
> Think for a moment what the Munich air crash meant to Matt Busby.
>
> If a painter spends a lifetime on a canvas and then has it destroyed by some malicious dauber, the world sympathises. Yet the painter can take up his brushes and create anew.
>
> If a ballet dancer falls and sprains an ankle, the balletomanes howl their anguish at such bad luck. In time the dancer may yet come back quite as good as ever.
>
> If an inventor wrecks his dream child, he deals with materials; it is possible to try, try and try again.
>
> In Busby's case his life work was founded on the skill of human beings. They were young men; they were his friends; they were as sons to him, as he watched them grow from boys into young men. He also lost close confidants like Walter Crickmer, the United secretary; Bert Whalley,

**Denis Law in action, a magnetic player and potent finisher.**

**Law evades Gordon Banks in the Cup Final, 1963.**

**Law (no 10) scores the first goal in United's 3-1 defeat of Leicester City in the Cup Final of 1963.**

the United coach; Willie Satinoff; a close personal friend like Frank Swift, and the sports writers too.

I sometimes wonder whether people fully realize what all this meant to Busby, who was, so to speak, the centre-piece of it all.

Let me be quite brutally frank. Only a very remarkable man would have recovered from his injuries at Busby's age. Only a man with a sense of a mission yet unfulfilled would have come back to his job as Busby has done. I believe that, deep in that thoughtful mind – in spite of Munich – Busby is determined to create another football team like the one that perished; a team which will win the European Cup for Britain. I think he feels he owes it to the lads that are gone.

I still marvel how, in a matter of weeks, he pulled himself back from the Vale of Shadows to become recognisable as the man football knows so well. I still see Busby, in the mind's eye, after the doctors had told him he could leave Munich and come back to see his team play in the Cup Final at Wembley against Bolton Wanderers.

In his first full season back at the helm, Manchester United, after a shocking start to the season, hit a phenomenal streak and finished runners-up to Wolves. No one was more surprised than Matt Busby. He told me at the time, 'All I was hoping for was a reasonably safe place in the First Division until we get things sorted out. These boys have played better than I dared hope. But a lot has to be done. It will take years to try and build up again.'

This is just what Busby, with Jimmy Murphy still at his side, is trying to do. Is he right or wrong, to try and build a great football team again after all the fearful hearbreak and the great human tragedy of Munich?

I am quite sure he is right. Busby's family and close friends know that his health almost cracked under the strain, trying to get back into top gear too soon after Munich. He had to give up his job as Scotland's team manager and was advised to take a prolonged rest from his duties with Manchester United. Why didn't he? Say what you like about the man, but he is no quitter.

Meanwhile, back in Manchester, the minutes of the board meetings of the directors scarcely told in their cold, matter-of-fact terms of all the drama and heartaches that surrounded the club. On the very morning after the crash it was recorded that Mr. Harold Hardman, the chairman, together with Mr. W. H. Petherbridge, had attended the funeral of a fellow director, Mr. George Whittaker. It truly was a time of unlimited sorrow.

Picking on random points in the minute book, it was revealed on February 13 that Jimmy Murphy, standing in as temporary manager for Busby, was about to interview Ernie Taylor, of Blackpool, with a view to his transfer to Old Trafford. Murphy got his man. At the same meeting it was agreed that Jack Crompton, United's former goalkeeper, should be appointed the new team trainer if available;

that Johnny Carey and Jack Rowley had offered their services to the club in any capacity; that a sum of £150 was to be forwarded to the visiting relatives detained in Munich; that Professor Maurer together with his wife and some members of his staff at the Rechts der Isar Hospital in Munich were to visit Old Trafford and attend the League match against West Bromwich Albion on March 8.

The latter event duly took place as the German party became guests of the City and the club and were warmly greeted by a 60,000 crowd in the stadium. It was also an appropriate occasion for the chairman, Harold Hardman, to state publicly, 'Words are inadequate to describe our thanks and appreciation of the truly magnificent work of the surgeons and nurses of the Rechts der Isar Hospital at Munich. But for their superb skill and deep compassion our casualties might have been greater. To Professor Georg Maurer, Chief Surgeon, we offer our eternal gratitude.'

Throughout this sad and difficult period messages of sympathy had poured into the club from many quarters: from Her Majesty the Queen, the King of Sweden, the Pope, the French and Italian Ambassadors, the Apostolic Delegate, and Lord Derby, the Lord Lieutenant of Lancashire; also from municipalities and sporting organisations in every part of the world. Beyond these official tributes were others which served to show the sense of personal loss felt by so many, and a general appreciation of the integrity for which the club stood. Among such condolences were those from public schools, private schools, secondary schools and primary schools; ships at sea, works and offices and even prisoners in H.M. prisons; the D'Oyly Carte and the Lirica Italiana Opera companies; the L.C.C. Tenants' Association, the Salvation Army, the Sikh Community of Manchester, the Soroptimists International Association, the Society of West End Theatre Managers; and among thousands of private individuals, the Bishop of Chester, Sir Thomas Beecham, and the Rector of the University of Bordeaux.[1]

In the midst of all this sorrowful upheaval a memorial service was held at St. Martin-in-the-Fields, London, on February 17, where the address was given by the Bishop of Chester. In a moving oration came these words:

> We are here today to express on behalf of a great company the sympathy which we feel at so sudden and grievous a blow. We may well ask why this particular accident has called for such widely spread expression of sympathy. It is, I think, due not solely to the drama of the setting or the

[1] *Manchester United* by Percy M. Young (William Heinemann, 1960).

fact that skilful players, officials and writers, well-known and admired, have been killed, though of course these factors are present in our minds. It is rather due, so I believe, to the character of the team to which those players belonged and the fine sport which they have created and upheld. Those well fitted to express an opinion have spoken of the quite outstanding quality which Manchester United has displayed and, during the last ten years under the genius of Matt Busby, young men have not only been trained to a high standard of technical efficiency but they have also been inspired with a loyalty to the club and to the game which has been a pattern for the best that man can achieve. This character has brought the team to the highest places in the game in this country. It has made the name of Manchester United a household word. It has also given the team an opportunity of travelling to many foreign countries and there, in addition to playing football, they have proved themselves fine ambassadors on the football ground and off it.

When we remember that during the season a million people each week in this country watch professional football, we can appreciate the responsibility which is laid upon these young players. They are admired, idolised, glamorised, imitated. They set a standard which, unseen perhaps, certainly leaves its mark upon the moral standards of our society. They have a responsibility not only to play efficiently but to play well, and it is because Manchester United have acquitted themselves so splendidly in the wider as well as the ultimate discharge of their duty that the team has become a byword for those who play a good game wherever football is played.

A week or so later came another memorial service to the fallen journalists, held before a packed congregation at St. Bride's Church in Fleet Street where it was my sad privilege to give the address to our departed colleagues. Walter Winterbottom read the second address. As I spoke I remember looking up at the tall church windows. Snow had begun to fall. It seemed highly symbolic at that moment.

On the Saturday following Munich – February 8, two days later – snow also came to blanket much of Britain's football. That, too, brought a symbolic hush, for it was a moment of mourning in sport as teams and spectators stood in a two-minute silence for Manchester United, not the least of them a 60,000 crowd at Twickenham for a Rugby International between England and Ireland. At many grounds 'Abide with me' was sung before the kick-off.

In the meantime there was a job still to be done at Old Trafford. The show concerned football and in the best traditions of the theatre the show had to go on. With Jimmy Murphy standing in for Matt Busby, and Les Olive the new secretary in succession to deceased Walter Crickmer, a loyal servant of the club for thirty-eight years, a patchwork United side, mostly from the reserves, was put together. With only Foulkes and Gregg as survivors from the seniors, two new acquisitions were drafted into the team – the experienced and clever little inside forward Ernie Taylor, who had played for England and won F.A. Cup medals with Newcastle United in 1951 and Blackpool in 1953; and Stan Crowther, a strong wing half from Aston Villa. Both were granted special dispensation by the F.A. to play in the Cup for United although Crowther had already appeared for his former club in an earlier round.

Having already won at Workington and beaten Ipswich Town, United were now in the fifth round of the competition, due to play at home against Sheffield Wednesday. Because they were clearly not yet ready for the fray the F.A. revealed some milk of human kindness by postponing the tie for some ten days. So it was that on the Wednesday night of February 19, under the floodlights of Old Trafford, a 60,000-crowd, every nerve end jangling, welcomed back the red shirts to a field of battle once more.

It was an eerie, emotional occasion dominated by the memories and ghosts of the past, a poignancy heightened by the fact that the United half of the programme showed eleven blank spaces. Each name had to be filled in with the help of the loudspeaker announcements before the kick-off so that the chosen team duly read: Gregg; Foulkes, Greaves; Goodwin, Cope, Crowther; Webster, E. Taylor, Dawson, M. Pearson, Brennan.

Denis Law, then a Huddersfield player, has since told how he travelled over the Pennines to be at Old Trafford that night, drawn by the drama of the occasion and paying a black market £1 for a 2/6d. standing place on the terraces at the Stretford End.

It is history now how United won 3–0; how Shay Brennan, then a reserve full back, played at outside left and scored two goals to become the hero of the hour – the same Brennan who ten years later was to win a European Cup Winners medal with United against Benfica at Wembley in his proper position of full back!

From that moment there was no stopping United. Carried forward on a gathering wave of emotion throughout the land they swept through the twin portals of Wembley to reach their second successive Cup Final against all conceivable odds, only to lose once more. At least Busby, frail and damaged by his terrible experience, was there sitting as a spectator on the touchline behind his old colleague Jimmy Murphy who had helped a new, inexperienced side over the treacherous rapids at a critical period. And when Nat

Lofthouse floored and barged Gregg into the United net, ball and all, for Bolton's second goal no word or gesture of protest came from a single Manchester player. In that very act they won distinction. Their old values had not died.

Eleven years later, in June 1969, the final findings of the Court of Inquiry into the Munich crash were published, after much controversy and backsliding by German officialdom.

The key witness in the inquiry which cleared Captain James Thain from blame for the disaster was a German pilot who was at Munich airport on the day of the crash. Herr Reinhard Meyer, a pilot since 1940 and an aircraft designer, was one of the first to reach the crashed aircraft. He told the British inquiry under Mr. E. S. Fay that he 'was thinking about possible reasons for it and . . . was considering whether aircraft icing could have been the reason'. He said there was nothing like frost or frozen deposit on the wing of the B.E.A. Elizabethan airliner as it lay at the end of the runway. 'There was melting snow only.'

The Fay Report comments: '. . . Herr Meyer was the only person to investigate the icing question within a short time of the accident. He looked with the eye of an experienced pilot and aircraft designer.' The inquiry finds that the cause of the crash was slush on the runway, and that it is 'possible but unlikely' that wing icing was a contributory cause.

Other findings of the inquiry, set up by the Prime Minister and the President of the Board of Trade in April last year, are that Captain Thain was not at fault with regard to runway slush, but that he was at fault with regard to wing icing. 'But,' the report adds, 'because wing icing is unlikely to have been a contributory cause of the accident, blame cannot be imputed to him.' The report also finds that Captain Thain, now aged forty-eight and a smallholder in Berkshire, was at fault in permitting his co-pilot – another captain – to occupy the left instead of the right-hand seat, 'but this played no part in causing the accident'. The report concludes: 'In accordance with our terms of reference, we therefore report that in our opinion blame for the accident is not to be imputed to Captain Thain.'

These findings are at variance with those of two inquiries conducted by the Germans, which declared that the decisive cause of the accident lay in wing icing and that runway slush was a further cause. The latest inquiry heard twenty-seven witnesses and the commission sat in London, Bremen and Frankfurt. The central witness was Captain Thain who, since the accident, has spent more than £1,000 trying to clear his name. He told the inquiry that before the unsuccessful take-off he and his co-pilot looked out of the windows and the wings looked clean. The Fay Commission examined a photograph produced by the German investigators. It was taken from the airport building just before the Elizabethan's departure. The photograph appeared to show no signs of snow on the wings. After examining an enlargement of the original negative, the Joint Air Reconnaissance Intelligence Centre decided that the whiteness on the wings may have been light reflected from the wet surface, and not ice as previously thought.

So ended a sad chapter in the story of a famous club. The most apt epitaph perhaps for all those fine young men cut off in the prime of life were the words of Laurence Binyon, reproduced in the United programme of February 19, 1958:

They shall not grow old
As we that are left grow old.
Age shall not weary them
    nor the years condemn.
At the going down of the sun,
    and in the morning
We will remember them.

# *Part Two*

# 4

# *Entry into Europe:*
# *Vision of Wider Horizons*

PERHAPS ONE OF the most momentous decisions ever made by United was to ignore the protest and opposition of the Football League Management committee in the matter of taking part in the European Champions Cup of 1956–57.

Here was a new competition engineered by the famous French newspaper *L'Equipe* under its football editor Gabriel Hanot. In fact, the germ of a similar idea could be traced back to 1927 when a proposal was laid before the executive committee of F.I.F.A.; one of the most fervent promoters of that suggestion had been the late Henri Delaunay, then secretary of the French Football Federation. But notwithstanding the readiness and breadth of support the proposal received at the time nothing came out of it. There were always too many other fixtures to make it practicable.

Following the Second World War, however, the extended use of air transport and the arrival of floodlighting removed some of the major objections and it was *L'Equipe* in an article of December 1954 who revived the idea. Having suggested that the champion League club of each of the European F.A.s should participate, the newspaper struck while the iron was hot, and four months later, in April 1955, had the representatives of clubs from sixteen nations sitting round a table in Paris and agreeing to the draw for the first round to be played in the 1955–56 season.

Further discussions took place in Vienna at the congress of the European Union at which *L'Equipe* representatives were also present and as a result the following clubs agreed to enter:

Rot Weiss, Essen – Germany
Rapid, Vienna – Austria
Royal Sporting Club d'Anderlecht – Belgium
Servette – Switzerland
Djurgaarden Idrottsforenning – Sweden
Partizan Belgrade – Yugoslavia

Aarhus Gymnastic Forening – Demark
Stade de Reims – France
Voros Lobogo – Hungary
A.C. Milan – Italy
F.C. Saarebrück – Saar
Gwardia – Poland
Real Madrid – Spain
Hibernian – Scotland
Philips Sport Vereinigung – Holland
Sporting Club, Lisbon – Portugal

In 1955 Chelsea, for the first time in their history, had become League champions of England and had entered their name for the competition. Sadly, however, they were forced to withdraw their entry at the insistence of the Football League whose insular outlook at the time had suggested that this new tournament would interfere with domestic commitments.

When Manchester United became champions the following season they, too, were forbidden by the League to join the European Cup. To their everlasting credit, however, United refused to bow to their masters' voice. They decided they were their own masters. They saw, too, the vast scope and added interest of such a challenge; they appreciated the experience to be gained in knowing how the other half lives, and they sensed the gold that lay hidden across the waters. They duly entered and soon enough were to unearth a rich vein that was not only to do themselves good but the rest of English club football too. Contrary to the limited vision of the Football League rulers, Continental competition in due course was to stimulate the game within these shores to such an extent that the goal of every club here is now to get into Europe by hook or by crook.

Certainly there have been times over the past fifteen years or so when certain people began to have doubts about the way things were developing. Even Hanot himself on occasion regretted letting loose what he felt was rapidly growing into a Frankenstein monster. The desire to win and the rivalry engendered as the prizes and the incentives increased, tended to spill over the bounds of fair play. There have been a number of unpleasant, unfortunate incidents here and there as passions and greed exploded into violence, the scandal of 1971–72 being the Munchengladbach – Inter Milan European Cup tie.[1]

Hanot's worst fears were at last being realised by the European Union itself. In a New Year edict to welcome 1972, U.E.F.A. belatedly showed that they were prepared to step into line with the disciplinary purge in England.

[1] The trouble between Borussia Munchengladbach and Inter-Milan was not caused by misbehaviour of the players, but by the throwing of a beer can from the German crowd which knocked out Boninsegna, the Italian World Cup centre forward.

Hans Bangerter, the U.E.F.A. secretary, gave all clubs in European competition this warning: 'Any and all undisciplined action must be punished. In order to stop further escalation of such lamentable events, the disciplinary committee has no alternative but to apply in full the increased sanctions.'

These included the automatic suspension of offending players and awarding the tie to the opposition in the event of crowd disorder. Bangerter claimed that the roots of the present disease are the exaggerated bonuses for players and the demand for prestige victories by managers and directors.

'The ideals of fair play and sport ethics are more and more trampled down by what can only be called criminal elements,' he said.

The biggest danger that still remains is when an Argentine side challenges a European winner for the unofficial club championship of the world. We have only to recall the bloody outcomes when Celtic, Manchester United and A.C. Milan met these South American rivals over recent years to make the point. In fact, Ajax, of Amsterdam, the European champions of 1971, refused to meet Nacional, of Uruguay, their New World counterparts, in the play-off the following season. Much to the anger of the South Americans the Dutchmen decided prudence to be the better part of valour, and they probably set a good example by doing so.

Yet, eager for attention and challenge, Ajax's place was later taken by Panathinaikos, of Athens, who under the managership of Ferenc Puskas, had been beaten by the Dutchmen in the European Cup Final at Wembley.

There are still many snags, of course, and money perhaps plays too big a part in it all, emphasised by the home and away two-match system, whereby victory goes to the side with the greater aggregate of goals. This leads to a massive inflection on defence by the club playing away and spoils the game. But it doubles the gate receipts, which in the end is what people are really after. Far more entertaining, I would say, would be a straight knock-out on the lines of our own F.A. Cup, with the luck of the draw playing a greater part and offering the weaker teams a chance for surprise. But this is by the way and probably a minority view.

Meanwhile English football must tip its collective hat to Manchester United for the stubborn stand they took after winning the League in 1956. They challenged the League, entered, and made their masters eat their words.

But, having received an invitation from U.E.F.A. to participate, let Busby tell the story in his own words: 'I was very keen on the idea and at one of our board meetings early in May 1956, Mr. Harold Hardman, the chairman, asked me whether I thought it wise that the club should go in for the added commitment. My reply was: "Well, Mr. Chairman, football has become a world game. It no longer exclusively belongs to England, Scotland and the British Isles. This is where the future of the game lies." "All right," said Mr. Hardman, "if that's what you really feel." "Yes I do," was my retort. "Anyway, let's just try it."

'It was at that point that a letter was received from the League forbidding us to enter. At our next board meeting I again repeated my keenness on the challenge and once more proposed that if the Football Association were willing to accept and back us we should enter. This was duly forthcoming and at another board meeting on May 22 we decided to step into new waters . . .'

At once United made their presence felt. Their first competitive match on the Continent was in Brussels on September 12, 1956, against Anderlecht, the Belgian champions, when goals by Viollet and Tommy Taylor saw them to a 2–0 win. A fortnight later the return tie was played at Maine Road, Manchester, because the Old Trafford floodlights were not yet ready.

United won that second leg by 10–0, the goals going to Viollet (4), Taylor (3), Whelan (2) and Berry (1) in what Matt Busby still regards as one of the purest, most flawless exhibitions ever given by the club. 'In spite of that cricket score,' he recalls, 'I can still see young Colman running to collect the ball for a throw-in with only two or three minutes left, as if we were losing and his whole life depended on it. That empitomised the keenness of the side that night.'

For myself I shall always remember David Pegg's part in it on the left wing. He ran absolutely wild that night, turning the opposition inside out and contributing directly to seven or eight of those goals. Long before the end, the rest of the Manchester attack were doing their utmost to get his name on the score sheet. He failed. But what a performance!

Next, in October and November, came two ties against Dortmund Borussia, of West Germany, won narrowly 3–2 in Manchester and drawn 0–0 away. In January and February, 1957 – February 6, ironically, just a year ahead of the Munich disaster – followed the quarter-finals against Athletico Bilbao, the first leg lost 3–5 amidst the slush and winter snows of Northern Spain, the return won excitingly 3–0 at Maine Road to put United into the semi-final on aggregate by 6–5.

Real Madrid – 'Real meaning 'Royal' in Spanish – at that period was truly a regal club. Set in a luxurious complex in the Chamartin district of the city, it is a club in the fullest sense of the word, complete with restaurants, library, concert hall, trophy museum, drawing rooms and the rest, all lavishly equipped with chandeliers and fine furniture – a palace of a place which made most English grounds seem like broken-down slums ready for clearance.

But beyond all this the club catered for a wide variety of sports including swimming, track athletics, pelota and tennis. It was there that Manuel Santana, Spain's first Wimbledon singles champion, learnt his game. It is the football section, however, that has the greatest following and provides the major slice of the club's revenue, together with membership fees.

The stadium itself is a sight for the gods. Named after the man whose vision took them to their fame, Señor Bernabeu, the Bernabeu Stadium is built of white concrete and stone, tier upon tier, almost vertically. It seems to reach up to the clouds, gleaming in the sunlight as if it were some massive wedding cake. At full capacity it holds something like 135,000 people and on the big occasion it throbs with a hot, juicy feeling.

It was like that for the semi-final on that April afternoon in 1957. There was not a square inch of free space anywhere. The stadium seemed to be bursting at the seams and when the hour arrived for the kick-off there were still thousands left outside milling in the surrounding streets.

The British journalists had been allocated their own special enclosure. At the rear of this comfortable press box long tables were set with fruit and drink. Waiters in white jackets attended our needs. Never before had any of us experienced such civilised working conditions. Before the start we fell to toasting the section of the Spanish crowd below us in our sector of the ground. The friendliest of relations were soon established. Some of the Madridlaneans even hurled up pigskin bladders filled with rough red wine for us to partake, which we did with considerable gusto and no little amusement as we spilled the crimson juice down our shirt fronts. There is a knack in squeezing those bladders so that the jet streams into the mouth and not over one's clothes. Anyway, both sides had become the ambassors of good will by the time the teams took the sunlit arena.

Real Madrid had a highly talented forward line of Kopa (the expensive World Cup player from France), Mateos, di Stefano (from Argentina), Rial, and Gento – a group valued at £250,000, big money in those days. Behind them was a powerful half back line of Munoz, Marquitos and Zarraga. Manchester United lined up at full strength: Wood; Foulkes, Byrne; Colman, Jackie Blanchflower, Edwards; Berry, Whelan, Taylor, Viollet and Pegg.

United that season found themselves at full stretch. They were riding a tricycle, as it were – going for the League championship at home, in the F.A. Cup Final and now in the semi-finals of the European Cup. It was a deep test of skill, stamina and character of a young side still in the process of development.

Bernabeu Stadium made a colourful setting that day. Against the green stage as background, Real Madrid, all in white from head to toe, pranced on pointed tread like elegant white peacocks. Manchester United were all in red – for all the world like some Mephistophelian chorus.

In the morning, discussing the possible outcome of the big battle, we had gone through a form of mime with a waiter in the hotel. The Spaniard made his ideas clear with all the inventiveness of a Jacques Tati, the French comedian. Balancing a stack of plates in one hand he danced a jig. Next he tapped his forehead with the index finger. The meaning was apparent. The artistry and footwork of Real, against the tactical plan of Manchester . . .

So it proved; and in the end Real's artistry triumphed by 3–1. But what a close finish it was! With an hour gone, United were still holding on with a superb rearguard action, in which Byrne, Blanchflower and Wood, in goal, were outstanding. The score stood at 0–0, and Real were becoming anxious with nothing to show for all their sophisticated, sensuous attack. Manchester had their backs to the wall, but they were playing to a plan.

Then, suddenly inside the last half hour, it all began to happen. Rial dived headlong like a torpedo to turn in a fast, low centre from Gento, galloping like the wind down the left, with his quick, short strides and upright body. With quarter of an hour to go the great di Stefano accelerated through a tiny gap to glide in goal number two.

But United refused to lie down. Only eight minutes were left when Tommy Taylor climbed some invisible ladder to nod in a chip from Whelan and, at 2–1 they were still in with a chance, since Real had yet to visit Manchester for the return leg. Real, however, also realised their danger. Turning their attacking screw even tighter, they regained their two-goal advantage as the last grains of time were running out, when Mateos shot home a clever short pass from Kopa.

Played out in an electric atmosphere, it had been a very fine match. As our waiter had forecast, Spanish artistry versus the British plan. But all that chasing and covering told in the end as

Manchester's legs began to wilt. However, a two-goal deficit still left them, on paper, in with a chance at home.

As it happened, it was not to be. Real showed their class in a 2–2 draw a fortnight later at Old Trafford, where the new floodlights at last were in commission. Indeed, they even took a 2–0 lead there through Kopa and Rial, to stretch their over-all lead to 5–1 before Taylor and the young Bobby Charlton, just beginning to make his mark then, hit back to give it all a more respectable look of 5–3 over the two games.

United were out of the European Cup. But they had made a commendable mark at their first attempt, and I believe that they learned much from the experience. For the first time they had tasted the skill and high artistry of a world-class attack. Those Real forwards had played before their own people with all the pride and even, at times, the touch of arrogance of grandees.

Towering above everyone else was di Stefano. I had never seen him before and to me he was a fabulous performer, a kind of super Hidegkuti, as he played a roving centre forward role, moving left, right and centre at will, always at the heart of the action, now in the rear, now up front. Creator as well as goalscorer, he was the very heart and soul of that Real side. Señor Bernabeu had persuaded him to Europe from South America with the express intention of making him the cornerstone of a new Real Madrid. It was a stroke of genius, and di Stefano answered the call by taking Real to the heights.

With quick, short, pitter-patter strides, fiendish acceleration, marvellous ball control, and a gift for being in the right place at the right time, he pulled all the strings. He was the puppet-master supreme. For me he was above reproach: above, even, the law. Little Colman, as part of the Manchester plan, was set to follow di Stefano everywhere like a watchdog. Though he must have felt in the end that he had padded all over Spain and most of the North of England, Colman was never able to apply the brakes on one of the most brilliant footballers of all time.

What had become abundantly apparent was that British sides, forbidden by the laws of the Ministry of Labour at home to tap the market of world players, found themselves at a disadvantage. Restricted only to the British Isles, it was hard to compete against Spanish and Italian clubs who could comb South America and elsewhere for their stars. We had entered an age of competition with highly-talented, expensive mercenaries from different lands, and it was beyond our reach.

Yet there was born in that first meeting a deep and lasting

friendship between Manchester United and Real Madrid – a friendship that has existed across the years. Yet, as Busby the realist, has said since, 'Real invited us to several friendly matches in Madrid and at Old Trafford in the seasons that followed. There were close ties between us, but deep down they were keeping a close watch on us. We were the ones they feared in Europe to end their reign of supremacy. But for Munich, I believe, we would have done it, too, dominating Britain and the Continent for a decade . . .'

The following season of 1957–58 saw United, as League champions for the second successive year, in the European Cup once more. It was a year destined to end in unimagined sorrow and the purple dignity of defeat.

Dealing first with Shamrock Rovers, of the Republic of Ireland, with an aggregate victory of 9–2 (6–0 away), United went on to dispose of a talented Dukla side 3–1 over-all, keeping the return leg in Prague down to a mere single goal defeat thanks to some fine wing half play by little Colman, the 'pocket Napoleon'.

Next followed Red Star, Belgrade, yet another talented, well-drilled Eastern European side with Beara, the classic one-time ballet dancer in goal, Zebec in attack and masterminded by the brilliant, fiery little gipsy Sekularac at inside forward. Winning only by 2–1 at Old Trafford there were many who put United's chances of surviving in Belgrade as minimal.

But, doubtless uplifted by that brilliant 5–4 victory at Arsenal on the previous Saturday, only four days earlier, United now raised their sights to meet the dangerous challenge. Playing the same side as at Highbury, they took the field with Gregg in goal; Foulkes and Byrne at full back; Colman, Jones and Edwards as the half back line; Morgans, Viollet, Taylor, Charlton and Scanlon in attack.

Here is the dispatch of Don Davies on February 5 – hiding under the pseudonym in the *Guardian* of 'An Old International' – the last he sent to his paper before perishing with so many others the next day in the snow of Munich.

> Who would be a weather prophet? At Belgrade today in warm sunshine and on a grass pitch where the last remnants of melting snow produced the effect of an English lawn flecked with daisies, Red Star and Manchester United began a battle of wits and courage and rugged tackling in the second leg of their quarter-final of the European Cup competition. It ended in a draw, 3–3, but as United had already won the first leg at Old Trafford by 2–1 they thus gained the right to pass into the semi-final round of the competition for the second year in succession on a 5-4 aggregate.

Much to the relief of the English party and to the consternation of the 52,000 home spectators, Viollet had the ball in the net past a dumbfounded Beara in ninety seconds. It was a beautifully taken goal – a characteristic effort by that player – but rather lucky in the way a rebound had run out in United's favour. But, as Jones remarked, 'You need luck at this game'; and he might have added, 'a suit of chain mail also would not have come amiss'. A second goal almost came fourteen minutes later, delightfully taken by Charlton after a corner kick by Scanlon had been headed by Viollet, but this was disallowed, because of offside, by the Austrian referee whose performance on the whistle so far had assumed the proportions of a flute obligato. That was due to the frequency with which fouls were being committed by both sides after Sekularac had set the fashion in shabbiness by stabbing Morgans on the knee. But in spite of the many stops and starts events in the first half ran smoothly for United, on whose behalf Taylor led his line like a true Hotspur from centre forward. Other factors telling strongly in Manchester's favour at this time were the clean hands and sound judgment of Gregg in goal.

Further success for United was impending. Charlton this time was the chosen instrument. Dispossessing Kostic about forty yards from goal, this gifted boy leaned beautifully into his stride, made ground rapidly for about ten yards, and then beat the finest goalkeeper on the Continent with a shot of tremendous power and superb placing. There, one thought, surely goes England's Bloomer of the future. Further evidence of Charlton's claim to that distinction was to emerge two minutes later. A smartly taken free kick got the Red Star defence into a real tangle. Edwards fastened on the ball and did his best to oblige his colleagues and supporters by bursting it (a feat, by the way, which he was to achieve later), but he muffed his kick this time and the ball rolled to Charlton, apprently lost in a thicket of Red Star defenders. Stalemate, surely. But not with Charlton about. His quick eye detected the one sure route through the circle of legs; his trusty foot drove the ball unerringly along it. 3–0 on the day: 5–1 on the aggregate. Nice going.

As was natural, the Red Star players completely lost their poise for a while. Their forwards flung themselves heatedly against a defence as firm and steady as a rock; even Sekularac, after a bright beginning in which he showed his undoubted skill, lost heart visibly and stumbled repeatedly. Never the less there was an upsurge of the old fighting spirit when Kostic scored a fine goal for Red Star two minutes after half time. It ought to have been followed by another one only three minutes later when Sekularac placed the ball perfectly for Cotic. Cotic's terrific shot cleared the bar by a foot – no more. Next, a curious mix-up by Foulkes and Tasic, Red Star's centre forward, ended in Foulkes falling flat on top of Tasic and blotting him completely out of view. According to Foulkes Tasic lost his footing, fell over, and pulled Foulkes over with him. But it looked bad and the whistle blew at once with attendant gestures indicating a penalty. Tasic had the satisfaction of converting that one, although his shot only just evaded Gregg's finger tips.

The score now was 3–2 and the crowd broke into an uncontrolled frenzy of jubilation and excitement. So much so that when Cotic failed to walk the ball into a completely unprotected goal – Gregg was lying hurt and helpless on the ground – a miniature repetition of the Bolton disaster seemed to occur at one corner of the arena. Down the terraces streamed a wild horde of excited spectators who hung limply along the concrete walls with the breath crushed out of their bodies, if indeed nothing else had befallen them.

A quarter of an hour from the end Red Star, with their confidence and self-respect restored, were wheeling and curvetting, passing and shooting in their best style, and the United's defenders had to fight their way out of a regular nightmare of desparate situations. It was significant hereabouts that United inside forwards were not coming back to chase the ball as they had done so effectively in the first half and this, of course, threw added pressure on the rearguard. As soon as this fault was rectified the Red Star attacks, though frequent enough, lost something of their sting. In fact, United began to pile on the pressure at the other end and once Morgans struck a post with a glorious shot.

The furious pace never slackened, and as England's champions tried to find their flowing, attacking play of the first half, they were pelted by a storm of snowballs. Two minutes from time Harry Gregg came racing out of his goal, and hurled himself full length at Zebec's feet. He grasped it safely, but the impetus of his rush took him outside the penalty area with the ball, and Red Star had a free kick some twenty yards out. Kostic watched Gregg position himself by the far post protected by a wall of United players. There was just a narrow ray of light, a gap, by the near post, and precision player Kostic threaded the ball through as Gregg catapulted himself across his goal. Too late. The ball eluded his grasping fingers, and hit the back of the net. The score was 3–3.

United were through to their second successive semi-final. Yet that match in Belgrade which produced soccer of sublime ease and artistry in the first half, and an unforgettable fight in the second, was the last time anyone saw this wonderful young side play.

The remainder of that season had an unreal quality about it. Although United reached the F.A. Cup Final for the second year running, they were now in fact a team of threads and patches, a platoon decimated in action and fighting a courageous rearguard battle under the leadership of Jimmy Murphy. Yet even if they kept their flag flying proudly, that great young side on its way to maturity and undreamed of honours was gone for ever. But for fate they could have developed into the finest club team in all English football history.

A week before Munich they were lying second in the League, four points behind Wolverhampton Wanderers and due to play

Wolves at Old Trafford on the Saturday following Belgrade. That would probably have reduced the gap to only two points and who is to say that before the end United would not have become champions for the third year in succession to equal the earlier feats of Huddersfield Town and Arsenal in the 1920s and 1930s?

As it was, understandably enough, they slipped to ninth position at the end of that season and duly lost their European Cup semi-final over-all to A.C. Milan, 2–1 at home and 0–4 away in the 80,000 San Siro Stadium. On each of those occasions Bobby Charlton – having made an astonishing recovery from his Munich experience – was missing since he was abroad travelling with England prior to the 1958 World Cup in Sweden.

At the end of that season there followed what I have always considered a shabby act on the part of the Football Association and the Football League.

As a mark of sympathy and respect the European Union forwarded a special invitation to United to compete in the European Cup again. Naturally it was cordially accepted by the club, with the original blessing of the F.A. But the League again objected to their entry and though the Board of Appeal upheld United's acceptance, the Football Association achieved a complete *volte face,* reversed their earlier decision and refused United's entry.

Two letters, extracted from the Old Trafford files of the time, put the picture into perspective.

Copy of letter from the Football Association to Manchester United Football Club:

29th August, 1958.

L. Olive, Esq.,
Manchester United F.C.,
Old Trafford,
Manchester 16.

Dear Mr. Olive,

European Champion Clubs Cup Competition
Season 1958/1959

With reference to your club's application to take part in the above Competition, the following decision has been reached by the F.A. Consultative Committee:

'The Consultative Committee of the Football Association has considered an application by Manchester United F.C. under F.A. Rule 18 (b) for consent to take part in the European Champion Clubs Competition during Season 1958/1959.

The Committee is of the opinion that, as by its name this is a competition of Champion Clubs, Manchester United F.C. does not qualify to take part in this season's Competition. Consent is therefore refused.'

Yours sincerely,
STANLEY ROUS
Secretary.

MANCHESTER UNITED FOOTBALL CLUB LIMITED.

To the Secretary,
The Football Association. 2nd September, 1958.

Sir,

Manchester United F.C. Ltd., whilst accepting the decision of the Football Association Consultative Committee feel they must in justification of their attitude and actions state the following facts:

The Football Association in their letter of the 5th July, 1958 stated they had no objection to Manchester United F.C. entering the European Champion Clubs Cup Competition for season 1958/1959.

The Football League wrote to the Club that they could not give consent to the Club entering this Competition. The Club appealed to the Board of Appeal of the Football League. The Board of Appeal upheld the Club's appeal. The decision of the Board of Appeal is, by the rules of The Football League, FINAL.

Therefore the Club were allowed by the Football Association to enter the Competition. By the decision of the Board of Appeal which is FINAL, The Football League were prevented from interfering with our entry.

In these circumstances there was no reason why the dates we submitted to The Football Association should not be approved, nor why The Football Association should depart from the terms of their letter of 5th July, 1958, in which they stated as before mentioned, 'The Football Association has no objection to your Club taking part'.

So much for the differing attitudes of the governing bodies.

It was eight long years – 1965–66 – before United were again qualified to enter the Continent's senior club competition. True, they had gained a place in the European Cup Winners' Cup of 1963/64 and the European Fairs Cup (now renamed U.E.F.A. Cup) in 1964/65. In the former they advanced to the quarter-final when they experienced a disasterous tie against Sporting Lisbon, throwing away a 4–1 lead at home by collapsing to an inexplicable 0–5 defeat in Portugal. I was with them on that occasion and will never forget their return to the Palazzio Hotel in Estoril to eat a dejected late supper in a cold painful silence. It was a night when the players avoided each other's eyes. They knew they had let the club down; they were ashamed and they could hardly swallow their food.

Yet, imperceptibly, the tide was on the turn. League runners-up in 1963/64, they qualified for the Fairs Cup the next season to reach the semi-final where they lost a play-off against the Hungarian Ferencváros. This was but the stepping stone to a revived and re-shaped United side boasting such great new Scottish players as Law and Crerand and a young Irish genius, George Best, with a mature Bobby Charlton switched from outside left, doing the spoon-feeding of attack as a deep-lying centre forward in the pattern of a di Stefano or Hidegkuti.

In 1965/66, as champions of England for the sixth time in their history, United were back in their rightful place in the European Cup and about to produce one of their most memorable performances across the English Channel.

Those who saw it that March night in Lisbon under the stars of the Iberian Peninsula will never forget. Those who read of it next morning at home over a breakfast of egg and coffee probably pinched themselves to confirm they were really awake.

It was a quarter-final tie against Benfica. United had won the first leg at Old Trafford only narrowly by 3–2, when the ebony Eusebio had kept the Portugese in touch by helping with two fine goals by Augusto and Torres. When the team set out for Lisbon in March, a fortnight later, everyone knew they had a dangerous task ahead to protect that slender lead.

Denis Law recalls how as the United team coach neared the Benfica stadium the expectant crowds, choking the streets and pavements, beat on the windows and mockingly raised the five fingers of their hands. They had not forgotten the Sporting Lisbon debacle. By the end of that night those same Portugese hands were wringing with anguish.

But to the story of the match.

Manchester United that night destroyed the white flower of Benfica in their Luz Stadium by 5–1 in a thrilling outburst of attacking football. 'Luz' is Portuguese for 'light', but Benfica – European Cup finalists four times in the previous five seasons and winners of the trophy twice – were consigned to darkness as Manchester reached the European Cup semi-final for the third time since 1957.

They reached that stage with the most inspired, inspiring, and controlled performance I had seen from any British side abroad, matched perhaps, only by England's 4–0 win over Italy in Turin in 1948. Had I not seen it, I would not have believed it.

That night of magic, then, saw Manchester, in the presence of 75,000, wipe out almost goal by goal the memory of their sorry show in the city two years earlier when they lost 0–5 to Sporting Lisbon in the European Cup Winners' Cup. That can be forgotten because it was shoddy. But this win still lives on in the minds of everyone who saw a masterly exposition of mobility and skill, a performance which tamed Benfica for the first time at home in any European Cup tie over the previous seven years.

With Madrid and Milan, Lisbon had become one of the power houses of the Continental club game. Above their stately stadium stands a gigantic eagle. For so many seasons it had been a predatory bird, but its feathers were painfully ruffled on this occasion.

Benfica passed quietly into the Lisbon night, heavily mourned by their followers. They passed with laboured, feverish movements, relying too much on Eusebio, the cunning dark leopard, who for once was caged by Stiles, his stealthy tracker around the edges of the Manchester penalty area. And because Eusebio could not fully express himself, and Torres could not dominate in the air, Benfica found themselves confined, and their only majesty at the last was that of tragedy.

The Manchester opening conditioned all that followed, In the first quarter of an hour Best, twice, and Connelly had charmed the ball past Costa-Pereira in brilliantly co-ordinated movements to take their 3–2 advantage of Old Trafford to the unbelievable position of 6–2. All was done in a twinkling, almost before the Portuguese had opened their eyes. Best, with his long dark mop of hair, became known in those parts as 'the Beatle'. He was the best of all, as he set a new, almost unexplored, beat. The rest caught his mood, and their refined actions flowed, unbelievably courtly and delicate – yet deadly.

Best seemed quite suddenly to be in love with the ball, and the whole side followed his lead. Before our astonished eyes came the disintegration of a great Benfica side. But football digs into the spirit and as Manchester were inspired, Benfica were demoralised. The powerful Portuguese lost their hearts, their minds, and their skilful presence.

At the kick-off, and for the first few moments, Eusebio and company began with a deceitful air of infallibility. But soon United were striking gold, the Portuguese beat around the Manchester goalmouth like a trapped bird, and long before half-time – 2–6 down on aggregate – time began to glide away from them.

Manchester lived up to their word. They went there to attack – not to defend. Their football was marvellously fluid, the ball stroked along the pitch, long or short, making space and time for themselves as they bemused the opposition. They might have been musicians extemporising in some modern jazz idiom.

Manchester soon struck. In the sixth minute Charlton was checked, Dunne curved a free kick into the penalty area, and Best, rising on spring heels, headed beautifully past everybody. After twelve minutes Charlton passed back to Gregg. The goalkeeper cleared straight down the middle of the field, Herd headed downwards and backwards, and there was Best, gliding like a dark ghost past three men to break clear and slide the ball home – a beautiful goal. Hardly had that made sense than a quick, triangular movement between Charlton, Law and Connelly ended with Connelly beating Costa-Pereira at close range.

There the score remained until half time, with Manchester surviving a series of free kicks by Eusebio, bent and chipped from the edge of the penalty area as the Italian referee punished the smallest action by United. Seven minutes after the interval the crowd came to life again as Benfica mounted a bombardment and Pinto lashed a shot just wide. Then Benfica got one foot back in the match as Brennan, under pressure from Eusebio, lobbed the ball backwards over the head of his advancing goalkeeper.

Came more massed attacks from Benfica as the crowd roared and Eusebio tried to break free, supported by the lively Simoes, with Pinto and Coluna the midfield links. But Manchester held on calmly, Foulkes covering the tall head of Torres. United broke free again and in the final minutes a quick build up saw Law's cutting pass put Crerand in for a fourth goal, and in the dying embers Charlton, a hero in midfield, burst free himself, and swept past three men to deliver the *coup de grace.*

Teams:
Benfica: Costa-Pereira; Cavem, Germano; Cruz, Pinto, Coluna; Augusto-Silva, Eusebio, Torres, José Augustó, Simoes.

Manchester United: Gregg; Brennan, Dunne; Crerand, Foulkes, Stiles; Best, Law, Charlton, Herd, Connelly.

In their third European Cup semi-final since 1957, with an over-all victory of 8–3, it was a result that set a cat among the European dovecots.

Everywhere there was utter astonishment. Even at home there

were those, seeing the result 'fudged' in the stop-press column of newspapers (the kick-off was so late and the telephone comunications so bad that only some of the late editions could carry the full story) thought that the score was a typographical error. Surely it couldn't be true? United 5–1 up in Lisbon against powerful Benfica and through by 8–3? Yet it was true, all right, and the impact of it reverberated across the Continent.

The Portuguese themselves were highly impressed and appreciative. They knew what good football was, fed liberally as they were by the likes of Eusebio, the black panther, a dynamic player of skill, power, acceleration, and shooting precision, whose free kicks alone, from any range up to forty yards or so, carried a deadly power. (All this the British public were to see for themselves within the next four months, as Portugal reached the semi-finals of the 1966 World Cup in England, when Eusebio was the top scorer of that global championship, and one of its outstanding performers.)

That World Cup, indeed, provided the true measure of Manchester United's performance. Six players of that same Benfica side destroyed by United, were in fact in the Portugal team that beat Brazil and Hungary at Goodison Park, Everton, and gave the full might of England such a run for their money in a great game at Wembley at the last stride before the world final itself. There can be no higher recommendation than that.

Amongst the flood of winged words that found their way into the newspapers of the Continent on United's astonishing win, came the following next morning in the *Diario de Noticias,* a Lisbon publication: 'Manchester United were fabulous in all that is most artistic, athletic, imaginative and pure in football.' United had made their point. They had struck gold.

It was in Lisbon, that night, that George Best, with his flowing locks, was first christened 'the Beatle' by the Portuguese fans. Though broken and disillusioned by events, they took him to their hearts. They knew that they were in the presence of the unusual. Best, that night, was again in love with the ball and, in a few minutes, like the genius that he was in those days, he destroyed the whole opposition.

Busby revealed later that, at the team conference before the game, he instructed the team to play it tight and defensively for the first twenty minutes or so and then attack, building up moves from the rear. Best, however, seemed to decide to play his own game – and, in a flash, he had beaten them on his own. It was fantastic, but Busby said that the performance of the whole side gave him one of the greatest football moments of his life.

Later I was to hear from one of them a little story from behind the scenes. While they were waiting the call from the referee to take the field, two or three of the players were fooling around with a ball in the dressing room. Suddenly Crerand miscued. The ball struck a full-length mirror beside one of the lockers and shattered it in a hundred pieces. At that very moment the call came to set forth and, as they filed out on to the pitch, someone said: 'Christ, Pat, we've got enough on our plate already, and you've got to go and do that . . .'

At half time, as they returned to their dressing room, Crerand said loud and clear: 'Anyone got another mirror . . .?' There was laughter in the air. But by then the Benfica eagle was caged, and United's football was swinging.

That was the year United really should have won the European Cup. Real Madrid by then were on the decline, with di Stefano and Puskas both departed into the scrapbook of golden memories.

Left in the field, too, were Partizan of Belgrade, a tough but untalented Yugoslav side, a team that lived up to its name – partisans prepared to fight every inch of the way no matter the odds, yet a combination lacking in flair. It was they whom United faced in the semi-final, but then sadly proceeded to play their poorest football of the competition.

Up to that point they had scored freely with creative attack – nine goals in all against H.I.K. Helsinki; five against A.S.K. Vorwaerts, of West Germany, eight against Benfica; a record of six wins in six matches with twenty-two goals against six. Perhaps it was all due to some curious psychological hangover from the past, or over-confidence, but United were far below form in Belgrade where Denis Law stumbled when it mattered most, to miss an open goal and where Best struggled with a damaged knee. As a result they returned home 2–0 down but convinced that they would put it all right at Old Trafford.

Yet once again they failed to put it together. They attacked for most of the night, but, in face of some highly questionable tactics by the Yugoslavs, found themselves drawn into a slogging match which reached its climax when the quick-tempered Crerand, retaliating to a cruel tackle, was sent off the field. A 1–0 win fell short of the mark so that for the third time United – without Best, absent with cartilage trouble – had failed a stride short of the final.

But history was just around the corner. The previous season (1966/67) Glasgow Celtic had broken the Latin hold on the European Cup for the first time when they beat Inter-Milan 2–1 at the climax in Lisbon. At last the trophy had come to the British

Isles and at once the very next year (1967/68), United joined the exclusive company by keeping the prize on these shores.

Having dealt first with Hibernian of Malta, and then a tough Yugoslav foe in F.K. Sarajevo, they found themselves drawn in the quarter-final against yet another Iron Curtain side, Gornik Zabrze, the Polish champions, who boasted a fine forward in a young man named Lubanski who was destined some years later to bring down Bobby Moore from his pedestal as England's captain and to help knock England out of the World Cup of 1974.

The first leg was at Old Trafford on February 28 and it needed an own goal from Florenski after one hour of incessant attack and another from Kidd in the last minutes before Manchester United could pack the sort of lead they needed in their bag for the return leg in Poland a fortnight later.

Denis Law did not see his team build up their two–goal lead. He was in bed with a knee 'swollen like a balloon', said the United manager, Matt Busby. Law, added Busby, was extremely doubtful for the second leg. For a long time, indeed, United looked as if they were qualifying for the obituary column as they bashed their heads, brains and feet against a solid defensive wall. There was also pyrotechnic brilliance from Kostka, one of the most agile goalkeepers Old Trafford had seen in many a year.

At the final whistle when that last goal perhaps changed the shape of things, a relieved Manchester side lined the field to the exit tunnel to applaud the visitors off the stage. The greatest roar of all from a 64,000 full house was reserved for the last Polish figure to leave the scene. Predictably it was this same Kostka who must have made at least half a dozen saves out of this world.

As it was, that final surge by United was to make all the difference.

When United went to Poland a fortnight later they knew that only a solid, sensible performance, free from mistakes, would see them through. But little did they bargain for the conditions that met them. The flight from Manchester to Cracow gave the first hint of what lay ahead as their aircraft droned into Eastern Europe. A two-hour coach trip from the airport to Katowice in the Silesian mining area merely confirmed their worst fears.

Deep snow lay everywhere, crisp but not very even. It was a Christmas-card scene. A blizzard was blowing and bent figures in the streets fought against the clawing elements.

For two days before the kick-off the snow flaked down. The pitch itself was a white coverlet with hard ice underneath. Busby and all the United players – except one – thought it would be too dangerous for football. Needless to say the one exception was George Best. As Irish as they come, he seemed to regard it all as a challenge to his skill and balance.

Busby, of course – quite apart from the dangers of bad injuries to his key players – had no wish to put United's two-goal lead at Old Trafford as a hostage to fortune. Clearly the Poles wanted to play as much as Busby did not. Gornik, used to such Silesian conditions, merely said, 'We shall sweep the pitch and put salt on it. It may not be perfect, but it will be playable.'

In the event, on the decision of Lo Bello, the Italian referee, who arrived on the overnight train via Vienna, the match *was* played, much against Busby's better judgment and genuine wishes. But thanks to a brave rearguard action, all turned out well in the end and United were through to their fourth semi-final in eleven years (in spite of the date – March 13!) after a round trip of some 14,000 miles, embracing Malta, Yugoslavia and Poland.

True, they lost that night in the vast Silesian stadium before a 100,000 demanding, noisy concourse by a single goal, scored by Lubanski, Gornik's vaunted bombardier, nineteen minutes from the end. But that was not enough to save the Poles. On aggregate United were through by 2–1. So United took care to beware the ides of March. They did so by biting on the nail, defending magnificently in the deepest, hardest conditions of winter to be imagined, and by keeping their heads and feet on a snow-covered pitch, icy below, which made the setting more fit for ice hockey than football.

Up to half time, indeed, they fought on in a semi-blizzard of snow which, within ten minutes, almost obliterated the red line markings. Later, the driving snowflakes, swirling like a necklace in the lights, fled to leave us in the grip of a dark, bitter night. It was so cold that even these hardy Poles, the miners of Gornik, turned to lighting bonfires on the open terraces. Lubanski's late goal was the first United had conceded after nearly three and a half hours play on the Continent in that season's competition. That spoke volumes for their tactical planning and defensive ability when the chips were down.

The Poles, for all their sporting, correct behaviour in a hard match, were at the end deeply sad, and their manager, with a face as long as a pessimistic horse, was disappointed at United's defensive covering in depth. But, as Busby said, 'This is European football. We had only a slender lead. We came to contain the foe and we did the job we set out to perform. The Poles themselves defended deeply at Old Trafford.'

That was true, and comparing the two matches, one could say without fear of contradiction that the pressure on the Gornik goalkeeper, Kostka, was far more severe in Manchester than anything Stepney had to endure in Poland. In fact, had it not been for Kostka's great performance a fortnight earlier, it would have been all over bar the shouting even before going to Katowice.

When the draw for the semi-final was made United found themselves paired with their old and respected rivals, Real Madrid. People licked their lips at the prospect but few could have imagined the dramatic finish that lay in store in Madrid. As it was, though, there was little joy in prospect for United after they had toiled all night at Old Trafford for the meagre reward of a 1–0 lead in the first leg. Real demonstrated clearly enough that they still knew what the European challenge was all about.

At Manchester there were two teams of high reputation and regard. For four-fifths of the night it was United moving forward against a deeply-laid defensive formation which saw Gonzalez, Zunzunegui, Zoco, Sanchis and the deeply withdrawn José Luis drawn out in an iron ring across the horizon of Betancort, under the Madrid crossbar.

In the end all United had to show for their driving work was a glorious goal by Best ten minutes from the interval. Aston broke on the left from Kidd's long pass, and as he pulled the ball back diagonally from the bye-line, in came Best to thunder a left-foot shot to the roof of the Real net.

It might have been Walter Hammond driving a half volley gloriously past extra cover off the full meat of the bat. In that moment Old Trafford exploded, a frightened cat ran the length of the pitch, and one felt that here at last, in another sense, the cat had really been set amongst the Spanish pigeons.

But that was the end as far as Manchester United's positive efforts were concerned. Real, relaxed and aristocratic, played with a certain simplicity and sophistication, working for space and position with all their experienced timing coming to their aid – all this in spite of the raging pressure that continued to explode around their penalty area.

Pirri was superb, an artist in midfield: Perez looked dangerous with his speed at outside right, and there, too, was Grosso, working the midfield with the tireless Pirri. And if anybody needed a special accolade, it was Sanchis, for the masterly way he followed the gyrations of the elusive Best.

In all respects it was a fine, sporting match, finely controlled with the minimum of fuss by a Russian referee who later said, 'The

Number One footballer and gentleman on the field for me was Bobby Charlton, and I have never had more pleasure in taking such a match.'

Teams:
Manchester United: A. Stepney; A. Dunne, F. Burns; P. Crerand, D. Sadler, N. Stiles; G. Best, B. Kidd, R. Charlton, D. Law, J. Aston.

Real Madrid: Betancort; Gonzalez, Zunzunegui; Zoco, Sanchis, Pirri; Grosso, José Luis, Perez, Velazquez, Gento.

Referee: T. Bakhramov (Russia)

It was May 15 when battle was joined in the Bernabeu Stadium for the return leg. All Spain held its breath that night. And seldom could there have been a more hazardous or remarkable journey than Manchester United made in the Spanish capital as they recovered from the depths of despair at half time to draw 3–3 and beat Real Madrid, the champions of Spain and the symbols of Spanish football power, on aggregate by 4–3.

In the end, that goal by Best at Old Trafford was worth its weight in gold after all. But in Madrid it was a fairy story.

It was a match of great character. In the first half, Real had the freedom of the game and built themselves into a 3–1 lead by goals from Pirri, Gento, and Amancio, to a lone and almost lame duckling by comparison from Dunne, for United, a long forward lob of some forty yards which trickled home past Betancort as he was muddled by Zoco, with Kidd challenging close in.

That goal hushed the stadium, but Real at that moment seemed in no danger. All that looked in prospect was this lead probably to be built on in the second half. After all, the great Amancio, like a matador, had teased the Manchester United defence with masterly footwork and passes of his cape, as it were. At his side, too, there were Grosso and Velazquez and Perez, building up an almost non-stop barrage.

For half an hour Manchester held out, with Stiles snapping angrily all the time at Amancio's heels, and often failing. Brooding disaster hung in the air and suddenly the storm broke. In the last quarter of an hour of that opening half, four goals suddenly tumbled out of the night – a header by Pirri, from Amancio's bending free kick; from Gento as he burst through after Brennan had missed a long through pass from Pirri; then that long straggler from Dunne; next a dazzling shot on the turn from Amancio out of a crowded ruck.

So it looked all over, with the Spaniards 3–2 ahead on aggregate, and with more to come, we thought. The vast crowd was in a symphony of sound. They resembled a man who has two bottles of wine inside him, pleasantly intoxicated and feeling that there is nothing much wrong with life.

Manchester, in that first half, had played a tactical formation of 5–3–2, with Sadler, wearing the number ten, drawn deep in defence at the side of Foulkes, and only Best and Kidd to forage up front. This gave Real Madrid the initiative as the night was peppered with goals and chances.

This was fiesta time for the hot-blooded crowd, whose wrath flamed out as Stiles stabbed at the fleeting Amancio. Flags and banners waved: the air was full of fireworks and rockets and there was a hot juicy feeling of expectant victory in the air.

The stadium at half time must have seemed to Manchester United like a sheer, granite cliff of sound that was falling about their ears. But the twist was in store. Now the fairy tale began to weave itself, and out of nothing a magical recovery was born.

It was born from a change of tactics which saw Sadler at last moving up into attack and Manchester stirring to 4–3–3 and even 4–2–4 as they almost threw caution to the winds. There was the crunch. It brought justice because in the end it was English temperament, fibre, and morale that won through.

Turning to attack, United came back into the match with just over a quarter of an hour left when Foulkes headed on a free kick by Crerand which the alert Sadler slipped in on the run. That made it 3–2 on the night and 3–3 on aggregate.

Then, with twelve minutes left, the remarkable story was completed. Crerand took a long throw down the right touchline, and Best showed his peerless skill as he beat Sanchis and Zoco in a corkscrew run, sped up to the right bye-line, pulled the ball back diagonally, and there, of all people, was Foulkes, that veteran warrior of sixteen years, the defensive centre half, now following up in a moment of inspiration to turn the pass in at the far corner. It was a brilliant stroke, and it won United the battle.

The hour and a half sped like five minutes, though the closing seconds seemed an eternity, with twenty-one players in the Manchester half, and Real Madrid battering their heads against a red wall to save themselves. But not even Amancio, supple, alert, industrious, and brilliant in footwork, could rescue the monarchs, and in the end the sleek, self-assured football of Real, which they unfurled in the first half, died in the dark.

Teams:
Manchester United: A. Stepney; S. Brennan, A. Dunne; P. Crerand, W. Foulkes, N. Stiles; G. Best, B. Kidd, R. Charlton, D. Sadler, J. Aston.

Real Madrid: Betancort; Gonzalez, Zunzunegui; Zoco, Sanchis, Pirri; Grosso, Perez, Amancio, Velazquez, Gento.

Referee: A. Sbardella (Italy)

It was at half time in the dressing room that Busby provided the real tonic to that extraordinary recovery. When most of his men sat drained and dejected, trailing 3–1 and facing an apparently overwhelming task against opponents living on cloud nine, the master spoke calmly to his team, 'Don't give up hope. Remember you are only 3–2 down over-all at the moment, just a single goal in it and anything can still happen. The thing now is to attack and from the re-start, David (Sadler), I want you to move upfield in an aggressive way. That might surprise them.'

So it all came to pass. Sadler and Foulkes, appearing unexpectedly out of defence, sneaked the two vital goals and United were through at the last breath. The scenes of joy and celebration as the hundreds of supporters who had made the trip from Manchester later crowded in on the players at their Fenix Hotel still remain a warm memory.

Now all that remained was the prospect of Wembley and Benfica on the night of May 29, the Epsom Derby, which the players duly watched on television at their headquarters at Wentworth outside London. All played it cool outwardly, no matter that their inner heart strings must have twanged like guitars.

Yet one important point needed to be cleared up in Busby's book – the interpretation of the goalkeeper four-pace rule. Lo Bello, of Italy, who was to referee, had controlled the earlier tie against Gornik in Poland and there had warned Stepney not to retain the ball for more than four *seconds* and in fact had penalised the goalkeeper then on this count which had led to Lubanski's goal near the end.

The day before the Wembley kick-off the matter still remained cloudy. But Busby, with his astute attention to detail, had it sorted out both for himself and his opposite number, the much-travelled Benfica manager, Otto Gloria, a man born forty-eight years before in Rio de Janeiro, who exuded bonhomie and sunshine. Of Busby, Gloria said: 'I know him well and respect him. He knows so much.' Of the United players Benfica were to face next day, the Brazilian generalissimo remarked: 'The one I specially admire is Best. He is what we say *"Muito Bon"*!' Within twenty-four hours his judgment was proved correct.

The one sadness for United was again the absence of Law from the occasion. A few days earlier he had undergone an operation for a piece of loose cartilage floating in the knee which had troubled him for most of that season. Busby visited the player in hospital that same week. Law was still foggy after the anaesthetic. But he recognised Busby sufficiently to smile and express relief that the trouble had at last been discovered.

As the after-effects of the operation began to overtake Law again he whispered: 'I'm going away now, boss, so you'd better be off . . .'

'That was the first time a player ever sacked a manager!' remarked Busby later with a smile. Meanwhile there was a big job to be done and they did it. With a 4–1 triumph over Benfica before a 100,000 crowd at Wembley, United reached their rainbow's end after eleven years of trial, effort and near miss. So they became the first English club to win the European Cup and followed the breakthrough achieved the previous year by Celtic against Internazionale-Milan.

And having won, with a dramatic burst of seven minutes in the first half of extra time, they helped to beat back the Latin domination that for so long had taken Continental football by the throat.

There have been many occasions of Wembley to remember, but few, apart perhaps from the final of the World Cup itself and the Stanley Matthews epic of 1953, to equal that night. Out of nothing eventually there grew a dramatic climax. The first half was episodic and a busy dullness as a spate of ruthless tackling by the Portuguese defence and a symphony of whistling by the Italian referee broke the match into a thousand pieces.

A waiter might well have dropped a tray of glasses, such was the clatter, the crash and the bang of it all, with football secondary and both teams clearly out of humour with each other and with officialdom. Yet this merely proved to be the crucible. Out of the fire and the cruelty there finally lived something to treasure.

It came to a boil in extra time as Manchester United, once heading for victory but robbed of their prize ten minutes from the end of normal time, suddenly found a fresh wind that took them home in full sail. In a magical spell of seven minutes Best, Kidd and then Charlton struck like cobras to add to the goal which Charlton had first glanced in with his head to give them the lead soon after the start of the second half.

F.A. Cup winners, 1963: back row l to r: Crompton (trainer), Brennan, Setters, Gregg, Gaskell, Foulkes, Herd, Charlton; front row: Dunne, Giles, Quixall, Cantwell, Law, Crerand, Stiles.

Charlton and Foulkes go up for the ball with Spurs centre half, Brown, in the United goal mouth, 1965.

Law scores at Tottenham, 1966.

Stepney makes a brilliant save at Highbury, 1968.

It should have been theirs, too, without the need of extra time had not Sadler given Henrique the chance to save an open goal with his feet after Best had mesmerised and opened the defence with a dazzling dribble and a shot which the goalkeeper could only partially parry.

Then there was Best himself, dancing clear of everyone and trying to dribble past the goalkeeper with a delicate touch only to be robbed at the last inch. So when all this had come and gone and United had failed to drive in their nails, there came the crux of the battle. With ten minutes left, the giant Torres rose like some Eiffel Tower to a diagonal cross to the right and head the ball square for Graca to crack in the equaliser.

How United survived those last ten minutes of normal time only Stepney, under their crossbar, could tell. But I doubt if even he knew much about two saves – both of instant reflex action which somehow or other kept out scorching shots from Eusebio in the last three minutes before the whistle, as Eusebio went through the United defence like a knife through butter. In my book United owed Stepney a debt that night for those two remarkable parries when all seemed lost.

So out of the gathering darkness, as Benfica seemed to gather new strength and a new poise, United rose. Once more, as in Spain in their return leg with Real Madrid, they fell back on their morale and unconquerable spirit.

Again it made giants of men who seemed to have given their last ounce of strength as they searched for the final yard to the summit. The scene before the beginning of extra time resembled some battlefield, as the players of both sides fell back upon the velvet surface of Wembley seemingly exhausted, their limbs taut with cramp and their last fibres of strength apparently gone.

But suddenly there came the miracle. Within seven minutes of the beginning of extra time United found their Camelot. First, Kidd nodded backwards a long clearance from Stepney from one end; at the other, suddenly, the dark-haired Best had wriggled his way like some will-o'-the-wisp past two tackles, drawn the goalkeeper in close to him as does the matador draw in the bull.

With a delicate, elusive swerve Best was past Henrique and he drove in the knife coldly and clinically. Almost at once Charlton's corner from the left was headed by Kidd to bring a brilliant save from Henrique, but the young Manchester man was alert to his duty. On his nineteenth birthday he rose once more at the second attempt to nod in the rebound.

That was 3–1 and hardly had the cheering died than Kidd and

Charlton worked another smooth movement down the right. Over came Kidd's cross and Charlton, somehow, with a wonderful, glancing flick, turned the ball into the far top corner for 4–1.

That was it and as the teams changed over once more for the second bit of that extra time, Wembley again resembled a battlefield while the players were given their last ministrations. It was over, apart from one more remarkable save by Stepney, left-handed, low down and at point-blank range from Eusebio. No wonder at the end Matt Busby said, 'I am the proudest man in England tonight.'

So an emotional night reached its climax. The struggle itself was crystallised with a duel at one end between the giant Torres and Eusebio against Foulkes and Stiles. The fact that neither, in the end, scored left the United men as the victors, though somehow I would have dearly wished a goal from Eusebio before the end as a tribute to his marvellous power and feline movement.

At the other end it was the elusive Best, being chopped, harried and bruised from start to finish as he tried to bring his artistry to full flower. But soon, trying to dominate his ruthless opponents, he began to play with a kind of fury which over-stretched itself as he attempted to beat the hordes of Benfica off his own bat.

Perhaps the greatest eye-opener of the struggle was Aston at outside left. Without any flowery touches, time after time he cut the right flank of the Portuguese defence open by sheer, uncomplicated speed. It was simple enough. He merely pushed the ball past Adolfo and showed his heels to the Portuguese. Long before the end the packed stadium was chanting his name. Certainly that was a night for him to remember always.

At the back Dunne was also masterly, as he covered every stray opening that presented itself; so, too, was the faithful Foulkes and the abrasive Stiles, who had a face to face duel with Eusebio.

Crerand, also, was calmly masterful as he ranged the central areas at the side of Charlton. But I suppose in the last analysis it was Charlton's night. With two goals off his own bat it was he who went at last to collect the giant European trophy as the stadium rocked with joyful noise.

Behind him weary, but happy, straggled his side, and when the moment for the lap of honour arrived, Charlton himself was too tired to carry the giant cup around the stadium. He handed it over to his lieutenants and slowly trotted at the rear, no doubt thinking of all the years that had gone to make up that moment of glory.

So ended a dramatic night, when the banners waved and turned the great stadium of Wembley into a scene of carnival.

Teams:
Manchester United: A. Stepney; S. Brennan, P. Dunne: P. Crerand, W. Foulkes, N. Stiles; G. Best, B. Kidd, R. Charlton, D. Sadler, J. Aston.

Benfica: Henrique; Adolfo, Humberton; Jacinto, Cruz, Graca; Coluna, Augusto, Torres, Eusebio, Simoes.

Referee: Concetto Lo Bello (Italy)

Although United reached the semi-final again next season (1968/69) only to lose 2–1 on aggregate to A.C. Milan – but for a shot squeezed over the line by Law and not given by Machin, the French referee, they would probably have won the cup once more – the place to leave the Manchester Odessy into Europe, I believe, is that unforgettable occasion at Wembley on May 29, 1968.

# 5

## *1959–1968:*

# *Bridge over troubled waters*

ASTON VILLA AND Sunderland had it; Newcastle United, in their golden age during the Edwardian midsummer, had it; so, too, have Liverpool, Arsenal and Tottenham Hotspur in their various ways and times – a spark of tradition handed on like an Olympic torch from one generation to another. But few, I would venture to say, have possessed this indefinable quality to quite the same degree as Manchester United, who have overstepped so many dangerous chasms in their existence as to suggest that they have been blessed with the nine lives of a cat.

Each time so far they have survived their various crises to reappear with a new inner strength. It has been a spiritual victory and none was greater than their recovery after Munich. After such a shattering blow most clubs would have sunk with despair to the underworld. But such was the deep, abiding morale of the club that the period of recuperation proved astonishingly rapid.

Reviewing this period after Munich in quiet retrospect Denis Law – who himself was to play such a key role in the revival – said, 'When you come to think of it there have been so many clubs who have achieved virtually nothing in almost a century. Yet here were United, having picked up the shattered pieces of their immediate past, out in front of the parade again and following their destiny. Within five years they were a force to be reckoned with once more by the best at home and abroad. That is a history – a fairy story if you like – in itself . . .'

Certainly money helped in restoring the mosaic of Old Trafford. It was in this following decade that Busby used his cheque book at a cost of some £310,000 in procuring Law (£115,000), Quixall (£45,000), Crerand (£43,000), Herd (£40,000), Setters (£30,000), Cantwell (£30,000), and Dunne (£5,000). These were the new pieces on the chessboard. Yet it was not so much the money spent in replacing the departed brilliant young men who had emerged from the club's youth policy, as the shrewd eye that chose their successors.

That was the measure of Busby's skill. In these replacements he saw the type of player who measured up to his own philosophy of the game; a new group of performers with character capable of continuing the Manchester United style of attacking football. Broadly speaking the secret of this style had been based on a highly developed flexibility of movement with certain basic principles to follow. These could be dissected as follows:

(a) Keep the ball moving forwards.
(b) Keep changing the line of approach if possible.
(c) Spring the element of surprise.
(d) Let the ball do the work and keep it moving into the open spaces where it could be taken at top speed.

The United, in fact, have gained their reputation by an insistence upon attack, always with the object within this general principle of trying to achieve a position in approach where they have one more man in attack than the opposing defence. When they have succeeded over the past thirty years – at a time when tactics have changed and developed scientifically to a degree – they have done so by making these principles work.

If the young Munich side was versatile in the extreme – and who is to know what heights it would have eventually reached – the more mature team that first set United's feet on the path again in the following decade possessed many of the same qualities. And to add to the charm and personality of any success there has always emerged an unbounded delight in a subtle flow of passes and a love of the surprise stroke. This streamlined, smooth, intellectual football has always been closest to Busby's heart.

Munich and its aftermath, indeed, closely echoed the lines of Omar Khayyam:

> Should we not shatter it to bits?
> And then
> Remould it nearer to the heart's desire?

Remould United Busby did in due course. But first, still lying in a German hospital a gravely injured man, the daunting task of keeping the remains of the club on its feet fell to a harassed and saddened Board of Directors under its chairman Mr. Harold Hardman and to the devoted Jimmy Murphy, the temporary navigator at the helm.

With generous offers of help with players from Liverpool, and Nottingham Forest and Bishop Auckland – clubs first into the field with this Christian approach – Murphy put together a scratch combination of reserves, plus two signings from Blackpool and Aston Villa, which not only assumed a new mask to hide the sorrow, but took the nation by emotional storm to reach the Cup Final for the second successive year against all chance and logic. 'It was God who got us to Wembley, not Murphy,' said the Welshman as he fulfilled his difficult stewardship.

When United ended as runners-up in the League championship the following season of 1958–59, the miracle was extended further. By that time Busby was back on duty and in partial harness though still a sick man, hiding his pain with the devoted, unflinching support of his wife Jean. Together with his son Sandy and daughter Sheena, the strength of the Busbys has always been the strength and closeness of a family unit. It was this, with his faith and inbred determination, that eventually saw him though the dark barriers of his mind after so traumatic an experience which left him on the threshold of death for months, his life's work seemingly smashed and so many of his young gladiators and friends, an integral part also of his larger family, gone beyond recall.

Later, on returning home, he was to say:

> Deep down the sorrow is there all the time. You never really rid yourself of it. It becomes part of you. You might be alone and it all comes back to you, like a kind of roundabout, and you weep. The first time was when I went back to the ground at Old Trafford after the accident, I just looked at the empty field and in all my life I have never felt such a terrible vacuum. And so I cried, and afterwards I felt better for the tears, and because I had forced myself to go back there. It was something I had done, something I'd conquered.[1]

It was the first step on a bridge over troubled waters. Little was anyone to know what further rich prizes lay on the far bank!

Meanwhile football, like the restless tides of the sea, never stands idle. On April 19, 1958, the immortal Billy Meredith, the Welsh bard of the right wing from Chirk, near Wrexham, who had reached his apogee of fame with Manchester City and United before the First World War, died at Withington, Manchester, aged eighty-one.

The record books regale posterity with information about his dazzling career. But all this pales beside his stature in the annals of the game. He was the giant of his time. To leave the statement there

[1] *Father of Football. The Story of Sir Matt Busby* by David Miller (Stanley Paul, 1970).

is not to dismiss baldly the fame of a man who was a Matthews, Finney and Best of his day rolled into one. One may as well dismiss Wellington, Nelson and Churchill in a single paragraph. His memorial is to be found in Chapter 9 where his place is in the spiral of time.

In June 1958, following his return from hospital, Busby was awarded the C.B.E in the Queen's Birthday Honours and soon enough team changes got under way at Old Trafford to meet the challenges ahead. Busby and Murphy at that point turned pragmatist.

They both knew that the side which had got to Wembley did so on emotion and that the real playing strength would need to be repaired. The first man turned to was the fair-haired Albert Quixall, an inside forward who had won his first cap for England at the age of nineteen as 'the golden boy' of Sheffield Wednesday, five years earlier. His signature cost United £45,000, a staggering sum in those days which handsomely beat the previous record of £35,000 paid out for Jackie Sewell to Notts County by Wednesday themselves, and by Tottenham Hotspur to Swansea for Cliff Jones.

Next to join the Old Trafford company that summer was Warren Bradley, an amateur international outside right who signed professional forms from Bishop Auckland and made such a quick advance from his initial appearance against Bolton Wanderers in November 1958 that he gained England caps in 1959 against Italy, the U.S.A. and Mexico.

Quixall, however, of whom so much was expected, took time to feel his way. A quick-witted, graceful user of the ball, he could not settle at first to the United style. By the end of October the side had gone seven matches without a win, but with the inclusion of Bradley as Quixall's partner on the right flank and the switching of Viollet to centre forward, United began to get some colour back to their cheeks.

Mid-November saw the beginning of the turn of the tide with a home win over Luton Town and a 4–0 triumph at St. Andrews against Birmingham City. Quixall and Charlton by now were thinking along the same lines and speaking the same language so that without another defeat suffered to the end of 1958, the United machine had again begun to purr smoothly like a well-oiled machine.

Eight successive League wins ended with an unexpected 3–0 reverse at Third Division Norwich City in the third round of the F.A. Cup. Yet it proved a blessing in disguise. Able to concentrate their energies on the League Championship, they set out in hot pursuit of the leaders, Wolverhampton Wanderers, for the title.

Thus within a year of Munich, United unbelievably were in the forefront of affairs again.

At the end of February 1959 a last-minute goal by Charlton achieved victory over Wolves before a packed, swaying crowd at Old Trafford. This brought United's rich haul to twenty-three points from twelve matches so that by April it was neck and neck at the top:

| | | | | | Goals | | |
|---|---|---|---|---|---|---|---|
| | P | W | D | L | F | A | Pts |
| Wolves | 37 | 24 | 4 | 9 | 98 | 47 | 52 |
| Manchester United | 39 | 23 | 6 | 10 | 101 | 64 | 52 |
| Arsenal | 37 | 18 | 7 | 12 | 77 | 59 | 43 |

Wolves, however, staged a grandstand finish; United drew at Luton and lost at Leicester and the title went to Molineux by six points. Had United settled earlier at the start they might have pulled it off. Yet it was an astonishing effort after Munich. Busby, however, knew there was still much to be done to achieve the true shape of the side he wanted. Still, there was no denying the charismatic appeal of the team at his command. A total of 103 goals to their name in a season of readjustment, together with the emotional involvement by the public at large with the Munich disaster, produced a Lorelei siren call wherever United appeared. It was homage on a grand scale. Gates were closed at many away grounds where they played, while Old Trafford itself passed the million mark in aggregate, with the highest average home attendance – 53,258 – in Britain.

The 1959–60 season began with a couple of messages in the programme for the opening home match against Chelsea. One was from the chairman Harold Hardman. It read:

> My dear Friends, Once again it is my privilege, on behalf of my fellow directors and all who form part of the club, to welcome you back to Old Trafford.
>
> On 23rd August 1958 I wrote in the first programme of the season that provided we received your tolerance in defeat as well as your cheers in victory United would win through. How well everybody responded! To be runners-up for the First Division Championship was a memorable achievement and we are grateful for your encouragement.
>
> Our aim will be to maintain the same high standard of football during the coming season and in accordance with our policy of bringing the best teams in Europe to Old Trafford, we are delighted to have arranged an October visit by that fabulous club Real Madrid. As the opportunity

arises we hope to bring other top-line sides to Old Trafford for your entertainment.

The close season has been a busy one. By now you will have seen the new covered accommodation at the Stretford End which, when completed, will give protection for over 12,000 supporters. Covered standing accommodation is now available at the minimum charge of 2s. for over 22,000 spectators.

Finally, the Munich Memorial. After considering many designs one has been selected and the work placed in hand. It will be unveiled during the season, and we feel will be a fitting tribute to those who lost their lives whilst serving the Club.

The other message belonged to Matt Busby in his weekly column of the club programme:

I would like to express the hope that we will always please you by playing top-quality football.

That has been, and always will be, our aim and in examining our prospects for the season I should say the outlook is very bright indeed. We did extremely well last season – certainly better that I had thought possible – and although we are still rebuilding and searching for the winning rhythm, the over-all position is improving every day . . .

So began the first steps into the 1960s. The Munich Memorial was duly unveiled on February 25, above the main entrance, the last simple act of a sad chapter. On October 1, too, as promised, the great Real Madrid side, winners of the European Cup for four successive seasons since its inception in 1956, arrived to unleash a devastating defeat on United by 6–1 to emphasise their position as the football monarchs of Europe. The teams for that game read:

Manchester United: Gregg; Foulkes, Carolan; Goodwin, Cope, McGuinness; Bradley, Quixall, Viollet, Charlton, Scanlon.

Real Madrid: Dominguez, Marquitos, Lesmes; Ruiz, Santamaria, Santisteban; Canario, Didi, di Stefano, Puskas, Gento.

The fact that the following month United only lost 5–6 to Real in Madrid after a dazzling exhibition of attacking play by both teams was some consolation. But the truth was that a wide gulf separated United from the Spanish masters, reinforced as they were by such brilliant South American mercenaries as di Stefano (Argentina), Santamaria (Uruguay) and Didi (Brazil).

In spite of a scintillating 6–3 win at Chelsea and a 6–0 triumph over Leeds early in September, which promised well for a good season, it proved to be little more than an Indian summer. The over-all position, was not improving as Busby had hoped. Three defeats out of the next four matches by Spurs at Old Trafford (1–5), 0–3 at Manchester City, and 0–4 at Preston North End showed that the survivors from Munich were suffering a reaction, while the defence as a whole had begun to labour on its heels. Busby read the signs and started to take urgent action.

Morgans and Scanlon departed to Swansea and Newcastle respectively; Viollet, a naturally delicate player and sharp finisher, lost form and was rested; Charlton was switched to outside left. Into the senior side were drafted some of the young reserves who had been setting the Central League alight with such talented performances that they were attacting 12,000 gates and more, youngsters like Mark Pearson, at inside left, Johnny Giles on the right wing, Seamus Brennan at wing half, Dawson at centre forward and Gaskell in goal in place of Gregg.

But still the blend was neither right nor experienced enough. The commanding stature and control Busby sought was missing and when McGuinness was badly injured in January 1960 the manager decided on wider action. By the time spring was bursting, seasoned reinforcements had arrived in the persons of Setters from West Bromwich Albion, Cantwell from West Ham, and Herd from Arsenal. With them too, came an unknown young little Irish full back from Shamrock Rovers, Tony Dunne, whom Busby snatched after only two viewings for some £5,000. At that moment his shrewd eye for a potential player gave him one of the best bargains of his life, which was to be proved to the hilt later.

That season ended with United standing seventh in the League – a position they repeated in 1961 – a respectable enough but unspectacular role for the club. But 1960 at least was marked by two particular events – the celebration on February 13 of the fiftieth anniversary of the opening of Old Trafford, an occasion marked by a brilliant goal from Viollet (back in form) in a 1–1 draw with Preston North End. It was his twenty-seventh strike of the season which put him on his way to beating Jack Rowley's record of thirty goals in 1951–52. Viollet's final total of thirty-two still remains unbeaten at Old Trafford to this day.

In contrast to his sanguine hopes expressed publicly, Busby in his heart of hearts well realised the hard struggles that lay ahead if United were to remain amidst the vanguard for the big prizes. These fears he shared with his Board of Directors. By now, too, the club's successful youth policy was being imitated by others so that their five consecutive wins of the F.A Youth Cup from 1953 to 1957 had come to an end as other clubs developed their youth policies with promising youngsters.

But something even more disturbing was afoot, as Busby pointed out in the 1960 edition of *The International Football Book* published by the Souvenir Press:

> Without wishing to belittle the achievements of any club, I feel certain methods of attaining success have influenced British football too much and in the wrong direction. I am thinking of the power game. Results are achieved by placing undue emphasis on speed, power and physical fitness. Such teams now have many imitators. We are breeding a number of teams whose outlook seems to be that pace, punch and fitness are all that is required to win all the honours in the game. They forget that, without pure skills, these virtues count for precisely nothing. The imitators do not realise that Wolves, for instance, needed something more than that to get their good results. I should like to see the honours in England won by a pure footballing side, the sort of team that concentrates on ball skills above all else. Such a team could inspire the other ninety-one clubs. But for the air disaster I like to feel that others would now be copying Manchester United to the benefit of the whole League.

Little did he know it, but the precise type of football Busby was pleading for lay just around the corner. It was Tottenham Hotspur, who ten years earlier had blossomed with their 'push and run' style under the erudite managership of Arthur Rowe, who now provided it. Putting their minds where others were putting their bodies, Spurs brought a cerebral quality to their game and immediately swept the board. With men in their sides like Danny Blanchflower – the most intelligent captain of any team in the last thirty years with that other Irishman, Johnny Carey – the sensitive John White, Dave MacKay the power house, and Jimmy Greaves (returning from Italy), the arch pickpocket of goals, the Fagin of the penalty area, they possessed the right players to answer Busby's anxious plea. Brute force they spurned. Instead, they brought brute mind to bear and immediately they bemused everyone to win the League and Cup double in 1961 – the first club to do so in the twentieth century – and then the F.A. Cup again the next year in 1962. In 1963 they won the European Cup Winners' Cup to become the first British club to lift a Continental trophy. It was all beyond the conception of others at the time. It was like hitting below the intellect.

The sadness was that this conception of football scarcely caught on in general, apart perhaps from West Ham United, whose manager, Ron Greenwood, was of the same way of thinking and stamped it on his team. For the rest of the field, however, it was all rather too obtruse. It was above their heads. They preferred to stick to the blood and guts, the thunder and lightning of the physical British game. It saddened the likes of Busby, Walter Winterbottom and Greenwood, and a handful of others who thought along similar lines.

Though this may sound treacherous and unpatriotic, but in a sense it was a pity that England were later to win the World Cup as the hosts of 1966. Doing so with a new tactical conception of a 4–3–3 formation on the field, devised by their national manager Alf Ramsey, they came to be known as the 'wingless wonders'.

Full marks no doubt to Ramsey – later dubbed Sir Alf for his achievement – for making a successful brick from the straw available to him (he was not satisfied with the wing players at his command). But the outcome was that this triumphant tactic was duly imitated by the rest of football with dire results. England at that time happened to possess the right players to make the design work.

Others did not. They merely followed the new fashion blindly with the result that football as a whole became stereotyped, arid and constricted. The joy of attack was suffocated, the backroom tactical boffins took over, and football became a game of numbers – 4–3–3; then 4–4–2; next 4–3–2–1, etc.

To prove the point it is only necessary to compare the number of goals scored in the First Division between two decades. Consider this:

TABLE A

| *YEAR* | *GOALS* |
|---|---|
| 1950 | 1247 |
| 1951 | 1413 |
| 1952 | 1490 |
| 1953 | 1518 |
| 1954 | 1626 |
| 1955 | 1572 |
| 1956 | 1529 |
| 1957 | 1612 |
| 1958 | 1721 |
| 1959 | 1692 |
| TOTAL | 15420 |

TABLE B

| *YEAR* | *GOALS* |
|---|---|
| 1964 | 1571 |
| 1965 | 1544 |
| 1966 | 1459 |
| 1967 | 1387 |
| 1968 | 1398 |
| 1969 | 1203 |
| 1970 | 1211 |
| 1971 | 1089 |
| 1972 | 1160 |
| 1973 | 1160 |
| TOTAL | 13182 |

The point surely is made. Table A encompassed the age of four or five forwards up in attack and of penetrating wing play on *both* flanks; Table B reflects the bleak desert when the winger largely went out of fashion (note particularly the downward graph of scoring from 1967 onwards – the year *after* the World Cup) and where the overcrowded midfield became the central area of dreary attrition. Significantly, only two clubs (both of minor divisions, incidentally) have managed to achieve a century of goals in a season since the World Cup of 1966. That is something that cannot be blinkered.

The fact that Manchester United and Manchester City have now in the late 1970s both reverted to the old principle of using *two* wingers – with happier results – is an encouraging sign for the future. There may, indeed, be more than a grain of truth in the saying that 'what Manchester thinks today, the rest of the country will be thinking tomorrow . . .'

All this, however, is to digress. Yet it is appropriate enough to what Busby was thinking and wishing in 1960.

Tottenham Hotspur of that era, however, remain a key to the situation. Theirs was the spark that relit Manchester United's ambitious fires for the 1960s.

Yet for a spell the tinder was damp and failed to catch alight. Indeed, the seasons 1961/2 and 1962/3 were United's worst showings in the First Division since being relegated in 1937. A great deal had been constructed and achieved in the intervening quarter of a century and there was now no intention of letting it all go to waste.

But ending fifteenth in the League in 1962 and, worse still, nineteenth in 1963, the alarm bells began to ring loud and clear at Old Trafford. Busby and his directors saw the red light as the shadows lengthened and the dark tentacles of relegation reached out ominously. Something had to be done and it was. But in no wild panic. The right type of player was needed to rekindle the latent embers and character of the club.

When Denis Law was acquired from Torino F.C. in Italy in July 1962 and then Paddy Crerand from Glasgow Celtic in February 1963 – an inside forward and creative wing half respectively, both Scotsmen, with fire in their bellies, football in their blood and mercury in their veins – the magic formula was found. The fuse was mended and for the next five years United flew over the rainbow.

At this point perhaps it will be appropriate to tell of these two men's associations with United in their own words. In the case of

Law, in particular, there was a certain James Bond element in the way he returned to England from Italy.

'By 1962 I had become disillusioned with Italian football. I could accept all the hard discipline, the monastic retreat to mountain quarters for about three or four days a week and so on. But it became very boring and to add to that I was not even enjoying my football.

'I suppose I became fractious and difficult. At any rate I began to fall out with the Torino coach, or manager as we call him in Britain. Matters came to a head at the end of the 1962 season when he pulled me off the park during a cup game. I was accused of not trying and was suspended by the club for a fortnight. When the team went off to Switzerland for a close-season tour I was left behind alone in Turin to kick my heels.

'It was at that point that I had a call from Gigi Peronace – the Italian agent who had first negotiated my move from Manchester City to Torino at a time when other players like John Charles, Jimmy Greaves, Joe Baker, Gerry Hitchens and one or two more were also syphoned off to the Italian scene – saying that Manchester United would like to talk to me. Matt Busby and the United chairman, Mr. Hardman, as well as Mr. Louis Edwards, a director, apparently were at that moment in Switzerland. Everything had already been settled for my move from Torino to Old Trafford, said Gigi, and all that remained was for me to agree the details and personal terms of a contract with United. I was to go immediately to Swizterland to see the Manchester United representatives there.

'I was delighted with the prospect of getting back to my own country since I had liked Manchester as a place in my year's stay there earlier with City. In fact, I was so happy with the turn of events I would probably have gone back for nothing. Anyway, after a tedious train journey to Switzerland I met Matt and his chairman and all the small print of a contract was quickly settled. I returned to Turin feeling like a two-year-old.

'At that time I was unmarried and sharing a lovely apartment in the city with Joe Baker overlooking the River Po. One morning a day or so after getting back, I was woken by a knock on the window. It was a former Torino player who then had an administrative job with the club. He got me up and said I was required at the office of Mr. Agnelli, the millionaire boss of the Fiat Motor Company, who ran the Juventus football team with his elder brother.

'Getting there, Agnelli confronted me with the news that

Juventus had bought me from Torino for £160,000. I replied that this was impossible. I had just signed with Manchester United who had negotiated the deal officially with Torino. There was a contract already sealed between the two clubs and myself. Whereupon Agnelli produced another contract between Torino and his club Juventus which merely needed my signature. I refused to sign, repeating the facts about the deal between Torino and United in which I was to be transferred to Manchester for a fee of £115,000.

'I remained adamant. I couldn't sign two separate contracts. I stood my ground, gambling on the fact that Torino would surely prefer a matter of £115,000 from United to having no player on the field.

'Returning to my flat I reviewed the situation. I couldn't discuss it with anyone, especially my pal Joe Baker who was down at the Torino club training at that time. I didn't want to go there because I felt I might be conned into staying or something. So I made a quick decision. I threw a few things into an overnight bag, took a taxi from Torino to Milan and flew back to Scotland and Aberdeen, my home. Behind me, I left all my suits, tape recorder and gramophone equipment – everything – though Gigi Peronace in due course did send on most of my things.

'Anyway, I kicked my heels in Scotland for most of that summer of 1962 until at last I got a call from United telling me to report to Manchester and that all was settled and above board. I discovered duly that Matt Busby had known nothing of that other business between Torino and Juventus which had taken place behind his back after he and Mr. Hardman had left Switzerland to rejoin the United party in Majorca during that close season.'

Meanwhile Gigi Peronace – who in 1961 was the Sporting Director of Torino – has since filled in his version of the whole tangled web of the affair.

It was he who originally negotiated Law's move from Manchester City to Italy, involving also the transfer of Joe Baker, an Englishman playing with Hibernian in Scotland.

'Torino instructed me to acquire two strikers for them,' he said. 'I chose these two, Law and Baker. But the trouble was Torino had no money so I had to arrange Law's £115,000 transfer on a basis of three instalments. It was on those terms that I took Denis from Maine Road to Italy.'

Now comes the other end of the story. 'To condense it all,' continued Peronace, 'the first step in the deterioration of relations between the Torino club and Law came when Denis and Joe Baker had a nasty car crash in the city in Baker's new, fast Alfa Romeo. Joe was badly injured and out of action for several months; Denis was merely concussed and shaken.

'Towards the end of that 1961–62 season Torino were due to play Naples in a cup tie. Denis demanded a written guarantee from the club that he would be released to play for Scotland at Hampden Park the following week. When this was not forthcoming he literally never tried a yard in that Cup tie.

'I was sitting on the bench when Santos, the coach, called over Enzo Bearzot the skipper (now better known as the successful manager of the Italian national team) and told him to pull Law off the field. This Enzo refused to do and it was left to Santos to do the dirty work.

'Following that Denis swore that he would never play for Torino again, whereupon he was suspended by the club who then flew off to Switzerland without him for a friendly match in Geneva.

'It was there that I ran into Matt Busby and his two directors Mr. Hardman, then the chairman, and Mr. Louis Edwards, to learn that they had agreed with Mr. Filliponi, the Torino chairman, for the transfer of Law to Manchester United for £115,000.

'The fact was, however, it was only a verbal agreement. And big business in football being what it is, Filliponi later changed his mind when Juventus offered Torino a larger sum of £160,000 for Law. This was a contract that was signed by both parties without the knowledge of either Manchester United or Law . . .

'The rest of Denis's story is substantially correct except that in all the various in and outs it was I who paid for his taxi to Milan and airfare back to England and had to clear up the web of events. Eventually Matt Busby, having heard of the Juventus twist, wanted to wash his hands of the whole affair. But I persuaded him to trust me and leave things in my hands – which he did.

'With Law back in Scotland and out of the way I cleared the decks in due course. But remember that Torino still owed Manchester City the last of three instalments on the original deal at Maine Road the previous May – a matter of some £45,000. I went to Old Trafford and got two cheques from Manchester United to cover the £115,000 transfer from Torino – one for £70,000 which I took back to Italy; the other for the outstanding £45,000 owed to Manchester City, which I duly handed to their chairman, Mr. Douglas. It was finished.

'To my own satisfaction, at least, I always felt my hands were clean in the affair and I must say that this was much appreciated by both United and City.'

Matt Busby with the Sword of Honour, 1966.

Leslie Olive, Club Secretary, points the way to Joe Royle, head groundsman at Old Trafford for fifty years.

The indoor practice pitch at the Cliff.

On their way to face Benfica in Lisbon, Law and Best pass the time with a game of crib.

United win the European Cup Final at Wembley in May 1968. Charlton watches his first goal beat the Benfica goalkeeper Henrique.

There it was, an example of some of the devious passages that occur in the background of big football. Law and I meanwhile sipped our umpteenth cup of coffee in the Old Trafford offices as he ranged over the memories of his eleven years at Old Trafford.

'Had I gone to Juventus,' he continued, 'it could have been fun teaming up with the likes of big John Charles, Boniperti and the brilliant little inside forward Sivori, the Argentinian, who could make the ball sit up and beg. I remember once asking Sivori why he didn't pull out all the stops throughout the ninety minutes of a match.

'He replied: "I turn it on at the beginning of a game. I miss the next forty and then it on just before the interval. I do the same in the second half. Do you know why? Because everyone remembers the beginning and the end . . ."

'But how happy I was to get back to England and Manchester and so lucky to enjoy our great years through the 1960s with players like Bobby Charlton, Paddy Crerand and, in due course, "Georgie" Best. Those were the best years of my professional life. In any case, how could you fail to be happy with Sir Matt as manager? He was different from everyone else in football that I knew anyway. Perhaps there were a couple more near him like Bill Shankly and Bill Nicholson. The fact is that here at Old Trafford "the boss" treated you like a human being – not just a player. If, for instance, you had some trouble or worry at home during the week this was often reflected in your play.

'But Sir Matt realised that. For most managers you are a number and if you don't perform then obviously something's going to be said. But he treated you as a human being, with understanding. That to me was ninety per cent of the secret of his success, more so even than his football knowledge, though even as a tactician he was very good.

'He did not represent the modern approach to the game, which has declined as it is – though it is coming back a bit now with the advent of wingers as used here these days by United and City. We had tactics in those 1960s in the sense that we picked up opponents as one would normally do at corner kicks, free kicks, throw-ins etc. – static plays. But as regards any fixed formation, especially in attack, he told us to play instinctively, the way we felt best. If you came off the field beaten but on your knees there'd be nothing said because you'd only done your best anyway. That's why in those 1960s we were such a good side. The forward line moved anywhere they wanted. We were absolutely fluid and it was this that made it so hard for opposing defences to mark us tight. In later years, certainly, we started to become static, concentrating as "strikers" – the fashionable new word – through the middle. But by then, of course, the game had changed – for the worst in my opinion.

'I have many memories of some great matches in that period 1963 to 1969. Mark you, United had a miserable time in the league in 1962 and 1963, ending fifteenth and nineteenth and nearly getting relegated. But the tide had slowly begun to stir deep down, even in 1962, when they reached the semi-final of the Cup, and lost 3–1 to that great Spurs side. Next year, of course, we won the Cup, and then reached three more semi-finals in succession, losing 3–1 to West Ham in 1964, to Leeds in 1965 after a replay, and to Everton in 1966.

'Hell, those were exciting years. Just consider what United did from 1962 to 1968 – fifteenth, nineteenth, second, Champions, fourth, Champions, and second in the League in seven successive seasons; and at the side of that, F.A. Cup winners in 1963 as well as reaching five consecutive semi-finals. All this, of course, was capped by winning the European Cup in 1968. It was a fabulous period and wherever we appeared the gates seemed to be closed on full houses.

'It was a joy to play football in those days. And it must have been great to watch for the rest of you. We used to have some tremendous matches with Spurs in particular. They'd get five against us down in London and we'd thrash them by five up at Old Trafford. We were both virtually unbeatable at home then. Also, we had many fine games with Liverpool, full of open, attacking football.

'There was one match, especially, I remember at White Hart Lane. With only four minutes left we were leading 2–1 and holding on comfortably. Then bang! bang! Greaves sneaked a couple in those dying minutes and we were beaten 3–2. He really was remarkable. He wouldn't be in a match for long periods, unemployed as it were, and suddenly you'd wake up to find he'd put two or three in your net! When he got the ball anywhere near the penalty area the lads would begin to shake. He was the deadliest finisher I ever played against.

'Do you know what was the turning point that made those years possible for us – put us on the right path? Winning that Cup Final of 1963. As I said, we'd nearly got relegated that season. But all the time we felt we only needed some little turn of the screw to get us going. Having scraped a 1–0 win over Southampton in the semi-final with a goal by me – it was a poor match; a schoolboy side could have beaten either of us that day – we got to Wembley as the outsiders against Leicester City who were aiming for the double that season.

'Then all at once it came right at Wembley on the big day. Everything suddenly clicked into place. We played some really good stuff at last. I got the first goal, David Herd banged in two others and we won the Cup handsomely by 3–1. If we'd lost that one it would probably have taken us another year or so to find our feet. As it was the gate suddenly swung open for us and we were through to the shining uplands. Yes, Wembley 1963 was the turning point without a doubt.'

Law certainly put his finger on the pulse of those years. Yet modestly he made little or no mention of the part he himself played in the transformation. Crerand for one has said that whenever Law was in the side the whole team felt they had a goal start at the kick-off. As for Jimmy Murphy, he put the Scottish bombshell on a par with Jimmy Greaves as a finisher – even at times a shade ahead. 'There were one or two goals Denis got which I don't believe even Pelé himself would have pulled off.'

All this, naturally, is a matter of opinion. What is irrefutable as hard fact is that Law was of a highly volatile, explosive temperament. In November 1963 he was suspended for twenty-eight days for kicking an opponent. A year later he was suspended again for another twenty-eight days, and then for six weeks in 1967. All this represented a dark record and gave him a bad name at the time. If this was fact, nevertheless the question of opinion once more became an intruding element. For instance in 1964 David Miller, then of *The Sunday Telegraph,* wrote that Law was more sinned against than sinning: that it was the very nature of his lightning reactions that resulted in his being consistently fouled by defenders who were too slow to match him: and that his unrivalled competitive instinct consequently made him react equally swiftly to injustices. Sometimes, certainly he did illegal, intentional things that deserved reprimand; but he was caught up, like other players, in a system which allowed, with the help of permissive referees, too much freedom to the destroyers of the game at the expense of its truly creative artists.[1] Further to this, Crerand, another quick-tempered Scot, has since revealed how it was known that some players were told to provoke Law and himself on purpose with the object of upsetting their equilibrium.

Be that as it may, there can be no denying the magnetic quality of Law's play or his ability to score many a breathtaking goal. The

[1] *Father of Football. The Story of Sir Matt Busby* by David Miller (Stanley Paul, 1970).

facts speak for themselves even if Law is modestly reticent about himself on the subject. In the year 1965, when United won the Championship, he claimed twenty-eight goals in thirty-six League games, and was top scorer. In 1964 his total was thirty goals in thirty appearances in the League – a remarkable average of a goal a game – as well as ten goals in six Cup ties. In 1962–3, his first season at Old Trafford after leaving Torino, he played thirty-eight League games and scored twenty-three times. All this adds up to eighty-one goals in 104 matches in his first three seasons back in English League football.

Nor was that the extent of his bag in the League. In 1966 he claimed fifteen; in 1967 he was top again for the fourth time in five seasons with twenty-three; in 1969, suffering a bad knee and much pain after a cartilage operation of the previous year, it was fourteen; then fifteen in 1971; and thirteen in 1972. No wonder the Old Trafford crowds took him to their hearts. Compelling and theatrical in all he did, to them he was 'Denis the Menace: The King'. Utterly brave and quick as light in snapping up half chances, he was particularly brilliant in the air. To me, when he went for a header, he seemed to hang like a star in the heavens.

Paddy Crerand was the next to ride into town on a white charger to save the old homestead. Coming from Glasgow Celtic and already a Scottish international, like Law, he arrived at Old Trafford on February 6, 1963. It is extraordinary, almost eerie, how often that tragic date occurs and is repeated in the Manchester United saga. In Crerand's case it turned out to be a lucky day. For the next ten seasons he played a major role in the success of the club before hanging up his boots and remaining to do his duty off-stage where he had been so happy for a decade. By the time Crerand retired in 1972 Busby had moved upstairs to the directors' lobby; Wilf McGuinness had had a brief, unsuccessful feel of the managerial hot-seat; and Frank O'Farrell had taken over the team at a difficult period. It was as overseer of the youth side that the former United wing half remained and when O'Farrell, too, had lost control of the situation, it was as assistant to the new manager, the stormy petrel Tommy Docherty, that Crerand continued. But sadly theirs was not a happy relationship. It was dissolved in 1976 and Crerand moved on to become manager of Northampton Town for a short spell before disillusion overtook him once again.

All his happy times, indeed, came at the beginning as a player. 'United and Matt Busby were always the magic names in Scotland,' he recalls. 'Maybe it was something to do with Munich and because Matt himself was a Scot. Anyway, having played for Celtic for six years I wanted to move on and since there was a tacit understanding, so I believe, between the club and Busby that should I ever wish to come south of the border I would go to Old Trafford, that's how I came here.'

Crerand at that time was regarded by many sound judges as one of the ablest wing halves in Britain if not even in all Europe. In acquiring him for a creative role in midfield Busby's judgment again hit the jackpot. The part he duly played in feeding the overflowing skills of the Manchester attack of those days cannot be over-estimated. A one-paced player of steady, measured stride, he glided smoothly over the ground rather than ran. His perception and reading of a game took him to the right places at the right time so that interception and creative distribution were his strong points, just as they had been Busby's in his own playing days.

Perhaps even Busby found an artistic echo of himself in this fellow Scot, though Crerand in due course proved to be quite a different, more fiery, quick-tempered player, apt to retaliate at the slightest provocation with unhappy results. There was the occasion he was sent off for kicking a Yugoslav Partizan player in a tough European Cup tie in 1966, and perhaps more distressing still, the time he was seen by millions of viewers on television to spit angrily in the face of a Stoke City opponent. That in the opinion of some outraged United supporters brought the name of their club into disrepute and they wished Crerand to be dismissed from Old Trafford altogether.

Busby, however, had a way of pouring oil on troubled waters and Crerand, much to his own relief, remained to serve the club he loved.

'In spite of what some people thought and said of Sir Matt – especially in the later years, when he was accused of being over-indulgent in his treatment of wrongdoers and lax in his discipline – he could be tough when he had you on the mat.' That was Crerand's memory. 'Of course, he had his own way of going about a wigging. After a while you found yourself agreeing with him in all he said and you would accept his judgment and sentence. But when you got home you'd think: "My God, he's conned me again . . ." But one thing. He'd never abuse you or dress you down in front of others, which we all appreciated greatly.

'Very often, if he had you on the carpet for something or other, or was about to drop you from the team, you'd find yourself summoned during the week to the referee's changing room which was only a few yards away down the corridor from the players' dressing rooms. Whenever we came back from training to bathe, shower or dress we'd all run past that ref's cubby hole in case the door opened and Sir Matt was there to request our presence inside. That was his punishment hole. Believe me, he could be stern all right, though I do suspect he let young Georgie Best get away with things too much.

'Believe me, Bestie was a dear lad. Lost perhaps and spoiled by the wrong people. But he was no dissolute beatnik, no hooligan. I liked him, but people, and especially the press, got on his back. Since he was sensitive, and ran away from troubles and even his own shadow, he kept doing his disappearing acts. What he really needed was to have married the right type of girl who would have made him a home and given him some stability, companionship and something worthwhile to hang on to. He built that lovely big house at Bramhall and then was as lonely as hell in it by himself.

'Of my many happy memories at Old Trafford I suppose the peak was when we won the European Cup against Benfica in 1968. That was great, though we nearly lost it in the last few minutes of normal time when Alex Stepney kept us alive with a tremendous save from Eusebio. While we were having our leg muscles massaged out on the pitch before the start of the extra half hour, Sir Matt came amongst us and, I remember, was particularly angry with myself and Bobby Charlton for giving the ball away too much in midfield. "Use the ball *properly,* get hold of the middle of the park again, and you'll find yourselves not nearly as tired as the others. Now go to it and play football . . ."

'I had a very lucky start, of course, with United. I'd only been with them about three months in that terrible winter of 1963 when we reached the Cup Final and beat Leicester City to most people's suprise. At the time I never fully appreciated an English Cup Final and ever afterwards wished I could get there again to savour the occasion to the full. But, in spite of a number of semi-finals in succession during those great years, I never made it again. Yet we had a fine side that year against Leicester and we played really well on the day: Gaskell; Dunne, Cantwell (Capt.); Crerand, Foulkes, Setters; Giles, Quixall, Herd, Law and Charlton.

'It was a freer moving game in those days, with wingers on both flanks. The best of that breed I ever saw were Tom Finney and George Best, greater even than Stanley Matthews who never scored like those other two. But there were many fine players around at that time – Jimmy Greaves and our Denis Law, of course, both of whom could conjure goals out of practically nothing; Bobby Charlton, John White and Danny Blanchflower of Spurs, and big John Charles. A pal of mine who is absolutely United mad still tells me that whenever Best or Law got the ball he used to find himself on the edge of his seat in a fever of excitement and anticipation. That feeling has died now. And in my opinion one of the key figures in our side of those days was Nobby Stiles. He was a great lad, very clean living off the field, always happy and smiling. Yet on the field he'd rant and roar and curse like blue murder to keep us going. He was a tremendous motivator.'

Bobby Charlton, too, is of this same opinion today, saying that there was no one better at tidying up dangerous situations at the back than Stiles, adding that the reputation he got for being a vigorous player was due largely to his bad eyesight which led him into mistimed tackling.

Be that as it may, while Law and Best were the star prima donnas up front in attack, the real heart of the side beat in the midfield relationship of Crerand and Charlton, once the latter had been switched from outside left and given the role of a deep lying, withdrawn inside or centre forward from 1964 onwards. They matched the Bozsik–Hidegkuti partnership for Hungary in the 1950s and United's success as an entertaining, attacking side from 1963 to 1968 sprung largely from their joint creative service from midfield. They were the true effective hub of the whole wheel.

Nobby Stiles was first spotted by Jimmy Murphy in 1956 in a schoolboys' trial. On coming to Old Trafford in due course, he captained the youth team and worked his way up steadily through the ranks. It is almost with a sense of shock that one now remembers that he first appeared in the League side as an inside forward. But like water finding its own level, Stiles eventually settled in defence where, as Crerand remarked, 'Probably only Sir Matt and Ramsey (for England) appreciated his true merit and influence on others.'

Second in the League in 1964, four points behind Liverpool for the championship title, Busby still kept chipping away at his United creation. Impatient with the advance of some of his younger players he plumped for John Connelly, the Burnley outside right, whom he acquired for £50,000.

It was at this point that he made one of the most decisive decisions of his career. Having originally moved Charlton to outside left after Munich, Busby now saw in him a more mature character capable of playing a dominating role in midfield. No matter what number he carried on his shirt – 8, 9, 10, or 11 – this was the new part cast for him at the heels of attack with himself free to come through from the back to unleash his powerful shooting from the edges of the box.

Meanwhile, unknown to the world in general, a new secret weapon was being prepared quietly in the background. It was George Best.

Originally alerted by Bob Bishop, United's agent in Northern Ireland, with the words 'I believe I've found you a genius', Busby was not slow to act. In the summer of 1961 the scrawny little youth, aged only fifteen, was brought over to Old Trafford. But so shy and homesick was the little chap that within twenty-four hours he had caught the boat home to Belfast. Almost a waif in appearance, he was eventually to stray from the fold once more, but not before he had set the world by the ears with many a glorious performance.

All that was to lie ahead, but in the meanwhile a quick call to his parents in Belfast saw the young rookie sent back to Manchester. 'Don't tinker with the boy's style. Let him develop his own way, naturally. He's something special,' was Busby's instruction to his coaching staff. The result is now past history.

It was in mid-September 1963, that Best first found his name on the first XI team sheet – as reserve against West Bromwich Albion. In truth, he had already been chosen to play in place of Moir who was nursing an injury. This was one of those psychological ploys by Busby who was anxious not to worry the boy overnight. He need not have bothered. Best from the start, despite his tender years, had not a shred of nerves. He had ice in his veins. He played outside right that day and though showing his potential quietly did not get another run in the League side until Boxing Day when he scored his opening goal in a 5–1 win over Burnley. It was the happiest Christmas present imaginable and from that moment he was never out of the team unless injured or disciplined.

The first time I ever set eyes on him was at The Dell where United went as holders to face Southampton in January 1964 in the third round of the F.A. Cup. Losing at half time, Manchester recovered to win 3–2 largely thanks to the efforts of their two teenage wingers – Anderson on the left and Best on the right. We were obviously in the presence of a presence.

New young faces were filling the background now in company with Best – players like the aforementioned Anderson; Gaskell, a goalkeeper; David Sadler, a very useful amateur all-rounder from Maidstone who turned professional and later played for England (he shared digs with Best in his earlier days); John Aston junior, a winger, son of United's former full back and coach; and Francis Burns, who could perform either at full back or wing half. So did United open a new chapter in the sixties.

That season of 1963/64 saw United end as League runners-up,

find their way to the quarter-final of the European Cup Winners' Cup and reach the F.A. Cup semi-final where they lost 3–1 to West Ham United after accounting on the way for Southampton, Bristol Rovers, Burnley and Sunderland, who were beaten 5–1 only after a second replay in a tough, exciting tie. But what gave them as much pleasure as anything was the winning once more of the F.A Youth Cup that season after an interval of some seven years.

In his manager's report at the A.G.M. of September 3, 1964, Busby referred to the venture of building an up-to-date new stand to provide seating and standing cover for over 20,000 spectators, which could well lead to Old Trafford being granted representative matches in the future quite apart from the three World Cup games already allocated for 1966. 'Manchester United,' he said, 'are a name in English football and we want to keep it that way. Also there have been many changes in the game recently such as the No Maximum wage and new contracts have been difficult to surmount. But the directors and the club have adapted to the situation. Clubs must give the public entertainment and this we will continue to try to do. The only way to survive is to meet change as it comes.'

It was the team on the field that mattered and here United stood head and shoulders above others as an attraction throughout the 1960s. In 1959 – after Munich – the homage was unmistakable. At away grounds Manchester United were the Pied Piper as they attracted youth in huge numbers. At Old Trafford the average gate was the best in Britain with the total attendances amounting to more than a million. In 1960/61 it grew further in spite of Tottenham's great feat in achieving the League and Cup double. United were still Top of the Pops at the box office. The biggest crowd that season in the league was 66,579 when United visited Chelsea at Stamford Bridge; the second largest came at White Hart Lane when Spurs and United entertained a gathering of 62,602. Busby and his golden boys may not have won any of the big prizes at that time, but – to use a contemporary idiom – they kept laughing all the way to the bank.

With the general public interest fired by England's victory in the World Cup of 1966, the graph curved even higher. By the Christmas of that year over a million people had watched United home and away; by April 1967 the million mark was again overstepped at Old Trafford itself, so that the average home gate for 1966–67 reached 53,800, a post-war record for the club. In 1967–68 it went even higher to a Football League record of 57,549, beating an earlier figure established by Newcastle United. It was a season which saw United dissipate a five-point lead in the championship at the very end to their neighbours, Manchester City. But for that sudden collapse in the League at the climax they would have pulled off the unique double of championships and European Cup achieved later by Liverpool in 1976–77.

However, in that period, 1965 to 1969, United were constantly in the forefront of events in one way or another. On the credit side they became League champions in 1965 and 1967, were fourth and runners-up in 1966 and 1968; again reached the semi-final of the F.A. Cup in 1965 and 1966 (the latter for the fifth year running); and rounded it all off by at last winning the European Champions' Trophy in 1968. They might even have pulled off the latter again in 1969 but for the doubtful decision of a French referee when he denied Law a goal in the second leg of the semi-final against A.C. Milan at Old Trafford.

On the debit side, however, there grew an uncomfortable feeling that United had begun to consider themselves the God-given masters of everything. There was a sense of some divine right about them. True, they became the prime target of everyone as others set out to knock them off their pedestal. The result was that with abrasive players like Law, Crerand, Stiles and soon enough another long-haired Scot, John Fitzpatrick – who came into the picture when Stiles was absent for two months following a knee operation – all prepared to go to excessive lengths of over-exuberance in defending their position, the side as a whole began to get a bad name.

It was the natural but sad corollary of trying to win everything. The prizes and the money at stake had begun to get too big. Retaliation and a veil of arrogance began to clothe United and those who had followed them faithfully became disturbed by this new trend.

It reached a distressing nadir in the Cup semi-final of 1965 when United and Leeds United, then clawing their way up the Eiger face of successful competition, met at Hillsborough, Sheffield, on the last stride to Wembley. From the very kick-off a kind of tribal war seemed to have been declared. Players lost their tempers, their shirtsleeves and almost their legs as football itself was cast to the four winds. Not surprisingly it was a goalless draw and a disgrace, not only to football but to both sides. As a match, indeed, it resembled an ugly, unmade bed.

Tempers had cooled somewhat for the replay four days later under the floodlights of the Nottingham Forest ground, when Windle the referee bent over backwards to make amends for his ealier lenience. If anything, he tended to over-correct in his effort to achieve discipline and it was with the last of a whole string of free kicks against United that Leeds won, when Bremner headed in a flighted ball from Giles in the last minute. That was United's third semi-final defeat in four successive years. There was yet another to follow the next season.

Meanwhile with the turnstiles ticking merrily and the bank manager smiling contentedly, a Development Fund had been refurbishing Old Trafford and improving facilities for spectators and the players. An immaculate indoor training area, 240 feet by 150, too, was provided at the Cliff, for so long the club's practice ground, while to meet the needs of the 1966 World Cup Executive Committee an imposing cantilever stand was constructed at a cost of some £300,000 to give Old Trafford a grandiose look. It really had become a palace amongst English club grounds.

## 1964–1965, A Summary[1]

With eight of the team that had won First Division title in 1957 either killed or seriously injured at Munich in 1958, Manchester United had rebuilt. A sum approaching £400,000 was spent in the transfer market in less than four years and when after two near misses they were back at the top again in 1965 only two survivors of the air disaster remained – Bobby Charlton and Bill Foulkes.

As always Charlton played his heart out: as link man he had to lie deep and concentrate on getting the ball through to Herd, Best or Denis Law, who was top scorer (for the third year in succession) with a total of twenty-eight League goals.

Even so, it was the defence firmly built around Foulkes that carried United through to the title. When the pressure was on in mid-season at a time when the attack was missing chances, men like Foulkes and the two full backs, Brennan and Tony Dunne (all of them ever-present throughout the season), really showed their mettle. The defence conceded only thirty-nine goals.

Fortunately the attack hit form again late in the season (Charlton got a hat trick in a 5–0 win at Blackburn) and United enjoyed a run of seven wins in a row, clinching the championship with a 3–1 victory over Arsenal at Old Trafford.

At that stage, with one game still to play, United were actually level on points with Leeds United who had ended their programme with a draw at Birmingham. But with a superior goal average

[1] From *We are the Champions* by Maurice Golesworthy (Pelham Books, 1972).

United had no need to worry about their last game, for in spite of losing 2–1 at Villa Park they took the championship by .686 of a goal.

Pat Dunne, Shay Brennan and Nobby Stiles all won their first caps this season so that every member of United's championship team was an international.

Team: Dunne, (P.); Brennan, Dunne (A.); Crerand; Foulkes, Stiles; Connelly, Charlton, Herd, Law, Best.

Pat Dunne (goalkeeper): United paid Shamrock Rovers about £10,000 for this player but he remained less than three years at Old Trafford before transfer to Plymouth Argyle in February 1967. Born Dublin. F.A. of Ireland Cup Winners' medal 1964. 5 Eire caps.

Shay Brennan (right back): One of the Busby Babes thrust into the side after Munich. Made debut at outside left two weeks after that disaster in 1958 and scored two goals in a 3–0 Cup victory over Sheffield Wednesday. Later played wing half before establishing himself at full back. 291 League games. Born Manchester but qualified for Eire and was capped eighteen times. European Cup medal 1968 and two League medals.

Tony Dunne (left back): Completed United's trio of Eire internationals in this rearguard. Born Dublin and recruited from Shelbourne in 1960. Cup Winners' medal 1963. League medals 1965 and 1967 and European Cup 1968. Over 350 League games. Small and quick. Twenty-three Eire caps.

Pat Crerand (right half): His accurate long ball turned defence into attack in the twinkling of an eye. This immaculate midfield schemer cost United £43,000 when transferred from Celtic in February 1963 and was one of the stars of their Cup victory that season. Well over 300 League games. Sixteen Scottish caps. European Cup 1968 and two League medals. Scottish Cup runners-up medal. Born Glasgow.

Bill Foulkes (centre half): See under season 1955–56.

Nobby Stiles (left half): Great-hearted player and human dynamo who became one of the keenest tacklers in the game. A local development who made League debut in 1960–61 and appeared in 311 League games before transfer to Middlesbrough 1971. European Cup and League medals. Twenty-eight England caps and a World Cup Winners' medal. Born Manchester.

John Connelly (outside right): Began as an inside left with St. Helen's Town – his birthplace – and was snapped up by Burnley in

1956. Switched to the wing and became one of the freest scoring wingers in the league. Championship winners' medal 1960 and Cup finalist 1962 with Burnley. Twenty England caps. Transferred to Manchester United in April 1964. Moved to Blackburn Rovers in September 1966, and later to Bury, 1970.

Bobby Charlton (inside right): Began as a winger and developed into a deep-lying inside or centre forward noted for the accuracy of his passes over a long distance and the power of his shooting. Excelled in the art of manoeuvring into position for a shot at goal. Signed professional for United in 1955 and scored twice when making League debut in October 1956. Has since scored over 200 League goals. Created world record by appearing in 106 internationals (since beaten). European Cup, three F.A. Cup finals (one winners' medal), and a World Cup Winners' medal. Assisted United in three championship wins – 1956/57, 1964/65, and 1966/67. Well over 560 League games. Born Ashington.

David Herd (centre forward): Son of former Manchester City and Stockport County inside forward, Alex Herd, and played alongside his father in the same Stockport side after turning professional in 1951. Joined Arsenal 1954, and Manchester United 1961. One of the hardest shots in the game and scored over 200 League goals. Went to Stoke City in July 1968 after collecting one Cup and two League medals with United. Five Scottish caps. Born Hamilton.

Denis Law (inside left): United paid Torino £115,000 for this great player in July 1962. Unpredictable, but his amazingly sharp reflexes and powerful finishing made him one of the finest forwards of his era. Made debut for Scotland when only eighteen and went on to collect fifty-five caps. One Cup and two League medals with United in over 300 appearances. Developed on Huddersfield Town's ground staff and moved to Manchester City in May 1960 for £53,000. Torino paid £100,000 for his services in June 1961.

George Best: An instinctive, natural ball player with unlimited talent who made his initial league appearance with United in 1963. Two League medals and over 300 League appearances before he announced his premature retirement in May 1972. A flamboyant character who went to Old Trafford straight from school in Belfast. Developed into one of the world's greatest footballers. Won European Cup medal in 1968. Twenty-nine caps for Northern Ireland and also represented the United Kingdom. Born Belfast.

# 1966–1967, A Summary[1]

United's team that won the championship again this season showed a number of changes from the one that carried off the trophy two years earlier.

Alex Stepney arrived in goal from Chelsea for a fee of over £50,000 soon after the start of the season, and a young local discovery, Bob Noble, came in at left back to begin what promised to be a brilliant career. But a car crash put him out of the game after only twenty-nine League appearances. New to the forward line were David Sadler at centre forward – with Herd moving to inside left – while another local development, John Aston, made twenty-five appearances at outside left with Best moving to the right wing to fill the gap left by Connelly's departure to Blackburn early in the season.

With a 4–3–3 set-up and with the right combination of brilliance and consistency, particularly in the second half of the season, United won the title with a margin of four points ahead of Nottingham Forest who enjoyed their best-ever season to finish runners-up.

For a time it looked as if Liverpool would again get their name on the trophy and they were on top of the table in January, but after holding Newcastle to a goal-less draw at St. James's Park on March 11, the Old Trafford side regained the lead and remained ahead for the rest of the season, being undefeated in their last twenty games and actually clinching the title with a fine 6–1 victory (Charlton, Crerand, Foulkes, Best, Law 2, 1 pen.) at West Ham – the biggest away win of the season in the first Division.

United were unbeaten at home this season and actually enjoyed a run of thirty-seven home First Division games without defeat between April 9, 1966, when they were beaten 2–1 by Leicester City, until March 2, 1968, when Chelsea won 3–1 at Old Trafford.

Team: Stepney; Dunne or Brennan, Noble; Crerand, Foulkes, Stiles; (from) Best, Law, Sadler, Charlton, Herd, Aston.

Having begun this decade in the painful shadows United went out with all flags flying. Their battle honours were there for all to see. At the end of the 1950s Wolverhampton Wanderers and then, in a season or two, Tottenham Hotspur had been their closest rivals. Now, in the 1960s, the wind of change had swung the weather vane

[1] From *We are the Champions* by Maurice Golesworthy (Pelham Books, 1972).

towards Liverpool and Leeds United. It had become a three-pronged Battle of the Roses – Lancashire against Yorkshire – where not a yard was conceded by the contestants without a struggle. None of them would have it any other way.

Were they to know it, however, dangerous rapids lay close ahead, on which United's reputation and playing strength were to founder. There were those – like Foulkes and Law – who now say that they felt the approaching troubles. 'In my opinion,' remarks Foulkes, helped perhaps by hindsight, 'Sir Matt should have started to break up our side as soon as we had won the European Cup.' 'Maybe so,' adds Law. 'But that might have been too drastic. In a year or two, certainly; in 1970 or '71, things should have been changed but by then, of course, the boss was not really fit and by January 1969 he had resigned as manager of the team.' But this is to anticipate the future.

Meanwhile, in June 1968, Busby was knighted in the Queen's Birthday Honours, much to the approval of the whole world of sport, though there were some dark mutterings north of the border as to why Jock Stein, who was the first to triumph in Europe with Celtic, had not been granted a similar accolade rather than a C.B.E. I don't suppose it worried these two old, old friends for a moment one way or the other.

While concluding this last phase before the approach of the 1970s a long-range view of events may perhaps touch more closely on the truth of things. After all it is easier to judge the shape of a mountain from the valley than while standing on its peak.

For one thing United were still able to draw on their reservoir of young players, in some instances perhaps sooner than Busby would have wished. In December 1966 the United side that drew 2–2 with Liverpool showed six players all under twenty who had emerged from the fledgling team which had won the F.A Youth Cup in 1964. On the field that afternoon were only three men who had cost the club any transfer fees – Crerand, Herd and Stepney. The line up was: Stepney; Brennan, Noble; Crerand, Sadler, Dunne; Best, Charlton, Ryan, Herd and Aston. When three months later Herd broke a leg against Leicester, Sadler moved up from centre half to centre forward to confirm his value as an all-rounder.

Of a far deeper significance and public concern, however, was the dubious reputation United had built up for themselves through the sixties. They still remained the North Star for so many to follow: a national institution to revere. Yet there were those, particularly in the press, who looked beyond all the aura and the glamour. The world tends to have a short memory when it wants. But the hard facts revealed that in the decade between the Munich crash and the winning of the European Cup more than twenty United players had been dismissed from the field while the various teams in that time had earned nearly seventy bookings. This was a sad toll that could not be ignored, and Busby more than once had to face the charge of a lack of discipline and a licence for his players to behave badly.

Doubtless it worried him greatly. Yet in defence he would point to the outrageously cruel treatment such natural ball players as Best, Charlton, Law and Crerand in particular had to suffer from the destroyers in the game. Of these only the long-suffering Charlton, with his world-wide reputation for sportsmanship, refused to be dragged down into a mire of contention. As for the others, their Celtic fires were quickly sparked into instinctive retaliation, while the likes of Stiles and Fitzpatrick, two tigers of the hard tackle, tended to add fuel to the flames.

There have always been hard men in football but what became an unwelcome new trait was the disease of retaliation on the field and crowd violence off it. Busby, I believe, in a sense became lost in this new age. To him it was a shift of space and time; behaviour became two-dimensional and he could not really come to grips with it. Paternal by instinct, Manchester United to him were his larger family. A man's character is his destiny and having himself survived Munich, he felt his destiny was to protect this tight-knit family with a fierce pride. Yet it was as if he wore a cowl of obedience, only to stand by to see the law broken by others.

**United v Benfica at Wembley, 1968: Tony Dunne is injured; Charlton and Crerand, left; Eusebio shows concern.**

**George Best (no 7) turns after scoring to put United back in front in extra time. Final score 4–1.**

A lap of honour at Wembley with the European Cup, 1968; Shay Brennan, left, and Bobby Charlton, right.

Matt Busby holds the cup, flanked by Paddy Crerand and George Best.

# 6

## *1969–1977*

# *Turmoil and Recovery*

AMONG HIS MANY writings Sigmund Freud once said that one might compare the relations of the ego to the id with that between a rider and his horse. The horse provides the locomotor energy and the rider has the prerogative of determining the goal and of guiding the movements of his powerful mount towards it. But all too often in the relations between the ego and the id we find a picture of the less ideal situation in which the rider is obliged to guide his horse in the direction in which the horse wants to go. In other words, instead of harnessing and directing one's life, life itself takes over suddenly and one is obliged to follow its footsteps.

In a sense this is what happened to United for a spell in the coming years. Having ridden high for most of the 1960s, the early 1970s all at once found them losing control of the reins, losing their way and, almost inevitably, taking a fall.

A variety of events helped to contribute towards this. At the heart of it all perhaps was the physical condition and health of Busby himself, the motivator supreme for so long. One cannot live on the mountain peak indefinitely. The air becomes too rarefied at the top and in the end there is only one way left to go – downwards.

In spite of possessing the constitution of an ox, the endless strains, tensions and emotions of his job – to say nothing of the long-range after-effects of the damage suffered at Munich – began to have their combined effect. He lived, breathed, slept and dreamed football. As he himself once remarked, 'The only time I get a break from it is when I can sneak a round of golf.' There was no escape even socially, and when he went to watch a match for the very pleasure of it, there were always those who were trying to put salt on his tail, convinced that he was up to something or other.

Having weighed the situation calmly and logically – as was always his way – and talked over things with his Board of Directors, Busby came to the conclusion that the time had at last arrived after twenty-four years in the saddle to hand over the reins to a younger man. In the presence of a massed press conference this decision was finally announced to the sporting world in January 1969. It was the end of an age and the nub of coming events.

What was to follow is best summarised briefly and then examined later in more detail. In this way the broader picture may emerge.

Having relinquished the day-to-day control of the United players and moved to a new role as general manager, Busby and his directors soon found that there was no one immediately capable of following in the footsteps of the master. In the event unlucky, perhaps even unwise, decisions of the board led to the entrance and exit of three managers, all of whom for various reasons failed to fill the bill,

After an unbroken reign of twenty-four years there came three contenders for the throne of Old Trafford – young Wilf McGuinness, himself a former player and a United man through and through; Frank O'Farrell; then Tommy Docherty. In a space of eight seasons all had come and gone. At the time of writing, a fourth, Dave Sexton, is at the helm. Whether he will prove to be the right man remains to be seen. The future is in his hands.

January 1969, however, was the key point. It was then that the club issued the following statement:

> Sir Matt has informed the Board that he wishes to relinquish the position of team manager at the end of the present season. The Chairman and Directors have tried to persuade him to carry on and it was only with great reluctance that his request has been accepted. The Board fully appreciates the reason for his decision and it was unanimously agreed that Sir Matt be appointed general manager of the club which he is very happy to accept.

To this Mr. Louis Edwards, the chairman, added:

> Of course, we knew that it had to come but this does not mean that Sir Matt will be any less involved with Manchester United. In fact the post of general manager carries even wider responsibilities and my Board are well content to think that in future they can call upon Sir Matt's unique football experience in both home and international fields.

Busby himself explained his decision rather more fully: 'For some time now, and largely since our victory in the European Cup, I have been looking to the future. I feel it is time for someone in a tracksuit to take over the players out on the training pitch. As it is United have become rather more than a football club. They are now an institution. I am finding less and less time to give to the thing I consider paramount, which is the playing side.'

It was not until the summer of 1969 that the actual change in the chain of command took place. In that last season when he remained effectively in the chair Busby acquired Willie Morgan, Burnley's ball-playing Scottish winger, for £110,000; then lived through the fires of those two controversial unofficial World Club championship matches against Estudiantes, of Argentina; and saw his United again reach the semi-final of the European Cup where they lost 2–1 on aggregate to A.C. Milan.

Those two ties against Estudiantes de la Plata must indeed have saddened and sharpened the weariness that was overtaking a man who had helped to make Manchester United a name to conjure with throughout the world. In almost quarter of a century he had taken them to the peak of success on the playing field with the European Cup, five League championship titles, and two F.A. Cup wins out of four Wembley finals. In the process, too, he had netted the club a profit of over one million pounds.

However, in spite of all that, his sensitivity and love for the game itself was deeply scarred by the behaviour of those two confrontations with Estudiantes. To lose 2–1 on aggregate was bearable: but to stomach some of the actions of those Argentinians on the pitch was more than he could digest. With Stiles sent off in the first tie in Buenos Aires and then George Best provoked into retaliation against defender Medina at Old Trafford on the night of October 16, 1968, which saw both players sent off, merely hastened his decision to withdraw from the firing line.

All the romantic jousts associated with ancient knights in armour had disappeared from the game he loved and he had had enough of it. Yet when that particular match was over he still found it within himself to say, 'You cannot stop playing these games because of certain incidents on the field. There have been no finer artists of footballer than the Brazilians in the last ten years and they, too, are South American. We can only solve these problems by playing more, not less.' Not everyone would have agreed with that at the time, or perhaps even now – especially Sir Alf Ramsey – but at least it had a statesmanlike ring about it.

So, at the end of the 1968–69 season – with United finishing only eleventh in the League – Sir Matt abdicated from his throne. Chosen as his successor was Wilf McGuinness. Yet he was not accorded the full title of club manager at the start. He was required to earn that some time in the future by performance.

On April 9, 1969, an official statement was issued by the chairman, Mr. Edwards:

> The Board has given further consideration to the changes which will occur at the end of the season and has decided to appoint a Chief Coach who will be responsible for team selection, coaching, training and tactics.
>
> Mr. Wilf McGuinness has been selected for this position and will take up his duties as from 1st June and in these circumstances it is not necessary to advertise for applications as was first intended.
>
> Sir Matt will be responsible for all other matters affecting the club and players and will continue as club spokesman.

Here was a great future opened to a young man of thirty-two. If things went right, McGuinness held the pearl in the oyster. As it was, he became one of the youngest coaches in charge of a First Division side.

At his original appointment McGuinness was assistant trainer to Jack Crompton. He was in charge of the reserve team with a special interest in the United youth side. He had always been a one-club man. A Manchester and England schoolboy international, he first played in the United League team in 1955 and continued his international career with the England Youth, and the Under-23 side before gaining two full caps. At that point, December 12, 1959, he broke a leg playing for the United reserves against Stoke City at Old Trafford. It was a bad break and though it virtually ended his playing career, it opened the way to a rise on the managerial side.

United duly appointed him assistant trainer with the reserves and it was not long before the Football Association chose him as England's Youth team trainer. In 1968 he was appointed manager of the international Youth squad having already served as one of Sir Alf Ramsey's training assistants during the 1966 World Cup.

On June 1, 1969, McGuinness took over his new duties at Old Trafford at a salary of £4,000 a year. The future was there for the taking by a personable young man of charm and ability who had shown in his lower coaching duties not only tactical ideas but a sense of authority and discipline. But above all he was a United man to the core, a loyal servant who understood the ways of the club and the story of its growth to fame. In fact, he had been a part of that growth and he was a part of the family.

Other men like Don Revie (Leeds), Johnny Carey (Everton) – once United's famous captain at the beginning of their reign of power – Jimmy Adamson (Burnley) and Ron Greenwood (West Ham United) had all achieved their successes and offered maturity in the testing world of football managership. They were obvious and attractive candidates to succeed Busby. Yet it was no real suprise when McGuinness, young and as yet untested, was chosen. He was a United person.

Within eighteen months, however, his short reign was ended. Yet in his first full season of 1969–70 he could point to some success which held promise. United finished a respectable eighth in the League, after a poor start, the improvement coinciding with the arrival of Ian Ure, Scotland's centre half, from Arsenal, McGuinness's first major signing; the club also reached the semi-finals of both the F.A. Cup and Football League Cup, losing respectively to Leeds United (after three matches) and Manchester City; and for a third season in succession over a million spectators thronged Old Trafford. All this was no bad start for a virtual beginner feeling his way quietly.

This was a period of transition and though United again reached the semi-final of the League Cup next season, only to lose to Aston Villa of the Third Division, by Christmas time the side had slumped to a position dangerously close to the relegation zone. Clearly all was not well. There was a hint of dissension in the dressing room; disturbing cliques had been formed by the players; and discipline was not all that it should have been.

As a result at a board meeting held on December 28, 1970, it was decided to relieve McGuinness of his post and offer him the position he held formerly as trainer coach to the Central League side. The disappointed young man accepted his downfall with admirable dignity and showed his character and loyalty by agreeing to remain with the club rather than take wing elsewhere in a fit of pique.

At the same time Busby was prevailed upon to take up the managerial reins of the first team again until such a time as a successor was found from outside. In the event the Busby alchemy began to work again almost at once and the side soon picked up to end again in eighth position.

When I once asked David Sadler the reason for all this rapid change in events he replied, 'Not everyone, sadly, would play for Wilf. The side as a whole did not give a hundred per cent effort for him. It was as simple as that. As soon as Sir Matt returned to the scene it changed at once.' To me it was inexplicable that anyone could pull on a Manchester United shirt and fail to give his all. But strange things go on behind the scenes at football clubs. Invariably they are caused by personality clashes.

In retrospect Busby has said, 'Probably it was our fault for choosing Wilf.' (It is virtually certain it was Sir Matt's own advice which influenced the board.) 'Wilf knew the club; he had grown up with us and understood our ways. He was one of the family. But it appears we had reckoned without the other players. He was probably too close to them. He had played with most of them and knew their habits and this they resented. Disharmony developed and team discipline waned. In a sense they resented Wilf and it did harm to the club. It was sad and regrettable, but we were left with no alternative but to admit the error of our choice and alter things.'

Now began a period of all-change at Old Trafford.

It was during the close season in the summer of 1971 that the next choice of manager fell on Frank O'Farrell, a soft-spoken Southern Irishman, who had played wing half in his day for West Ham and Preston North End and had recently shown his abilities by taking Leicester City up to the First Division again. He took over on July 1, with Malcolm Musgrove, also a former West Ham player, as his chief coach.

Busby himself now withdrew permanently from any further direct control of the team, though his massive presence and influence remained in the background. Whether he wished it or not his shadow reached out everywhere, over everybody and everything. After all, he *was* Manchester United, past and present.

These days, of course, he is a member of the United Board of Directors, a member of the Football League Management committee and as such an automatic member of the Football Association, where his wide experience and knowledge of things football has opened the door to his presence on the senior England International Selection Committee. That in a sense gained him the Nobel Prize for the game in which he has won every other conceivable honour. If only his father could have been spared to see it all!

This perhaps is the point at which to reflect on Busby's contribution to football.

It is as difficult to speak of a good man as it is of an evil one. The one may seem to possess no single redeeming vice, the other no single redeeming virtue. Patently this is untrue when we are dealing with any human being. The man who is always right is clearly out of touch with a world which is so often wrong; the man who never forgets will never remember, the man who never gets lost will never find.

Busby learned all this, and because he has been both to heaven and to hell, and back again, been tempered in the fires and remained true to his principles, he is what he is: a good man.

In his playing days before the war – soon after his move from

Manchester City to Liverpool – *The Guardian* once wrote of him: 'Busby is the gentlest mannered and most philosophical of footballers.' That rings true, a fitting tribute indeed, not only to a sage and seasoned wing half who played for his native Scotland, but also to the man himself who came to find after early stark years in the dark belly of a coal mine. He has been engrained by life, smiled at it, realising that victory and defeat are but brother and sister who walk hand in hand, and been blessed with a sense of style. He is the epigram that 'genius is born, not made'.

Now he has become the father figure. Relying on the advice of his own intuition, he has brought the breath of inspiration to his own stolid virtues and to those around him. Three qualities are strongly marked in him – humility, compassion, and calmness in a crisis. Others have remarked upon this and sought the secret within themselves, but lacking a rich philosophy, have failed.

Although an almost legendary eminence Matt has had time to spare for everybody. Always approachable and modest to a degree, no one was too small or insignificant for a kindly smile and the answer to a question. It is a humility born of early struggle and given only to those few who found the truth when the way ahead looked bleak and life itself a mountain impossible to scale.

His compassion embraces a deep friendship, understanding, and sympathy for the problems, moods and requirements of his players. Remembering his own younger days of doubt, depression, and loneliness in the bad times, he never forgot the lesson.

Supported by a humane and progressive Board of Directors he helped to rebuild United into a *club* in the finest sense of the word. He did it by the wise process of having all his staff, from the biggest star to the groundstaff boy, treated equally well as 'a Manchester United player'.

It was because of this very thing, this deep sense of family, that United were able to rise like a phoenix from the molten ashes of Munich. I doubt whether any other club in the land, let alone the world, would have stood so firm and upright amidst those bitter, tragic ruins as did the proud survivors of Old Trafford.

The secret of that survival lay, perhaps both directly and indirectly, in Busby's calmness in a crisis. He faced many crises of varying pressure in his life, but all with the same stoic fortitude. There has been the crisis of a match when things were going wrong. Out went the command, 'Keep playing football.' There have been the nagging problems of positional changes required to make the machine tick smoothly again. Matt faced these, too, with a calmly taken, calculated risk.

Yet his influence has spread wider than Manchester itself. By challenging the parochial authority of the League he was first, with his Manchester United, into Europe and its growing Cup competitions. He helped to widen the horizons of English football; he brought the Continent to these shores and with it a vision and a wealth undreamed of before at club level.

Having stepped aside for the second time, Busby and the Board of Directors were immediately uplifted as O'Farrell, the new man, projected United into the best start they had made in the League for many years. One of football's quiet men, O'Farrell did it, as it were, with a whisper and in stockinged feet. There were no grandiose statements of a new promised land; no immediate big money transfer deals; and no fanfare of trumpets. All O'Farrell did was to switch Morgan and Gowling from the forward firing line to become midfield creative providers and the side at once fell into a smooth, winning groove.

All this was achieved in spite of the fact that the long-serving 'Nobby' Stiles had been allowed to depart to Middlesbrough, while Crerand, in the last stages of his playing career, had taken over as coach to the youth side – the immediate loss of two wing half backs who in their various ways had played such a key role to the success of the 1960s.

Besides this, too, Old Trafford had been banned by the F.A. for a spell at the start of the 1971/72 season because of the senseless behaviour of a spectator who had thrown a knife on the pitch during the Newcastle match some months earlier. With all clubs responsible for the behaviour of their supporters, United found themselves fined a sum of £7,000 for that stupid act while for some weeks they were forced to play all their home matches on neutral grounds not less than twenty-five miles distant from Manchester.

Brushing all this aside like some insult best ignored, United started in full sail. Bobby Charlton, Denis Law, George Best, Alex Stepney and others were still on parade and, with seven points from their opening four matches, they swept into an early lead. By the end of December United had firmly established themselves at the head of the championship with only two defeats by the turn of the year and Best again in magical form with seventeen goals to his name.

But the New Year of 1972 brought a depressing change. The rosy future changed pallor to a dingy grey. Seven defeats in a row followed each other like a gaggle of geese and O'Farrell was forced into the transfer market. He procured Martin Buchan from Aberdeen for £130,000 to stiffen the defence – a wise investment which was to pay handsome dividends in the years ahead – and Ian Storey-Moore, a goalscoring winger from Nottingham Forest for £200,000, who soon was chosen to play for England at Wembley.

Though a break was applied to the downhill run, a finishing place of eighth in the championship for the third year running was a disappointment after all that early promise. It was clear that much remained to be done if United were to regain their former status.

Ominous confirmation of this soon arrived at the start of the 1972–73 season. Failing to win any of their opening nine games – a violent contrast to the previous year – United sank like a stone to the bottom of the League. Manchester United in twenty-second place! It was unthinkable.

In an effort to cure the illness O'Farrell bought two forwards to get on the goal standard again. They were Ted MacDougall from Bournemouth for £170,000, and Wyn Davies from Manchester City for £65,000. Scottish and Welsh internationals respectively with a reputation for scoring, they were in the nature of short-term cures. For the future O'Farrell picked up a promising Irish youngster, Trevor Anderson from Portadown, for £20,000.

But United's illness was now not so much organic as mental.

Once again things had begun to go wrong in the dressing room. George Best at this stage began to lose himself in a welter of bad publicity. Followed by the media wherever he moved, the wandering minstrel went on the blink as time after time he either failed to appear for training or missed trains with the team. Often enough, like some elusive leprechaun, he would be dug out of some hiding place with some sympathetic female to whom he had turned for comfort. A little boy lost, unable to face the mounting pressures as United sank, he contributed largely to the club's decline by his own behaviour. The fact that he escaped full punishment for his adventures angered the other players so that the poison ran deep.

Accustomed to being a winner since his earliest years at Old Trafford, Best has since confessed that he spent some of the worst nights of his life at that time, sitting alone into the dark hours at his luxurious new home built at Bramhall, riling against the change of the fates. 'I was expected to do it all. People looked to me to win matches on my own and it was just not possible. I thought of our great days when, for instance, we were able to go to West Ham and win 6–1 gloriously, to take the League title. We never considered defeat for an instant then. Being a winner by instinct, I became depressed beyond measure by the team's failure. I wanted to hide away from it all in some dark corner.'

It was at the height of this crisis that I visited O'Farrell at Old

Trafford one November day in 1972, and spoke to one or two senior players at the same time. My reactions to that trip were recorded in print the next morning:

> The autumn sun warmed the afternoon. The taxi driver, nosing his cab through busy Manchester traffic, said out of the corner of his mouth: 'It's going cold'. I agreed absently, my mind on the coming talks with Frank O'Farrell. 'I don't think you've got it, friend, I said, "It's going cold." The temperature's dropping. We're approaching Old Trafford.'
>
> He laughed the sardonic laugh of a world which has a short memory. 'Me, I'm a City supporter, really. Now they're both in trouble. I'll tell you for why. City should never have let Joe Mercer go. United: they should have started rebuilding immediately they won the European Cup four years ago. It's not O'Farrell's fault. It's the chap before, the one they knighted.'
>
> To start excavating the sort of troubled situation now facing Manchester United is not original. Others have been having their personal dig for some time past. Whatever has been uncovered can be interpreted in a variety of ways, which only makes things more complicated.
>
> In trying to establish an Identikit of the whole problem, one is soon caught up in a web of conflicting opinion. It is as elusive as trying to imprison a shaft of sunlight in a matchbox. All that remains clear is that United are facing the problem of past success and, while their jealous enemies may be gloating, a far larger, sympathetic company are sad and confused.
>
> To the world O'Farrell is wearing his troubles well. Perhaps he has a public and private mask. At any rate he looked fit, relaxed and geared for the fight when I called on him. His oak-panelled office at Old Trafford on the first floor, adjoining the inner boardroom, is much the same as Sir Matt Busby left it.
>
> The obvious change is that the desk has been shifted to the windows, suggesting more space. On it lay a squash racket and three balls. 'I've been having a sweat this morning. It helps to keep me in trim.' On a low mahogany table a bottle of whisky stood between us. It was a friend, not an obstacle.
>
> As the end of his Panatella cigar glowed O'Farrell nibbled at a soft drink. ('The TV boys are coming to interview me so I'd better watch it.') 'Of course we're having a rough time. So are others.
>
> 'We had a bad start. We lost the opening match at home to Ipswich. Then followed a couple of 2–0 defeats at Liverpool and Everton and there we were. Three games and not a point. "Manchester United bottom" is a good headline for you press chaps. If we had been tucked anonymously somewhere in the middle it wouldn't have been so easy for you. And there we were, with the screws on us right away.'
>
> O'Farrell's eyes were steady: the southern Irish lilt continued the diagnosis softly behind a smile. Once, just after the war, I remember,

some of us were presented with a visiting England team to Mr. de Valera at Government Buildings in Dublin. The blue eyes, almost transparent, and the soft brogue of the tall man were lulling and scarcely belonged to a fiery revolutionary.

O'Farrell talked on quietly.

'I've been criticised for buying forwards when the defence has looked fragile. But I've shopped around in that direction without success.' He ticked off names on the fingers of a hand – Nish, Mills, of Ipswich, Currie, of Sheffield United, a midfield man. 'In any case we were also short on goals and United's reputation was founded on attack.'

The anatomy of a football club is complex. Ideas, opinions and voices conflict. 'I have tried to keep out of Frank's way these days,' says Busby. 'But I hear whispers here and there and things seem to have gone sour in the dressing room. As for buying, I must say I'm concerned.'

'Don't make a fool of yourself and put all the blame on the manager,' says Bobby Charlton. 'He was left a difficult legacy.' It is compounded of many things. First, probably, was the cult of the individual, at once a strength and weakness of Busby's sides and which O'Farrell is attempting to modify quietly. 'I have my own long-term plans,' he says. 'Meanwhile we need a survival kit.'

Now, too, the fear of the future gnaws at some of the big names who, having scaled the heights through the 1960s, should have been phased out earlier. It is a ruthless business. This fear has bred a certain dissension, jealousy and opposing factions behind the scenes which have eroded the team spirit. There is a worm in this apple, and it must be rooted out if United are to recover.

'First things first,' says O'Farrell. 'Our immediate need is a little luck and two or three wins strung together to restore a bit of confidence. What disturbs me is the way we're letting down our loyal supporters. And don't forget, after everyone's own club we are still the second best loved team in the country. We still draw the crowds on our travels.'

Here again is that universal emotional link with United, the key being the Munich disaster. Bill Foulkes is a survivor with Charlton of that black day. Now in charge of the youth at Old Trafford, he has given his whole career, like Charlton, to United. A realist, he puts his finger on some of the causes of the present decline. 'When George Best first went off the rails Sir Matt was sympathetic and lenient. George, who says he hates publicity but attracts it like a lightning conductor, wouldn't have got away with it the second time. But by then Mr. O'Farrell was in the chair and being an important player whom he needed that was that. All this has helped undermine morale.'

Without any show of false modesty Foulkes added: 'Secondly, United have never really replaced me at centre half.' True, they badly need a rock of Gibraltar at the heart of their defence. 'Actually we should have started rebuilding in 1967, *before* we won the European Cup. And finally, what we need now are more players of character, like Bremner, for instance, who drives Leeds. There is still pride in the club but spirit is low. The horizon is dark and if Mr. O'Farrell can restore things he deserves a knighthood.'

As I left Old Trafford a long crocodile of schoolchildren were being guided around the stadium backstage as if it were a museum. No one would wish it to become that, a place of relics and memories.

On a downward path streams broaden and mountains shrink. For United, however, the streams are deeper, the mountains steeper. An aristocrat fallen on hard times, they have no Divine Right to anything. Like everyone else they just have to keep working – together.

O'Farrell was clearly in the hot seat and he knew it. He could feel and hear it sizzling beneath him.

With Storey-Moore largely out of action with a damaged knee, which eventually led to an early retirement – a sad blow both to United and to football – Best, having already departed to Spain to return only once, and then announce positively that he was turning his back on the game for good and all, United were in deep trouble by Christmas 1972. This was only a month after I had visited O'Farrell.

When they were well and truly crushed by unfashionable Crystal Palace 5–0 at Selhurst Park it was a case of pouring more hot coals on their heads.

One should have picked up the scent when Tommy Docherty was to be seen watching the match at Crystal Palace that Saturday. At any rate it was all soon enough to come out in the open.

On the morning of December 20, 1972, at least half of Manchester must have felt very much like the morning after Munich fourteen years earlier. The world of football, too, as a whole stood with bowed heads at United's disarray. The reason was that the previous evening their Board of Directors had announced after a crisis meeting the dismissal of Frank O'Farrell as manager. With him, too, Malcolm Musgrove, the trainer, and John Aston, the coach, were relieved of their positions forthwith.

At the same meeting it was revealed that George Best, around whose errant behaviour the crisis had come to a head, would remain on the transfer list. The player himself was reported to have said that he would never play football again.

Part of the official statement gave one main reason for these decisions: 'Because of the bad position of the club in the League.' Furthemore, it was felt by the board that it was in the best interests of the club and of Best himself that the player leave the club. Meanwhile the board would assume full responsibility for team selection, and the position of manager would be advertised.

All this was decided at a meeting in the morning but not disclosed publicly until the evening, after further consideration of the situation following the receipt of a letter from Best saying that he was unable to continue as a player at Old Trafford, or indeed anywhere. It was decided, too, in the wake of the humiliating 5–0 defeat at Crystal Palace three days earlier which had left the club bottom but one in the First Division of the Football League. A year earlier they led the table by four points.

So a great club stood at the crossroads, as it did on February 7, 1958. Munich, however, was a physical disaster, an act of God. Now they faced a challenge of the spirit, in many ways brought upon themselves. To understand the dark thread of events that brought them to this pitch is to solve the puzzle of a nest of Chinese boxes.

Only four years earlier Manchester United became the first English club to win the European Cup, having proved themselves in 1956 as the first club to challenge the authority of the League who had forbidden entry into Europe. In 1957, 1958 and 1966 they reached the semi-final of this great Continental competition. In 1968, after eleven years, the Odyssey was ended under the captaincy of Bobby Charlton and the managership of Matt Busby.

Since winning the European Cup four years earlier – in spite of reaching the European semi-final again the next season (1969) – a slow decay had been taking place. Five, four, three, two years ago were all the salad days of George Best. He was an individual par excellence who glittered within a basic system of team framework.

He became 'El Beatle', so nicknamed by the Portugese on the night he and United destroyed the flower of Benfica 5–1 in Lisbon.

Best was the first folk hero of football, a pop idol, glamorised, lionised and hunted wherever he moved, finally to become a playboy of the Western world. If his contribution to United over those years was brought to ruins by his behaviour, that is only part of the sad story of decline.

The real point, however, was who would be brave enough to succeed Mr. O'Farrell? It seemed very much to be a case of dead men's shoes. Since Sir Matt Busby released the managerial reins two years earlier, Wilf McGuinness (himself once one of the Busby Babes) had come and gone. Now Mr. O'Farrell had come and gone.

The chairman said he hoped to attract a top man who had already proved successful. But Mr. O'Farrell himself was successful enough elsewhere before putting his head on the chopping block at Old Trafford. As John Bond, the manager of Bournemouth, who had bid £250,000 for Best a fortnight earlier and who was a former playing colleague and friend of Mr. O'Farrell since their days together at West Ham, said, 'When I heard the news my feeling was one of total amazement. He is still a very good manager. You don't become a bad manager in a matter of weeks.'

Another side of this sad and complex affair, which contained not only a clash of personalities but revealed some of the human dilemmas involved, could be gauged by some of the things written by Best in his letter to the board.

> I had thought seriously of coming personally and asking for a chance to speak at the board meeting but once again, I am afraid, when it came to saying things face-to-face I might not have been completely honest.
>
> While in Spain I received a lot of letters from both friends and well-wishers, quite a few asking me to reconsider. I did so and after weeks of thinking it over I decided to give it another try. It was an even harder decision to make than the original one.
>
> I came back hoping my appetite for the game would return and even though in every game I like to think I gave a hundred per cent there was something missing. Even now I am not quite sure what.
>
> Therefore I have decided not to play football again and this time no one will change my mind.
>
> In conclusion I would like to wish the club the best of luck for the remainder of the season and for the future. Because even though I personally have tarnished the club's name in recent times, to me and thousands of others Manchester United still means something special.

The point it seems, was that Busby's shadow loomed over the place and hard though it comes to say it, that influence in a sense may have helped finally to create the situation of those years.

Manchester United were paying for the aura they themselves had shed across the game.

The first reaction of Mr. O'Farrell on being dismissed was to ask the board about the position of his assistant, Musgrove. This was disclosed when board members gave a press conference. Mr. Edwards said, 'He asked two questions – what the position of Mr. Musgrove would be and if his own contract would be honoured. He was told Mr. Musgrove would also be relieved and that his own contract would be honoured.'

Sir Matt said, 'The situation reached a stage where we wanted to clear the air completely. We had to sweep the board clean. That is the reason for the outgoings and the George Best decision.' He said the club had already taken the decision that Best would remain transfer-listed and not be picked for the team again, before the player told them by letter of his decision never to play again.

'Best did not know anything about our decision but when the club secretary got back to Old Trafford, Best's letter was on his desk.

Somehow it did not surprise me,' added Sir Matt. Mr. Edwards said Best's registration would remain with United. The board had not discussed whether or not to sue him.

Sir Matt said that United would be looking for a successor to Mr. O'Farrell, who was a top man of proven ability, and ruled out an appointment from within the club.

'We will have to try to get the lads to respond and do something for us until an appointment is made. Managers don't mind moving to a club at the bottom because they know it cannot get any worse and there is always a chance of improving things.'

Asked if his own presence at the club would be an embarrassment to potential applicants for the job, Sir Matt said, 'I cannot understand this. I have always given full co-operation, and since Frank O'Farrell came here he has had a completely free hand to do as he wished.'

Another director, Mr. Denzil Haroun said: 'Mr. O'Farrell has bought players, trained the team and managed the team. From my personal knowledge Matt Busby has never interfered in any way. He has never been to the training ground since he became a director and he has never been in the dressing room before or after a match in the past eighteen months. No other director could say that.'

O'Farrell's failure was a lack of communication. A withdrawn, quiet, sensitive person, he stood apart from his men and was seldom to be seen fraternising even in the most cursory way with any of them. Seemingly chained to desk work, he resembled a prisoner in some ivory tower.

The players scarcely knew him. When asked his opinion of his manager Denis Law, the extrovert, once quipped, 'Frank O'Farrell – who's he?' Later he had said more seriously, 'Mr. O'Farrell came as a stranger and went as a stranger.'

In 1973 Matt Busby in his book, *Soccer at the Top,* wrote of O'Farrell: 'He was brought to the club to manage players. It seemed as if he wanted to manage the board, too.' Whether or not it was this which upset O'Farrell after his dismissal, but at a United board meeting on January 15, 1974, it was reported that a letter had been received from O'Farrell's solicitors to the effect that he considered that because of comments made by Busby in his book, O'Farrell felt that he was now released from the agreement signed by the two parties. Whatever that agreement was – it was private and not revealed in the minutes – the Old Trafford directors considered that it had not been broken and their solicitor, Mr. Royle, was instructed to reply accordingly. Some bad blood clearly remained after O'Farrell's departure.

The cat was out of the bag, and the situation being what it was, the grass was not allowed to grow under their feet by the United Board. Early in the New Year Tommy Docherty, the brash, abrasive, loquacious Scot, a man always with his ear to the ground, was appointed to succeed O'Farrell. Clearly here was the type of motivator needed at Old Trafford at that moment. Never short of a word to say, a fighting little Jimmy Cagney of a character, he was always good news to the media as he provided the headlines. It had been so ever since playing for Preston, Arsenal and Scotland and managing at Chelsea, Aston Villa, Queens Park Rangers, Rotherham and in Portugal. His had been a somewhat stormy career but he had proved himself able to make teams play, whatever the turmoils and cost in human relationships.

Under Docherty's early galvanic leadership the sudden comings and goings of players began to turn Old Trafford into something of a railway terminus. In no time at all, Docherty lashed out transfer cheques to the total of some £420,000 in surrounding himself with Scotsmen he had known at club and international level – men like Forsyth (Partick), Graham (Arsenal), Lou Macari (Celtic), all of them Scottish caps, and a big centre half, Jim Holton, from Third Division Shrewsbury Town, a raw-boned, powerful youngster also destined to win a Scottish cap. With them, too, came left back Houston and McCalliog, a midfield motivator.

A new enthusiasm was fired, but it was several weeks before the last shadow of relegation was dispersed. A late, finishing run of eight matches without defeat got United off the hangman's trap door, with refreshing performances from developing young players like Brian Greenhoff, Sammy McIlroy and Gerry Daly. This new blend of youth and experience augured well for the future. But 1972–73 had been a narrow squeak, with United ending eighteenth in the league – their worst position for precisely ten years.

The seasons 1972 and 1973, in fact, proved something of a watershed in affairs at Old Trafford. Apart from the traffic in managers, those two seasons saw the end of three of the club's finest-ever players. To put them in alphabetical order they were Best, Charlton and Law. Here were three vibrant artists, dazzling match winners on their day, each of whom had been voted by the Continental press to the prestigious award of European Footballer of the Year – Law in 1964, Charlton in 1966, and Best in 1968. For some inexplicable reason only Law of this elite company failed also to gain the accolade of Footballer of the Year in England.

The break-up of this triumvirate in its way was an historic moment. Each chose his own path and for differing reasons. Best, for one,

A "goal" by Law against A.C. Milan, disallowed by an unsighted referee in the semi-final of the European Cup at Old Trafford, 1969.

Best scores the only goal of the match, despite being well marked by Ipswich in the third round of the F.A. Cup, January 1970.

Bobby Charlton plays his last League match and his 751st for United, April 1973, against Chelsea at Stamford Bridge.

emotionally disturbed, decided to turn his back on United and on the game itself and departed to Spain in search of sunshine and of peace, which sadly was to elude him even in the years ahead. As Bill Foulkes had said of him, his destiny was that of a lightning conductor that attracted problems and trouble. Denis Law, once 'the King', never really recovered from knee trouble at the end of his reign and moved over briefly to his earlier home at Maine Road with Manchester City, having already given United eleven of the best years of his life.

Charlton – the faithful, loyal through thick and thin from his schooldays as a fifteen-year-old – had been at Old Trafford since 1953. One of nature's gentlemen, no words could accurately reflect what he meant to United and what United meant to him.

The great performer of his time and hero of the game on the field, he was hero off it also as a human being. In the flesh he was what Gary Cooper and James Stewart were in the movies, each one the gentle, chivalrous, wholly self-sufficient male – Jefferson's lost American hero, the wise innocent.

Denis Law was quite a different personality. Fearless and brave to a degree, his speed of reaction in tight situations was electric and his instinct for the half chance quite feline. When he was on your side there was always the hope of victory, no matter how dark the situation. I once saw him score all six goals in pouring rain for Manchester City in a Cup tie at Luton only to find them all wiped out when the match was abandoned in deep mud and water. He opened the scoring again for City in the replay – seven goals in a row – only to find himself, ironically, on the losing side at the end as Luton recovered to win against all the odds. Denis was very much the menace and it was some sardonic fate that reserved for him the role of scoring the goal for Manchester City at Old Trafford in 1974 which finally sent United grovelling down to the Second Division. It was a match in which he did not want to play, for at heart he was still a United man.

George Best is a Gemini. He is two people and, like his football, one has never known what the other was about to do at any given moment. He has lived and played with tension and apparently thrived on it. That is the nature of this animal who has always shunned being caged.

Born in Belfast on May 22, 1946, Best played his first match for United on September 14, 1963, aged seventeen. Five years later he was at the height of his powers. The world was at his feet. At that time one only had to thumb through the glossy magazines or the humblest football rag, the odds were he would be staring out of a page, fixing attention with luminous eyes, a lush Beatle hairstyle and a quizzical expression which suggested that while he alone may know the hundredth name of Allah, it was all a bit of a joke anyway.

Words, words, words: analysed, X-rayed and photographed, it has all been said before about this modern phenomenon of the football scene. In six years he became a cult for youth, a rebel, a living James Dean. The cause was clearly defined – the welfare of his club and country and to prove himself the greatest player in all history one day.

The rebel in him was contrary – the creator of a new image for football – yet one who turned back the clock in a search for individual freedom in an age of conformity and method within the game. He remains a son of instinct rather than logic.

The fact that he was a Pied Piper followed by an ever growing army worried him not a bit. He was touched, mauled and buffeted by the admiring crowd off stage: he faced an equivalent treatment on the field. Yet, in neither case did he suffer an inflated ego nor a wounded sense of revenge. Like breathing in and breathing out, it was all merely part of the business of life.

Certainly there were and are flaws in the complex anatomy. There came the sudden upsurge of angry retaliation to something brutal; sometimes a childish, taunting provocation, the figurative thumbing of the nose at some frustrated opponent; a mischievous irreverence, difficult to pin down in personal affairs. A Pied Piper in one sense, he was an elusive pimpernel in another.

Football lifted him from a humble background without forfeiting the grass roots of his upbringing. Mammon did not obliterate his basic loyalties. But as he owed his fame first to football, that is where we must look.

People persistently wonder about his place in the hierarchy of the game. Where does he stand in relationship to Stanley Matthews, Tom Finney and the rest of the cavalcade of the past? Everything is relative from age to age. The genius of one would not be the genius in another. Recently, Reuben Bennett, the scout of Liverpool, a Scotsman, remarked to me, 'Wee Patsy Gallacher, of Celtic, was as good as Pele and Eusebio rolled into one.' Colleagues laughed at that. But even Bennett was prepared to concede the gifts of Best in the modern game. 'Aye, he was hard to pin down,' he agreed unemotionally. 'George was different. All the others were just footballers,' says Malcolm Allison. 'Probably his greatest quality was his courage,' says Stanley Cullis. So the pyramid of opinion grows.

I put the question to Arthur Rowe, the architect of Tottenham's fine 'push and run' days, and to Blanchflower, later his captain, who carried forward the White Hart Lane spark into the 1960s: 'Place in order of preference Matthews, Finney and Best.' Rowe at first hedged: 'Diamonds are diamonds, rubies are rubies, and pearls are pearls,' he replied evasively. But when Blanchflower voted for Best, Rowe was inclined to agree.

Blanchflower's reasoning ran: 'Stanley was a supreme dribbler who would tax even the most ruthless, sophisticated defences of today. But he was primarily a provider. Finney was perhaps a better all-rounder than Matthews. He could play anywhere in a forward line, and besides that was a free goalscorer. But George Best gets my vote. A master of control and manipulation, he was also a superb combination of creator and finisher: he, too, could play anywhere along the line.

'But more than the others, he seemed to have a wider, more appreciative eye for any situation. He seldom passed to a colleague in a poor position. He was prepared to carry the responsibility himself.

'But basically, Best made a greater appeal to the senses than the other two. His movements were quicker, lighter, more balletic. He offered the greater surprise to the mind and eye. Though you could do nothing about it, you usually knew how Matthews would beat you. In those terms, he was more predictable to the audience. Best, I feel, had the more refined, unexpected range. And with it all, there was his utter disregard of physical danger. Think of his ability to beat giants like Ron Yeats, well over six foot, in the air. He had ice in his veins, warmth in his heart, and timing and balance in his feet.'

It was a difficult choice, indeed – Matthews, Finney or Best. I would second Blanchflower's proposition. And among the wingers, there still remains that elusive figure of Garrincha, the Brazilian with the corkscrew legs, who made his mark as perhaps the most formidable winger yet in any World Cup finals.

Now Busby draws on his pipe and says, 'George Best is possibly the greatest player on the ball I have ever seen. You can remember Matthews, Finney, Mannion and all the great players of that era, but I cannot think of one who took the ball so close to an opponent to beat him with it as Best did.'

As for Best, his personal hero remains di Stefano, of Real Madrid days.

Yet, until he started to 'wander' in the 1970s, his own dedication was complete, his nerves non-existent. Once, before a big European Cup tie, he was calmly drinking Bovril with me at a crowded bar under the Old Trafford stands while other players, already changed, were anxiously living out the last tense moments before the kick-off in the dressing room.

With only twenty minutes to the whistle, he had to be reminded that he was playing and still unchanged. Whereupon he departed to perform in a kind of radiance, destroying the opposition as he had done so often. Benfica, among others, will always have cause to remember him.

Best's mother played hockey for Ireland. He himself has taken other kinds of stick for his pains. He regarded himself an entertainer, and he shared the gift with the world. Other games interest him only obliquely. Indeed, he seldom even shares a relaxing round of golf with a friend. 'It's understandable,' said a wag. 'He doesn't really like parting with the ball.'

In so many ways the Best story has been a tragedy. Although he still plays, his football now is a parody of its former self. At his height he raised the game to an art form then threw it all away, almost wantonly. He realises it now, of course. But six years the older he can now talk about it dispassionately, as he did to me over an extravagant luncheon at his favourite bistro down the London King's Road.

Back from Los Angeles where he had been playing for the Aztecs, he was helping Fulham at that point. The young man who once said during his golden days at Manchester United that he hated to hear the final whistle remains deeply grateful to the Americans.

'They offered me a part on stage again after I'd been kicking my heels for too long and eating out my heart with disillusion at Old Trafford's eventual fall from grace. United should have started to change their side after we'd won the European Cup in 1968. After that, we started to go downhill slowly.

'People were getting old and bit by bit things began to turn sour. I could see it coming. I hung on, hoping. Eventually I had to speak up. Then came the explosion and the rift. I suppose I was spoilt at the beginning, but those were some of the unhappiest nights of my life. Each time United got beaten, it was like some national disaster to me. If I'd been a poet I would have felt I had run out of thoughts and words. I got sick of the very game itself.'

When finally he turned his back on United – and, so he thought, on football – he departed to Spain a second time. Disturbed, lonely and uprooted, what he needed then was a firm guiding hand. In a state of mental confusion and physical exhaustion, he wished to stop the world in order to get off. To him – as to others far less miscellaneously gifted – football was life and brute judgment suggested that he was bound to regret his decision to retire bitterly sooner rather than later.

After a heavy season of many personal turmoils, which included I.R.A. threats on his life and the wounding of his sister in the leg when leaving a dance hall in Belfast – 'that wouldn't have happened had she not been my sister' – this complex and, in various ways, poignant character suffered deeply. His unique qualities as a player brought him fame and fortune: perhaps too much of both. That, no doubt was much of the trouble. Over-exposed to the mass media, his privacy invaded, his very life became public property. Yet the rebel in him still remains strong.

The departure of Bobby Charlton on the other hand was something quite different. But then he was cast in a different mould as a person. His last season as a player at Old Trafford was 1972–73 when United just escaped relegation with a fighting finish.

It was on September 18, 1972, that a testimonial match was staged for him on the ground he loved so much and where he had given his all. Glasgow Celtic were the chosen opposition and though no goals were scored it was a night to remember. A 60,538 crowd, paying over £40,000, enjoyed the celebration which was laced with emotion and a fine competitive spirit.

Old Trafford was aglow as the concourse came to pay tribute to a man who had been an example to the game. There were admirers from all over Britain: thousands from Glasgow and visitors also from Europe. When it was all over Charlton did a personal lap of honour followed by an army of youth while the rafters rang.

Writing a tribute to him in the Sovenir Testimonial Programme, Sir Matt Busby said:

> When Bobby first came to Old Trafford he was a very shy lad, but it never showed on the field of play. I remember the goals he scored when he was only 18. I have vividly implanted in my mind the sight of him volleying David Pegg's centre home in the F.A. Cup semi-final against Birmingham at Hillsborough. It was a tremendously hit shot and he repeated it in his first international, playing for England against Scotland at Hampden Park when he half-volleyed the ball into the back of the net.
>
> I cannot begin to describe all the other wonderful goals he has scored or list his proud international career, except to say what a marvellous contribution he made in the World Cup of 1966 with his valuable goals.
>
> Could I also ever forget his header in the final of the European Cup, a goal that set us on the path towards the victory that had been our aim for so long.
>
> He has broken all records and won everything possible that there is to

win. Yet he has remained completely unspoiled, still prepared to do more than his fair share for the cause of Manchester United. The shy boy has blossomed now into a man with a great sense of assurance, confidence and responsibility.

Booked only once in a first-class playing career of almost twenty years – and then never officially reported to higher authority – Charlton gained a unique position in football. He was as world famous in his way as Pele, a distinction he shared with the Brazilian when the Governor of the State of Jalisco presented each man with a gold medal at Guadalajara during the World Cup of 1970 in Mexico 'for services to football and to sportsmanship'. That remains one of his most treasured gifts.

If style is the man, then Charlton repays a long, close look. His flowing movements when surging into attack suggested a hidden poetic line; the ceaseless support for each colleague on the field, while himself was rotating as the midfield hub of the wheel, reflected a selfless loyalty to a cause; his high standard of behaviour on stage still remains an example and a reproach to others in a game of violence, and as such remains a mirror of deeper values.

Sitting quietly in the corner of a crowded, noisy room some years ago, he said ruefully, 'I wish I could play music and talk the way I feel football.' There was the real man, searching for a wider dialogue, sensitive and emotional beneath a steady surface of calmness.

Voted both English and European Footballer of the year in 1966, the owner of winning medals for the World Cup, the European Cup, F.A. Cup and League Championship, he went through the card. No one in the global game can match such a record. Yet perhaps the most appealing of all his qualities was the unaffected modesty with which he has worn these varied honours.

Born in Northumberland, he came of mining stock. His mother belongs to a progeny that produced four generations of players, one of the most remarkable footballing families in the land – the Milburns of Leeds United, Newcastle United and Leicester City, to which Bobby and Jack, of Leeds, added a new distinction when they became the first pair of brothers to play in the same England side since the Formans, of Nottingham Forest, in 1899. Nature's gentleman, one day Bobby will be remembered as the jewel of them all.

From the time that he and the elder Jack first attended the same Ashington Junior School, he was a natural. Jack went to the

'Downies' (the ground-floor section) and the younger one to the 'Uppies' (the upstairs group), and throughout his schooldays Bobby played in every one of the many representative sides for which he was eligible, starting with the under-nines of those 'Uppies' and completing the pattern as an England schoolboy cap. It was at that junior school that the young Charlton received his first complete football strip. It was run up by a female teacher from war-time blackout curtaining.

In a long career, he carved a name as a chivalrous, scrupulous opponent. Yet it was the explosive facets of his play that will remain fresh in memory. His thinning fair hair streaming in the wind, he moved like a ship in full sail. He always possessed an elemental quality, jinking, changing feet and direction, turning gracefully on the ball, or accelerating through a gap surrendered by a confused enemy, he could be gone like the wind.

Once an outside left, he was later deployed as a deep-lying centre forward, leading the United and England attack from the rear, a Telstar off which each succeeding attacking message bounced. It was an exacting role that would have tested many a younger man. It would be interesting to have fixed a pedometer to his heels to establish the mileage covered in a match as he worked the midfield like an artist.

Spotted playing for England in a youth international, he became an early and obvious target for a host of clubs. But he had set his heart on Manchester United and he joined them at the tender age of fifteen in 1953. Inside five years he had stumbled out of the holocaust of Munich, and two months later stepped into the full England side for the first time. It was against Scotland at Hampden Park where he began his run of goals in the international field that now sees him as the record English scorer of all time, with a tally of forty-nine.

After only three seasons, he was a veteran by the age of twenty-two, with seven of his 106 England caps behind him, together with a League championship title and two appearances in a Cup Final. Since then, his museum of trophies has swollen as he ranged every corner of the world's football fields.

In Britain, Sir Stanley Matthews, Tom Finney and John Charles all earned a special niche in their day. Bobby Charlton long since was elected to that exclusive club.

It was that lethal shooting that first took the eye. He celebrated his opening senior game in a Manchester United shirt with two goals as the curtain went up on his career. Appropriately enough, the opponents were Charlton Athletic. Since then, many were the memorable strikes with both feet from the edges of the penalty area.

People still talk about the thirty-yard thunderbolt against Mexico which pointed the way ahead for England in the World Cup of 1966 at Wembley. Others, longer in the tooth, recall his first England goal of all – a left-foot volley to Finney's centre from the edge of the box. Even the astonished Scottish goalkeeper ran half the length of the pitch to shake the new boy's hand. It knocked the breath out of that crowd of 134,000 at Hampden.

Left to fret in disappointment on the sidelines without a kick as one of the World Cup party of 1958 in Sweden, he found that the years brought their truthful reward. Yet, of all the triumphs shared, I doubt if any gave him more satisfaction than the carnival night of May 29, 1968, when, as captain, he led Manchester United as the respected figurehead of the first English club to win the European Cup. That night, I am sure, he played as much for the lost past as for the living present.

His long, bony face can wear an elusive look of anxiety or of fun, and as much as he longs for relaxation, he does not allow himself to unwind unduly: just for a spell after Munich his nerves were shattered. It was necessary at the time to talk to him like a Dutch uncle.

Without Charlton, Law or Best in their ranks – not to mention Crerand, Stiles and Foulkes – it was a strange-looking United that took the field in 1973–74. Having just escaped relegation the previous season the fates were now creeping up behind them with a hatchet. They were about to learn the lesson that no one in football has a divine right to anything. By the spring of 1974 they had plunged down to the Second Division.

It was a bitter blow, especially since near the end of the season the side began to show some promise with wins over Chelsea (away, 3–1), Norwich (away, 2–0), Newcastle (home, 1–0), Everton (home, 3–0), and a 3–3 draw against Burnley at Old Trafford.

That run lifted United into twentieth position, with only Southampton to overtake for safety. The Saints were two points ahead, with an extra game played and, as the fates would have it, United had still to play them at the Dell. Victory then would virtually have ensured safety. Yet a 1–1 draw still left hope since all the other stragglers – West Ham, Southampton, Birmingham and Norwich – had played an extra match.

A 0–1 reverse at Everton took United into the vital meeting with Manchester City at Old Trafford. It was all or nothing for the Reds now. A point was unlikely to have been any use – even though they still had a final match to play at Stoke. Yet, as time ran out even a point might have been some consolation. If Birmingham had lost at home to Norwich; and if Southampton were beaten at Everton; then a point might still be vital. With the situation so electrifying, Old Trafford fans were grasping for every straw to keep hope burning.

Then, with eight minutes to go, the knock-out blow was delivered. And by none other than a former United favourite, Denis Law. As he back-heeled the ball home, realising its consequences, the great Scottish international had grave difficulties in hiding his real feelings.

It was the Second Division for United. No argument now.

Even so, some youngsters in the crowd could not wait for the final whistle and invaded the pitch, causing the match to be abandoned. The Football League later ruled that the result should stand. As a consequence fences were erected behind each goal at Old Trafford to prevent supporters from entering the pitch.

It was a graceless ending. But, sadly, by then United had already become something of a tarnished symbol of British football. By becoming a hard, ruthless side as they tried to save themselves, they had slipped from their lofty pinnacle. To many people this slow decline seemed a disaster second only to Munich. Some indeed took a sterner view, considering events in their long-term effects to be worse even than Munich. Certainly in 1958 United were uplifted by a universal sympathy which knew no bounds.

Now it was just the reverse. As United slowly went down the hill amidst a welter of bad publicity and a series of internal crises the general feeling was that they deserved their fate. Worse still, they lost much of the good name they once enjoyed and there was little sympathy for them. Indeed, in some places there could be detected a positive gloating as the dark clouds gathered over Old Trafford. As United struggled like a fish on a hook to escape what clearly lay ahead, a harder element entered their game. Where once they had won fame with their classic pure football, based on attack with great players like Bobby Charlton, the late Duncan Edwards and Tommy Taylor, Law, Crerand and – yes – Best in the vanguard, on the departure of that exciting brood they took on wolf's clothing as a hard side intent only on survival.

It must have scarred the very soul of Busby, who around that time said this in an interview with *The Observer*:

> The way things are going alarms me deeply. What is new and frightening about the present is that you have entire sides – not just one or two men – that have physical hardness for their main asset. It's true there are

still a few teams who believe the game is about talent and technique and imagination, but for every one of these you'll find ten who rely on runners and hard men.

Also to add fuel to the fire Manchester United's army of so-called supporters had gained for themselves the ugly reputation of being one of the most vicious mobs. The club still disowns them fiercely but there seems to have been a welcome improvement of late.

Manchester United, passing through the fires, should have pondered the words of the Bishop of Chester in his address at the memorial service to their colleagues stricken at Munich:

> When we remember how many millions of people in this country watch professional football every season, we can appreciate the responsibility which is laid upon these young players. They are admired, idolised, glamourised, imitated. They set a standard which, unseen perhaps, certainly leaves its mark upon the moral standards of our society. They have a responsibility.

As for the supporters of Old Trafford they should even now read what Dr. Percy Young wrote in his history of the club they purport to follow: 'In one sense Manchester United grows from the centre of the parish. The parishioners look over the wall, see the wider vision, and learn. They benefit from two worlds.' It is something worth living up to.

United's return to the Second Division for the first time in thirty-seven years, however, happily did not prove to be a farewell to all their yesterdays. If anything, it stood them in good stead. Indeed, it had a cauterising effect, for it helped them to shed fear and return to a positive, aggressive policy of attack upon which the club's success and fame had been built. It was a return to character. It helped, too, to underline the basic loyalty of their *true* supporters. An average home gate of 48,388 at Old Trafford proved to be the best Second Division following for twenty-five years.

The scent of victory filled the air from the very first match of the 1974–75 season. Indeed, they led the race from start to finish, throwing off all opposition. The only setbacks were the breaking of a leg by Holton in November which put the Scottish centre half out for much of the season, and a surprising defeat by Third Division Walsall in the third round of the F.A Cup.

The semi-final of the League Cup, however, was reached for the third time in six seasons and though Norwich City then kept Wembley still that last vital step out of range, United were able to concentrate all their energies on the League. With a finishing burst as powerful as their start, United duly clinched promotion at the first attempt, when a goal by Lou Macari gave them a 1–0 win at Southampton.

At that Tommy Docherty declared in ringing tones, 'We are back where we belong. Our fans deserve First Division football.' He might have added also that the First Division needed United and the splendour of Old Trafford as an added attraction to the top drawer of the game. However, he added a cautionary note, 'Don't expect too much too soon, though. We are a young team and I have more young players I want to introduce. I anticipate three years of mediocrity – then watch us go!'

However, little did even Docherty – the ebullient extrovert, never short of a word – realise how over-cautious was his optimism. In a trice United were up and over the rainbow once more. Back in the big time again after only the briefest of stays below stairs, 1975–76 found them, to universal surprise, actually in the running for the League and Cup double.

But even more pleasant was the fact that United returned to their old standard of behaviour on the field, no matter what the violent fringe element of some of their so-called supporters got up to. For two years running – 1975–76 and 1976–77 – they were well top of the Fair Play League, run by Vernons Pools and the *Daily Mail,* which carried with it a prize of £1,000 shared amongst the team. As I write now in 1977–78 they are again up amongst the leaders for this award.

In all, 1976 proved to be a rewarding return to the top flight. As it turned out, they failed in their attempt at the double. However, to end third in the League and reach Wembley for their sixth Cup Final in history was fulsome enough, even though to lose to Second Division Southampton at Wembley proved a sad disappointment. Against all the odds United as a young team froze on that sunny afternoon, losing to a snap goal by Bobby Stokes, the Southampton left winger. Yet had the ball run kindly for them that day they would have won comfortably enough, chances being missed in the early stages, while in the second half a glancing header by McIlroy rebounded from the Southampton crossbar.

Whatever the respective merits of both sides before the kick-off, the Cup Final is usually an even money bet for an upset of some sort. The year of 1976 proved to be no exception.

Against all logic and predictions the unexpected happened once more. It was Southampton's planning and a snap goal by Stokes seven minutes from the end that did the trick. They aimed to cut out

United's two wingers, Coppell and Hill, and though Coppell's speed and footwork down the right frequently threatened to win the match, too often he was crowded out at the last stride as, unsupported, he cut in for the bye-line. They aimed, too, to prevent Macari and Daly slipping behind their defence on blind side runs. It all worked like a charm as the Manchester attack, for all Pearson's clever, close distribution, tended to hold the ball too long and over-elaborated in tight patterns as they ran endlessly into contracting, solid defence.

So ended a match which truly caught alight only after the interval. But it was a clean and well mannered affair, fit to set before the Queen, uplifted not least by the sporting behaviour of the Manchester throngs in their hour of disappointment and by the dignified manner in which Tommy Docherty and his young side swallowed their defeat. They had given much pleasure and entertainment all season.

Teams:
Southampton: I. Turner; P. Rodrigues, D. Peach; N. Holmes, M. Blyth, J. Steele; P. Gilchrist, M. Channon, P. Osgood, J. McCalliog, R. Stokes.

Manchester United: A. Stepney; A. Forsyth, S. Houston; G. Daly, B. Greenhoff, M. Buchan; S. Coppell, S. McIlroy, S. Pearson, L. Macari, G. Hill, (sub D. McCreery).

Referee: C. Thomas (Treorchy)

This sudden, successful turn of events after the relegation decline of 1973–74 was due largely to some subtle tinkering with the team line up by Docherty. The sad season when they fought desperately to stay up had seen little Lou Macari left up front virtually as a lone striker, a role which never really suited him and where his ball playing skills were suffocated with no close support.

At the end of that season Docherty acquired Stuart Pearson, a goalscorer, from Hull City for £200,000 and having got his man proceeded to switch Macari to midfield as a provider. With a wide vision of the field Macari became a new player and an immediate success as United set sail for instant promotion out of the Second Division, while again reaching the semi-final of the League Cup.

By then the side had slipped into a settled formation – Stepney in goal; Forsyth, Brian Greenhoff, Buchan and Houston as the back four; Daly, Macari and Willie Morgan in midfield; with Pearson and

McIlroy joined in attack by a new acquisition from Tranmere Rovers, Steve Coppell, playing wide on the flank at outside right.

Meanwhile there were changes amongst the staff. Anderson departed to Swindon, McCalliog to Southampton, whom he duly helped to beat United in the Cup Final – and ironic twist!

Next, having returned to the top drawer, other reinforcements arrived at Old Trafford: Tommy Jackson, an experienced player on a free transfer from Nottingham Forest; a teenage Irish lad, Jimmy Nicholl, who soon showed such skill and maturity that for a spell he took over from Forsyth at right back. ('He reminds me of Johnny Carey,' said Busby to me one evening at Elland Road after United had won at Leeds. No praise could come higher than that!) David McCreery, another Irishman, a young all-rounder often used as a substitute either in midfield or attack; and finally Gordon Hill, a left winger and a £70,000 buy from Third Division Millwall.

This last deal proved to be the key in a brave new concept by Docherty. With Coppell and Hill, two inexperienced wingers from Third Division clubs, Docherty now set out to surprise the football world by switching to an all-out 4–2–4 attacking formation which involved the use of two wingers on the flanks to give width to his forward line.

Here was a return to earlier days, to the 1950s, with a line up that had seemed as extinct as the dodo. It was this refreshing approach that surprised the rest of the field and took United to within touching distance of the double. Apart from which it brought back some life and entertainment for the crowds. For the second season in succession, indeed, Old Trafford was top of the list with an average home gate of 54,750. On nine other grounds the visit of United attracted their largest attendances of the season, while United's lowest home crowd was 44,269 and that against lowly-placed Wolverhampton Wanderers on the Saturday before Christmas, traditionally the worst Saturday of the season when father is out with the family attending to the last-minute festive shopping. In fact, it is three years since United last had a crowd under 40,000 for a League match, a figure which must make every other club green with envy.

Another distinction came Old Trafford's way when thirteen United players were called for international duty in one season: Brian Greenhoff, Pearson and Hill for England; Forsyth, Buchan, Houston and Macari for Scotland; McIlroy, Jackson, McCreery, Nicholl for Northern Ireland; Roche, the club's reserve goalkeeper, for Eire. To this company could be added Coppell, who won Under-23 honours for England and, later, full caps.

Thus, with a fresh breeze in their sails, United looked to be set fair for the future, particularly since Docherty stuck to his attacking 4–2–4 conception which seemed to give a lead to the rest of football for better days and more enjoyment, not only for supporters, but also to players who were encouraged to express their talents more freely instead of being imprisoned in a defensive straitjacket.

Docherty's philosophy was simple and straightforward. He said, 'This defensive football is a bore. Spectators want to watch goals. That is what we try to supply.'

The vast army of United supporters proved that he was right. 'It is other managers who are wrong. They score a goal, go one up and then close the back rank so tightly that it would be easier to get into Fort Knox.'

In particular the Reds didn't close the ranks at Ipswich, where they lost 0–3. In his disappointment, Docherty said, 'I am proud of my lads. They kept trying to score away from home and they never went on the defensive. Someone has to lose, so why not give the fans a match to remember?

'We didn't like losing. Who does? The point is that we lost and could still keep our heads up because we didn't pull all our men back. The only aim in football is to score goals, and if in defeat we score fewer than our opponents that's just the way it happens.'

It was good thinking. But still others hold back, preferring safety first methods.

The 1976–77 season, however, saw one more major adjustment to the team. The talented Gerry Daly was transferred to Derby County for £188,888, the sad departure of an instinctive, creative midfield player. But Docherty found the answer. He acquired Brian Greenhoff's older brother, Jimmy, from Stoke for £100,000, an experienced clever striker to take the weight off Pearson in the centre of attack, and proceeded to switch McIlroy to midfield in place of the departed Daly. It worked like a charm.

For most of the season United were up with Liverpool, Manchester City, Ipswich, Newcastle and Aston Villa in the vanguard of the League championship, ending eventually in sixth place, a slight decline from the previous year. Yet they gained a place in Europe for the second year running.

The previous season the U.E.F.A. Cup was their goal where, however, they lost in the second round to Juventus of Italy, a seasoned combination which supplied six men to their national team challenging England in the same qualifying group for the World Cup finals in Argentina in 1978.

Now it was the European Cup Winners' Cup as a result of getting to Wembley for the second year in succession, there to beat their great rivals, Liverpool, the favourites, who were aiming for a fabulous treble of the League title, the F.A Cup and European Cup. This time, however, having been thwarted themselves in the past, it was United's turn to prick the bubble with a great and surprising 2–1 victory over the League champions.

Yet it was not a final when sympathy ranked high among the emotions. Similarly, it would have been less interesting had the majority of predictions been satisfied. On the day little went according to preconceptions except the fulfilment of hopes for a match to restore the full value of the occasion.

Although Liverpool set off in character, carefully preparing their ground, they expanded into an attacking style far earlier than was expected. Manchester United began by looking better than at any time since their defeat by Southampton a year before but, surprisingly, it was doing what came unnaturally, defending, that formed a foundation for victory.

Near the end of a goalless first half of sufficient if quiet interest, the feeling was that United were ill-equipped for the second when Liverpool could hardly fail to take the chances they were making. United had conceded midfield and were magnificently saved from a slaughter by the composure of Brian Greenoff, Buchan and Albiston, the young replacement for Houston.

The proposal that Liverpool would do no more than absorb United's attacks until well into the second half was clearly not their own. Kennedy's header down towards the near corner of United's goal was instantly denied by Stepney's goalpost or else they would have received rightful reward for unquestionable superiority, but as the half ended Jimmy Greenhoff was almost able to score as a direct result of a careless interception by Hughes. Five minutes into the second half, the match seemed to breast the hill and suddenly there was a new horizon, totally different to the one we had expected. Hughes and Smith failed to hold Jimmy Greenhoff, who had always troubled them. His back header dropped under Pearson's control but he was moving too wide. Clemence would surely cover the angle. The shot was too late, too close to Clemence and aimed at the remnants of a target at the near post. But the ball was well struck. Clemence was still moving too quickly to turn on his side and it hit the net before he fell.

As the 'Stretford End' at Wembley celebrated, one wondered whether this goal was not also an invitation to United's downfall. Liverpool's counter-punch is their speciality and, sure enough, within three minutes Case was allowed time to control a lob, turn and shoot past Stepney for another goal plucked from the eye of a crisis. It was at this moment that Liverpool would normally have begun to stride out. Here, though, their powers failed. In another two minutes Smith was caught out by the speed of Macari and Jimmy Greenhoff and his own advancing years. Macari came alongside in support of Greenhoff and took over. His shot hit Greenhoff sufficiently hard to deflect wide of Clemence and into the Liverpool goal.

Tension, too often the enemy of such occasions, now held the game in a fascinating grip. There was still plenty of time for Liverpool and too much for United. Buchan had the responsibility for planning Manchester's long defence. Liverpool planned their long attack from the bench. They withdrew Johnson and sent Callaghan into the field, but it was Fairclough, the unpredictable youngster, who was really needed to challenge Greenhoff's command in the penalty area. They missed more chances and so United survived. If Liverpool's dream was finished in five minutes, the day and domestic season was completed to perfection by the generosity of their players and supporters in defeat and the delight of United's manager, Tommy Docherty.

Teams:
Liverpool: R. Clemence; P. Neal, J. Jones; T. Smith, R. Kennedy, E. Hughes; K. Keegan, J. Case, S. Heighway, D. Johnson, (sub I. Callaghan), T. McDermott.

Manchester United: A. Stepney; J. Nicholl, A. Albiston; S. McIlroy, B. Greenhoff, M. Buchan; S. Coppell, J. Greenhoff, S. Pearson, L. Macari, G. Hill, (sub D. McCreery).

Referee: R. Matthewson (Bolton).

Docherty – at last a winner after all those visits to Wembley with Scotland, Chelsea and United. Yet within two months he was a loser in another way. Once, surveying his empire at Old Trafford, he had said to me, 'After becoming a cardinal in this cathedral, who could return to be being a parish priest?'

Yet in so short a time after marching triumphant from Wembley with his team, he virtually excommunicated himself by declaring his love for Mary Brown, wife of the United physiotherapist, Laurie Brown, and mother of two young children, and the breaking up of two homes which meant the end of his own marriage of twenty-five years. As the situation was uncovered, skin by skin like the peeling of an onion, a parting of the ways became inevitable. But whatever the background storms Docherty had put United back on the map.

The next incumbent at Old Trafford was Dave Sexton from Queens Park Rangers, whom United had approached seven years earlier to succeed Wilf McGuinness. At that time Sexton, though keen to join United, had said that he could not desert Chelsea who had only recently won the F.A. Cup for the first time under his leadership. He felt a strong obligation to stay with them and refused the Manchester offer. This had impressed United. Loyalty was always a quality close to their heart. Now seven years later they had got their man. The future holds the answer as to the wisdom or otherwise of the choice.

At least the way is now clear for Dave Sexton, the quiet man, to get on with the challenging duty of keeping United on the gold standard.

During all this turbulent period there had come in 1971 the retirement of Jimmy Murphy, the faithful right-hand man, as assistant manager. This followed, almost naturally, the resignation of Busby as team manager. Now Murphy is a scout still with the club, but no longer scanning the horizon for promising youth. Front line players are his target these days and it was he who alerted United to the latent possibilities of Coppell and Hill, the wingers, a contribution of considerable influence to the club.

One of the continuing blots on the Manchester horizon, however, has been the violent behaviour of certain elements who call themselves United supporters. It has been a problem to exercise the minds of the government and in particular of Mr. Denis Howell, the Minister of Sport. Chelsea and one or two other clubs have proved headaches, too, over recent years. 'But,' said Mr. Howell, 'the worst hooligans have little connection with Manchester. They travel from all over the country as if on a pilgrimage. We really cannot allow support for a football team to become a cult if it develops to the point of threatening the peace of towns and creates intolerable problems for both police and clubs.'

To explain the explosive psyche of certain followers of the game, I approached two students of human behaviour who have made an objective study of the situation and not fallen into the emotional trap of taking sides.

One was Dr. Desmond Morris, the anthropologist, author of *The Naked Ape,* a Fellow of Wolfson College, Oxford, and a director of Oxford United Football Club; the other was Mr. Peter Marsh, who at the time was preparing a thesis on the subject for his doctorate at the Oxford Department of Experimental Psychology. He said: 'It's a spin off from the mods and rockers, bovver boys, hell's angels, and America's *West Side Story,* which has moved from arena to arena from the tribal atmosphere of the 1960s. Now we have the punk rockers.'

'Certainly people need peak moments of excitement as relief from systematised boredom of work,' added Dr. Morris. 'The vast majority of the half million or so who watch football every Saturday are not thugs. Their fan behaviour on the terraces is a ritual rudeness between factions. There is little or no bloodletting, merely threat displays as in the animal world. It is only a minority who overstep the mark.

'The danger of dealing with these thugs, of course, is that we may push the rest over the top. Herded into train carriages and guarded by police dogs, they may decide to become animals, too. The politicians must be careful here. In fact, I see in much of football crowds a quasi-religious element, the trappings of church-going as it used to be – the chanting on the terraces, special costumes, rhythmic clapping and the rest. The singing of the Liverpool Kop, for instance, resembles a cathedral choir.

'There are measures afoot such as the issue of identity cards to supporters which could be withdrawn by clubs for misbehaviour – like the issue of disciplinary yellow or red cards to players on the field; also the conversion of grounds with more seating accommodation to reduce violence.'

With this last Mr. Marsh disagrees. 'There is an upright intimacy about football which it would be sad to lose. In fact, the extremists are subject to certain internal controls on the terraces.

'I believe the best solution for dealing with these hard cases lies in the dynamics of restraint exercised by this terrace culture. We should tap the social mechanism of this internal control.'

'Indeed, on balance,' added Dr. Morris, 'football reduces violence in life. If there was no game I doubt if people would sit quietly at home reading Proust. They would merely look around somewhere else to let off steam. More honest, relevant reporting by the media, too, would help in controls before we turn to a policy of despair. The mass of true fans should receive better publicity and the thugs deglamourised and ostracised.

'As it is, the group loyalty of the terraces has no mechanism and no organisation to point a finger at the thug. Sophisticated society on the other hand protects itself. Doctors are struck off for misbehaviour and the rest . . .'

'In fact, the violence at chariot races in Byzantine times was far worse than anything we see now at football,' went on Marsh.

Here were the views of liberal-minded intellectuals, which would find small echo from those who have been mugged, stabbed, had property smashed and generally been terrorised by wild mobs. These would call for sterner punishments than the puny fines handed out by magistrates. Docherty himself, on the occasion of rioting at Derby and at Norwich in 1976 and 1977, advocated a return of the birch or the cat. 'That would give the thugs something to think about.'

But still the violence of a fringe minority continues to dominate the scene. To cap it all United – having returned to Continental competition in the European Cup Winners' Cup of 1977–78 – were at first thrown out of European football by U.E.F.A. in the September because of the rioting of some of their so-called supporters in the Cup tie against St. Etienne in France. It was hard on the United players who themselves had behaved and played well in a 1–1 draw only to find themselves expelled from Europe because of the ill-behaviour of their countrymen on the terraces. Yet the action of U.E.F.A. was fully approved by the mass of sober-minded followers of the game at home. At any cost these things must somehow or other be exterminated whatever liberal intellectuals may say or think. Upon appeal, however, U.E.F.A. rescinded their expulsion and ordered United to play the return leg against St. Etienne on a neutral ground 125 miles distant from Manchester. The choice fell on Home Park, Plymouth. However, as Brian Scovell wrote in the *Daily Mail*:

> British football fans are the worst behaved in Europe.
>
> The original ban on Manchester United was the third expulsion of a British club from European competition because of spectator violence at away matches.
>
> They follow Leeds (in Paris in 1975) and Glasgow Rangers (in Barcelona in 1972) into the sin bin of soccer.
>
> The full score sheet for bans imposed by U.E.F.A. on clubs is:
>
> BRITAIN 3: Glasgow Rangers 1972 (rioting fans – banned two seasons, reduced to one on appeal). Leeds 1975 (rioting fans – banned two seasons, reduced to one). Manchester Utd. 1977 (rioting fans – ejected from Cup Winners' Cup – later amended on appeal).
>
> ITALY 2: A.S. Roma 1965 (spectator violence – banned two seasons). Lazio 1974 (spectator violence – banned one season).

GREECE 1: Panionios 1971 (players' misbehaviour – banned one season).

SPAIN 1: Real Madrid 1976 (spectator violence – banned on season, reduced to playing next three European matches 300 km. from Madrid).

In addition Tottenham Hotspur were fined £500 and ordered to play their next three European matches at away grounds after their fans had rioted in Holland in 1974.

And Wales were banned from the European Championship after disturbances in the match against Yugoslavia at Cardiff last year. They appealed and were reinstated on condition they played away from Ninian Park.

Hooliganism has been a curse on Manchester United for the past 10 years.

In 1969, the club were ordered by U.E.F.A. to erect a wire fence behind the goal area at Old Trafford after A.C. Milan's goalkeeper had been hit by a missile.

Two years later, an F.A. commission ordered the club to close its ground for a fortnight following an alleged knife-throwing incident.

The worst incident came at the end of the 1973–74 season, when there was a pitch invasion late in the match against Manchester City at Old Trafford.

The match was abandoned minutes before the end, City were awarded both points, and an F.A. Commission ordered the club to cage in the fans with eight-foot high fences, something the club had already decided to do.

Meanwhile on the financial front, by the end of 1977 Manchester United had wiped out a half-million pound overdraft with a season of record profits. It was the end of a five-year battle to get out of the red and balance the books following the frenzied spending spree to try and escape relegation.

United first plunged into debt at the bank in 1972 with a £234,000 overdraft, and they had been in the red ever since. Frank O'Farrell and then Tommy Docherty, when he first swept into Old Trafford, spent heavily in the transfer market. In two successive seasons United lost a total of more than £600,000. The overdraft rose steadily until in 1976 it stood at £495,188. But the Reds battled back financially and on the strength of big profits for the last two years and the 1977 money-spinning run in the League and Cup they were in the black again.

Chairman Louis Edwards said at the time, 'It looks safe to say now that we have just about cleared our overdraft at the bank. It could have been done sooner, but in 1975 we incurred a lot of expenditure in the building of the Executive Suite and Grill Room.

These have become very popular and the costs involved have been fully justified. The club will reap the benefit in future years. However, it kept our overdraft very high and in 1976 we spent £70,000 on new lights, £30,000 on new railings and a number of other things.'

The bonanza was a triumph for Docherty's determined efforts to balance the transfer books. The Reds' manager bought only Stuart Pearson to help win promotion from the Second Division, and in 1977 he more than balanced the arrival of Jimmy Greenhoff by selling Gerry Daly for £188,888 and, of course, Jim Holton and Colin Waldron (on a free transfer) to Sunderland.

Docherty did much for United. Then threw it all away.

The difficulty in attempting a football book is that hardly is the ink dry than something new has happened and the thing is out of date. To illustrate the point. While still re-drafting the original manuscript of this effort, the directors of Manchester United decided to pay Leeds United the gross sum of £388,888 for the signature and transfer of their Scottish international forward Joe Jordan. It was a negotiation successfully completed.

And while writing these very words the news came of another deal between these same two clubs. It had been in the pipeline for some time and conditioned by the fact that the player in question would only join Manchester United, turning his back on offers by other clubs. The man was Gordon McQueen, the giant Scottish international centre half. The gross transfer figure in his case proved to be £495,000, so that with two strokes of a pen, much hard bargaining and an outlay of nearly one million pounds, Manchester United revealed their plans and hopes for the future: the acquisition of a powerful, goalscoring striker and a defensive Goliath, strong in the air at the back, a United weakness in recent times.

All this is to underline the fact that a giant like Manchester United can never afford to slumber if it is to maintain its authority in the ceaseless urge for success and security in a game that has long since become big business. In a sense it resembles the arms race between East and West.

To change the simile, Old Trafford may be likened to the vast complex of a modern aircraft carrier. Its playing staff represent the aeroplanes on the flight deck, always at the ready for action and constantly replaced with more up-to-date machines.

The staff officers high on the bridge are the Board of Directors. The captain is the chairman. He directs the planning and tactics and together they keep their collective hand on the helm to steer the ship on a safe course through dangerous waters. All play their parts in the chain of command.

Under their control come the rest of the crew, each with a specific part to play if the ship is to be kept seaworthy, efficient and happy – the officer of the flight deck who is the manager of the team; the engineers and technical staff, who represent the coaches, trainers and physiotherapists; the administrative staff in the person of the club secretary and his entourage, and so on. It is a complex hierarchy, closely linked like the large and small interlocking wheels of a piece of machinery. Below decks are the rest of the able-bodied seamen upon whose loyalty, efficiency and discipline a good ship depends.

The chairman is Mr. Louis Edwards, who joined the United board on February 7, 1958 – the day after the Munich disaster – and succeeded to the throne on the death of his predecessor, Mr. Harold Hardman on June 9, 1965. A powerful, successful man whose Rolls-Royce tells of his business acumen, he is the elder brother of a former Lord Mayor of Manchester. He is the leader of this inner cabinet of six members whose collective decisions, taken in a democratic way, direct the club along the desired lines.

Finance – the delicate business of profit and loss – is his strength. It is reinforced by a positive attitude towards problems. Friendly and generous to his fellow men, he is difficult to shift once he has got his teeth, terrier-like, into a situation. This is the strength of his leadership. The growth and success of United under his direction remains his monument.

Consider for a moment. Since his taking of command in 1965, United have won the League Championship twice, lifted the European Cup in 1968, and reached two Cup Finals at Wembley. In the process, the ground and its facilities have grown enormously – a magnificent modern cantilever stand now decorates what used to be open terracing; the old scoreboard end behind one goal is now also an enclosed stand with spacious accommodation so that the whole of Old Trafford is now covered on four sides. Where once there were 8,000 seats there are now 24,000, with eighty furnished boxes rented on lease to individuals and commercial businesses, all this in a ground capacity reduced from an uncomfortable 76,000 to 58,500 for safety purposes. To crown it all, there is now also a luxurious executive suite and grill room for members, an eyrie where a match can be watched in comfort, as well as a fine indoor, covered pitch at the Cliff training ground. Old Trafford has stepped into the future, and if Louis Edwards has his way it will remain at or near the head of the parade.

On his board are numbered five other dedicated men whose guiding passions are the love and welfare of United. They are Mr. Alan Gibson, the vice-chairman, son of James Gibson, the chairman and saviour of United in the parlous days of the 1930s, whose service to the club now stretches to thirty years. He was one of the lucky ones who missed the Munich crash because he was recovering from a broken leg. Around the table, too, is to be found Mr. W. A. ('Bill') Young. Holding a seat on the Central League Management Committee, he is a farmer who can gauge the extent and value of a crop as well as he can sense the turning of the leaves and the change of the seasons. It is a gift in valuing the worth of a team.

At his side is Mr. Denzil Haroun, Justice of the Peace, debonair and cigar-smoking, a brother-in-law of Edwards, who keeps his shrewd eyes mostly on the reserves and whose great interest is in the youth players, the stars of tomorrow. He is a front man in representing the club at official banquets, an enjoyable aside to his other commitments.

Youngest on the board is Louis Edward's son, Martin. An all-round sportsman, who played Rugby Union for Wilmslow until injuries ended his activity, he offers fresh ideas and injects modern executive thinking to the company. He is able to balance the needs of tomorrow with the requirements of tradition.

Last but not least is Sir Matt Busby, who was elected to the board on October 14, 1971, after a distinguished career of a quarter of a century as United's manager. It was to him that Louis Edwards surrendered his seat on the Football League Management Committee which opened a door to the Football Association itself, on whose Senior Selection Committee he now sits.

Enough has already been said of Sir Matt's contribution to the club in the managerial field, which led to a knighthood in 1968. To the world at large he is the epitome of Manchester United itself, as intimately linked with its modern history as the moving memory of Munich and the deeds of John Carey, Bobby Charlton, Denis Law, George Best, and the rest of a famous cavalcade on the field.

A compassionate man of the world who has known the good and the bad times, his expertise in football matters is invaluable to his fellow members. Destiny and character won him a place in helping to direct the affairs of the club: he gained the accolade of leadership because he is the servant to a cause close to his heart. It is as a servant that he now supports his fellow members on the bridge. His hand is on the wheel, but so are other hands. His voice is only one of others. Decisions are taken only by a majority, which is the way of democracy.

Loyalty is the keynote of a successful and contented crew. From top to bottom it is to be found at Old Trafford. Leslie Olive, once a goalkeeper, now the hard-working, dedicated, helpful secretary, has been with the club for thirty-six years and has seen all its remarkable growth. He has represented the club on the Council of the Manchester County Football Association since 1969 and is now one of the Association's senior vice-presidents. He keeps his finger on the pulse of the multifarious workings of Old Trafford. His assistant for the past seven years is Ken Merrett, whose service began twelve seasons ago. Among his responsibilities can be counted the weekly basic wage bill of £6,000 for the players; and keeping a weather eye on the electronic turnstile control machinery which is linked to every entrance all round the ground. This is of prime importance in keeping a safety limit on United's fanatical support. 'One day last season,' he says, 'a lady knocked on my door to ask permission to scatter her dead husband's ashes on the pitch. She had travelled all the way from Bristol for this touching request.' There is no end to the things that happen in football.

The players apart, one of United's nerve centres is its Development Association. It is administered by Mr. Bill Burke with a staff of forty. He came from an equivalent job at Edgbaston which he helped set up and organise for Warwickshire County Cricket Club. Arriving at Old Trafford on August 19, 1961, he recalls the day well. 'There was no office for me in those days, so I commandeered the then assistant secretary's room. I came with a pile of paperclips, rubber bands and a bottle of ink.'

Now he is at the centre of a well-equipped two-storey building at the main entrance to the ground, set beside the adjacent railway line and station that feeds Old Trafford on one of its side, a visionary project of Chairman James Gibson in the 1930s, an artery that links the stadium with Victoria Station in the heart of the city. It was the first of its kind in the country.

The object of the Development Association is to extend United's tentacles in the area of finance. Based on the pools system, it can now claim 250,000 members, some of them as far away as Bermuda, Mauritius, Malta and Germany, the business drummed up by its army of agents in many parts of the world.

'In our first week of operating we took £480 in receipts and paid out prize money of £240. Now we take £20,000 a week which will increase when our new lottery, begun only at the end of this January, gets into top gear. Weekly prize money on our pools is £5,000, to which we hope to add another £4,000 with our lottery.'

It is all big business for the club, but there is a wider object with the lottery. It is intended also to provide cash for youth. Profits in this new venture will be earmarked not only for United but to support amateur sport in the Manchester area. In particular it is hoped to finance the completion of the Melland Road Sports Hall near Belle Vue, a project that ground to a halt through lack of public money, leaving the building for an indoor centre an empty shell for the past two years.

Now United have promised a rescue operation for £10,000 from their first lottery profits to get work started again, with the Sports Council providing another £10,000 matching grant, with a further £19,000 expected from the Local Council as part of the inner city construction project.

What with pools, royalties and advertising, the Development Association has so far provided United with over one million pounds for ground improvement facilities, contributing extensively to the cost of £400,000 for the executive suite and the £350,000 needed for the covering and seating provided in 'K' stand at the former open scoreboard sector of the ground, opposite the Stretford end.

In every way United in these days of inflation are a going, healthy financial concern and the continuing envy of others.

From the top to the humblest employee at Old Trafford, the club has always maintained its family spirit and sense of involvement. All are considered valued members of Manchester United. The pride of it is reflected in continuity and long service. Joe Royle was head groundsman for fifty years, his brother David for twenty-eight. Joe Royle has been followed as groundsman by Gordon Loughnane, another long-serving member who has more than twenty years service with the club. Ken Ramsden, manager of the ticket office – who works closely with David Smith, Chairman of the Supporters' Club with its 40,000 members around the country – joined United from school at the age of fifteen and now has eighteen years under his belt.

'The seating accommodation has trebled since I have been here and it has become a non-stop, seven-day-a-week job, especially when the team is successful. If it weren't for our computer, we'd be swamped.'

In charge of the ladies serving refreshments in the guest lounges on a match day is Lily Leinster, who also looks after the needs of the manager and his staff during the week. Lily's first association with the club was as a landlady looking after young players. This began some fourteen years ago and she has been on the full-time staff for the last nine years.

Ken Ramsden's mother, and his aunt, Mrs. Taylor, work the club laundry. Between them they boast fifty-two years of service and still think nostalgically of days gone by. As does Mrs. Burgess, who makes tea and coffee in her large kitchen in the administrative block. She too has twenty years behind her and recalls the days when 'my boys' (as she calls them) used to scrounge tea in her kitchen before and after morning training. 'Bobby Charlton, Tommy Taylor, Eddie Colman, Duncan Edwards and the rest. Later, Denis Law, the friendly, laughing one. Once upon a time they used to come to the ground by bus. Not like the moderns in their expensive motor cars. Duncan Edwards used to arrive on a bicycle.'

Mrs. Ramsden has that same feeling for yesterday. 'Today's stars move in a pop entertainment world. I hardly see them except when they're playing. It's a different world. But what tricks the lads once used to get up to in my laundry, which, of course, is now very modernised. They would sit around and chat after training and I'd lend them a two bob piece if they wanted to back a horse. Aye, but it's been grand! We've never been forgotten by the top brass. We've always been taken to Wembley with the players' wives for a Cup Final and been a part of the celebration afterwards.

'I can say this, too. I've shared the sorrow and the joy of the club. When the victims of Munich came home and were laid out in the old gymnasium, I was told to polish all the coffins. I did that. And ten years later I also polished the European Cup.'

Sorrow and joy are, indeed, indivisible. But it is people, all the people, who unite to make Manchester United the club that it is.

So we arrive at the watershed of the United story. This has been the modern sector of it. The beginnings of it all, largely wrapped in shadow, are about to be excavated in part. Meanwhile, let it be said, this great club has crept out from its recent shadows to feel the sun again.

# *Part Three*

# 7

# *1878–1892:*

# The Birth of an Empire

From the wee and tiny acorn grows
the impressive and stately oak

THE SCENE CHANGES with dramatic impact. In turning back the calendar a hundred years a measure of imaginative licence is permissible, as we attempt to recreate the world of our fathers and grandfathers.

1878: It is Mid-Victorian England – the age of Gladstone and Disraeli which saw the beginnings of social and industrial reform; the age of the horse and carriage; of the top hat and the cloth cap; of extravagant beards and mutton-chop whiskers; of Dickens; which brought the curtailment of long working hours and, more important, that unique social creation, the Saturday half-holiday.

When the age began prosperous men, as often as not, went to the City on Saturday afternoons. By the time it closed, a working carpenter at two o'clock on any Saturday afternoon might expect to be strolling round with his pipe to the 'Dog and Duck' or perhaps pushing his way into a crowd at a football match.

Those free Saturday afternoons did more than anything to make the game popular with all sections of the community. It was during this period, too, that football was for the first time fashioned from a chaos of varying rules and regulations into some semblance of order. There had, it is true, been earlier attempts at coordination, but the first enduring step in this direction came with the formation of the Football Association in 1863, so named because it was an association of clubs who held an identity of views and together set down a code of laws.

It was, too, the age of the true-blue amateur of the south who dominated the game until the rising tide of professionalism in the north could no longer be contained and was finally legalised in 1885, an historic act which led to the foundation of the Football League three years later. Indeed, for some twenty years at the start of organised football it had been products of the public school system and young men from the Universities of Oxford and Cambridge who ruled the roost, helping to form the Football Association and formulating the original laws of the game.

It was, to be sure, an upper-class game at the time, civilised and organised out of the hurly-burly of the rough and tumble so enjoyed for centuries – in spite of many a Royal edict against it – by the ordinary man on the streets and open fields of the countryside. Yet it was an Old Harrovian, C. W. Alcock, the secretary of the Football Association, who started the F.A. Cup competition in 1872, adapting on a national scale the knock-out House tournament he had known at Harrow School.

Today we live in a meritocracy where success and a worthwhile place in the community is open to all with natural gifts, ambition and a will to work. Be that as it may, the age of the common man now owes Alcock an inestimable debt, for out of his simple idea and from a closed society all else in football has since grown.

It is all the more romantic, then, to look back at the beginnings of what has now grown to be the wide empire known around the world as Manchester United. It is romantic because its birth was not attended by kings and princes, nor by wise men bearing gifts.

Its origins, indeed, belonged to humble artisans, working men, attached to the Lancashire and Yorkshire Railway. They were formed into a team by the Dining Room Committe of the Carriage and Wagon Works and set forth on their historic stride into the future under the name of Newton Heath (L.Y.R.) Football Club, playing on a strip of land in North Road, Monsall Road, Newton Heath, a north-east suburb of Manchester, situated not far distant from the railway works and facing Oldham.

The precise date of the birth is buried in the mists of time. As well search for a footstep on a sandy beach, long since washed away by the sea. A variety of reference books over the years have invariably pointed to 1885 as the start of it all, due probably to the fact that it was in that year that Newton Heath (L.Y.R.) first came to some attention by reaching the final of the Manchester Senior Cup where they lost to another local side called Hurst.

But in *The History of the Lancashire Football Association* it is stated in black and white that the Newton Heath (L.Y.R.) club was founded in 1878, though no evidence seems available as precise proof of this, beyond a reference to be found in the souvenir programme of a bazaar held at St. James's Hall, Manchester, from February 27 to March 2, 1901, to raise a sum of £1,000 to help the club.

Mr. Louis Edwards, the present chairman of United, has been kind enough to loan his copy of this precious document, from which I take liberty to quote the following old-fashioned opening paragraph:

> Very ancient people will refer you to the existence of a Newton Heath Football Club some time during 1878, and they will tell you that the lads who kicked a ball often got into trouble with others who preferred the summer game, because the former often spoilt the ground for the 'wielders of the willow'. Side games were mostly played, and football proper was in its infancy, few then having any idea it would grow into such a fine healthy man. Side games were not exciting enough, and local clubs were invited to do battle, among them such teams as Manchester Arcadians, Dalton Hall, Naughton Dale, Hurst Brook Rovers, Oughtringham Park, and Blackburn Olympic 2nd, the latter being a big standing dish for a long time . . .

Further to this, it might seem apposite to echo the sentiments of that souvenir Bazaar Brochure. The clear object, of course, was the raising of money to help Newton Heath (L.Y.R.). But rather more striking was the drive, enthusiasm, and ambition of those Manchester stalwarts so long ago. In those terms there is not a whit of difference between yesterday and today. Again I quote:

> At a large and enthusiastic meeting, held in April last, 1900, it was unanimously resolved to hold a GRAND BAZAAR, with the object of raising sufficient funds to place the Club on a sound financial basis, and which would enable the Management to obtain a team capable of securing and maintaining a position in the First Division of the Football League.
>
> There is a strong feeling that Newton Heath and District ought to have, and can, support a First Division Club, and the co-operation is, therefore, earnestly requested of all who take an interest in the popular winter pastime, and who desire the attainment of this object.
>
> To fully achieve, it is necessary that at least £1,000 should be forthcoming as the outcome of this Bazaar, and the Committee look forward to the realization of, what they trust will prove to be, their well-based hopes.

Whether or not 1878 is the exact starting point of it all, it is a good enough tee for the first drive. To this day there still exists a Newton Heath Loco Football Club which has always maintained close ties with United, especially during the reign of Walter Crickmer and Louis Rocca, 'who', writes the Loco secretary, 'was to be seen on our ground at every home game – scouting'.

The secretary's letter lifted another small corner of the veil, though most of the club's records were lost in a fire at its headquarters in 1976 – another odd coincidence to set beside United's own earliest minute books bombed and burnt in the war damage of Old Trafford.

It appears that the old Lancashire and Yorkshire Railway started what were known as 'Improvement Classes' in 1859 from which the men formed sports clubs. 'The Carriage and Wagon Department,' continued the letter, 'became known as Newton Heath L.Y.R. and had a ground in North Road – now called Northampton Road. We of the Motive Power section beame Newton Heath Loco and played at Ceylon Street.'

> For a start friendly matches were played in Railway competitions. However, the Carriage and Wagon Department had a very good team and finally opted out of Railway competition to join other local league football, eventually going on to win the Manchester Senior Cup in 1886. In fact, from 1885 to 1891 they were in the final every year, winning four times in 1886, 1888, 1889 and 1890 and losing in 1885, 1887 and 1891.

Those were the embryonic years of formation and struggle as football passed through its age of tender growth and dynamic change – the crosstape of 1872 becoming the crossbar of 1892; goalnets, first used in the Cup Final of 1892 when West Bromwich Albion beat Aston Villa 1–0 before a 25,000 crowd at the Kennington Oval in London; referee and umpires to referee and linesmen; the introduction of the penalty kick and the two-handed throw-in; the change of formation on the field of play from seven forwards to five; the changing phases of dribbling and passing; knickerbockers to shorts and shin pads; the decline of the amateur and the growth of power of Lancashire, the original home of professionalism. It was, in fact, Preston North End who started the tide with undercover payments to two Scotsmen, James Love and Fergus Suter.

All this and more did those years see, years first dominated in Lancashire by the Rugby football code until the arrival of the F.A. Cup lit a bonfire for soccer, as more and more clubs sprung up with enthusiasm in a desire to win the 'little tin Idol', as the original cup was affectionately called.

When Newton Heath (L.Y.R.) first came into existence it was all a matter of sport for sport's sake. To be a member of a team in those days meant that a player had to provide his own outfit, pay all incidental expenses and even subscribe to the upkeep of the playing pitch.

The enthusiasm of those Newton Heath railway men was of the

United v Liverpool in the 1977 Cup Final. Lou Macari's shot loops into the net off Jimmy Greenhoff (hidden).

United Directors holding trophies won in 1977. Martin Edwards and Sir Matt Busby hold the Fair Play trophy; Louis Edwards, the Club Chairman, and Alan Gibson hold the F.A. Cup; Bill Young and Denzil Haroun the F.A. Charity Shield.

**Past and present. Four Chairmen of Manchester United: J. H. Davies, 1902–27; J. W. Gibson, 1932–51; H. P. Hardman, 1951–65; Louis Edwards, 1965 to the present.**

kind influenced by a true sporting spirit: such was it, indeed, that when evening matches were played the team members, it is said, were so eager that they hurried to the ground at the end of work with blackened faces and carrying their supper baskets. They were the hardy breed who toiled for their daily bread and played football like demons on Saturdays.

As for the North Road ground itself at Newton Heath, it was a test even for the hardiest soul. To say that it was bad appears to have been an understatement. As *The History of the Lancashire Football Association* described it, 'In places it was as hard as flint, with ashes underneath that had become like iron, and in others thick with mud.'

The Souvenir programme for the bazaar of 1901 put it another way:

> The ground was little more than a clay pit, its surroundings a quagmire. After you had entered the bottom gate it was quite a work of art to steer clear of the pools of water. But when once you got there you were all right – if it didn't rain. If it *did* rain – well, if you've never experienced it you cannot possibly be enlightened.

Needless to say there was no dressing tent on the ground. Facilities were far too primitive for that. The players were required to use the limited arrangements first of 'The Three Crowns' public house in the Oldham Road, and then of the club headquarters situated at that time in the Shears Hotel, a good half mile distant from the North Road. It was a matter of a sharp run to the ground, then after a hard match a sharp run back, and a wash and rub down. It all made for fitness, enlivened by a brass band on the field which 'hailed the conquering hero . . .'

Close to the surface of the subconcious are the homes where people have lived – or merely existed. In the case of Newton Heath, the chrysalis, and later the butterfly itself, Manchester United, there have been three in all – the original humble North Road; next, Bank Lane, Clayton; and finally mighty Old Trafford. The first and last of these were about as similar as Bleriot's old bi-plane to a modern space rocket. The mind boggles as imagination stumbles at the contrast. Yet yesterday is the father of today and it is yesterday we are now dealing with as we tiptoe back through a century of development and change.

'Tiptoe' perhaps is scarcely the correct expression. Rather it is a case of hacking a way through a jungle of tangled facts; of digging here and there for stray clues to the reality of the past.

One of the major steps was taken in 1878 with the formation of the Lancashire Football Association under the presidency of the Marquess of Hartington. Six years earlier – at the time the F.A. Cup competition was begun – a football club had been launched in the village of Turton by a number of boys from Harrow School. One of the pioneer members of Turton was J. J. Bentley, later President of the Football League and a one-time secretary of Manchester United from 1912 to 1916 at a critical period of the club's life.

It was his enthusiasm, supported by others, which helped to activate the interest of football in the county so that the many new clubs formed through the impulse created by Turton were finally banded together in the Lancashire F.A. A year later, in 1879, a Cup was offered by this body for competition amongst its constituent members. So the ripples widened from the stone originally dropped in the pond.

Meanwhile Newton Heath (L.Y.R.) were quietly gaining strength in the background. Nicknamed either 'the Newtonians', 'the Heathens', or 'the Coachbuilders', they satisfied their growing ambitions by arranging fixtures with opponents like Astley Bridge (already competing in the F.A. Cup itself), with whom they drew in January 1883; against Dalton Hall, whom they beat 4–1; against Haughton Dale, whose impertinence in fielding their reserve team was punished to the tune of 7–0; and with Oughtringham Park, who were vanquished 4–2 by a Newton Heath side which lined up: C. Fulton; S. Black, E. Moran; W. Siddons, T. Kay, E. Howles; T. Davies, W. Jordan, J. Blears, J. Gotheridge, and T. Beach.

On March 22, 1884, came the club's first representative recognition when four of the team – the redoubtable and enthusiastic Sam Black, Moran, Fulton and Blears – were selected to play for Manchester and District against Liverpool and District on the Bootle Cricket Ground at Old Hullard Lane. Here were the forerunners of all the individual honours that were to be won in the years ahead.

The shadows of coming events were cast over 1885 when Newton Heath (L.Y.R.) first reached the final of the Manchester Cup. They lost then to Hurst, but it mattered little. The point was that their name was being projected and even the *Manchester Guardian* took note of them with a ten-line notice.

It was in that year that professionalism, after a bitter fight, was at last legalised and Newton Heath lost no time in strengthening their forces by offering jobs on the railway to prominent players from far afield, several of them Welshmen.

While one half of Lancashire at that time lived on a higher plane in the persons of Preston North End, Blackburn Rovers and Olympic, Bolton and Burnley, the Manchester area was gradually flexing its muscles as the bonfire of football spread rapidly, much to the chagrin of the followers of the Rugby game.

In Newton Heath's world the year 1886 stood out in letters of gold. With the glowing reputation of being a goalscoring team, they began to attract a growing following which was rewarded when between January and March of that year 'the Coachbuilders' won five matches in a row with a tally of twenty-seven goals against three. This led eventually to the Newton Heath (L.Y.R.) triumph in the final of the Manchester Cup before an 8,000 crowd at Whalley Range.

The team of the latter part of 1886 was much strengthened, both physically and otherwise, by the arrival of a certain Jack Powell, a full back of more than fourteen stone and over six feet in height. With him there lined up this side: Becket; Powell, Mitchell; J. Davies, Burke, Howles; Gotheridge, L. Davies, R. Doughty, Lowton and Earp.

All these are but names to us now, but they remain part of a rich cavalcade which is difficult to pigeon-hole with precision. Yet history bows to them.

In August 1887 a Scotsman named Pat McDonnell was acquired, a fellow so down on his luck that he walked all the way to Manchester from Glasgow to gain employment with the Wagon Works and play with Newton Heath (L.Y.R.). A month later, September, there arrived Tom Hay from Staveley, a man destined to win fame with the 'Heathens' as a great goalkeeper, a specialist role where United have often been fortunate over the past century, down to the long-serving Alex Stepney of the present.

Another abiding quality which runs through the whole story like a silver thread has been the spirit of family and comradeship which has always bound the club. Without doubt it has been this sense of fraternity which has existed between the officials and the players from its earliest Wagon Works days to the present that has helped to ride the many storms on the way. It has provided both buoyancy and stability when the going became hard.

Before turning to some of the players who made their mark over this opening decade notice must be taken of Newton Heath's general rise in the world, both socially and on the field. From its birth in 1878 the president of the club had been Mr. F. Attock, Carriage and Wagon Superintendent of the Lancashire and Yorkshire Railway. By 1888–89 he had gathered round him as vice-presidents many distinguished names in the political world of Manchester, some of whom, indeed, had shown interest in the club since its earliest railway days.

In every way it was a compliment, not only to Mr. Attock, but to these men themselves who were far-seeing enough to pin their loyalties to so young and as yet undistinguished – judged by the larger world – a sporting body. It was, indeed, a feather in the Newton Heath (L.Y.R.) cap to have won the support and attention of such eminent men as the Hon. A. J. Balfour, M.P. the Hon. C. E. Schwann M.P.; Sir James Fergusson, Bart, M.P., the Member for North-East Manchester, who later lost his life in the Jamaica earthquake; not least, C. P. Scott, J.P., the distinguished and powerful editor of the *Manchester Guardian,* whose journalistic fame lives to this day; and a number of other influential aldermen, councillors and businessmen.

Nor were these mere figureheads. They took an active interest in the welfare of the club as the team did its best to live up to such excellent support. In October 1887, for instance, Sir James Fergusson added to the importance of the occasion by attending when Burnley paid their first visit to the North Road ground, where Bolton Wanders and Blackburn Rovers had succumbed in friendlies. He was present, too, a year later when a Canadian touring side arrived to relieve Newton Heath of their unbeaten home record before a 3,000 crowd, a result which the 'Heathens' duly avenged in 1890 with a 5–1 victory over a second visiting Canadian team.

In 1888 the club lifted the Manchester Cup for the second time with a record 7–1 win over Denton when J. Doughty scored three of the goals in a side which read: J. Pedley; J. Powell, J. Mitchell; T. Burke, J. Davies, J. Owen; J. Earp, I. Wright, J. Doughty, J. Gotheridge and R. Doughty. There soon followed two further major battle honours when Aston Villa were beaten in a friendly (though lacking five players of their First XI), and a year later – March 1889 – the defeat of Nottingham Forest. By then there were three changes in the team which did such noble duty: Hay; Powell, Mitchell; Burke, Davies, J. Owen; Tait, Gotheridge, J. Doughty, R. Doughty, and G. Owen.

Things clearly were on the move. The butterfly had already begun to stir within the chrysalis, anxious to lend its colour to the outside world. The next step came when the name of Newton Heath (L.Y.R.) was found among the entries for the F.A. Cup of 1889. Though considered worthy of entry by the Cup Committee of the day, they were made to eat humble pie 6–1 by the League and Cup holders of the day, the 'Invincibles' of Preston North End.

The F.A. Cup, however, was one thing, a mere brief spoonful of jam in the season. What was really needed was a steady ration of bread and butter with League competition to attract paying customers through the gate to help make ends meet. The answer came with the inauguration of the Football Alliance in the autumn of 1889, a league inferior only to the Football League itself and destined to become the future Second Division.

This was what Newton Heath (L.Y.R.) needed. Their application to join was accepted and in a company twelve strong they played their first match under Alliance rules against Sunderland Albion on September 21. With a 4–1 win the 'Heathens' set sail bravely towards a distant and exciting new horizon. This was a major signpost in their life and the *Manchester Guardian* noted it faithfully with a 400 word report, something of an extravagance in those early days, especially by a newspaper heavily inclined towards Rugby football. Newton Heath (L.Y.R.) had caught the eye of the mighty and the men who took their share of the limelight were: T. Hay; J. Mitchell, J. Powell; R. Doughty, J. Davies, J. Owen; W. Tait, W. Stewart, J. Doughty, E. Wilson and J. Gotheridge.

No matter the drive, the planning, the attention to worrying detail and the financial problems of directors and committee members, the heart and soul of a club lies in its players. They are the ones who provide the character and etch history on the field. As time like an ever rolling stream bears its sons away, there is usually one who stands fast to hand on tradition to a rising generation. That remains as true then as it does today.

Among such a gallant band stands pre-eminently one, Sam Black, for six years a member of the original 'Heathens' and for four years the club captain. Sturdy of stature, with thighs like tree trunks, one has only to study the old photograph of him to sense the pride of the man. Posed in a studio portrait, left hand on hip, long white tights above black stockings and boots, he looked capable of conquering the four corners of the world, come what may.

In the words of H. P. Renshaw – a respected and well loved pressman, who for thirty-six years faithfully followed and chronicled the deeds of Manchester United from its simple origins as an offspring of the Lancashire and Yorkshire Railway; the first historian of the club, in fact – Sam Black in his day was 'one of the finest backs that ever kicked a ball'. He came as a boy from Burton and threw in his lot with Newton Heath (L.Y.R.).

A consistent and popular player and an inspiring captain, he took part in the final of the Manchester Cup in the year of its inauguration in 1885. Twice he captained the Manchester Association representative side against Liverpool Association and during this spell declined to join Blackburn Olympic in the season of 1883 when they won the F.A. Cup, finally to break the power of the old amateur south in the competion. He also refused to throw in his lot with Mitchells and Crewe Alexandra at that time.

Playing always as an amateur, he finally returned to Burton where he joined the local Wanderers before giving up the game to become secretary of the Derby Town Club. Also a cricketer of no little ability and able, too, to hold his own with the best at quoits and bowls, he finally turned to refereeing in 1889. Even there he made his mark with one particularly astute decision in a match between Woolwich Arsenal and Burnley. Arsenal – so the story went – had scored, but when the Burnley goalkeeper produced the ball it was found that the case had split and the bladder was protruding. At once Black disallowed the goal, holding the opinion that the ball at that moment was not a ball within the meaning of the law. He might have done well in the legal profession.

Another outstanding captain was Jack Powell who led the side into the Alliance League. A native of Frwd, near Wrexham, he was one of a number of Welshmen who came to Manchester to find jobs with the Lancashire and Yorkshire Railway and to play football. In 1879, although never having played the game, he joined the famous Druids club of Ruabon. After only three games he was chosen to play for Wales against England, a fact which doubtless would make the modern footballer smile indulgently.

In 1883 Powell joined Bolton Wanderers and three years later, because of a residential irregularity, moved to Manchester where, as a fitter by trade, he joined the Newton Heath 'Coachbuilders'. Registering as a professional in 1887, he proceeded to give his all to his new club and to his native Wales for whom he played fifteen times.

While modern United have often turned to Scottish and Irish talent – the likes of Delaney, Law, Buchan, Macari, and Willie Morgan on the one hand; Carey, Whelan, Best, Gregg, Tony Dunne and McIlroy on the other, to name but a few – in the closing years of the nineteenth century it was Wales that took the attention of Newton Heath. Manchester and its Wagon Works depot of the Lancashire and Yorkshire Railway, of course, was the El Dorado where jobs and money were the attraction.

High in this list stand the names of the brothers Jack and Roger Doughty. Although not originally in search of employment, they came in fact as boys to the old Newton Heath at North Road, and in due course helped to put football on the map in the Manchester area.

Jack first lent his aid for a return of ten shillings a week for tea and train fares. Later, when he turned professional, his highest salary was thirty shillings per week. Both brothers played for Wales, Jack as centre forward and Roger as inside left and when Ireland were once beaten 11–0 in 1888 they claimed six of the goals between them, Jack hitting four – this in spite of the fact that three of their side had left the field early to catch a train!

In those days Wales used to honour its players with a badge and jersey and when in due course it was decided to present a cap instead, Jack was to receive the first of the new award. In all he appeared nineteen times for his country while Roger was chosen on four occasions. As members of the Druids in their teenage days, both gained a couple of medals for winning the Welsh Cup.

Nor were they the only sons of the Principality playing in Manchester at that time and helping to fashion local history. On one occasion five members of Newton Heath (L.Y.R.) turned out for Wales against Scotland at Edinburgh. They were the two Doughtys, Jack Powell, Tom Burke and Joe Davies. Among others to represent Wales were the brothers Jack and Billy Owen, Lot Jones and Hagan. The last named later moved to Fairfield (another club of local repute) and then to Burnley where a broken leg finally ended his career.

As for Jack Doughty, the warrior, he was still alive and well in the mid-1920s and still working for the railway company. Very fast with the ball at his toes, he led the Newton Heath (L.Y.R.) attack three times when they won the Manchester Cup and it was seldom that he failed to score.

Most clubs across the years have had their fanatical supporters, some of them sparing nothing to become closely identified with a team. In a sense they play the role of a Walter Mitty, dreaming of a heroic part which they can never play. The modern Manchester United has never been short of one of these. Nor, in fact, were the original Newton Heath.

One of the closest of these was a certain Mr. Bird, a local chimney sweep who on occasion even posed with the team in a group photograph. He loved the players and they loved him and with good reason. His stentorian exhortations during a game of 'Play up the lads!' always generated an extra effort; and when some special match was in the offing he would invite the whole side to his home two or three times in the week, there to regale them with a substantial meal of Lancashire hotpot or potato pie, followed by a smoking concert to soothe any over-anxious soul. Father Bird, as he was known, spared no effort to feather the Newton Heath nest.

Another of this ilk was a Mr. Sedgwick. In silk hat and frock coat he cut a stately figure as he attended North Road to support his favourites. And they in their turn owed him much, since he was the all-powerful stationmaster at Manchester Victoria Station and was always able to supply them with reserved carriages on their journeys to away matches. In this same league of dedicated stalwarts, too, was George Dale, one of the early directors, who never wavered in his support of Newton Heath throughout a long life. Even up to the 1920s he used to organise an annual cricket match between the players of Manchester United and City on the Gentlemen of Cheshire's ground at Chelford.

In a sense those may have been carefree, uncomplicated days exempt from the pressures and demands of our modern life. Yet they were anxious days. There was always a shortage of money; a struggle to make ends meet and keep the wolf from the door. Yet somehow or other Newton Heath (L.Y.R.) managed to stay alive, living from hand to mouth and surmounting each succeeding crisis. Loyalty, a love of club, pride and a family spirit combined to keep the ship afloat.

As 'gates' increased so, however, did the overheads too – as many clubs now find to their cost in our days of inflation. On February 3, 1888, for instance, a throng of 8,000 witnessed a friendly against Preston North End, the giants of the time; and when in 1889–90 the Alliance League matches got under way, crowds of 10,000 were not infrequent. At that time, too, an element of roughness had entered the game so that it was not uncommon to see the referee lecturing both teams.

With crowds on the increase and both stamina and enthusiasm fully tested by the inadequacies of the North Road ground, funds were raised from local dignitaries to build a stand to accommodate 1,000 spectators in 1891, a great relief to those able to afford such comfort on a bleak winter's day.

This was but a straw in the wind. Change was on the way and the first transition came in 1892 when the uncomfortable suffix of the letters L.Y.R. was disposed of. Henceforth the club became known simply as Newton Heath. At this point a new limited company was formed – but floated on insufficient capital – which for the first time required the close attention of a paid official. This proved to be A. H. Albut, who arrived as secretary from Aston Villa.

A man of drive and some experience of company matters, he required an office away from the distractions of the headquarters at the Shears Hotel. In due course a cottage was first leased at six shillings a week at 33 Oldham Road, then later larger accommodation in a disused schoolroom at The Institute, Silver Street, Miles Platting.

Being a man with a sense of public relations, Albut persuaded his directors to turn this into a social centre where players and supporters could mingle freely. To this end a billiard table was supplied to help in the cementing of friendship and understanding. All too soon, however, this venture came to a dead end when all the cues became conspicuous by their absence. With nothing else to play for, these had all been claimed by the winners of contests.

Those indeed were days when life was hard, life was earnest and lived on a shoestring. Yet in a curious way things have a way of levelling out. What is lost on the swings may well be gained on the roundabouts. Newton Heath were about to discover this on the field of play.

Their first two season in the Alliance had been anything but successful when they had ended eighth and ninth in a field of twelve. Yet with the help of a new outside right in Farmer – a scintillating dribbler, an entertainer of the crowds and as such a popular hero for several seasons – Newton Heath suddenly caught a fresh wind in their sails.

Doubtless their appalling pitch at North Road continued to be their closest ally and an enemy to all visiting opposition. But whatever the reason, at the end of the 1891–92 season they found themselves runners-up in the Alliance to Nottingham Forest with the following figures:

| | | | | | Goals | | |
|---|---|---|---|---|---|---|---|
| | P | W | D | L | F | A | Pts. |
| Nottingham Forest | 22 | 14 | 5 | 3 | 59 | 22 | 33 |
| Newton Heath | 22 | 12 | 7 | 3 | 69 | 33 | 31 |

Left behind in the field were Small Heath (later Birmingham City), Sheffield Wednesday, Burton Swifts, Crewe Alexandra, Ardwick (later Manchester City), Bootle, Lincoln City, Grimsby Town, Walsall Town Swifts, and Birmingham St. George's.

It was at that psychological moment that fate dealt a card into Newton Heath's hands. The Football League decided to form a Second Division and at the same time to extend their First Division (in existence only since 1888/9) from fourteen to sixteen clubs.

So it was that Nottingham Forest and Newton Heath suddenly found themselves moved upstairs to the First Division in the company of the Aston Villas, Preston North Ends, Evertons and Sunderlands of this world. The green and gold jerseys of Newton Heath were at last among the aristocrats.

# 8

# *1893–1906:*

# *Change of Scenario*

HISTORY BELONGS NOT only to the past. It belongs to today. Even the future is now. Time is open-ended, like a river without banks. Everything is interlocked. To review a century is like pouring a hundred years into an hour glass. Yet in all such a lengthening mountain range of time certain high peaks of achievement and dark valleys of crisis stand out. We now move into a decade at the turn of the century full of such turbulent events.

Having been elevated from the Alliance to the First Division of the Football League at the end of the season 1891–92, the green and gold jersey of Newton Heath was now to be seen disporting itself amongst the aristocrats of the day. But like someone who has raised himself from one class to another – from below stairs, as it were, from the servants' quarters to the master's drawing room upstairs – Newton Heath were soon discomfited and ill at ease in their strange surroundings after a bright enough start.

That new start came on September 3, 1892, when the 'Heathens' travelled to Blackburn, where they lost their opening match to the Rovers only by 4–3. However, the real red-letter day in Manchester football came a week later, when on September 10, the first ever Football League match was played in the city. Burnley were the visitors and the result a 1–1 draw, with the Newton Heath side lining up: Warner; Mitchell, Brown; Perrins, Stewart, Erentz; Hood, Donaldson, Coupar, Carson, Matthieson.

A month later came the really big one. On October 15, Wolverhampton Wanderers were given a humiliating thrashing by 10–1, the Wolves, not unnaturally, but unavailingly protesting about the fearful conditions of the North Road ground. On December 31, 1892, followed one more major performance when Derby County were well beaten 7–1 in the days when a sharp, but friendly, rivalry existed between the railway centres – Newton, Derby and Crewe.

Yet by the end of that opening season Newton Heath lay bottom of the League, a full five points behind Accrington in fifteenth place above them. A haul of only six wins and six draws from thirty matches (18 points) was all that they could muster and it was only a 5–2 win over Small Heath (after a 1–1 draw) in the Test Matches of those days that kept them in the top drawer.

But not for long. Next year, 1893–94, they ended in sixteenth and bottom place again with even fewer points – a mere fourteen from six wins and two draws. This time, losing their Test Match 2–0 against Liverpool, they found themselves relegated to the Second Division which had been formed only the previous season. For the next twelve years they were destined to stay there while the world and events around them – including the South African war – stepped into the approaching turmoil of the twentieth century.

It was in September 1893 that Newton Heath at last moved home from their original North Road ground. In a sense it proved a mere step or two from the frying pan into the fire. In exchange for the cloying mud of the past the supporters of the club were now offered the overwhelming stench of nearby chemical works which polluted the environment.

The new ground was at Bank Lane, Clayton, lying to the windward side of an army of thirty chimney stacks which belched forth acrid fumes. The foul atmosphere found itself canonised in rhyme:

> As Satan was flying over Clayton for Hell,
> He was chained in the breeze, likewise the smell.
> Quoth he: 'I'm not sure in what country I roam,
> But I'm sure by the smell I'm not far from home.'

Yet the housewarming of the new home, with its enlarged enclosure, offered better things when Burnley were overcome 3–2 in the presence of a 10,000 crowd. Annoyed though they were at being shifted from North Road, the supporters at least were prepared at the start to accept the inconvenience of a three-mile jaunt to Clayton provided the future was to hold better things.

It was not the mud and the rugged conditions that brought about the move. It was, in fact, the Church. The later Souvenir Bazaar Programme of 1901 explained it in these words:

> When the company took over the Club and its liabilities, matches were played at North Road, the ground belonging to the Cathedral authorities. On the same ground was a cricket pitch and the winter pastime interfered with the summer game. The ground was held by the

Lancashire and Yorkshire Railway people, who received, what was held to be, a very handsome rent from the Newton Heath Club, they, in turn paying a nominal rent to the Dean and Canons. So that the railwaymen might have their ground to themselves, there was nothing for it but that the footballers must find another field of play. The Dean and Canons were approached by a very influential deputation, among whom may be mentioned Sir James Fergusson, M.P., C. P. Scott, Esq., Rev. B. Reedy (St. Luke's), Councillors Bowers and Rothwell, W. H. Hughes, Esq., J.P., and many other influential gentlemen. These gentlemen met the Cathedral authorities, but without success. They had already granted one piece of land for recreative purposes, and could not see their way to allowing another. Owners of every available piece of land were visited, with a similar result. If football was to continue, we must have a considerable space of ground, and this was found at Clayton. The Bradford and Clayton Recreative Committee were approached, terms were made, and the ground was let to the Club for eight months of the year, with an occasional evening for practice, preceding the opening of the football season. Now the ground is held on a favourable lease, but the expenditure incurred has financially crippled the directors. The stands at North Road belonged to the Newton Heath Directors, these they left behind them, receiving for them less than £100. The alternative being, in case of taking stands, away, to leave the ground as they found it when they took possession; this was found to be impracticable.

The better things hoped for, however, turned out to be pricked balloons. The opening weeks (which proved to be the outriders of eventual relegation at the end of 1893/94) in fact embraced much trouble. A 3–1 defeat at West Bromwich Albion, followed by a 2–0 loss in a tough match at Derby (which led to an F.A. inquiry) were forerunners of the return game against West Bromwich at Clayton on October 14, 1893. This time Newton Heath won 4–1, but such was the critical report and the comments on the game written by 'Observer' in the *Birmingham Daily Gazette* in respect of Newton Heath that the Manchester club decided to take legal action against the Midlands newspaper concerned.

While the *Manchester Guardian* considered that the directors were taking things too seriously, Newton Heath thought differently. Albut, the secretary, approached J. R. Strawson, of Lincoln, the referee of the match, for his comments and upon the receipt of a reply asked the *Guardian* to print the letter.

It duly appeared on October 20:

I have read [wrote Strawson] the newspaper cuttings you have sent me with much surprise, for more untruthful and groundless accusations were never made against any club, and such abominable scurrility can only be the outcome of an unhealthy imagination produced by gross partisanship. Reduced to plain facts, the charges are simply that Reader was kicked and Geddes injured, and if these two occurrences did take place, they cannot fairly form the basis of charges of brutality and ruffianism in a game that has always possessed elements of danger. My own impressions of the game are diametrically opposed to those of the Birmingham reporter, for instead of roughness and brutality being prevalent, there was a total absence of these very objectionable qualities from the game, and although the victory was undoubtedly largely due to the dash shown by the Newton Heath players, no unnecessary force was used and not a single vicious foul occurred during the whole game on either side. In the dashing rush made by the home team when the first goal was scored Reader was slightly hurt but to say he was purposely kicked is quite untrue, for I was not two yards from the spot and was watching intently for any such conduct. With respect to Geddes's injury no appeal even was made for a foul. So, however that occurred it is quite certain it was accidental.

After hearing the reports of the Derby match I went to Manchester on Saturday expecting a rough and unpleasant experience, and it is quite certain on that particular day I should have put a sudden stoppage to anything like foulness: but never during an experience of fourteen years among all sorts of clubs and in all sorts of contests have I had a pleasanter afternoon when refereeing a football match. Not once was any decision that I gave questioned, the play of both sides was a credit to their clubs and a credit to the game, and while the Newton Heath players continue the same straight forward, manly work they can afford to pass over with contempt all such cowardly attacks as you have brought under my notice.

I am pleased to be able to inform you that several of the West Bromwich players after the match expressed themselves highly pleased with the conduct of the Newton Heath team. I shall be pleased to give you any further information on any particular point you may require with reference to this game . . .

The offending comments printed in the *Birmingham Daily Gazette* of October 16, 1893 and written by 'Observer' – William Jephcott, a respected and experienced journalist in the Midlands – were these:

It wasn't football, it was simply brutality and if these are the tactics Newton Heath are compelled to adopt to win their matches, the sooner the Football Association deal severely with them the better it will be for the game generally . . .

Strong words. But four months after the action had been brought by Newton Heath on March 2, 1894, in the Manchester Civil Court, following the usual legal jockeying and play on words, Mr. Justice Day, the judge, with a verdict which might have made Solomon raise an eyebrow, awarded Newton Heath, the plaintiffs, damages of only a farthing, with costs to be paid by both parties – yet another blow for the club's finances. The trial, played as it were on their home ground, was a defeat for Newton Heath at a time when they were beset by many shafts of misfortune. Having lost that one the Heathens, as said earlier, lost the Test Match to Liverpool at the end of that 1894 season and packed their bags for the Second Division.

Those two sad years were summed up by *The Guardian* in what read more like an obituary than a leading article:

> Newton Heath, who have for two season been at the bottom of the table, have perhaps not much to complain of. They have at times shown form which would have justified their inclusion in the First Division, notably in the West Bromwich match which led to so much litigation; but a club which has remained at the bottom of the table for two seasons has no reason to complain if a rising club which heads the list so easily as Liverpool has done should usurp its place.

The relapse into the Second Division, for all the loss of face, proved not to be as bleak as expected. For all but two of the dozen years that Newton Heath remained down they were constantly in a position amongst the vanguard fighting for promotion. Indeed, from 1895 until at last they regained First Division status in 1906, they ended successively third, sixth, second (at the end of 1897–98 Test Matches were ended and the First and Second Divisions increased to eighteen clubs each, with the promotion and relegation system of two clubs introduced), fourth, fourth, tenth, fifteenth, fifth, third, third, second.

Throughout those years not only was there a steady turnover of players, some of whom left a major mark on the field of play, but much went on backstage.

The unending battle, of course, was against penury. In all that time no more than three or four clubs could really be said to be solvent – a distant echo of the present. There is, after all, little that is new in the world of football. Newton Heath for one were certainly not amongst the affluent. Their role was that of the beggar with the begging bowl, a hard fact of life that endlessly exercised the minds and ingenuity of the club officials, and particularly that of Albut the secretary.

Albut, it appears, was a man quick to turn a dark situation to advantage. Legend has it that on one occasion a directors' meeting was held by the light of three candles fixed in ginger beer bottles. The Corporation had cut off the gas supply and served the club with a summons. The piece of blue paper, however, came as a blessing in disguise to Albut. With the court summons in his pocket he approached a player of a neighbouring club whom he wanted and who he knew had received no wages for weeks.

Explaining his plot, he told the player to demand of his own secretary the immediate payment of the money owed him otherwise he would have to serve a summons on him. To support the demand he was to wave the blue paper in the official's face. The demand naturally could not be met, whereupon the player gained his release from the club. The following Saturday he turned out for Albut and Newton Heath and being something of a celebrity put another £10 or more on the North Street 'gate'.

Apocryphal or not, it reflected the constant struggle for money that weighed heavily on the game.

When the club moved to Clayton they still could scarcely bless themselves with a penny piece so that there arose the difficulty of a registered office. But again a tenuous lifeline was at hand. The *Manchester Evening News* erected a wooden building on the ground as a telephone box for their reporters and this the newspaper kindly allowed the club to use as an office.

At the completion of the box H. P. Renshaw, the Manchester journalist, was invited to the opening ceremony. He later recalled how he duly arrived at the new Bank Lane ground only to find secretary Albut and a director, both wearing clogs, engaged in whitewashing the goalposts and the palings round the pitch. Albut apologised that the christening ceremony was cancelled since a postal order for a pound which he had expected in the morning post had not arrived. But with the generous help of the licensee of a neighbouring tavern the baby's head was wetted and the new office duly declared open.

It truly was a case of living from hand to mouth, yet perhaps good for the soul. It was love, pride and determination that kept things going.

Among achievements on the field there were many stirring battles to recall with illustrious Blackburn Rovers. In the successive years of 1893 and 1894 Newton Heath met them in the early rounds of the F.A. Cup. The first of these the Rovers won handsomely after the Blackburn medical authorities had tried to postpone the tie because of an outbreak of smallpox in the Manchester area. The following season brought a goalless draw at Clayton before an 18,000 crowd but a clear 5–1 victory for Blackburn in the replay.

The first season of 1895 in the Second Division brought one particular highlight. On March 9 Walsall came to Clayton and were

1889–90, Newton Heath (L.Y.R.) with the Manchester Cup. Back row: Mitchell, Slater, McMillan; middle row: R. Doughty, Ramsey, Owen; bottom row: Smith (umpire), Farman, J. Doughty, Evans, Malarvie, Sharp, Priday (trainer).

A red letter day. The team that played the first ever Football League match in Manchester on September 10th, 1892. Back row: Massey (trainer), Warner, Davies; middle row: T. Taylor (Director), Alf Albut (Secretary), T. Fairbrother (Director), Mitchell, Perrins, Stewart, Brown, Erentz, Clements, J. Lateward (Director); bottom row: Farman, Coupar, Donaldson, Carson, Hood, Mathieson. Final score a 1–1 draw with Burnley.

An artist's impression of Old Trafford on its opening day. 19th February 1910, drawn from what is now the scoreboard end. The stand on the right was never actually built.

The first team 1905–06: back row, Downie, Moger, Bonthron; centre: J. E. Magnall (Secretary), Picken, Sagar, Blackstock, Peddie, Bacon (trainer); sitting: Beddow, Roberts (captain), Bell, Arkesden.

trounced 14–0, a match in which Cassidy, arrived from Glasgow Celtic, made his debut with four goals. However, Walsall's protest against the ground conditions was upheld, and the match replayed on April 3. To make their point positive Newton Heath won again, next time by 9–0 but, ending third in the league, failed in their Test Match for promotion 3–0 to Stoke. Their disgruntled supporters felt they had been cheated since the game was played on the Port Vale ground, a mere half hour walk from Stoke. One silver lining, however, came with the news that the club's debts had been reduced from £593 9s. 5d. to £323 17s. 6d.

One other honour fell to the 'Heathens' before the turn of the century. On February 26, 1898, mighty Blackburn Rovers were beaten 2–1 so that at last the then much coveted Lancashire Cup stood on the Newton Heath sideboard for the first time.

The wonder of it was that with so little money at hand Newton Heath were able to unearth any worthwhile players. The grooming of home-grown talent was then a thing of the future. Yet the club was blessed with having wise men of discrimination as organisers. Prime amongst them was Mr. Crompton, of Miles Platting, one of six presidents in succession to F. Attock between the years 1891 and 1902, who rendered yeoman service.

On the retirement of the alert A. H. Albut after a decade as secretary in 1900, there followed in his place another enthusiastic worker in James West, who came to Clayton from Lincoln. Though staying only three years he, too, worked like a beaver to keep the ship afloat on the stormy waters of those days.

It was all this collective and keen discernment that helped to bring to Clayton players like McNaught, who later went to Tottenham Hotspur in 1898; the Scot Joe Cassidy, the demon shot of Middlesbrough and Celtic; the Erentz brothers; Billy Bryant, 'a rare Sheffield United blade'; Walter Cartwright, the Cheshire half back, and Harry Stafford at full back, a man destined to play a key, even decisive, role in the fortunes of Newton Heath. A statue should be raised to him and to a certain dog to mark their place in the destiny of Manchester United. But that is another story and will duly fall into its allotted place.

Of all these men it was perhaps McNaught who played the best football in his fine career at Clayton. His masterly strokes at half back earned him the title of 'the little wonder'. He was admired not only for his play but for his gentlemanly behaviour on all occasions and for his intelligent command of subjects outside the game, a man who played his part as a leader in the newly formed Players' Union. Another notable figure also was Peden, an Irishman formerly with

Linfield & Distillery. An international in 1888, he was a clever but emotional and unreliable left winger. Yet on his day he was a virtuoso match winner as when once he mesmerised Blackburn Rovers to such a degree that at the final whistle he was carried shoulder high from the field by a mob of enchanted, exhilarated Newton Heath supporters. Nor should one forget Caesar Jenkins, later to move to Small Heath and Walsall, a burly fellow whose bark was worse than his bite. However, he expressed his feelings in no uncertain way and once caused a goalkeeper to return to his native Scotland after having heard Caesar's opinion of his prowess – or lack of it – under the crossbar!

In those days of poverty and trouble the arrival of a new player would excite the whole of Clayton. Crowds would gather at the railway station to greet the new capture. Financial support at the ground, however, slowly declined and became so slim that finally the professional players' wages were assessed on a percentage of the gate receipts. Before stripping for a game one of them was known to ask: 'Many people on the ground?' When informed that the crowd was thin, he would add: 'Oh, well, I don't think I am fit to play today. My foot isn't right . . .' Fortunately he was an exception, since the vast majority played on nobly with a fine, sporting spirit.

With their livelihood constantly in jeopardy and tossed here and there like a feather in the breeze the time was approaching when footballers clearly would unite in some form of common protection of their security, rights, and interests. It came in 1898 with the formation of the Players' Union and on January 12 a meeting was held in the Spread Eagle Hotel, Corporation Street, Manchester, where players from Newton Heath and Manchester City played prominent parts in the new movement. In later years this union was to run foul of the Football Association, with players suspended by the national governing body and in retaliation themselves threatening a strike.

All this was but part of the changing pattern of life as a whole. Trade unionism at large was on the rise and gaining in strength, a form of collective protection that would have refused to countenance the treatment meted out to professional footballers. What trade, for instance, would accept the fate of a Newton Heath player who on one occasion found his week's pay to be three half crowns? When the man remarked, 'Now I shall have to spend another Sunday indoors', a director queried, 'How's that?' Back came the reply, 'Because my best suit is in pledge for fifteen shillings.' Whereupon it was decided, rather than he should suffer this indignity, to give the player sufficient money to redeem his clothes, plus a couple of shillings for what the directors called 'spending brass'.

That may appear amusing now in our affluent society but then life was very real and earnest. There was the tale, too, of an enterprising tailor in the town who offered a free overcoat to any Newton Heath player who scored a goal. One of them, indeed, earned a couple of these garments in an afternoon, but soon enough games became a farce as even full backs started surging forward to take pot shots at goal. In due course the directors persuaded the tailor to end his generosity. But he had made his point. The well-advertised publicity gave his business a healthy boost!

If times had been hard previously, by 1901–2 they threatened catastrophe and even possible extinction of the club. Lying fifteenth in the Second Division only the inadequacies of Gainsborough Trinity and Stockport County saved Newton Heath from oblivion. Even so, they managed to beat Manchester City at Hyde Road to lift the Manchester Cup for the sixth time in their existence, thereby avenging the defeat by their neighbours in the final of the previous season. The team on duty on that occasion was: Saunders; Stafford, Erentz; Morgan, Griffiths, Cartwright; Schofield, Couper, Preston, Hayes, Lappin.

But in essence the turn of the century found the club scraping the very bottom of the barrel. Non-existent money had been spent with the freedom of a drunken sailor on players, most of whom failed to live up to their previous reputations, and on ground improvements. So-called guarantees for all this outlay proved worthless, while the four-day Grand Bazaar held at St. James's Hall between February and March 1901 to raise at least £1,000 to help repair the situation, turned out to be more colourful than profitable. Attended by the Northern Military Band and the Besses-o'th-Barn Brass Band, there were sections to illuminate Italian, Nile, Indian, Eastern, Mediterranean and Riviera craftsmanship. Prices of admission ranged from two shillings and six pence at the opening to sixpence all day at the close. There was the attendance of such luminaries as the M.P.s Sir James Fergusson, C. E. Schwann, W. Joynson-Hicks, and Councillor Bishop; while even exhorting rhymes printed in the programme such as

Come, my masters, young and old
Here are things that must be sold;
Your kind support we now await,
Another day you'll be too late.

failed to separate people from their purses to the extent expected and required. Much to their credit, however, among the patrons of this affair were the local rivals, Manchester City. Here shown was a sense of civic pride and an offer of support for a club on its beam ends.

In the early months of 1902 the creditors duly foreclosed and a move was made by the contractors who had refurbished the Clayton North Lane ground to bankrupt the club. A statement issued by the Official Receiver on February 22 showed that Newton Heath were in debt to the tune of £2,670, and bailiffs attached the few existing assets of value at the Silver Street office. Yet somehow the club limped on, using every available crutch until at last on March 18 a shareholders' meeting was called.

It proved to be a historic turning point.

The meeting place was the New Islington Hall with Mr. F. Palmer in the chair. He announced that the Football Association had agreed to the re-forming of the club and that no blame attached to the directors for the state of the bankruptcy, though one is entitled to ask at this distance of time the question – if not them, then who?

James West reported that no tradesmen's debts were left outstanding through the receipts of £402 3s. 8d. since the date of the winding-up order, whereupon Harry Stafford, the club captain, arose to enquire in straight terms just how much money was needed to make the club solvent.

When the chairman suggested a figure of £2,000 Stafford proceeded to drop a bombshell that shook the meeting. He knew, he said, of four gentlemen each of whom was prepared to invest £500 in the club, a figure he himself was also ready to match. In a sense it was a statement as far reaching as the Gettysburg Address and probably unique by a professional player in all the long, tangled history of football. Here, indeed, was a man of outstanding loyalty who put club before self. I repeat my earlier words: a statue should be raised to him outside the Old Trafford of today. The following year Stafford was reinstated as an amateur and later, when he had hung up his boots, he was elected to the board of directors.

The four men in question were Mr. J. H. Davies, of Old Trafford; Mr. J. Taylor, of Sale; Mr. W. Deakin, of Manchester; and Mr. J. Brown, of Denton. The meeting was adjourned, the assembled company fell with delight on Stafford's neck and the officials of the club forthwith met with their new benefactors to review the situation. On April 28 the *Manchester Guardian* announced: 'The Newton Heath combination will now be renamed

Manchester United' and history took what has proved to be a giant forward stride.

The new title, it appears, caused some disputation. Some favoured 'Manchester Central' others 'Manchester Celtic'. According to the redoubtable Louis Rocca it was he who hit on the title now made famous through the land. 'I got up and suggested Manchester United. The name was taken.'

The die was cast and Manchester United born, with J. H. Davies the new man at the helm.

If the loyal Stafford sowed the fresh seed it was Davies who duly tended and reaped the new harvest. He was a remarkable, highly able man whose very touch seemed able to turn copper to gold. Equally extraordinary was his relationship with Stafford and the way in which fate brought the two of them together.

Romantic fairy tale or not, the story has come down the years that a beautiful St. Bernard dog belonging to Stafford became lost as it rambled round the premises of the Grand Bazaar of 1901, a barrel fastened to its collar for the purposes of collecting money from the crowds. The animal was found by a Mr. Thomas, the licencee of a hostel belonging to Mr. Davies. Thomas showed the dog to Davies who bought it as a birthday present for his daughter and later, having done business with its lawful owner, proceeded to install Stafford in yet another of his public houses. Thus began the fateful meeting of two men that was to change the course of Manchester's football history.

But the gods had something more in store. In September 1903 James West, his policies in question, resigned as secretary and in his succession there followed J. E. Mangnall as secretary-manager, having given up a similar post at Burnley.

At that moment was forged between Davies and Mangnall a partnership that duly brought national fame to United for the first time on a grand scale – the one a shrewd businessman, a self-made near millionaire, once an agent's clerk, innkeeper, and later brewer, thriving on hard work and discipline and with an instinct for long-range, future development; the other a clever pragmatist with an unerring eye for a natural footballer and a persuasive personality that could charm the birds out of the trees and players out of the arms of other clubs. It is perhaps not too wide of the mark to suggest that Mangnall lives on today in the person of Sir Matt Busby.

Fanciful or not, Davies, as president, and Mangnall between them put Manchester United on the map. While Mangall got his results on the field – where it matters for success in the long run – Davies, by his generosity to many charities and to individual players in the club, built up the corporate spirit which still underpins the modern Manchester United. In this sense the United of yesterday and today hold hands firmly – united in deed and in spirit whatever the problems of the hour.

At the start Davies knew and cared nothing for football. But once at the helm his shrewd instinct told him that with sufficient capital outlay the club could harness a massive potential public. Furthermore, noting the oversea visits of Southern clubs to countries like Holland, Belgium, France, Germany, Bohemia, and the Austro-Hungarian Empire, he correctly read the future development of football on a wider international stage. Here again is an echo of Busby and Harold Hardman, the chairman, as they took United into Europe in 1957 against the wishes of the Football League.

The initial major triumphs under Davies and Mangnall were to come during the following decade and will be dealt with later. But meanwhile, turning a brief page on the future, it is worth recording a leader written in April 1909 in the *Manchester Guardian.* Taking a backward look over the shoulder, the paper patted itself on the back with the double-jointed ease of a contortionist with the words:

> It seems quite a long interval from the days when the assets, the liabilities and the players' contracts of the Manchester United club were bought for little more than £100, to the winning by the same club of the League Championship[1] and now of the Association Cup.[2] Yet really only a few years have passed since Mr. J. H. Davies, by making what was thought to be a risky bargain, saved the Clayton organisation from disruption and set himself the task of building up a team second to none in the country.
>
> In these latter days, and after so many other peaks of achievement, it tends to be overlooked that in the first decade of this twentieth century Manchester United became exactly what the *Guardian* said it was: 'second to none in the country.' The recipe was 'hard work and unwavering perseverance'.

With Davies as president of the new, re-formed company, there came as chairman, J. J. Bentley, president of the Football League itself, controller of the Lancashire F.A. and an earlier power behind the throne at Bolton Wanderers, who signed the minutes of board meetings until December 3, 1908 – yet another valuable ally

[1] 1908
[2] 1909

of the club. It was he who recommended Mangnall to succeed James West as secretary-manager and an inspired choice it proved.

Meanwhile, to return to Stafford and his colleague Cartwright, the half back. Both were from Crewe; both were faithful, dedicated players who never failed the club even though they were never certain of having their railway fares reimbursed. So indebted to Stafford in particular were United that towards the end of his playing career they rewarded him with a benefit match.

The famous back and captain of the team for many years – he later emigrated overseas – was always something of an extrovert and he now displayed his sense of theatre by deciding on the novelty of playing a night match with the aid of Wells' lights and a gilded ball.

Sadly, however, the night chosen brought a gale of hurricane force so that no sooner had one light been got working than another was extinguished. The sides chosen were the representatives of both Manchester United and City and when the workmen had finally thrown in their hands trying to keep the lights working, the referee, with only one lamp flickering, called it all off. On reaching the dressing rooms it was discovered that half the players had already left the field in the dark and were fully dressed enjoying a smoke in comfort. That was the one and only attempt at artificial lighting at Clayton.

Davies's first act was to put down £3,000 out of his own pocket for the purchase of new players. With Stafford as his first scout (before the arrival of Mangnall) to help James West in his duties, Davies could point, among others, to the arrival of T. Arkesden from Burton United, a former partner of the immortal Steve Bloomer at Derby County; James Peddie, from Third Lanark and Newcastle, a clever forward who was both a provider and a goalscorer with a dynamic shot; and J. W. Sutcliffe, at one time a Rugby football international expelled from that code for suspected professionalism, who turned to Association first as a forward and later as a goalkeeper good enough to be selected for the English League against the Irish League in 1903.

Ending fifth in the Second Division in 1903, with an F.A. Cup victory over Liverpool and gates above the average – there were 25,000 for a key match against a Small Heath side seeking promotion, and over 40,000 to see Bristol City in September 1903 – it would appear that James West had achieved a fair measure of success during the awkward period of transition. But as is the way with human nature, there were many impatient, dyed-in-the-wool supporters who demanded even quicker success.

Thus, with the pressures on him mounting, West surrendered his seat of office to open the way for the arrival of Mangnall.

Mangnall himself had had a hard time at Burnley keeping the club afloat. As always lack of money was the problem. But on his arrival at Clayton, with the wealthy, generous Mr. Davies behind him, he played for big stakes. He spent widely, but wisely and well with the full support of his board.

Within three years he had done the trick for which everyone had been clamouring. In 1906 Manchester United won promotion to return again to the First Division and the flags were out at Clayton. Even the chemical fumes nearby bore the sweet smell of success. Just as they had languished in the Second Division for twelve years, now also United were to remain in the top drawer for a dozen seasons, but that is another part of the unfolding story.

To reach this step towards eminence Mangnall had acquired a number of new men who were to play a major role in the coming years. From Southampton came Moger, regarded as one of the outstanding goalkeepers in the south. At his side were others like Bonthron, Robertson, Roberts, Duckworth and Bell. The guiding star here proved to be Charlie Roberts, centre half and one of the more notable captains in all United's history. His influence on the team was as great as that in later generations of John Carey and Bobby Charlton; of Meredith on Manchester City in that era; in after years of Danny Blanchflower on Tottenham Hotspur; John Charles on Leeds; Stanley Matthews and Tom Finney on Stoke and Preston respectively; of Billy Wright on Wolves; and of di Stefano and Pele, the South American maestros, on the world game. With Duckworth and Bell to either side of him there was formed a half backline that was to become one of the immortal club triumvirates of football history. In their day they were regarded with the same bated breath as were Colman, Jones and Duncan Edwards in the 1950s.

Roberts, emerging originally from Darlington, was signed in the mysterious dark hours of April 22, 1904 from Grimsby. It was a typically sensational stroke by Mangnall which not only outflanked representatives from Derby County, Nottingham Forest and Manchester City but hoodwinked the sharp eyes of football journalists, usually quick to pick up the scent of impending action. Roberts himself wanted to join only Manchester United (like others after him) and he cost the club £400.

Aged twenty, just under six feet tall and weighing twelve stone six lbs, he was one of the best centre halves in the country. With the skilful qualities of a true, natural footballer, he put his brains where others put their bodies in a game where physical strength counted for too much (as it does today). Interception and creation were his metier, though he played only three times for England, taking second place for much of the time to Billy Wedlock, of Bristol City. But it was as a leader of character that his real influence lay and to him United owed a depth of gratitude.

But Mangnall, the manager, was the effective driving force. When United won promotion at the end of the 1905–6 season the *Manchester Evening News* wrote of him on September 1, 1906:

> For a team to be successful a good secretary is almost as necessary as a good centre forward, and Manchester United are fortunate to possess a gentleman of the ability of Mr. J. E. Mangnall. Prior to coming to Clayton, Mr. Mangnall carried the Burnley club through a most serious crisis, and the honourable position the United now occupy is in a large measure due to his untiring efforts and enterprise. Only those who are acquainted with the inner working of the club can have any conception of the important duties he has been called upon to fulfil, and the fact that since Mr. Mangnall took office the period has been one of steady and continuous progress is sufficient testimony of his ability. Careful to a degree, Mr. Mangnall is yet one of the most keen and enthusiastic sportsmen connected with the game, and by his tact and unfailing courtesy he has done much for the club. His extensive knowledge of the game and its players has been placed unsparingly before his employers, and as a judge of players he has few superiors. Upon Mr. Mangnall fall the duties of secretary and manager, and during his three years' connection with the club he has proved himself a model official. The esteem in which he is held by the players was shown last Saturday when he received a most flattering reception on rising to receive one of the promotion medals.

Having emerged from the careworn chrysalis of Newton Heath to become the Manchester United of 1902 in colours of red and white, their first match was away on September 6 at Gainsborough Trinity whom they beat 1–0 with a goal by Richards with this side: Whitehouse; Stafford (capt.), Read; Morgan, Griffiths, Cartwright; Schofield, Richards, Peddie, Williams, Hurst.

The following Saturday brought the first home game under their new identification. A 20,000 crowd – 8,000 of them under cover as a result of the ground improvements during the fallow months of summer – gathered to see them on their way with another narrow 1–0 win over Burton United, a side then on the slippery slope downwards. That season United ended in fifth position – a leap of ten places on the previous year – and at the end of it there came Mangnall to the managerial hot seat.

A new spirit was abroad and with hope in the air the crowds grew, a 40,000 gate attending a match against Woolwich Arsenal on January 30, 1904. Soon Clayton was chosen for its first representative match, that between the English and Scottish Leagues which moved the directors to have new stands erected on the ground, a task speedily achieved by a hundred workmen.

In 1904, however, there came trouble. The root of it all was a feeling by the players that they were being used as sweated labour, earning no more than £3 a week (and sometimes not that) in winter and £2 in the close season of summer, a poor return when gates reached the 40,000 mark. As a result investigations were held into the affairs of a number of clubs, amongst them Manchester United.

But the real sensation came in the October of that year when a Consultative Committee of the F.A. found Manchester City guilty not only of illegal payments to their players but irregularities in transfer deals with the Glossop club. As a result five directors were suspended for three years and the team – apart from three away matches – were banned at home for a month between October and November.

In 1905 G. H. Lawton, later to become chairman, took Harry Stafford's place on the United board and Mangnall's weekly salary was raised to £5. But rather more dramatic was an F.A. edict which stated: 'W. Meredith to be suspended from August 4, 1905, to April 30, 1908 for having offered a sum of money to an Aston Villa player – A. Leake – to let Manchester City win the match.' Meredith in his defence said that he acted on behalf of the club secretary while Leake added that he took Meredith's suggestion as a joke.

Seven months later another F.A. Commission enquired into a charge that Meredith had demanded his wages while under suspension and had visited the club's dressing rooms. As a result Manchester City put their great man on the transfer list in May 1906. On May 24, United signed him for £500 in spite of the fact that his suspension still had nearly two years to run.

At the end of that same sad month of May the curtain fell on the Manchester City tragedy. Seventeen of their players, who were judged to have received illegal monies, were fined, suspended until January 1, 1907, and further barred from ever playing for City again.

As a consequence the directors put all of them up for sale and a meeting for their disposal was arranged for a particular evening at the Queen's Hotel in Manchester, Piccadilly, a historic building now sadly demolished for redevelopment.

Little can the many visitors who stayed there over the years have pictured, or even known of, the events of that evening. Officials and managers arrived there from all parts of the country and waited patiently in an outer room for the sale to begin. None of them at the time knew that the wily Mangnall of United, had received permission to approach the players in advance so that when at last he emerged from the inner sanctum to march through a silent, weary and dumbfounded gathering outside he had in his pocket the signatures of the Manchester City men he wanted – Sandy Turnbull, the talented forward, Herbert Burgess, George Livingstone, and Jimmie Bannister. Negotiations duly completed, they eventually wore United's red shirts.

So ended a cause célèbre, with United the richer with reinforcements who were to take them to the top of the tree in the near future.

Meanwhile promotion to the First Division (as runners-up to Bristol City) made 1906 a gala year for them. The feat was clinched on April 28 with a 6–0 win over Burton United with the following team: Moger; Holden, Blackstock; Downie, Roberts, Duckworth; Wombwell, Peddie, Sagar, Picken and Wall.

A snowstorm added to the gay feeling of a belated Yuletide in spring; brass bands saluted the heroes; fireworks decorated the sky; the pavilion was awash with red and white balloons, flowers and bunting, and for the first time in history both the Manchester clubs found themselves side by side in the First Division.

In a year of elections local politicians also jumped on the bandwagon of football, realising its hold over the man in the street. A. J. Balfour kicked off in a match against Grimsby, while even Winston Churchill and J. R. Clynes attended a first round F. A. Cup tie against Staple Hill. In every way, indeed, it was a red-letter season for United. Promotion apart, they trounced famous Aston Villa (the holders of the trophy) by 5–1 to reach the last eight of the Cup for the first time since 1897, there to lose 3–2 at home to Woolwich Arsenal.

But even bigger things were just around the corner. As Alfred Gibson and William Pickford wrote of United in Volume 3 of their massive joint work, *Association Football and the men who made it:* 'there never was a more robust "sick child".'

# 9

## *1907–1922*

# *A Taste of Wine and Roses*

THIS WAS THE Edwardian mid-summer which was said to have brought forth football's golden age. On the English international stage alone were giants like Sam Hardy, Aston Villa's famous goalkeeper; the immortal full back partnership of Bob Crompton of Blackburn Rovers, and Jesse Pennington of West Bromwich Albion, the latter a robust octogenarian after the Second World War who once told me as we stood in the board room of the Hawthorns that he remembered the floor under our feet when it was a cornfield in youth; the two outstanding centre halves of their day Charlie Roberts, the Manchester United captain, and little Billy Wedlock, the Bristol City master; Colin Veitch, the classic Newcastle United wing half; the one and only Steve Bloomer, the Derby County goalscoring ace, the Jimmy Greaves of his era; and the stylish amateur, Vivian Woodward, of Tottenham Hotspur, who took over as England's centre forward from that other historic amateur G. O. Smith of the Corinthians and Old Carthusians.

All these are part of the fabric of the game, to say nothing of Billy Meredith, of Wales, and Peter McWilliam and Bobby Walker, of Scotland. There will be things to say still of Meredith as he helped Manchester United to the heights in the years ahead.

In terms of clubs, too, this was the golden age of Newcastle United when in a remarkable spell of seven seasons between 1905 and 1911 they reached five Cup Finals at the Crystal Palace – oddly enough to win only one of them, and that a replay against Barnsley at Everton – and at the same period became League Champions three times. We now also approach the first halcyon days of Manchester United.

This indeed was the turn of the wheel as major honours at last fell to the club who for three decades had fought penury, bankruptcy and hardship, yet somehow survived to come through the mill. Their eventual greatness was enshrined by their corporate club spirit and by giving to others in distress the bone which so often they had needed themselves, so that by 1911 the *Manchester Guardian* was able to write: 'With the same management and many of the same players United have fought their way out of the Second Division of the League, won the English Cup and twice gained the Championship of the First League. Most of the achievements of the eleven have been carried out under the captaincy of Roberts.'

The success of governments, commerce and the armed forces inevitably depends on special men who offer a special leadership. They may be said to be the captains of industry in the broadest sense. In these terms United owe an imperishable debt at this stage of their life to two men off the field – J. H. Davies, the president-chairman of the company for quarter of a century from 1902, and J. E. Mangnall, the secretary-manager from 1903–1912; on the field to Charlie Roberts, the captain, and Billy Meredith. Here was a quartet that raised United to the heights of their day.

One of Mr. Davies's most ambitious and visionary projects was to move the club from Clayton to Old Trafford, where a new ground had to be constructed. This took place in 1910 and it was H. P. Renshaw, the faithful United chronicler, who wrote of Davies in these terms in the mid-1920s:

> It is to this outstanding man that the Manchester public owe one of the best equipped grounds in the country. It was a daring move that Mr. Davies made when he decided to take football into a district only thinly populated and where the 'soccer' code had very few supporters. The removal meant a considerable personal risk, but Mr. Davies, as a sportsman, was anxious to provide the working man with a ground where he could watch a game played under practically ideal conditions. That his vision was a wide and deserving one has been proved by the gradual course of events.
>
> When he took over the reins of office the club was not too strong in a playing sense, but although he had very little knowledge of the Association game he made many wise selections and, helped of course by those with experience, he gradually got together a team which proved itself second to none in the country. It was a remarkable performance when it is considered that within a space of nine or ten years Mr. Davies converted what was a bankrupt concern into one of the most successful clubs in the land.
>
> Mr. Davies, as the head of a very important business concern, spends a surprising amount of time in the interests of the club and in sport generally. When Bramhall Hall looked likely to go the way of many famous mansions, he stepped into the breach to save this beautiful old mansion and made it now his own residence.
>
> A man with a big heart, Mr. Davies has been a real friend of many

> charities, not only in Manchester and Salford, but the surrounding districts. Recently he arranged a special practice match at Old Trafford and when the receipts were counted he doubled the sum out of his own pocket to help the funds of a Maternity Home opened in Stretford. The Salford Royal Hospital, the Ancoats Hospital, Nurses' Homes, and a variety of institutions have always found in him a valuable contributor and it may safely be said that since the United club came into existence the gate receipts of trial games and collections on the ground have realised something like £30,000 for charity.

Clearly charity – in so many ways – has always begun at home with Manchester United. Perhaps it is a trait strongly developed in the north. One has only to glance down the years to discover that Manchester City's help to their neighbour after the blitz of the Second World War had laid Old Trafford waste was matched in reverse a quarter of a century earlier. In October 1920, when Hyde Road became a danger to Manchester City supporters, United promptly offered Old Trafford to their friends across the way for their home fixtures. Furthermore, Mr. Davies recommended strongly that no charge whatsoever, either in rent or percentage of receipts, should be made upon City. It was a free, open and generous offer which however, was finally declined by the City supporters who were prepared to suffocate and be trampled down at Hyde Road rather than luxuriate in the wide spaces of their rivals. But Mr. Furniss, the City chairman, much appreciated 'the kindly and friendly spirit of United which has promoted what we feel to be a most generous offer'.

Some years later (we seem to be leaping ahead; but it is all in this same vein of help to those in need), just before the Second World War, a distastrous fire occurred at Stockport County in 1935. In a later Stockport club programme they remembered: 'It was Manchester United who immediately telephoned us that we could go down each afternoon and use their ground and rooms for training . . . We Stockport people believe that Manchester United are jolly good sports.'

And while one is on the subject, there were the special charity matches arranged by United for the Lord Mayor's Unemployment Relief Fund of 1921 during the period of recession after the First World War, and the game against Airdrieonians on behalf of the Mayor's Million Shilling Fund for hospitals.

All this allusion to charitable works and the fair treatment of players as human beings strikes an answering echo, indeed, in the attitudes today of Busby and his board of directors of the modern United. Remember, in fact, what the likes of Johnny Carey, Bobby

Charlton, Law and others have had to say about being regarded as human beings at Old Trafford and not as mere numbers in a system. This vertebra has been central to United throughout their existence and it has perhaps been their saviour in times of crisis.

The season 1907–8, which was to prove historic, began with a new Manchester United being floated as a limited public company. For a lengthy period, too, the Football Association supervised the affairs of the club until at last a note in the minute book of November 20, 1911 stated: 'The Commission has gone exhaustively into the position of the club and satisfactory arrangements have now been made which will put the club in a proper working condition.' At that point shares were issued to the general public with a capital of £15,000 in £1 shares, while arrangements with the firm of Walker and Pomfray, the brewers (of whom Davies was the head) – the owners of the Old Trafford land – resulted in twenty-four acres and twelves poles being leased to the club at an annual rent of £1,492, with the directors holding the option of purchase within seven years. All these actions were underwritten by the personal guarantee of the generous Mr. Davies which, as it proved, was to lead to problems in the distant future.

In 1907, of course, the first steps towards a limited company had only just begun, while the idea of a move away from Clayton to a new ground was little more than a hopeful whisper. The prospects of all this and of the coming season (which was to be a triumph) were reflected in an article by 'Wanderer' in the *Manchester Evening News* of August 1907:

> Perhaps I had better state at once what I consider the most interesting facts concerning the club at the present time. First, then, the work of making the concern a limited company, in accordance with the desire of the F.A., is now in progress, and will not be finished until we are well into October. Mr. W. R. Deakin has been added to the Board, and the arrangements made will come before the next meeting of the Football Association. Secondly, the club is sure to remain at Clayton another season, but the intention is to move to a new ground as soon as possible, and it is just about a thousand to one that the home chosen will be at Old Trafford, and that when erected it will compare with any ground in the kingdom.
>
> There can be no better site than Old Trafford, where the City and Salford cars meet, the Sale and Altrincham service is tapped, and the cricket ground station would be available. The air will be purer for both the crowd and the players, and everything seems in favour of such a change and a choice. My third fact is that the United have never in their history opened a season with so strong a playing combination as they have at the present time.

> There can be no doubt about this. Only really bad luck with players and injuries can prevent the United from having a successful season. Moger, Bloomfield and Wilcox are all goalkeepers of class, and this position has been more than well looked after by Mr. Mangnall. When Bonthron left for Sunderland Mr. Mangnall, who secured Wall from Barnsley, again went to the Yorkshire colliery town and brought away Stacey, a full back who fairly won his spurs last winter. Thus we have Holden and Burgess as backs, and Stacey as first reserve.
>
> Coming to the half backs, the first thing to be said is that Alec Downie takes a well-deserved benefit during the campaign. A loyal servant, a terrier at work, and a right-down good player – all these compliments have been well earned by the right half back, and Clayton people must make it their business to see that the benefit is a big success. Downie will understudy that fine trio, Duckworth, Roberts and Bell, all of whom are at the top of their profession, and in the prime of life. After his promise of last season, the first-named of the three should win a cap before we see cricket at Old Trafford next May. McGillivray, the second team centre half, is a most promising player, and a good-class reserve left half would remove the only weakness I can see at Clayton.
>
> It was no secret that Bell last season often played when hardly fit because of the lack of a suitable substitute. The forward line ought to be very strong. No club on either side of the Border will have so dangerous an outside pair as Meredith and Wall, and Picken, the two Turnbulls, and Menzies are four fine and robust inside forwards.

Here for the first time United were about to enter a period of genuine stability and success on and off the field. For the younger generation of today only the Manchester after the Second World War – during the 1940s, '50s and '60s – has meant much. Yet that modern spell was no isolated phenomenon. By wise judgment and a shrewd blend of individual abilities Mangnall the secretary-manager – the Busby of his day – was able to build a team that dominated the country for a period of four seasons some seventy years ago. With Meredith, the unforgettable, on the right flank of attack and Wall, another international on the left, both goalscorers, supported by a masterly half back line of Duckworth, Roberts and Bell, United possessed all the ingredients for an outstanding side – five artists and six other good players (plus a strength in depth of reserves) who blended into a composite whole.

When Meredith turned out for the first time in United's red shirt, there seemed to be some premonition that great things lay just around the corner. There was a strange tingle in the air. It was New Year's Day 1907 and vaunted Aston Villa were the visitors. As clear as a signpost to the future, it was Meredith who took the ball almost to the right-hand corner flag, centred to the last refined inch to the unmarked Sandy Turnbull and Villa were beaten 1–0. It was the first rung of a ladder that was to lead to the top.

The Clayton ground was filled with a 40,000 crowd that day and such was the emotive feeling of the occasion that even the normally subdued *Manchester Guardian* dipped its pen in purple ink:

> When Roberts led the United team with its famous recruits on to the field there was a scene of wonderful enthusiasm. A greater roar of cheering has probably never sounded over a football ground, nor probably has a football crowd ever been seen in more remarkable animation. The vast motionless expanse of faces which stretched upwards from the snow-heaped sides became suddenly moved and transformed almost as a sea under a hurricane, and one saw nothing but an amazing tumult of waving arms and handkerchiefs.

United finished eighth that season of 1906–7 to confirm their worthiness of a return to the First Division. It was a case of coming events casting their shadows before them. With only Bonthron, the full back, gone to Sunderland and James Turnbull a new centre forward arrived from Leyton, it was virtually the same side that gave United a flying start to the 1907–8 season.

By the end of Christmas Day they led the field with figures that read:

| | | | | GOALS | | |
|---|---|---|---|---|---|---|
| P | W | D | L | F | A | P |
| 19 | 16 | 1 | 2 | 56 | 24 | 33 |

The only defeats had been 1–2 at Middlesbrough on September 14, and 0–2 at Sheffield Wednesday on November 30, with a 1–1 draw at Notts County on December 14. At one stage they won ten matches in a row.

Things, however, did not run smoothly over the second half of the season. Seven defeats followed – three of them at home – and when Wall missed a penalty kick to lose 0–1 against humble Notts County and was roundly congratulated by several players there was a distinct feeling that the players were not trying.

Patently there was restlessness within the ranks, probably caused by economic worries and the vile playing conditions at Clayton. Yet when it became clear that there was some fire beneath the whispered smoke rings of a move to Old Trafford with the promise of a new stadium planned to hold 100,000 people (that figure was always a grandiose aim; an attempt, I suspect, to move the power of the Football Association from the south to the north and shift the

Cup Final away from the traditional Crystal Palace) oil was poured upon the troubled waters. United duly returned to an even keel and by the end of April they had become League Champions for the first time, a full nine points ahead of the runners-up Aston Villa, with Manchester City third.

## 1907–08, A Summary[1]

The half back line of Duckworth, Roberts and Bell was the real seat of power in this triumphant side which read:

> Moger; Holden, Burgess; Duckworth, Roberts (capt), Bell; Meredith, Bannister, Turnbull (J), Turnbull (A), Wall.

With George Stacey and Vince Hayes in the full back position in place of Holden and Burgess, and Harold Halse taking over from Bannister, this team also won the F.A. Cup the following year.

Harry Moger (goalkeeper): Joined United from Southampton in 1903 and made 242 League appearances in nine seasons. Got another League medal 1910–11 and one F.A. Cup winners' medal 1909.

Dick Holden (right back): A local discovery who was introduced into the side in 1904–05. Career cut short by a knee injury eight years later after 106 League games.

Herbert Burgess (left back): Was capped four times by England during his stay with Manchester City and also helped them win the Cup (1904) before his transfer to United in January, 1907.

Dick Duckworth (right half): 225 League appearances for United as a member of their great half back line. Had remarkable understanding with Billy Meredith. One Cup winners' and two League medals.

Charlie Roberts (centre half): The king-pin of the side and one of the outstanding personalities in the League at this time. There was no more wholehearted player than Charlie Roberts who captained United during this successful period and spurred them on through thick and thin. He was reckoned to have been one of the first men to introduce real craft to the centre half position. His international appearances were limited to three, probably because his outspoken leadership of the newly formed Players' Union (he was their chairman) put him out of favour with the selectors. Born

[1] From *We are the Champions* by Maurice Golesworthy (Pelham Books, 1972).

Darlington and began with his local club before joining Grimsby. Moved to Manchester in 1904 for a fee of £400 and remained until 1913 when he went to Oldham Athletic whom he later managed. Played 291 league games for United; two League medals and one Cup winners' medal.

Alan Bell (left half): The quiet member of United's famous half back line. Born in South Africa but capped for Scotland in eleven seasons with United. After World War I he served as trainer to Manchester City until his death. 297 appearances for United; two League medals and one Cup winners' medal.

Billy Meredith (outside right): Born Chirk. One of the greatest outside rights in the game's history. Created a record number of appearances in the Home International Championship since unbeaten, he played his last match for Wales when in his forty-third year. Joined Manchester City from Northwich Victoria in October 1894, and was one of the City players to move to United in 1906/7. Played for City again during World War I and was officially re-signed by them in July 1921. Completed 682 League appearances before his retirement in 1924, 303 of them for United. Two Cup winners' medals (one with City) and two League medals.

Jim Bannister (inside right): One of the players signed from Manchester City in 1906/7. Remained only two and a half years before his transfer to Preston North End early in season 1909/10.

Jim Turnbull (centre forward): This Scot stayed long enough with United to collect a League medal and a Cup medal before moving on to Bradford in 1910. Had joined United three years earlier from Leyton.

Alec 'Sandy' Turnbull (inside left): Signed from Manchester City in the 1906/7 troubles at Hyde Road, he already had an excellent understanding with Meredith and was well drilled in converting the winger's pin-point centres. Two League medals and two Cup winners' medals (one with City). Killed at Arras during World War I while serving with the Manchester Regiment.

George Wall (outside left): Came from Barnsley in the spring of 1906 and remained until the outbreak of World War I. A winger with a powerful shot, he won seven England caps, two League and one Cup winners' medal.

It had been a memorable season and it was reviewed in some length by 'Wanderer' in the Manchester press:

> When Charles Roberts puts away tonight the big ball so far as League strife in 1907–8 is concerned, he will have much cause for pride and

pleasure, and much on which to reflect in the quiet moments of the future. He will realise that he is the captain of the League Champions, and, if he knows as much of himself as others know of him, he will feel that he more than any man has played a big hand in the winning of the League honours by a club only in its second season as a First Division member.

It may be, too, that the young man from the Darlington district will find his thoughts going back to the day when he left Grimsby Town to come to Manchester of the hard and strenuous years that followed in the Second Division, of the final winning of promotion after desperate fighting, of the proud day on which England chose him to play against Scotland and of other events in his wonderful career in this city. To Charles Roberts more than any man Manchester United owed their promotion, and to him again they chiefly owe their success in heading the League. Yes, I know well the splendid spirit shown by the team as a whole, the fine work done by every man on the side week after week, the wonderful skill and devotion to duty of Meredith, and the brilliant goalscoring and nursing of George Wall shown by Alec Turnbull.

Realising all this, I yet feel it to be my opinion that Roberts has been the man of the club. He has led the side with an enthusiasm that has put life and confidence into the team. In match after match his energy has been remarkable, and he has been great alike in attack and defence – a sixth forward and a third back, Roberts missed caps this season because of injury at an unfortunate time. That he is the greatest centre half playing, a man of the judgment of Meredith will tell you without hesitation. In the loss of the caps he might have had he will be solaced by the medal of the captain of the League of Champions.

No one will ever know – they cannot – how bitterly William Meredith felt the ingratitude of the Manchester City crowd to him during his appearances at Hyde Road in the Manchester United colours. A man proud of his prowess, proud of all he has done for gallant little Wales, for the City and for United, Meredith felt very deeply the unkindness of those who once made him their idol. And before the recent League match at Hyde Road he told both the United officials and the players that he did not wish to face such an ordeal. They had hard work to persuade him to play, and it was in a reluctant spirit that he took the field.

How fortunate it was that he did so. To the delight of Meredith, of the United team, and, surely, also of every true sportman on the ground, the crowd seemed most anxious to convince the famous Welshman that he still had a warm corner in their hearts, and as he left the field at the interval and again at the close of the game they simply rose to him, and gave him a magnificent reception. Everyone felt as pleased as Punch about it, and I believe that Meredith himself could not speak all that he felt in those great minutes, for him, if he were to talk for a week. It would be impossible to speak too highly of all that Meredith had done for the United. Played on as he never was before by opponents, in the last half of the season especially, he has yet maintained his world-wide reputation as the greatest forward playing. There can be no doubt that in the course of a season many fouls were perpetrated on a man like Meredith, and his escape from injury is a tribute to his agility and his watchfulness.

Not long ago Colin Veitch, of Newcastle, remarked in my hearing, 'Ah, well, you know, Meredith can carry a forward line along himself' – a fine tribute from a good judge. The only benefit Meredith ever had did not realise more than £70 years ago. I hope to see him have a great benefit with his present club some day, and also to see the Welsh Association recognise in a practical way all that this loyal son of the Land of the Leek has done for them.

I should like to say something also about Alex Turnbull, who has scored so many goals himself and has made Wall a reputation. I hope the latter realises the fact. A man of big shoulders and quick feet and active brain, 'Sandy' is a great player, and a more unselfish inside man I never saw. A great opportunist, with 'class' written all over his football! A Scot said to me the other day, 'Glasgow folk say that if Scotland had played Quinn in the centre with Sandy Turnbull and Wilson on his left, England would have been heavily beaten.'

The falling-off in form after the defeat at Fulham in the fourth round of the Cup ties was noticeable and I suggest it was but natural. The men had set their hearts on going further, and the failure, where they had not expected it, was a great blow to them. I shall not forget how desperately Meredith and Sandy Turnbull tried to turn the tide of the game. Then came the disappointing benefit for Bell and Downie, and this undoubtedly greatly upset the men, who thought the match a poor reward for such services as had been rendered by the two players concerned.

All the time the players had been justly dissatisfied with the Clayton ground, and the prospect of a new home by next Christmas has helped Mr. Mangnall in the signing-on task. The bad conduct of a section of the spectators too, has at times incensed the players. This class of spectator is unfortunately to be found in most big crowds, and they do great harm to the game. It would be a very proper action on the part of officials to retaliate by ejecting from the ground persons who do not behave decently.

That reference to bad crowd behaviour may come as an eye-opener to those who have come to regard hooliganism and violence as a modern trend. Not so. To be sure, there were no instances of stabbing and blood-letting, or the destruction of public property as nowadays. But crowds could be bad-tempered, as was reported in the *Manchester Evening Chronicle* on February 12, 1906, under headlines of 'Manchester United men mobbed. Mud and stones thrown'.

The South-West corner of Yorkshire is obtaining an unenviable notoriety for unsportsmanlike methods. First the Preston footballers were given a bad 'quarter of an hour' at Sheffield, and on Saturday evening the Manchester United team met with an even worse experience.

The Manchester men had signally defeated the Bradford City team in the afternoon, and the vigour enthused into the game evidently had its effect on the spectators, a large section of whom waited outside the enclosures until the visiting team appeared and expressed their disapproval in no uncertain fashion.

Bonthron, the Manchester full back, came in for a large share of the crowd's attention. Escorted by police and surrounded by his colleagues, he was making for the vehicle which was to convey them away when he was struck by one of the crowd, who was immediately seized and made to give his name and address.

To reach vehicles the Manchester players had to walk up a narrow thoroughfare leading to the main road. Here it was that people congregated, and the appearance of the United players was the signal for hooting and an angry demonstration. Stones and mud were thrown, and players and officials were quickly bespattered with the black slime.

The attitude of the Bradford officials and players cannot be too highly commended. They protected Bonthron from the mob at great personal risk, and some were said to have been struck by missiles thrown by someone in the crowd.

The uproar was great, and mud was thrown until Bonthron's clothes were splashed from head to foot. Finally that player was escorted into the yard of the Belle Vue Hotel by his friends. Here he entered a cab, and Mr. P. O'Rourke seating himself on the box, the vehicle was driven through the crowd assembled outside the hotel at a rapid rate.

The other Manchester players and officials followed in cabs, and a stone was hurled through the window of the conveyance in which were the president of the Football League, Mr. J. J. Bentley; the secretary to the Manchester United club, Mr. E. Mangnall; and Mr. J. Taylor, a member of the committee.

Charlie Roberts, the Manchester United captain, said: 'You can't imagine what it was like. I have never experienced anything like it. I pushed several men away who were going for Bonthron. I was glad to get out of it. I feel sorry for Peter O'Rourke (the Bradford secretary) and the other officials. There is no doubt they did all in their power.'

Mr. J. H. Davies, the president of the Manchester club, was present at the match with several ladies. He says it is the worst experience he has ever passed through, and the lesson taught him, so far as Bradford is concerned, was a severe one, and he will certainly never repeat the experiment of taking ladies to Valley Parade.

Mr. Mangnall, the secretary of the Manchester club, has written to the Bradford City directors as follows:

'Our directors desire me to express extreme regret at the unpleasant proceedings which took place after our match on Saturday. They were disgraceful. At the same time they wish to exonerate your directors, and indeed beg to thank them most heartily for the steps they took to protect the members of our team and officials.'

Nor was this crowd unruliness confined to England. In May 1908, perhaps as a reward for winning the League title, the United team were taken on a Continental tour of eight matches played in Prague, Vienna and Budapest. In the last of these a 12,000 crowd – the biggest seen in Hungary until then – got out of control as United ran up a 7–0 victory under a Magyar referee who seemed to play to his own rules, could not speak English and gave ridiculous foul after foul against the United team.

Clearly the assembly did not relish the dribbling nor the supposed hard play of the visitors. At the final whistle they made an ugly rush at the Manchester players, one of whom later described it all in a letter to the *Daily Dispatch* of May 18, 1908:

> Although mounted police and others with swords did their best to protect us a few of us were hit by people standing near the entrance to the dressing tent.
>
> The fun really commenced when we were leaving the ground. As soon as we got into the landaus waiting outside the gates a wild and apparently uncivilised mob did all they possibly could to maim us. Stones and brickbats were thrown at the occupants of each carriage on leaving the ground for our hotel, and although some of the party received rather nasty knocks, fortunately nobody was seriously hurt.
>
> The matter will probably be reported to the British Consul here. As things stand it is not safe to be left to the mercy of a howling mob who make no secret of carrying revolvers and daggers about with them.

So much for the passions aroused by a game of football. All too grimly we have come to live with it in our times. But to read of it happening seventy years ago changes the gentle picture of the so called 'good old days'.

Meanwhile at home there was much activity back stage as the 1908–9 season got under way. There were the details of the United as a new limited company, with many a busy F.A. legal eagle shoving his oar into the arrangements. More exciting, however, to the general public and to the players themselves were the proposed plans for the new Old Trafford ground to be erected.

It was to hold 80,000 people (not 100,000, the original dream); there were to be refreshment bars, even a tea room for the customers, and an electric lift for the use of officials and reporters – a far cry from the days not long before when it was decided to put in a single telephone at Clayton for the use of the secretary only and not the press. One can only guess how match reports reached newspaper offices then. As for the players, there were plans for hot and cold plunge baths in tiled changing rooms; a gymnasium and massage room; and rooms for recreation and billiards. All this was to be a paradise compared with the old Newton Heath days with the half mile trot from the changing room and single tin bath tub of the Three Crowns Hotel; a sharp change, too, from Bank Street, Clayton, where only a short time ago it was agreed to instal a fan in the dressing room! Old Trafford was to be a palace fit for champions.

To underline their quality as a side United now also proceeded to win the F.A. Cup in 1908/9 for the first time in their history – two of the major prizes of the game in successive seasons. They achieved it with Clayton still as their home but with one eye on their promised new land.

The previous season – when they won the League – had seen them fall to Fulham 2–1 in London in the quarter-final of the Cup, a tie they should have won hands down but for the outstanding goalkeeping of Leslie Skene under the Fulham crossbar. This time, however, United made no mistake as they dealt with Brighton and Hove 1–0, Everton 1–0, Blackburn Rovers 6–1, Burnley 3–2 in a replay, Newcastle United 1–0 in the semi-final at Bramall Lane, Sheffield, and finally Bristol City 1–0 before a 67,000 crowd at the Crystal Palace.

If there was one slice of luck on the way it came at Turf Moor, Burnley, in the quarter-final. The ground was a sheet of ice and many thought that the referee, W. H. Bamlett, should never have started the match. To add to the difficulties snow began to fall soon after the kick-off and grew thicker as time wore on. Finally, with only eighteen minutes left and Burnley leading 1–0, Bamlett called it a day but was so exhausted himself that he required Charlie Roberts to blow the final whistle for him. So did the elements and the fates conspire to rescue United. A fatalist would have said that the trophy was destined for them from that moment.

Two other incidents on the way deserve a note. In the opening tie against Brighton the normally studious Meredith was judged to have charged an opponent, E. Stewart, unfairly, was reported to the F.A. and in spite of a strong plea by United, was suspended for one month from February 2.

The other event was one of true sportsmanship worthy of a side like Newcastle. Already they had reached the final three times in the previous four seasons; now in 1909 they were heading for their third League championship title in five years. What a scalp to acquire as United faced them in the semi-final!

Again the elements were partly involved. Manchester United held on to a 1–0 lead as the heavens opened over the closing stages. Having survived to reach the final at last United were in no hurry to leave the ground: there was some celebrating to be done first in the dressing room. Yet when at last they emerged, with the rain still bucketing down, they found the Newcastle men sitting in an open brake to see them off, soaked to the skin after a wait of a full quarter hour. As their conquerors drove away every Geordie was on his feet cheering the United team to the echo and wishing them good luck for the final. It is a moment like that which lifts man above himself.

The climax itself came at the Crystal Palace on April 24. Although Bristol City stood eighth in the First Division and Manchester had slumped from their pinnacle of the previous year to thirteenth, it was United who took the field as favourites. They had experience and the big names and that victory over Newcastle behind them; Bristol could only point to the redoubtable little Billy Wedlock at centre half.

At any rate to add interest to the occasion here were two newcomers to the final and after a number of years the element of North v. South rivalry was renewed. But first, on the morning of the match, came these impressions of a correspondent on a London newspaper:

> The pleasant, open surroundings of the Crystal Palace make for humour and gaiety. The masses of people on the slopes present an illusion of shrubberies with here and there a rhododendron blossom – really a gigantic, heavily coloured hat worn by some London working girl. When the Spurs played Sheffield United it was possible to follow the play merely by listening to the cheers and counter cheers. So it should be again today thanks to the renewal of the North and South *motif*. The voice of the North is deeper, more resonant than that of the South, the latter being pitched high above the former and having a distinctly nasal intonation. When both are heard during a prolonged episode of exciting play the northern basses and baritones supply a pulsating drone-note in the fantasia of enthusiasm. A piece of foul play elicits a colossal yelp from the many-eyed monster – it is a singularly alarming and ugly sound which shows that it is an English monster after all. Instances of physical mimicry (such as the lifting of a leg on the part of a score of spectators when a high kick is made) are frequent.
>
> The northern contingent pay great attention to the matter of commissariat. They bring stone jars of strong ale and sandwiches an inch thick, packed in the little wicker baskets which are also used for conveying carrier pigeons. As a rule the northerners and southerners,

> though they never fraternise, suffer each other gladly. Now and again there is an altercation when the expression of a London clerk, described as a 'gormless gooby' by some Lancashire factory hand, is worth studying. The writer remembers a big Yorkshireman, accosted by a mechanical brain worker in a high stiff collar, hit off the other in the charming phrase 'more clout nor pudding . . .'
>
> Assuredly every student of humanity will find much to interest him in the crowd of a Cup Final.

That may have been so, but there was little to interest the student of the game in that Final. United won a disappointing, hard game with a single goal scored by Sandy Turnbull before half time. Only two men shone for their skill – Wedlock of Bristol, and Meredith, who thus added a second Cup winners' medal to the one he had gained with Manchester City five years earlier.

Turnbull's fitness had been in doubt up to the last. The final decision was left not to the player himself but to Charlie Roberts. 'Let him play,' said the skipper. 'He might get a goal and if he does we can afford to carry a passenger.' In the event it proved to be the wisdom of Solomon in a match where United provided most of the skill and Bristol all the physical challenge. Of Meredith even *The Times* lowered its guard to enthuse: 'He played beautiful football; his clever footwork, rare control of the ball, sure passes and long shots at goal gave the deadliness to his side's attack.'

United's accent was on attack even then.

Though that was the end of a United triumph in the Cup for thirty-nine long years until Johnny Carey led his side up to the Wembley Royal Box in 1948, it was not quite the end of this particular story. There was a sting in its tail.

For the season 1910–11 a new trophy was presented for competition by the F.A. and the other presented to Lord Kinnaird to mark the completion of his twenty-one years as President of the Association. The reason was that the F.A. discovered that the design, without their authority, had been pirated two years earlier by wealthy United well-wishers in Manchester.

Naturally the Association disapproved strongly, but could take no steps in the matter since the design of the Cup at that time was not copyright. Their answer was to pass the following resolution at Overstrand on July 9, 1910: 'That the present Football Association Challenge Cup, having been duplicated without the consent of the Association; be withdrawn from Competition and a new Cup offered, the design of which should be registered.'

The Finance Committee, having been requested to obtain designs for the approval of the Council, reported on September 5, 1910 that they had decided to ask for such designs to be submitted not later than December 1. The value of the Cup was to be fifty guineas, and they stipulated that the pattern and workmanship should be of greater consideration than the weight. So was a new trophy fashioned.

This third Cup bought by the F.A. is perhaps rather more handsome than its predecessors. It is after the style of an antique votive urn, weighs 175 ounces, and is nineteen inches high, exclusive of plinth. The body has a serious of bold flutings, surmounted by four panels decorated with rich bunches of grapes and vine leaves. The lid is decorated similarly to match the body, and is surmounted by a knob which is practically a small replica of the Cup itself. The only lettering upon the body of the trophy is the inscription on the front, 'The Football Association Challenge Cup'. The ebony plinth bears a massive silver band on which are inscribed the names of all previous winners. Chosen from an enormous number of designs and models submitted by the most renowned silversmiths in the kingdom, it was the work of Messrs. Fattorini and Sons, of Bradford. What could have been more appropriate that its first winners should be Bradford City? An odd coincidence somehow when one considers that never before or since has this Yorkshire town been concerned with the Cup Final!

Those were days of succeeding stress and strain in a changing social and economic scene. Trouble fed on trouble. The next major crisis to darken the horizon involved the Players' Union. Revived as an active body, it re-entered the picture in season 1907–8. At a meeting on March 9, 1908, F.A. consent was given to the Union with the proviso that its balance sheet be submitted to the Association annually.

But no sooner had this consent and protestation of good wishes been expressed than a new problem was precipitated by the affiliation of the Players' Union with the Federation of Trades Unions in 1909. Feeling themselves at the mercy of a federation which might suspend football operations at any time because of a strike of any of its other bodies, the F.A., the League and the clubs for once closed ranks.

The F.A. withdrew its recognition of the Union, suspended its chairman and secretary, and ordered all its members to resign from the Union or their registrations would be cancelled. The players stood firm and at a mass meeting of 200 of them at the Albion Hotel, Manchester, on August 28, under the chairmanship of J. T. Jones, of the Municipal Employers' Association, a vote of thanks was accorded to the Manchester United players in particular –

twenty-seven of whom were then under suspension – for the firm stand they had taken on behalf of the Union.

With only three days left to the start of the season there was deadlock. A strike threatened. It was anticipated that players at Newcastle, Sunderland, Middlesbrough Everton, Liverpool, Chelsea and others would follow the Manchester United lead and there was a possibility that the clubs would have to break from the F.A. Meanwhile United officials had already cancelled their opening fixture against Bradford City and with two other home games also due to be played at Clayton within six days against Bury and Notts County the club would expect to lose some £2,000 in receipts.

Happily on August 31, the very eve of the season's start, a truce was reached. The Players' Union was given recognition again; cases were to be permitted to be taken to court under the Workmen's Compensation Act; all suspensions were to be removed; and arrears of lost pay to be made good. In all this turmoil the United players, led stoutly by Charlie Roberts, came out with flying colours and when they duly took the field to face Bradford City on September 1, they were given a rousing reception for sticking to their principles. By their determination these United pioneers came to be known as 'the Thin Red Line'.

On January 22, 1910, United played their last match at Clayton. There was little nostalgia, no shedding of tears. The nearby chimney stacks as ever belched forth their fumes; Tottenham Hotspur were well beaten 5–0; Meredith, who had not been on the mark for a year, scored at last; and only 5,000 sturdy people turned up to take a last thankful sniff of the chemical vapours.

A month later, on February 19, Old Trafford raised its curtain on a glittering new stage. Liverpool were the visitors and a 50,000 crowd invaded the stadium, 5,000 of whom it was estimated sneaked in without paying.

Admission was 6d; to the covered stand 1s., 1s. 6d. and 2s.; while a number of reserved seats in the centre of the stand cost 5s. As the *Manchester Guardian* wrote on the following Monday morning:

> Along Clayton Road they came and over Trafford Bridge in trams, buses, cabs, taxis, costers' carts, coal lorries, and all manner of strange things on wheels. Those who had not had the good fortune to find a cab or to meet a friend with a costers' cart walked it – a great stream spreading wide over the footpaths into the road, the despair of already over-harassed tram drivers, the delight of sundry small boys who trotted alongside cheerfully offering to do 'twenty cart-wheels an' a "roll-over" for a 'a'penny'.

> The grandstand itself was a new luxury unknown till then, with stewards to direct V.I.P.s to 'plush tip-up seats' as though in a theatre or cinema. The pitch itself – after the years of mud and glue at Newton Heath and Clayton – resembled the surface of a bowling green.

United, in red, began brilliantly with two goals from Sandy Turnbull (fed as usual by Meredith's exact centre) and Homer inside quarter of an hour. Liverpool, in white, reduced the lead, but Wall put Manchester two ahead again with an oblique shot from the left wing. Yet, as so often over the years, it was Liverpool's stamina and team spirit that told in the end as goals by Goddard and Stewart (two) gave them a great 4–3 win.

It was a disappointment for the hosts, but as the *Manchester Guardian* remarked:

> In point of fact the United were no more 'at home' than Liverpool were. This was merely a house-warming, so to speak, and of the two teams Liverpool seemed the better suited by the extraordinary 'fastness' of the ground. It is a long stride, of course, from the quagmires of Clayton to the springy lawns of Old Trafford. It is more than likely that when United do begin to feel at home on their new pitch visiting sides will fare as the United themselves fared on Saturday. The team will have to see to it. These 'swell' grounds need some living up to.

In due course this is precisely what United proceeded to do. Meanwhile in that summer of 1910 permission was granted to *Pathe Gazette* to take cinematograph pictures on the ground – a first step into wider publicity – as a fresh harvest of new players were signed on the staff under the vigilant eye of Louis Rocca, who had advanced from tea-boy at the tender age of ten years at the original Newton Heath home to the position of chief scout by 1907. For forty years, until his death in 1950, that had been his vital role – the man who picked good apples or tender apples for United's barrel and saw them grow. His service to the club as he watched it develop from one century to the next will forever remain a memorial to his loyalty.

The new men were Hofton, a full back from Glossop; 'Knocker' West, centre forward from Nottingham Forest; Dean, a goalkeeper from Eccles; Green and Hodge, half backs respectively from Chesterfield and Scotland; Aspinall, an all-rounder from Southport, and Nuttall, son of the club's assistant trainer. Of these West made the biggest mark as he took over at centre forward to become the leading scorer in 1910–11 with nineteen goals and the best marksman in four of the five seasons leading up to the First World

War. Sadly his outstanding career was ended by an alleged complicity in a bribery scandal on the outbreak of hostilities. He never played football again.

When United beat Newcastle 2–0 at Old Trafford on October 15, 1910 – a match set aside for the benefit of two long-serving and popular players Holden and Picken – they again stood on the threshold of success. It was their seventh win in eight opening matches of the season and it took them to the top of the League, a point ahead of Sunderland. Although money was still tight with rising overheads and an overdraft of £11,000, the season unwound on rising hopes.

In the end it proved to be a dramatic climax, with the outcome decided on the very last day and Aston Villa again going for their second successive title.

On the final day Villa had one more point than the United, but while the Midland club were defeated 3–1 at Liverpool, the United's players rose to the occasion and soundly thrashed a powerful Sunderland side 5–1 at Old Trafford. Since Sunderland finished in third position on this score alone United fully deserved their second League title in four years.

## 1910–11, A Summary[1]

Their points total this season was identical to that of 1907–8 but now there were no long runs of success as had been enjoyed on that earlier occasion.

The mantle of goalscorer-in-chief was taken over this season by Enoch 'Knocker' West, a centre forward with a cannon-ball shot who had previously claimed nearly a century of League goals for Nottingham Forest.

Other changes in the side from that which had won the title in 1908 were at full back where Holden and Burgess had been succeeded by Stacey and Donnelly, while Harold Halse was preferred to Bannister at inside right.

Team: Moger; Donnelly, Stacey; Duckworth, Roberts, Bell; Meredith, Halse, West, Turnbull (A.), Wall.

The new men were:

Arthur Donnelly (full back): Never really established himself as a first team regular with United although in this, his best season with the club, he made fifteen First Division appearances.

George Stacey (full back): One of the most reliable full backs in

[1] From *We are the Champions* by Maurice Golesworthy (Pelham Books, 1972).

the First Division, this cool and resourceful defender was signed from Barnsley in 1907 and was in the Cup winning team of 1909. Remained at Old Trafford until the war, making 239 League appearances.

Harold Halse (inside right): Born Leytonstone and began his career with Barking. Southend United secured him and in 1906–7 alone he scored a record ninety-one goals for that club. Joined United in 1907 and won a Cup and League medal. Had a season with Aston Villa in 1912–13, leading their scoring list and gaining another Cup medal before moving to Chelsea and appearing on the losing side in the Cup Final of 1915. Ended his league career with Charlton Athletic from 1921 to 1923. One England cap.

Enoch West (centre forward): One of the most prolific goalscorers in the immediate pre-World War I period. He had been a great favourite at Nottingham Forest for five seasons before joining United in 1910. Born Hucknall, he was later suspended by the F.A. for the alleged 'fixing' of a match, but his libel case against two newspapers was dismissed by the judge.

It had been a close thing, indeed, but what an end to a season, with the final table reading:

| | | | | | Goals | | |
|---|---|---|---|---|---|---|---|
| | P | W | D | L | F | A | Pts |
| Manchester United | 38 | 22 | 8 | 8 | 72 | 40 | 52 |
| Aston Villa | 38 | 22 | 7 | 9 | 69 | 41 | 51 |
| Sunderland | 38 | 15 | 15 | 8 | 67 | 48 | 45 |

This triumph led United to an outing by motor to the Chester races, yet another example of thoughtful appreciation for a job well done, shown by Mr. Davies and his fellow directors at Old Trafford.

Yet all this was to prove the end of a beginning for United. Having lived at the heights for a spell they were now about to return to the shadows of the valley. This is the nature of football which tends to move in cycles, either short or long. In the case of United it proved to be the latter – forty-one years before the League title returned to Old Trafford; thirty-nine years before the Cup was recaptured.

Life itself for ever remains restless. The old order changes. War clouds were now gathering on the far horizon and all too soon the Europe that had found a measure of stability and peace was to be lost for ever. New forces of aggressive nationalism were on the march; new ideologies were to infest the world.

In football terms, too, the shining raiment that had clothed Manchester United for a period of six years now began to tarnish and wither. The first step in this disintegration came with the departure of J. E. Mangnall, the manager, who took his magic touch across the way to Manchester City in August 1912.

A wise man, able to see through and beyond situations, perhaps Mangall sensed what was in the wind. At Meredith's benefit match at Old Trafford in September 1912 it had already become clear for one thing that the stupendous United half back line of Duckworth, Roberts and Bell was on the wane. A year later, with age beginning to show its mark, it was broken up.

Roberts, the giant and inspiring leader of the halcyon days, was transferred to Oldham though he continued to live for a number of years in Manchester where he opened a thriving tobacconist business (established 1907) which his grandson, Ted Roberts, still runs to this day. Bell went to Blackburn Rovers, and Duckworth, left to his own devices and memories, at first declined to play on but later withdrew his refusal.

At the heart of it all, though, it was the departure of Mangnall, a much sought after character, that seemed to start the decline. It was the collapse of a pack of cards. From the moment that he left until United almost inevitably suffered relegation at the end of season 1921–22, their final placings in the First Division (with the war intervening) were thirteenth, fourth, fourteenth, eighteenth, twelfth, thirteenth, and twenty-second. In this same phase, too, they reached the quarter-final of the Cup only once and were knocked out of the first round on four occasions. How strange the change from major to minor as Old Trafford began to play in a doleful key.

When Mangall left even Meredith – himself well beyond the first flush of youth – wrote an appreciation of him in the *Weekly News* of August 31, 1912:

> The Manchester United team will, of course, greatly miss Ernest Mangnall, who has left us to manage Manchester City with an advance on the already handsome salary he was receiving. Even though he and the Directors of the Manchester United have not agreed on a number of matters, there is no doubt that Ernest Mangnall was a very fine manager. No man in the country, except perhaps Will Cuffe, of Everton, could have run such a club with so much success on so low a cost. I should say that Mr. Mangnall and Mr. Cuffe stand alone in the managerial world. Mr. Cuffe is the best man at the clerical side of the business – his legal training has, of course, been of great value to him in

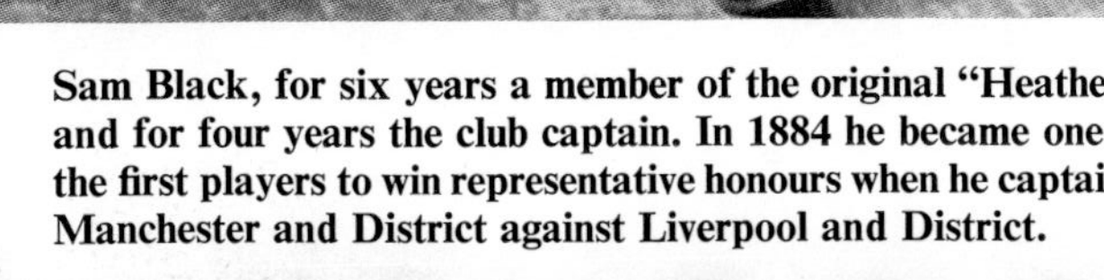

Sam Black, for six years a member of the original "Heathens" and for four years the club captain. In 1884 he became one of the first players to win representative honours when he captained Manchester and District against Liverpool and District.

The goal that won the F.A. Cup against Bristol City at Crystal Palace in April 1909. Halse, right, hammered a shot which came back off the underside of the bar to Turnbull, left, who volleyed home over goalkeeper Clay's head.

F.A. Cup winners 1908–09: back row, J. E. Magnall (Secretary), Bacon, Picken, Edmonds, Mr Murray (Director), Moger, Mr J. H. Davies (Chairman), Homer, Mr Lawton (Director), Bell, Mr Deakin (Director); centre: Meredith, Duckworth, Roberts, Turnbull, West, Stacey; front row: Whalley, Hofton, Halse, Wall.
The triumphant return to Manchester, Charlie Roberts holding the F.A. Cup.

> his work – and Mr. Mangnall is about the best judge of a player serving a club in England. Apart from that, the new Manchester City manager knows how to buy and sell at the best profit to his own club. He should do well at Hyde Road, although it is obvious that he has a very great task there. If he succeeds he will probably make enemies, because it is well known that he is to have a free hand. I know him, and I feel confident that he will not be content until the club is run at a big profit.

Nor was Meredith inclined to leave his opinions there. The pen in his hand and, as it were, the ball at his feet, he branched out into the subject of rising transfer fees, a matter which still exercises many minds in this age of senseless, ultra inflation.

> Still, although Ernest Mangnall has gone there is nothing wrong with Old Trafford. Manchester United are quietly ready for the season, and know that a new manager will be soon appointed. Mr. J. H. Davies, the man at the wheel, who has found all the money in advance, is more confident than ever he was. The club actually paid £12,000 off the ground debt last season, although a profit of £800 remains, and there is to be a bridge into the adjoining town of Salford, with a big car shed on the ground for Salford cars before the season closes. Even now the United are tempting certain clubs to part with men at offers of over £1,000 for each player.
>
> And this brings me to a matter much in my mind. Has it ever struck the reader how tremendously the value of the first-class player has ascended of late? Take twelve or fifteen years back. Were the giants of those days ever transferred at £800 or at four figures at £1,600? Rather not. Was Tom Brandon, one of the greatest backs who ever did or ever will kick a ball ever worth to his club a four-figure transfer fee? or Doig at his best, Jimmy Cowan, Steve Smith, Dunning, Jack Reynolds, Jimmy Crabtree, Charlie Sagar, Darrock, Fred Geary, ay, or any of the old-time stalwarts? No, my friends. Clubs had not the money and had not the necessity then to produce before their patrons the best possible talent they could get hold of. Why is it today? Because, great though the interest in the game was fifteen, twelve, and ten years ago, it is now four-fold. There is no comparison. Gates are three times the size. Clubs have to make bigger grounds and get better talent, and for years the clubs have been cutting each other's throats in the race for success, and they have run the price of good palyers up to their present figures. The harder the clubs compete the bigger grows the price of the men who draw the gates. Only the other day a club manager said to me, 'If we sign a new player he will have to be a man who will be an advertisement in himself, and that is four figures or nothing'. Now, I think that remark was very significant, and that shows the tendency of the clubs at the present time and shows it rightly. The bigger the price, of course, the greater the iniquity of the transfer fee.

That was Meredith talking sixty-five years ago. It might have all been said only yesterday!

What took place on the field of play in the seasons shortly before the outbreak of war was virtually nothing. The end of the 'golden age' was on its way. Yet in spite of it, Old Trafford remained a Mecca.

In 1911 the replayed Cup Final between Bradford City and Newcastle United was held there. In 1915 it was also the scene of the last final before the curtain was lowered for four years on serious football. On a grey, wet Manchester afternoon Sheffield United took the trophy back to Yorkshire with a 3–0 win over Chelsea. In a drab, strained, off-key atmosphere it became known as the 'Khaki Cup Final' and when Lord Derby presented the prize and the medals at the finish he took the opportunity for some military recruiting and an appeal for national loyalty, 'You have played', he said, 'with one another and against one another for the Cup. Play with one another for England now.'

Old Trafford itself, indeed, must for ever stand as a memorial to the vision and financial help of J. H. Davies. It was his dream of a stately home worthy of a club and of a game he had come to love. It was a dream fulfilled in reality.

Before its construction J. J. Bentley was consulted and it was as well that he was since the original scheme would have made the ground twice as costly. The first plans aimed at making the terraces far higher all the way round and also included a cycle track. Bentley wisely reduced these plans. Even so the ground cost some £60,000.

The site itself, however, had been decided by Davies himself and the stadium lay on land of great and constantly increasing value. Its main drawback was that no entrance existed on the Salford side and for this there came lengthy negotiations.

Old Trafford, however, soon became a magnet. The 50,000 crowd for the 1915 Cup Final apart, other major attractions at that time proved to be:

1911 – Manchester United v. Aston Villa: Attendance 65,101; receipts £2,464 4s. 10d.

1911 – Bradford City v. Newcastle United (replayed Cup Final): Attendance 56,607; receipts £3,487.

1912 – Manchester United v. Blackburn Rovers: Attendance 59,300; receipts £3,114 5s.

The ground was designed by Mr. Leach, an architect who for many years made a study of this class of work, and with its gangways, huge terraces, splendid barrier system, great stand containing 750 tip-up cushioned chairs in the centre, and holding altogether over 15,000 people it made a magnificent spectacle at any time. Apart from the fine arrangement and construction of the stands the turf was remarkably good, recovering from bad weather, and heavy usage very quickly. The players' dressing rooms and bathrooms had no equal in the country, and altogether Old Trafford constituted a monument to the progress of football and an athletic arena of which Manchester could well be proud.

The man who eats cake has to pay for the luxury, and so the Manchester United directors found the task of paying off the debt on the ground a heavy burden on the club, leaving little on which to run the concern. This was an anxious task. Many changes had taken place since Old Trafford was opened. Mr. J. E. Mangnall was now the Manchester City secretary, and the secretary at Old Trafford was Mr. J. J. Bentley, while Mr. John Robson became the club manager. The directors were Mr. J. H. Davies (president), Mr. W. R. Deakin (chairman), Mr. G. H. Lawton, and Mr. H. P. Hardman.

It was now a time of troubles, change and farewell. The gradual break-up of a fine team and the departure of Mangnall apart, it was like the spin of a roulette wheel as figures came and went, some claimed by death.

In 1911 Harry Stafford, the former captain of the 1890s, who had played so major a role in interesting Mr. Davies in the club and turning him into a fairy godfather, waved goodbye to his not inconsiderable past as he departed overseas to a new life for reasons of health. In consideration of his unswerving loyalty over the years the directors voted him £50 as a helping hand in his new venture.

In 1914 J. R. Robson came from Brighton as manager until in 1921 he retired through ill health to give way to John Chapman, who arrived from Airdrieonians. In 1916 J. J. Bentley, a grand old man of football, president of the League, resigned as secretary and died on September 2, 1918. In 1920 W. R. Deakin also passed away to be succeeded as chairman by G. H. Lawton. Father Time was busy with his scythe.

Before moving on one cannot fail to mention two attendances at Old Trafford of remarkable contrast. Boxing Day, 1920, a massive crowd of 70,504, paying £4,824, saw United play Aston Villa in a League match. At the end of that season 1920–21, Old Trafford returned the lowest official crowd ever recorded in the Football League – thirteen people! United, themselves, were not involved. The directors had loaned the ground to Stockport County whose own arena was under suspension at the time. The Second Division game was between Stockport and Leicester City and proved a goalless draw. Unlucky thirteen indeed!

At the end of that 1921 season, too, there came the great parting of the ways. In every degree it was a sad farewell after so much triumph and so many imperishable memories. In a squabble over back pay, in which Meredith showed his pig-headed, inflexible determination over what he considered to be his rights, the United directors regrettably decided to give him a free transfer.

So it was that at the age of forty-eight Meredith reverted to the second chapter of his three lives as a player in a career which had begun with Northwich Victoria in 1894. After that had followed Manchester City, then Manchester United. Now, in August 1921, he retraced his steps to become once more a City player, and on August 25, a 35,000 crowd gathered at Hyde Road to see the return not of a prodigal son, but of a living legend.

It was an event that nearly forty years on was to be echoed when another immortal outside right Stanley Matthews – later knighted – returned from Blackpool to his native Stoke City. The average gate at the Victoria Grounds was quadrupled that day while bill posters in the town carried two simple words: 'He's back'.

Reams have been written over the years about Meredith. To those who would doubt his ability to survive in the modern game it is sufficient surely to say that a true genius will survive in his own time in any age.

His knack of running outside the touchline while keeping the ball in play within the boundaries was a trick to confound many a full back – something which he copied perhaps from Billy Bassett, the famous West Bromwich Albion outside right.

The incessant chewing of a tooth pick, the devilish accuracy of his centres from the corner flag, and his sudden changes of course inwards instead to shoot a goal were other facets of his play always harped upon. He himself once wrote: 'A wing man who never attempts a shot, and who always requires to "shake hands" with the corner flag before centring will soon find that he invites far closer attention than if he left the defence in complete ignorance whether he intended to shoot, centre, or pass. It is the player of originality and initiative . . . who will make his mark.'

To uncover something different about Meredith I am grateful to Peter Corrigan, of *The Observer,* who wrote the official centenary history of the F.A. of Wales in 1976, published by Welsh Brewers Ltd.:

> His career was prodigious whichever way it is looked at. Some estimate that he played as many as 2,000 games. More likely was the figure that he

himself claimed of 1,568, of which 857 were League matches played in the 31 years between making his League debut in 1894 and when he eventually retired in 1925. Before he died in 1958 at the age of 81, he was asked what he thought of Stanley Matthews that other evergreen right winger whose brilliance challenged Meredith's. The reply was most complimentary until the famous Welshman concluded: 'But I do wish Stan could have scored a few more goals.'

There was the great difference. Meredith scored 470 goals in his career and many were match-winners. But his record was unassailable from so many directions. He became the oldest player to appear in the Home International championship in a game against England in London in March 1920. which was his 48th appearance in the championship.

Later when he kept a pub in Manchester and his customers drank thirstily at his stories about the game, he could be persuaded to lay out his medals and caps along the bar and, as he pointed out, the caps were all the same size – 6⅞ths!

Yet there was frequent controversy over the number of caps Meredith gained. Even he thought he had won over 50, a confusion he was entitled to because the Football Association of Wales made a presentation of his 50th cap to him in February 1920 and he played for Wales once more after that.

The Welsh F.A, however, were misled. Although Meredith was chosen against Ireland in 1899 his club refused to release him at the last minute and somehow his name stayed in the records as having played. His official total was 48, made up of 20 matches against England, 12 against Scotland, and 16 against Ireland. Also he appeared in two 'victory' internationals against England in 1918 which are not recognised as official games.

By 1900, he was established both in the Football League and internationally as a winger of exceptional class. He made his Welsh debut at the age of 20 in Ireland in 1895 where, despite being seasick on the voyage to Belfast, he played well in a 2–2 draw. On the following Monday they had to play England at Queen's Club in London where, he said, 'I saw more top hats than I had ever seen in my life'.

England had an all amateur team out that day and Meredith met the famous C. B. Fry and W. J. Oakley, the left back, the latter giving him a hard time of it. 'He made me gallop that day. Once he kept shoulder to shoulder with me for half the pitch which was 150 yards long.'

The following year Meredith was included in the Welsh team to meet England in the first soccer international ever played at Cardiff and which as a missionary project was a disaster since England won 9–1, the legendary Steve Bloomer scoring five of the goals.

The South Walians who looked askance upon that performance probably didn't even notice the young right winger because Billy Meredith was not the sort of player to excite interest at first glance. His sparse, erect body was perched on legs so spindly they did not look capable of supporting a piano stool. His face was drawn and unremarkable apart from the eyes that were direct and challenging. Overall the impression he gave to the stranger was more likely to attract sympathy than admiration.

But once he started playing the transformation must have been staggering. He didn't have great speed but he had that vital quickness over the first few yards and those legs provided so much balance and manoeuvrability that he could take the ball past you in a telephone kiosk. Once in flight and free of challenge he had hair-splitting accuracy, whether placing a cross with great precision or letting fly with a shot that had surprise as its first ally and force as its second.

And all the time his teeth were champing on a toothpick, deftly transferring it from one side of his mouth to the other as his feet and brain worked their miracles. Some thought the toothpick served some mystical, calming purpose but the reason was more basic.

When he worked down the mines he chewed tobacco constantly and carried on the habit when he went to play for Manchester City. But his dribbling must have been fairly fluent all round for soon the laundry were complaining at the state of his jersey front and he was kindly asked would he chew something else. He chose a toothpick.

By the time the Welsh F.A. bucked up enough courage to play in Cardiff again, which was in March 1900, Meredith was far better known. 'The finest right winger living,' said the *Western Mail* in passing.

Wales borrowed Cardiff Arms Park for the occasion, which meant they had to play on a Monday because Cardiff R.F.C. were playing Newport there on the Saturday and even though the rugby hero of the day, Gwyn Nicholls, was not playing because of injury there was a crowd of 10,000 for the game.

The F.A.W. were expecting 20,000 for the soccer international with excursions coming from all over the country. The *South Wales Echo* reported, somewhat haughtily, 'The kick-off has been arranged for 4 p.m. to allow the artisan classes to see the game without undue sacrifice of working time.'

Wales, dressed as they were in those days in shirts of white and green halves, took the field to a slight sprinkling of snow and within three minutes were a goal down. According to the reports they would have stayed that way had it not been for Meredith. He had gone very close with a shot from the touchline in the first half but in the second half the following happened: 'Morgan Owen gave Meredith a beautiful long pass and he dribbled prettily past Oakley and getting close to Robinson put in a drive which no man on earth could have stopped. The ball hit the crossbar and bounced into the net amid immense cheering.'

The score remained 1–1 and the crowd went away happy at having Meredith's greatness confirmed before their eyes. It was enough to prove that here was a man, and here was a game, worth some attention.

A man of few words off the field, when the ball was at his feet his movements became as lyrical as the poetry of a Dylan Thomas. He was emotional too, as he showed at the end of his last international in that match against England at Highbury in 1920. It was a poignant occasion. Almost forty-six years old, he stood by before the start as a presentation was made to his old headmaster, who watched proudly as five of his former pupils wore the red shirt of Wales that day.

And what a memorable day, too, it was for Wales. They beat England 2–1 for the first time in their history and when it was over the usually calm Meredith walked into the dressing room with tears streaming down his face. No one could have staged a more theatrical climax to a wonderful international career.

Nor was that all. He offered a broader contribution to his profession off the field by remaining a powerful supporter of the Players' Union from its birth until the end of his life. And at heart, too, he always remained a United man, returning in 1931 as a coach, often helping to spot budding talent in the public parks, and sometimes even attending an Annual General Meeting.

On his death in 1958, at Withington, Manchester, he still owed a small sum on the purchase of his house and this the United directors cleared with the consent of the Football Association; the final grateful, worthy gesture to a man who straddled the world like a giant in football boots.

If it was a time of parting, it was a time, too, of slump for the club. In 1922 United ended bottom of the First Division and were relegated for the second time in their history. Once more it was challenge, a case of having to pick themselves up off the floor with the help of men like Mew, a small but talented goalkeeper, Silcock, a classic full back from Eccles, Hilditch, a cultured half back, and Spence a centre forward who scored four goals against Burnley within a week of signing professional.

All these were to be part of the future. Meanwhile the old order had changed and it was a sad case of *sic transit gloria.*

# 10

# *1923–1939:*

# *Walking a Tightrope*

THE PHOENIX RENEWS herself only when she is burnt. In this concluding phase before the Second World War the Phoenix of United was badly singed several times as the club walked a precarious tight rope.

To build a successful football side brings thirty per cent joy and seventy per cent despair. For much of the 1930s it proved to be mostly despair and little joy as United sank to their lowest ebb in 1934, a nadir which almost swept them into the Third Division. Three years earlier, too, relegation and a massive financial crisis combined to lead not only to a threatened revolt by the shareholders but the possibility of a move away from the comfortable surroundings of Old Trafford. Had that happened they were threatened with the gutter.

But as the saying is, 'Cometh the hour, cometh the man'. He proved to be James W. Gibson, whose son Alan has carried on the family name these many years on the United board. When others would have bowed silently to the inevitable, thinking the end to be inevitable, the spirit of Old Trafford – a home where football and a sense of community exist in its very bricks and mortar – arose and transcended all obstacles.

But first things first, and having departed into the Second Division at the end of the season 1921–22, the first priority of the club was to climb back as quickly as possible to what they regarded as their rightful place in society. To this end they put all their eggs in one basket.

The man they felt who could lead them out of the wilderness was Frank Barson, the Aston Villa attacking centre half, who had already gained an England cap against Wales in 1920 and collected a Cup Winners' medal with Villa that same season at the side of great men like Sam Hardy, Andy Ducat (the Surrey cricketer),

Billy Walker and Clem Stephenson. He possessed the pedigree, it was argued.

Barson, however, was a highly controversial figure. Born in Sheffield and schooled rigorously by 'Battling' Barnsley, where survival of the fittest was the first and only law, he was looked upon with some circumspection as a trouble shooter, a kind of Jesse James ready to terrorise the local populace. There was even the story, doubtless apocryphal, that he had once threatened his manager at Villa Park with a pistol. Off field, if one is to believe it, he was a mild mannered, considerate man.

'But at Barnsley,' he once told the *Empire News* in February, 1939, 'they taught me to be a robust player. I was a weighty player, too. I shirked no collision and I got up with more respect for the man who had put me down. I had my nose broken four times and was twice in hospital with injuries to my back.' His critics, however, failed to differentiate between toughness and roughness. The true definition of him perhaps should have been 'rumbustuous'.

When United opened negotiations for his transfer in July 1922 Aston Villa asked a fee of £5,500 as against an offer of £4,000. As so often it became a matter of horse trading until eventually a sum of £5,000 was agreed – a huge price for United at that time. Yet the urgent need was there and Barson was promised the licence of a public house if he could lead his new club back to the First Division. Within three seasons he had achieved it.

A simple soul off field, the generous character of the man was really shown when he left Barnsley, who parted with him to Villa only because of their financial difficulties. On that move he refused to take from his Yorkshire club his share of the transfer fee. Yet when he next left for Old Trafford, Aston Villa, for some unexplained reason, withheld from him the percentage of the deal due to him.

He was not one to forget or overlook such injustices, as he showed even on the field. If a colleague was fouled unduly, he would take it upon himself to exact retribution and would often first inform a referee of his intentions. With it all, however, he possessed one of the best football brains of his time; he was an inspiring leader who won the admiration and respect of colleagues who followed him through fire until he left for Watford in 1928, finally to become a trainer at Swansea.

A former blacksmith, Barson was as hard as nails. He once headed a goal for Aston Villa from a thirty-yard range and on another occasion when still a Villa player, trekked seven miles through deep snow after missing a train to arrive at Old Trafford only minutes before the kick-off. Even so, he proved a key Villa figure as United were beaten. No wonder the Lancastrians wanted him. He would go through a brick wall if need be.

As the *Manchester Guardian* once wrote of him in February 1926 following a match against Sunderland at Old Trafford – United were back in the First Division then; a crowd of 58,661, paying £4,823, attended the affair – 'Barson was a commanding figure: he held the side together at a critical time, and set the example of bold tackling, well-judged passing, and not a little daring that was of incalculable value.'

Having surrendered their First Division status there followed a spring clean at Old Trafford in 1923. Mew, who had given illustrious service over many years, retired with a presentation from the club of an inscribed gold watch as a memento of 500 League appearances. He was succeeded in goal by Alf Steward, an all-round games player also on the staff of the Lancashire County Cricket Club, who had joined United three years earlier from Stalybridge Celtic.

At full back now were Charlie Moore and Jack Silcock, a determined, reliable partnership; the half back line read Hilditch, Barson and first J. B. Grimwood, next Frank Mann (a member of Huddersfield's Cup Final side of 1922) and then Ray Bennion, a Welsh international.

It was this defensive department that took most of the weight, since the forwards – the lion-hearted Joe Spence apart – though gifted individually like McBain, Myerscough, Lockhead and Partridge, were disjointed and short on scoring power. To go a goal down at that period more often than not meant defeat for United. Yet of this company Barson, Silcock, Hilditch and Spence all won England caps.

Little of note came to pass for two years while the side was gathering strength around the central figure of Barson. Yet Old Trafford itself remained a magnet for others. In September 1924 Manchester County hired the ground to play the New Zealand All Blacks at rugby football (they paid United 20 per cent of the gross gate), as interesting a diversion as had been the appearance of American troops playing baseball on the pitch during the First World War. Later, in 1927, there even came a week's exhibition of lawn tennis by the famous Wimbledon champion Suzanne Lenglen, staged by that theatrical entrepreneur, C. B. Cochran. If nothing else, that at least was a testimonial to the quality of the Old Trafford grass.

In 1925 there came a curious transfer. On February 7, Albert

Pape, the Clapton Orient centre forward, travelled to Old Trafford for the first time prepared to face United. But officials got together after his arrival, negotiations for his transfer were settled and approved by the League over the telephone, and before the player fully realised it he found himself taking the field to play for United instead of against them – an event which could not happen today when a transfer has to be registered forty-eight hours before a player can appear for a new club.

By the end of that 1924–25 season, there arrived the moment United had been working for. The earlier Barson deal duly paid its dividend in full. Promotion to the First Division was achieved again thanks to a storming finish and a defensive record of only twenty-three goals conceded, never since equalled in either the First or Second Divisions.

The final table read:

| | | | | | Goals | | |
|---|---|---|---|---|---|---|---|
| | P | W | D | L | F | A | Pts |
| Leicester City | 42 | 24 | 11 | 7 | 90 | 32 | 59 |
| Manchester United | 42 | 23 | 11 | 8 | 57 | 23 | 57 |
| Derby County | 42 | 22 | 11 | 9 | 71 | 36 | 55 |

With Derby breathing down their necks, it all hinged on the last match of the season on May 2. The mathematicians and Senior Wranglers had all their slide rules ready with a variety of possibilities hanging on the scores. In the event both drew – United 0–0 at Barnsley, with a side which lined up: Steward; Moore, Jones; Bennion, Barson, Grimwood; Spence, Smith, Pape, Lockhead and McPherson. Derby drew 2–2 at home against Blackpool.

If United heads were high again as they rejoined the elite, little did they know that troubles and crises were again to stalk them in the coming years. Yet having emerged from the fires of the past like tempered steel they again refused to crack, although at one point they came very close to it.

Meanwhile 1926 seemed to offer the vision of better things. They ended respectably enough in ninth position in the League, and for the first time in seventeen years fought their way to the semi-final of the F.A. Cup, there to be faced with a local derby against Manchester City.

The whole community was agog at the prospect. When the great day arrived at last Manchester resembled Goldsmith's deserted village as a vast exodus made its way across the Pennines to Sheffield and Bramall Lane. United, sound and reliable, were taken as the favourites to beat a City side of eccentric quality who were fighting relegation. However, as so often happens, it was the favourites who fell.

The United defence had an off-day and it was City, brilliantly inspired by Jimmy McMullan, who went on to Wembley with the feather of a 3–0 win in their caps. Once there, however, the bell tolled for them as Bolton Wanderers, with a goal by David Jack, took the Cup 1–0 and City in due course sank to the Second Division. Such is the irony of football.

On April 17, Old Trafford gained another honour. The England v. Scotland match – always a historic fixture in the sporting calendar – was staged there and to mark the occasion the Manchester United board authorised the publication by the Service Guild of a souvenir programme for the event, which also included a potted history of the United club. Printed by Allied Newspapers of Withy Grove, the whole of the proceeds from its sale, without any deduction whatever, were given by the club to local medical charities. J. H. Davies and his colleagues were probably intent on earning a place in heaven.

That the English and Scottish Associations should agree to use Old Trafford when the recently built national stadium of Wembley was available needless to say gave great satisfaction in Manchester, especially since this was the fiftieth official meeting between the countries. It was the first full international ever held within the city, but there was some resentment against an increase in prices. 'Yet,' as the publication remarked, 'it will not be the fault of the United officials – Mr. John Chapman and his lieutenant, Mr. Walter Crickmer – if those who put in an attendance do not watch the game with comfort.'

The year 1926, however, did not pass without its black mark. On October 8 a telegram arrived at Old Trafford from the Football Association. The bleak wording of it read: 'For improper conduct in his position as secretary-manager of your club Mr. J. A. Chapman is suspended from taking any part in football or football management during the present season.'

What Chapman's crime was is not precisely clear. A guess could be unfair and well wide of the mark. At any rate the United directors took a stern view and forthwith ended his connections with the club. Upon the recommendation of Mr. H. P. Hardman, Hilditch meanwhile acted as player-manager until the appointment of Herbert Bamlett as manager in April 1927, with Walter Crickmer the official secretary from 1928, a post he held with meticulous dedication until his tragic death thirty years later in Munich.

Having returned to the First Division in 1926, achieved a respectable position of ninth in the Championship, and reached the semi-final of the F.A. Cup, not even the most dedicated supporter, shielded against pessimism by red-tinted glasses, would have foreseen that United were about to suffer the most depressing phase of their life.

Yet this, precisely, is what lay ahead until the outbreak of the Second World War interfered with a bleak, checkered existence. The wind of change was about to blow hard and cruel. One moment United were riding along on the crest of a wave: the next they would disappear from view deep in a trough. For much of the time it was a case of the latter.

Henceforth, until the outbreak of the 1939 Hitler war, United lived the life of a see-saw. It was a case of down, up, down and up, a gipsy existence of being harried from pillar to post. Too good for one life, not good enough for another, they became a sandwich pressed between the First and Second Divisions.

The bare bones of it all were these:

1931 Relegated to Division 2
1936 Promoted to Division 1
1937 Relegated at once
1938 Promoted again immediately.

It was a form of limbo, yet though a life of uncertain activity it was preferable perhaps to being buried in a tomb of anonymity somewhere in the middle of a League table. At least it was something to keep the general interest alive, however disturbing at times. And through it all United never lost their essential identity.

Simplest perhaps is to divide these closing years into three phases before the world moved into a new nuclear age. There was still much flesh and blood to clothe the skeleton.

## Phase I (1927–1931)

It was from 1927 that the thunder clouds started to gather. It began with the death of the great benefactor J. H. Davies, who, since 1902, had kept the club afloat for a quarter of a century through thick and thin. As both chairman and president he has seen the good days and the bad; he had dug deep into his personal bank account; but above all he had fostered and kept alive the spirit of comradeship and family within the club.

Shortly before his death the financial position had seemed to take an upward curve for the better. In 1923, for instance, there was a loan amounting to £20,424, an overdraft at the bank of £3,355, and sundry debts of £15,091. By 1926/27 the loan had been reduced to £2,248, the overdraft had disappeared, and the sundry debts stood at £13,170 – in all a gain of some £23,000 in three years.

It was at this point that it was resolved at last to purchase the freehold of Old Trafford – rent and rates there annually cost some £1,300 – a long cherished desire. Hardly had the decision been taken, the project completed, than sadly Davies died after all those years of financial struggle.

The minute book of February 23, carries this important statement:

> Mr. Lawton (Chairman) reported that in accordance with the instructions of the Board he had seen the Manchester Brewery Co. with a view to this Company (i.e. M.U.F.C.) exercising (sic) the option to purchase the land forming the site of the ground contained in the lease of 30th December 1914. He stated that the Brewery Co., were prepared to sell the said land to this Company in accordance with the terms of the option, namely for £10,150 and a yearly ground rent of £48 in respect of the leasehold portion, conditionally on this Company giving to the Brewery Co. a charge on all its assets to accrue the payment to the Brewery Co. not only the said £10,150, but also the further sum of £11,199.18.8 being the sum agreed between the parties as owing for rent of ground to the 25th March, 1927, such charge to carry interest at the rate of 7½ per cent per annum, and the purchase date as from the 25th March, 1927.

The business was carried through by C. E. Sutcliffe, solicitor of Rawtenstall and a distinguished football administrator, and confirmed on June 30.

Although at last United had bought the roof over their head, underfoot they began again to skate on thin ice. Successive positions since 1927 of fifteenth, eighteenth, twelfth, and seventeenth in the First Division were writings on the wall for those who could read. By 1931 they could no longer hold back the inevitable. Bottom of the League, they were relegated for the third time in their history.

It was clear from the beginning of that season where United were heading. In fact, they set an unenviable League record – never since challenged – of losing every one of their opening twelve matches. The depressing catalogue ran: v. Aston Villa (H) 3–4; Middlesbrough (A) 1–3; Chelsea (A) 2–6; Huddersfield (A) 0–6; Newcastle (H) 3–7; Huddersfield (A) 0–3; Sheffield Wednesday

(A) 0–3; Grimsby Town (H) 0–2; Manchester City (A) 1–4; West Ham (A) 1–5; Arsenal (H) 1–2; and Portsmouth (A) 1–4. A tally of thirteen goals scored against forty-nine conceded.

At last, at the thirteenth attempt, a match was won 2–0 against Birmingham in pouring rain. Although soaked to the skin a 12,000 crowd gave United a rousing welcome fit for a winner of the Derby or Grand National. But by the end of the season they sat like a stone at the bottom, nine points adrift and having conceded 115 goals, which would also now stand as an unwanted record but for the fact that Blackpool, who unbelievably escaped relegation in twentieth place, in that same season gave away 125 goals!

By now, with Barson gone, there were new faces in the side – most of them doubtless blushing with embarrassment – men like Reid, a centre forward who did at least manage seventeen goals off his own bat; Dale at left back; and H. Rowley at inside left. Spence, Steward, Silcock and Hilditch all kept going still but in a minor key.

In April 1931 Bamlett's worrying time as manager came to an expected close and those two ever-present helpers in trouble, Walter Crickmer and Louis Rocca, held the reins lightly until relief arrived.

Earlier that season, however, on October 17, 1930, there came a meeting of 3,000 supporters at the Hulme Town Hall under the chairmanship of Mr. S. Mason. Dissatisfaction and even revolution was in the air as the team suffered that deplorable run of defeats. By then ten matches had come and gone and United were bottom of the championship without a single point to their name.

Two resolutions were carried – a lack of confidence in the board; a boycott of the following day's match against Arsenal. Charlie Roberts, the old hero, however, opposed the latter proposition. He had, he said, 'the deepest sympathy with the players'. He blamed the directors wholly for the bleak position. 'The management had created their own trouble and they could not say they had never been warned.' He could not understand why the management called themselves 'businessmen yet were losing large sums of money every week through a lack of enterprise'.

As it proved the boycott turned out a damp squib. Indeed, a 30,000 crowd gathered silently to watch their team lose for the eleventh successive time. All Manchester was in a ferment, including even some City followers. What was the underlying cause of the decline and what was being done about it? The board blamed ill-luck and an unusual run of injuries which led to an unsettled team. Nor had any new talent been unearthed anywhere.

No dividend was paid that season but a note of hope for the future was struck at the A.G.M. Recorded by the *Manchester Guardian,* it was to this effect: 'The United's first business is to build up an efficient side from youth.' Those, indeed, were prophetic words that were to bear fruit in the future.

In the autumn of 1931 a financial crash seemed inevitable. Following the Wall Street Collapse in America of 1930, the succeeding recession of world trade and the mounting figure of unemployment in the capitalist world there was no reason why a football club should escape the natural consequences. United had to cry poor mouth and go cap in hand, requesting the Brewery Company to allow the payment of mortgage interest to be suspended; also the Stretford Urban District Council permission to meet certain road charges by instalments.

By December the bank withheld any further credit and nothing remained in the kitty to meet the players' wages.

It was at this critical moment that yet another fairy came upon the scene. Long ago it had been J. H. Davies. Now it was J. W. Gibson, a director of the clothing firm of Briggs, Jones and Gibson Ltd.

His first step was to pay the players and put £2,000 at the disposal of the club. Provided public interest was shown with full backing all round, arrangements could be made, he suggested, to acquire a new manager and a sum of up to £20,000 made available to buy new players. Meanwhile he guaranteed to be responsible for the liabilities of the club until January 9, 1932. At that the reigning directors – Messrs. Lawton (chairman), Hardman, Yates, H. Davies and Bedford – offered to resign to facilitate Gibson's proposed reorganisation of the company.

It was on January 5 that there was another directors' meeting when Gibson was co-opted and stated his terms of help.

This vital operation has been clearly set out in Dr. Young's *History of Manchester United:*

1. Mr. Gibson will give an undertaking to the Club that he will take over the whole of the liabilities, subject to the first and second mortgagers agreeing to withhold demand for payment of principal for two years unless the assets of the Club are placed in jeopardy.

2. Mr. Gibson to have the option of repaying the mortgages within two years.

3. On the present Board of Directors retiring, Mr. Gibson will undertake to form a Board of Directors acceptable to the shareholders.

4. Mr. Gibson is prepared to send a letter to the present directors of the Club embodying these terms, but subject to this appeal for £20,000 being successful.

**A promotion goal. Bamford (centre) scores the equaliser that gives United the Second Division championship against Hull City at Boothferry Park, May 1936.**

**Actress Josie Collins kicking off in the testimonial match for J. E. Magnall at Maine Road, September 1924. Players from Liverpool and Everton faced a combined team from Manchester United and City.**

Old Trafford today.

5. The proceeds of the appeal for £20,000 are to be put into a separate account at the National Provincial Bank Limited, Spring Gardens, Manchester, in trust and earmarked 'solely for trasnfer fees'.

On 6 January Gibson held a press conference, at which he proposed a new issue of 'Patron's Tickets' (independent of season tickets), whereby he hoped to raise £30,000. He spoke with competence and enthusiasm, telling how his scheme had the approval of C. E. Sutcliffe, Vice-President of the Football League, and how he had been deeply touched by the receipt of the sportsman's equivalent of the proverbial widow's offering – 'a postal order for one shilling from a working man who said he was never able to get to the matches on Saturdays, but hoped that his mite would help to keep the old Club together'.

On January 11 there followed another board meeting at which Lawton took the chair for the last time and at which Gibson, with a far-seeing eye, warned even of a possible decline into the Third Division unless urgent action was taken to strengthen the team.

Meanwhile there was disappointing response to his scheme of 'Patron's Tickets' with its object of raising £30,000. However, Gibson had another card up his sleeve. He named four men who were prepared to join him with financial help. They were Colonel George Westcott, Matthew Newton, A. E. Thomson and Hugh Shaw. They joined the board; Gibson became chairman and within a week president of the company.

So once more the flame that was Manchester United flickered like a candle in the wind, was almost extinguished, but steadied to burn until at last it shed a light that glowed to the furthest corners of the land. That, however, was still a long way off. But it was J. H. Davies and 1902 once more. It seemed like a reincarnation.

## Phase II (1932–1934)

United, it proved, were still not out of the wood. The old cliché about it being 'darkest before the dawn' applied now. Casting around desperately for fresh talent there were several new faces at Old Trafford. Among them, in July 1932, was A. Scott Duncan, a former player with Dumbarton, who came at a salary of £800 as the latest in a long line of managers, only one of whom as yet had taken the club to the stars – J. E. Mangnall.

Gibson for his part remained his ebullient, confident self in public, no matter what his private opinions were. At the July

A.G.M. of 1932 he was able to announce a trebling of gate receipts, and the proposed provision of improved covered accommodation for the popular terraces. The *Manchester Guardian* reported him as saying: 'That a new type of spectator had taken the place of the old fair-weather sort, and he did not fear the competition of the motor cycle or the "dog chasing dummies", provided the club supplied the right type of football.'

Alas, the right type of football continued to be elusive. In 1931–32, ending twelfth in the Second Division, United in fact used thirty-four players in a vain attempt for some cohesion and success. The scrum of players who passed through the portals of Old Trafford at that period resembled the crowds who scrimmage for bargains at New Year sales in the big department stores.

Although the bank overdraft stood at £15,286 money continued to be spent frantically – £5,000 on Neil Dewar from Third Lanark; £2,500 on Stewart from Cowdenbeath; McGillivray from Glasgow Celtic; Byrne from Shamrock Rovers and McMillen from Cliftonville; Fame and Chalmers from Cowdenbeath. Scott Duncan, a Scot, perhaps could be excused, if not forgiven, for his belief in Scottish skill; Celtic skill at large, indeed, with the Irish also involved. Not forgiven for the reason that the men he chose north of the border and in Erin's isle simply were not good enough.

In the meantime amongst those who departed from United was the long serving Hilditch, who returned home to Cheshire, while Spence, the big hearted, faithful servant, joined Chesterfield. Even though United ended sixth in 1933, a respectable enough position, life for them was in truth a grand illusion. Though creditors held back sympathetically from pressing their demands too hard, only the realists could sense that United were seemingly heading for disaster.

Having spent some £20,000 on new players with nothing to show for it, the directors continued to find themselves under fire from the press as 1933–34 found the team drifting towards the rapids. As a result Westcott and Thomson resigned from the board and their places taken by Harold Hardman and Dr. W. McLean.

At this point Mr. Gibson drew in his horns. He no longer wished to guarantee the bank overdraft – now £17,705, of which the widow of J. H. Davies stood guarantor for £5,000. On reflection, however, Gibson withdrew his objection and continued his help as before on condition that the club gave him control over its assets.

The climax to all this turmoil arrived on May 5, 1934. At that moment – and to this day – United stood at the lowest point in the whole of their history since joining the Football League in 1892. On the last day of that season they virtually had one foot already in the Third Division as they went to London to face Millwall at the Den.

On the morning of that fateful match the position at the bottom of the Second Division read:

| | | Goals | | |
|---|---|---|---|---|
| | P | F | A | Pts |
| Swansea | 41 | 49 | 59 | 33 |
| Millwall | 41 | 39 | 66 | 33 |
| United | 41 | 57 | 85 | 32 |
| Lincoln City | 41 | 42 | 73 | 25 |

As the fates would have it Millwall, their opponents, were also deeply involved in the quicksands. United's duty was clear. They had to win to escape, otherwise the palace of Old Trafford, the scene of Cup Finals, an England-Scotland international and several F.A. Cup semi-finals, with its 70,000 plus capacity and its amenities, would have to open its doors to the likes of New Brighton, Barrow and others of the lower orders. It would be a case of sheer prostitution.

This was the life or death struggle that faced the following men as they took the field: Hacking (an international from Oldham); Griffiths, Jones; Robertson (ex-Stoke), Vose, McKay (ex-Bolton); Cape (from Newcastle), McLenahan, Ball (ex-Sheffield Wednesday), Hine (from Huddersfield) and Manley (ex-Northwich Victoria). What a motley crew; a team virtually unrecognisable as thirty-eight players were used that season.

Yet each man deserves his small niche in the history of the club. By determination and spirit they met and overcame a situation that could have daunted even the finest of teams.

Although reduced to ten fit men early on with an injury to Hine, who changed places with Manley on the wing, each man played as if prepared to die. Manley scored before half time, and, gaining in confidence, Cape added a second at the change of ends.

So the miracle was achieved. United won 2–0, escaped with the skin of their teeth, and it was poor Millwall who accompanied Lincoln to the Third Division.

United were welcomed home as heroes and the jubilation was communal. Even the Manchester City supporters sighed with a civic pride. They at least had something of which truly to be proud since a week earlier, April 28, City had brought back the F.A. Cup to Maine Road. In their side was a certain right half, a talented Scottish ball player by the name of Matthew Busby. Little could he have known as United limped from an embattled season, which could so easily have doused their flame, what the fates had in store for him in the years to come.

One well-loved character was missing from that final titanic struggle in London's dockland. He was Spence who left at the end of the previous season. For fourteen years he had been a front liner in the first team. Joining Old Trafford after the First World War, he was leading scorer on five occasions (and twice joint top), even as a right winger where he had been switched to make good the departure of Meredith. By the time he left he had set up a new club record of 481 League appearances – a figure which stood until surpassed later in the 1960s by Bill Foulkes – and scored 157 League goals, with twenty-two his top mark in 1927–28.

## Phase III (1935–1939)

Now comes what in many ways is one of the most inexplicable, disjointed passages of the United story. Having just escaped excommunication to the Third Division they proceeded to bounce back and forth between the First and Second Division like an echo in a deep valley. In three successive seasons – 1936, 1937, 1938 – they went up, then down, and up again as if unable to decide where they wanted to exist.

Ironically it was the war that put an end to their beachcombing and when that was concluded United proceeded to drop anchor in the top drawer until 1974–75. Only Sunderland and Arsenal have achieved a longer unbroken stay in the First Division.

Only James Gibson, the patriarch, seemed unmoved as he stood above the passing storms wearing, as it were, two masks – public confidence and private concern.

Scott Duncan, however, the manager, made little impact. Though he worked hard to create stability it eluded him and soon enough, perhaps finding the over-all responsibilities, pressure and press criticisms too disturbing to his nature, he resigned in November 1937 in spite of having signed a lucrative five-year contract only the previous season. After much heart-searching the directors released him and he departed to a quieter life in East Anglia where he helped to steer Ipswich Town from the Southern League into the Football League in 1938.

On his departure United survived without a manager until the arrival at Old Trafford of Matt Busby in 1945. Until that dramatic turning point it was the long-serving, efficient Walter Crickmer, a man for all seasons and of all trades, who attended to the day-to-day running of the club for the next eight years, most of them spanning the difficulties of war time, and the air-raid destruction of Old Trafford.

Scott Duncan, however, in his stay from the autumn of 1932, saw much of the action. In 1936 he navigated United through the rapids to return to the First Division with a side which generally lined up: Hall; Griffiths, Porter; Brown, Vose, McKay; Bryant, Mutch, Bamford, H. Rowley, Manley.

Of these it was he who signed Vose on professional forms; McKay, a ball playing wing half, he picked up from Bolton; Mutch from Arbroath; Bryant and Bamford, a goalscoring centre forward, from Wrexham as a result of United playing a charity match in Wales in aid of the Gresford Colliery disaster fund – a case of casting bread upon the waters.

That 1936 success ended with a run of nineteen unbeaten matches, climaxed by a 3–2 victory at Bury on April 28 when 'Old International' – Don Davies to those in the know – wrote in the *Manchester Guardian*:

> . . . One last shot from Bamford, a daisy-cutter past the post, and the referee's whistle formally announced Manchester United's happy return to their proper sphere. Thousands of oily, begrimed and jubilant Manchester workmen poured on to the field eager for 'Red Shirts' to chair. And whom do you think they collared? Of all men, Bamford and KcKay, true knights of the 'Rueful Countenance', both sadly enjoying their hour of triumph.

United, however, were not yet ripe for their proper sphere, as Don Davies had written. In a trice they were back whence they had come, relegated with Sheffield Wednesday. Again it was a long, hard haul while their neighbours City, with a fluent attack of over a century of goals, were lording it at the top of the League and heading for the championship title.

A number of others like Liverpool, Leeds, Bolton and Wednesday were in the shadows with United as the last day approached. United travelled to West Bromwich hoping that victory might save them. They lost 0–1. Yet still they clutched at a last straw. Leeds had one game to play. If they lost at Portsmouth United could survive by a hairsbreadth. In the event Leeds won 3–1 and for the fourth time in their life United, dogged by injuries and ill luck, were back to Division Two.

The game of snakes and ladders, however, was not yet done. United not only went down in 1937 but they returned to the drawing board and to the work bench. Now Breen had come to them in goal via Belfast Celtic; Roughton, a determined full back, from Huddersfield; and two on the left flank of attack from Bournemouth who were to make their considerable mark in the renaissance after the war.

They were Stanley Pearson and Jack Rowley. The former soon hit a jackpot with four goals from outside left against Swansea Town; the latter with a thunderbolt in either foot, inexplicably had not caught the eye of the shrewd Major Buckley, the 'star maker' of Wolverhampton Wanderers, and had slipped through the fingers of Molineux to migrate to the home of retired colonels and refined spinsters on the south coast.

The followers of United in this hectic period had become battle hardened, already conditioned no doubt for the war that was on the near horizon. There was scarcely the miss of a heartbeat as the team, after an unpromising start, found themselves once more in a tense finish. This time they were heading in the right direction. Once more everything hinged on the last match, with Sheffield United having completed their programme.

On the morning of the final day of that season 1937–38, May 7, the top of the Second Division table read:

| | | | | | Goals | | |
|---|---|---|---|---|---|---|---|
| | P | W | D | L | F | A | Pts |
| Aston Villa | 41 | 24 | 7 | 10 | 71 | 35 | 55 |
| Sheffield United | 42 | 22 | 9 | 11 | 73 | 56 | 53 |
| Manchester United | 41 | 21 | 9 | 11 | 80 | 50 | 51 |
| Coventry City | 41 | 20 | 11 | 10 | 65 | 44 | 51 |

Villa already were assured of promotion. It was merely a question of which of the other three would accompany them. Goal average seemed likely to decide and here United held a fractional advantage – 1.60 against Sheffield's 1.30 and Coventry's 1.47.

By nightfall it was settled. United beat Bury 2–0 at home, Coventry drew 1–1, and the flags were out at Old Trafford. Yet the gods of chance had not quite finished their sport. With one last cast of the dice they sent United up and dragged Manchester City down, one of the most extraordinary reversals in the long history of the League. The previous season City had become Champions; now with virtually the same side they were relegated and that with a better goal average than half the First Division.

The United team that faced that last decisive challenge was: Breen; Redwood, Roughton; Brown, Vose, McKay; Bryant, Baird, Smith, Pearson, J. Rowley.

People are the lifeblood of any club and no one was more aware of this than Mr. Gibson. In his speech at the Annual General Meeting of August 17, 1938, he praised effusively the work done backstage by Walter Crickmer as secretary and caretaker of the vacant role of manager; of Curry, as trainer, and Inglis, as coach, both of whom had joined the club in the summer of 1934 following the narrow escape from the tentacles of the Third Division. In the spring of 1940 Tom Curry became masseur.

Financially the club was sounder but still in debt over-all. In 1934–35, with greater support on the terraces, United showed a working profit on the season of £4,490, the best return since 1928. In 1937 the season's profit was £10,486, but hanging over their heads like a sword of Damocles was a new mortgage of £25,000 on the clearance of the old one. Yet for the last five years up to the outbreak of war profits had been shown on the annual balance sheets: 1935, £4,490; 1936, £6,528; 1937, £10,486; 1938, £6,615; 1939, £5,993.

Notwithstanding the expensive mortgage and high interest rates, United continued to think big. Like theatre owners they were constantly on the search for star names to attract audiences and ways and means to improve the comfort and amenities of their emporium. Like Arsenal in the south – winning prizes and gaining support at Highbury through success – United realised that football had become an entertainment industry.

By the mid-1930s Old Trafford itself had become a magnet for F.A Cup semi-finals and representative matches, so much so that Gibson began to take a grandiose, inflated view that it could be enlarged to become the Wembley and the Hampden Park of the north of England. It was a dream that proved to be stillborn.

Yet in November 1938 Old Trafford was a fitting, shining stage for one of Stanley Matthews's virtuoso performances. Northern Ireland fell under his hypnotic spell as England won 7–0, with Willie Hall, of Spurs, playing inside right to the maestro, scoring five of the goals, three in a spell of four minutes at one stage, each one from a Matthews pass. Matthews himself, rounded off the jamboree by going through on his own to complete the score.

At the start of that season, indeed, Old Trafford had been refurbished. The wing terraces had been given new roofing which now helped to give cover for some 40,000 spectators. At ground level, beneath the stand, there was a new treatment room for injuries, a new cobbler's shop, and redecorated dressing rooms. All this had cost more than £35,000.

To fill this fine theatre eager eyes swept the land for well established stars. Tentative enquiries were made for men like

Connor, Sunderland's outside left, Duncan (Derby County), Worrall (Portsmouth), Delaney (Glasgow Celtic) and Birkett (Arsenal). Even Matthews became one of the wanted men when he tried to move from Stoke, an event that led to mass meetings of protest all over the Black Country. To them it was as unthinkable as the shifting of Nelson's Column, Big Ben or St. Paul's Cathedral to new sites. United offered £6,000 plus a player for the great man, but public outrage and demand kept him at home. It is significant that all the players in United's mind at that stage were wingers.

In a sense the circle has now been completed. But before lowering the curtain on the United of 1939, two important points must be made.

First, the earlier words of Sir Matt return to mind – that when he came as manager to the ruins of Old Trafford in 1945 he was lucky to find on the staff not only someone like Walter Crickmer – tutored in his time by experts like J. E. Mangnall and J. J. Bentley – a wholly dedicated and invaluable servant who knew more about the inner workings of the club than any other individual in Manchester, but also some players who were to take a major part in the rebuilding and success of the club after the war. They were, of course, John Carey, Stan Pearson, Jack Rowley, Allenby Chilton (who was wounded on active service) and John Aston, a product of the youth policy.

Beyond this, too, after the war there was now established for the first time at the headquarters of the Football Association a national manager of the England team who also combined that duty with Director of Coaching, a long overdue appointment established by the F.A. Secretary, Sir Stanley Rous. The man in question was Walter Winterbottom, himself a former amateur centre half with United whose brief career at Old Trafford was cut short by spinal trouble.

Discovered playing for Mossley in the Cheshire League he got his chance at Old Trafford when Vose was injured. Having first dominated Barker, the Derby County and England centre forward, one week, he followed this in January 1937 by shutting out Tilson, of Manchester City, in his first traditional local derby. As the *Manchester Guardian* said of him: 'An outstanding success in the game was young Winterbottom, who beat Tilson in the air, on the ground, short-circuited most of Tilson's passes, and relieved Tilson of the others with the neatness, suavity, and good manners of a well-trained gentleman's gentleman removing an overcoat.'

A veritable Jeeves of the football field, in fact, Winterbottom was no rugged 'stopper' of his day. He sought style and creativity, qualities he later brought to his appointment with England. Yet another United product who contributed much to the game as a whole, Winterbottom always had a close and sympathetic feel for his old Manchester. United in their turn always held his ear and commanded his attention, which was reflected in a sense by the England caps won later by Cockburn, Pearson, Rowley, Byrne, Aston, Foulkes, Chilton, Berry, Bobby Charlton, Duncan Edwards, Viollet, Warren Bradley, McGuinness and Ray Wood.

The other fact to remember – also pointed out by Busby earlier – was the policy of youth training established before the war. All he did, he stressed, was to develop later the foundations already laid.

Indeed, it was as far back as 1909 in the reign of J. H. Davies, and later in 1931 when J. W. Gibson was at the helm, that the idea of a youth policy was mooted. Finally, in February 1938 it was proposed: 'With reference to the formation of a Junior Athletic Club for cultivating young players after they leave school a scheme submitted was approved and the matter left with the secretary.'

So the Manchester United Junior Athletic Club (M.U.J.A.C.) came into being, at first helped by a committee of teachers and by instructors from Manchester University. As Mr. Davies stressed at the time, 'Manchester United assume no possessive attitude over these boys. We merely tell them that we hope that if as a result of what the club has done for them they should rise to anything like fame they will bear United in mind . . .' A year later the scheme had got going and in 1939 M.U.J.A.C. had won their Division of the Chorlton League. It was the orchard that helped to produce many of the great names of the future.

So the curtain came down with James Gibson, in a mood of civic optimism, asserting, 'United have no intention of buying any more mediocrities. Our aim is a United composed of Manchester players.'

Yet with it came a sad ending. A month before war was declared and the lights went out in Europe for the second time in a quarter of a century, news came of the death of Charlie Roberts. In the *Manchester Guardian* obituary he was spoken of as the greatest captain Manchester United ever possessed, while mention was made of his wider influences on the game as a whole and the leading role he played in the Players' Union dispute of 1909. 'Today,' wrote the paper, 'the Union flourishes: Roberts became its first Chairman and later a Vice-President and trustee. It is a worthy memorial to a great player and a great sportsman.'

All three homes of United – North Street, Newton Heath; Bank

Street, Clayton, and Old Trafford – are memorials to an army of young men who have worn the club colours, which have not always been the red shirts and white shorts we have come to know so well. At one time or another these have changed from the original green and gold jerseys of the 1880s and 1890s, to plain white, then white shirts with a red V sign across the chest, and next briefly to white with cherry hoops in the mid-1930s.

Heraldry is the folk art of the upper classes; and the football strip is the heraldry of the folk. It was invented for exactly the same reason as the gorgeous martial liveries of the Middle Ages from which the art and science of heraldry derived: to distinguish two parties of combatants from each other.

Now Manchester United celebrate their centenary and are poised to move into the next hundred years. As in the past they will doubtless pass through the good and the bad times. That is the law of the human condition.

What will it all be like in the future: what changes will occur in the structure of the game as a whole? Bobby Charlton, pondering quietly one sunny morning in the offices of modern Old Trafford, put his thoughts into words:

'I'll always have a great affection for this place. I suppose I put a lot of blood and tears into it: I put my youth into it. And to see the place now as opposed to when I first arrived makes me realise that I had a little part in all the change. I find that very rewarding. Look at it now. It must be the envy of every club in the country.

'United have the right set up: it is the proper way to watch football, sitting in comfort, having a meal. And still it's not finished. I can see it carrying on and they'll keep building new stands, and another one on top and another one on top of that. And so on. It all seems a part of the never ending story. Where will it finish?

'Other clubs, who don't have this United aura, have to graft for every penny they can get. They are the ones I worry about. If only someone could tell me what future there is for football in fifty years time. Is there a hope for teams with little wooden stands: can they replace them with safe modern structures? I can't see it.

'I believe it all revolves back to directors, to the Football League, to share issues, and who controls what. If a manager does badly he's sacked; if a coach does badly he's sacked; a scout who does badly is sacked. But a director, if he does badly, *stays*. That is what has to be changed.

'As for the man in the street, the guys on the terraces, they're everything. They are what it's all about. They're not a part of the backroom politics and all the in-fighting. They don't understand that. All they understand is that they've got their team and their whole life revolves around coming down here.

'I believe successful managers should move on to boards of directors – like Sir Matt here, Joe Mercer at Coventry and Alec Stock at Queens Park Rangers – to bring some expertise to the control of affairs, some opposition to the ideas of men who may be good at running businesses but know little about football.

'As for United, in good times or bad, they're always news. Now they boast eighty private boxes around the ground costing either £780 or £850, plus V.A.T., per season. They have supporters' clubs in seventy-three countries from Russia, Mexico, Iceland, the Canaries, Japan, Hong Kong, to Vietnam and Mauritius. They employ an office staff of forty and there is a thriving Development Association. As I said earlier, they're part of a never ending story. They are a theatre of dreams . . .'

Basically it is the loyalty of the genuine supporter, following fortune through thick and thin, who provides the moral strength to a club. Like a conifer tree, bent down by the weight of trouble in the face of heavy snow and the elements, the tree suddenly springs upright again at the very moment it appears likely to snap in two. Such was United in those traumatic days, and such in the main, too, is the genuine loyalty of the man on the terraces.

Before me lies a letter in spidery handwriting from just such a true-blue devotee. It is signed, obviously with some amused relish, H. Dutton ('Legs of Mutton'). A pensioner of seventy-four years of age, he supported United in the open for over half a century and takes us back to the early 1920s with some of his shared memories. The mind plays funny tricks over such a length of time and on occasion he may have confused certain events. Even so, how much more worthwhile, warm and expressive this is in evoking a picture of the past than a mass of cold facts and figures. He wrote:

> When I look back and think of the days of United I think what happy days. Then you could get in for a bob (1s.), ladies a tanner (6d). At three-quarter time the gates were opened and those out of work and unable to afford the bob were let in free. You could get wet for nothing, as there was no cover in those days. The only covered stand was beside the railway and that was blitzed in the Second World War.
>
> On the top of the terraces on the popular side were two or three wooden huts where you could get a pint and a wad (meat pie). Then there were the players as that time such as Joe Spence, a good goalscorer; Tommy Meehan, a wing half, who was transferred to Chelsea after scoring two penalties against them one Saturday and who died tragically young; Billy Henderson, who arrived from Airdrieonians;

and Frank Barson, the famous centre half who came to Old Trafford from Aston Villa. I remember in one match against Villa Henderson being fouled by him, getting up and threatening to 'do' him there and then. Two or three weeks later Barson joined United!

What trips you could have if you could afford the fare – to Bury, Bolton, Stockport and Liverpool. You could not afford to go very far in those days. What a difference now with all the cantilever stands, private boxes, air travel and money etc.

At Bury and Bolton you could get black puddings at halftime with mustard. A fellow brought them around in a bucket. At Oldham you could buy roast potatoes. A pal of mine once got one and put it in his pocket, forgetting he had a bar of chocolate there already. You should have seen the state he was in!

At this point the old gentleman's mind took a sudden leap forward some thirty years, like an evening gone. Memories have a way of finding their own convenient pigeon holes. He recalls the Cup Final of 1948.

Then there was the Wembley final against Blackpool which United won 4–2 after being 2–1 down. When captain John Carey was presented with the Cup he dropped the lid. I wonder how he felt in front of 100,000 spectators! He was a great player. The team at that final was: Crompton; Carey, Aston; Anderson, Chilton, Cockburn; Delaney, Morris, Rowley, Pearson, Mitten.

Other players I can still remember were Mew in goal; Moore and Silcock at full back; Meehan, Hilditch, Whalley, Grimwood, Montgomery, Neil McBain, and 'Tiny' Haslam, who stood 6ft 6ins. All these I think were half backs. Then there was the great Spence ('Give it to Joe'). Those were the days when if a goalie held on to the ball too long he could be barged into the back of the net and it was a goal.

Then there were forwards like Lockhead, Hopkins, Thomas, Cape, Sapsford (who once scored eight goals for the reserves in a match against Stockport County), Bamford, Mutch, Patridge, Bissett, a Scot, and Myerscough. Oh! there are so many names to conjur with at my age.

But I must mention Radford, who was a left full back. His knickers were so tight I don't know how he got them on or took them off. It was not just fat but hard muscle. He was tragically killed in a motor cycle accident.

I must relate a story about him. United were playing Hull City at Old Trafford. It was just after half-time. United got a free-kick on the stand side near the players' entrance. Up comes Charlie Radford to take it. Bang it goes towards the Hull City goal with a terrific wind blowing behind it. One of the Hull players tried to head it. It knocked him unconscious and the next moment the ball was in the back of the Hull net. I am not sure but I think United won 3–2. What players to try and remember! It is impossible.

Now they are carrying the torch for England in Europe. Good luck to them and to the chairman, directors and manager. They are all concerned with United. So even are the ground staff and ball boys. That's how we feel at Old Trafford. We're warm-hearted here in Manchester. They have had their sad days as we all know, but they always get over them because they give of their heart. They are a family.

I have supported United for 52 years and I used to come with my married son, who is now out of work, until the crowd trouble got too much, not to mention the price. Also I have arthritis and cannot stand for long now. This is not a begging letter. It is all true. There is only *one* United!

What enjoyment, sadness and happiness United must have given 'Legs of Mutton' Harry Dutton over all those years. Every stroke of his pen must have brought a quickened heart beat as he retraced the past.

There are those, too, who perhaps unable to attend personally, fan their fanaticism from afar by keeping endless statistics and cutting books of their favourite club. There must be thousands of examples of this up and down the country, each one a veritable museum in its own right.

One such person, Mr. J. A. James, living in Surrey, kindly wrote offering help in the compilation of this United story.

I have set in bound volumes and indexed, some 2,500 action photographs of United, including about 120 or so which cover the period of promotion in 1906 to the Second World War. I believe my collection of the early days is unique and certainly covers important events in the history of the club – the winning goal in the 1909 Cup Final; a Joe Spence goal when we (*note the pronoun 'we'*!) once beat Liverpool 6–1 to stave off relegation; the 1926 Cup semi-final against Manchester City etc., etc.

I also have in bound volumes a record of every match United have played. This includes matches in 1878 and is illustrated with newspaper cuttings and reports of the early Manchester Cup Finals which the 'Heathens' dominated. There are also League tables of the Football Alliance prior to United achieving League status in 1892, with especially good coverage of the really early days – fixtures against Haydock Temperance, and 'derbies' against West Manchester on the Manchester Rugby Union football ground.

All this took me 15 years to collect and compile and involved a great deal of hard work not to say money. Each volume probably cost me £50 to compile. I wonder how many other eccentrics there are around who collect this kind of material, but I should be surprised if anyone has been more thorough than I.

This clearly has been a labour of love and the material being too valuable and unwieldly to move I visited the shrine itself. The collection was overpowering in its attention to detail and its devotion to the expanding life of the club. I suggest to Mr. James that he should bequeath this remarkable museum in his will to Old Trafford, where it could finally rest in United's handsome trophy showcase.

Supporters are the lifeblood of the game. They are attracted to it like moths around a flame, perhaps acting out fantasies of their own, either because they are not good enough performers or cannot find time to play and train seriously. To be a part of a swaying crowd is a substitute for the real thing. It is personal involvement. You are ready to forfeit yourself for a short span to the heart of a battle.

Football has a quality and an atmosphere surrounding it that is all its own. What is its magic? Consider. For most of the week the curved wall of the arena, any arena, is still and lonely, a big cement circle surrounding emptiness with only the wind to rattle its hoardings. But on Saturday afternoons, or a midweek night under floodlights, during the season the curve of that wall comes to life. It reaches out in a big sweep like a magnet and draws into itself something vibrant, full of warmth and powerful feeling.

The life of the whole community, high, middle and low, pours with you into that bowl, filling it to the topmost brim. As you take your place the crowd is in the last moments of savouring the flavour of itself and its rich expectation before impatience sets in. It matches your sense of being glad you're there with the noise, the colour and the expectation spreading all over you. The arena, that sunlit, floodlit, shaded or wet stage for a drama no one can foretell, is touched of a sudden with a magic colour and hum from the crowd.

J. B. Priestley, that Grand Old Man of literature, put his finger on it when he wrote this in his lovely book of some years ago *The Good Companions*:

> Something very queer is happening in that narrow thoroughfare to the west of the town. It is called Manchester Road because it actually leads you to that city, though in order to get there you will have to climb to the windy roof of England and spend an hour or two with the curlews. What is so queer about it now is that the road itself cannot be seen at all. A grey-green tide flows sluggishly down its length. It is a tide of cloth caps. These caps have just left the ground of the Bruddersford United Association Football Club. Thirty-five thousand men and boys have just seen what most of them call 't' United' play Bolton Wanderers . . .
>
> To say that these men paid their shillings merely to watch twenty-two hirelings kick a ball is merely to say that a violin is wood and cat-gut, that *Hamlet* is so much paper and ink.

> For a shilling Bruddersford United A.F.C. offered you Conflict and Art: it turned you into a critic, happy in your judgment of fine points, ready in a second to estimate the worth of a well-judged pass, a run down the touchline, a lightning shot, a clearance kick by back or goalkeeper. It turned you into a partisan holding your breath when the ball came sailing into your own goalmouth, ecstatic when your forwards raced away towards the opposite goal, elated, downcast, bitter, triumphant by turns at the fortunes of your side.
>
> What is more it turned you into a member of a new community, all brothers together for an hour and a half, for not only had you escaped from the clanking machinery of this lesser life, from work, wages, rent, doles, sick pay, insurance cards, nagging wives, ailing children, bad bosses, idle workmen, but you had escaped with most of your mates and neighbours, with half the town, and there you were cheering together, thumping one another on the shoulders, swapping judgments like lords of the earth, having pushed your way through a turnstile into another and altogether more splendid kind of life, hurtling with conflict and yet passionate and beautiful in its Art.

As for United they stand for something more than any person, any player, any supporter. They are – as was once written in the club programme of 1937 – the soul of a sporting organisation which goes on from year to year, making history all the time. They remain a club with a rich vein of character and faith. Because of that they have no fear of the morrow.

Though no longer choked by the chemical fumes of Clayton even now the odd chimney stack prods the air like an accusing finger close to Old Trafford. To one side of the ground, near by, runs the Manchester Ship Canal spanned by a revolving bridge. Thousands pour over this canal towards Old Trafford. Thousands pour in from the opposite direction, from Warwick Road and the city centre; Lancastrians, warm-hearted, selective, generous, yet fanatical in a dedication to their men in red. So loyal through triumph or adversity, at times, indeed, this loyalty to United reaches a pitch of fanaticism that is frightening. It is tribal.

Yet who can forget the panoply of the club's battle honours or the cavalcade of players who have passed under its care: who, too, can forget the tide of men, women and children who have swarmed across that Ship Canal or passed the cricket ground near by, that other, gentler Old Trafford of Hornby and Barlow?

In rain, snow and mist they have stood their ground on the mighty terraces, cold of hand but warm of heart. To be in Old Trafford and to see their beloved men in red, is for them a momentary taste of honey.

Statistical appendices as at end of Season 1978

# Appendix 1

## OFFICERS OF MANCHESTER UNITED F.C.

### PRESIDENT OR CHAIRMAN

| | |
|---|---|
| c. 1882–1891 | F. Attock |
| 1891–1902 | T. Connolly |
| | Councillor James Bowes |
| | James Taylor |
| | W. Crompton |
| | W. Healey |
| | James Taylor |
| 1902–1927 | J. H. Davies[1] |
| 1927–1932 | G. H. Lawton |
| 1932–1951 | J. W. Gibson |
| 1951–1965 | H. P. Hardman |
| 1965– | L. C. Edwards |

### MANAGER AND/OR SECRETARY

| | | |
|---|---|---|
| c. 1890–1900 | A. H. Albut *Secretary* | Resigned 1900 – probably in consequence of financial crisis of 1899, reported in *Athletic News*, August 28, 1899. |
| 1900–1903 | James West *Secretary* | Appointment noted in *Athletic News*, August 27, 1900; resignation in minute book, September 29, 1903. |
| 1903–1912 | J. E. Mangnall *Secretary* | Note of appointment to Manchester City in *Athletic News,* August 26, 1912. In May 1921 Mangnall received a long service medal from the Football League at the conclusion of 21 years in management. |
| 1912 | T. J. Wallworth *Secretary* | Assistant Secretary, acting as Secretary *pro tem* from September 9, 1912 – when Mangnall's contract officially ended, to October 28. |
| 1912–1916 | J. J. Bentley *Secretary* | Appointed from October 28, 1912, resigned September 16, 1916. |
| 1914–1921 | J. R. Robson *Manager* | Appointed Manager from December 28, 1914; Secretary-Manager from September 16, 1916; resigned October 31, 1921, but appointed Assistant Manager. |

[1] From September 23, 1909, until October 28, 1919, W. R. Deakin was Chairman and J. H. Davies President.

| | | |
|---|---|---|
| 1921–1926 | John A. Chapman *Secretary-Manager* | Appointed October 31, 1921; suspended by F.A. from October 8, 1926. |
| 1928–1958 | Walter Crickmer *Secretary* | Appointed Secretary *pro tem* October 8, 1926; new agreement made May 29, 1946; killed at Munich, February 6, 1958. |
| 1926–1927 | Clarence G. Hilditch *Player-Manager* | Temporary appointment from October 8, 1926. |
| 1927–1931 | Herbert S. Bamlett *Manager* | Appointed April 13, 1927; resigned November 9, 1937. |
| 1927– ? | L. Rocca *Assistant Manager* | Appointed on an annual contract from October 4, 1927; no mention of termination of office in minute book. |
| 1932–1937 | A. Scott Duncan *Manager* | Appointed August 1, 1932; resigned November 9, 1937 to become Manager of non-League Club, Ipswich Town. |
| 1945–1969 | M. Busby *Manager* | Appointed February 15, 1945. |
| 1955–1970 | J. Murphy[1] *Assistant Manager* | Appointed March 22, 1955; acting in place of Manager from February 6, 1958 until beginning of 1958–59 season. |
| 1955–1958 | L. Olive *Assistant Secretary* | Appointed March 22, 1955; Acting Secretary February 7, 1958. |
| 1958– | L. Olive *Secretary* | Appointed May 6, 1958. |
| 1969–1970 | W. McGuinness *Chief Coach* | Appointed April 9, 1969 |
| 1970 | W. McGuinness *Team Manager* | Appointed August 11, 1970. Sir Matt Busby takes up the post of General Manager. McGuinness relieved of duties, December 29, 1970. |
| 1970–1971 | Sir Matt Busby *Manager* | Sir Matt takes over team duties till the end of the season. |
| 1971–1972 | F. O'Farrell *Manager* | Appointed June 8, 1971. Sir Matt accepts place on Board of Directors. O'Farrell relieved of duties, December 19, 1972. |
| 1972–1977 | T. Docherty *Manager* | Appointed December 22, 1972. Dismissed July 4, 1977. |
| 1977– | D. Sexton *Manager* | Appointed July 14, 1977. |

[1] Coach from 1946.

# Appendix 2

## UNITED'S RECORD

### THE ALLIANCE

| Season | P | W | D | L | F | A | Pts. | Posn. |
|---|---|---|---|---|---|---|---|---|
| 1889/90 | 22 | 9 | 2 | 11 | 40 | 45 | 20 | 8th[1] |
| 1890/91 | 22 | 7 | 3 | 12 | 36 | 55 | 17 | 9th |
| 1891/92 | 22 | 12 | 7 | 3 | 69 | 33 | 31 | 2nd |

### FOOTBALL LEAGUE
### DIVISION I

| Season | P | W | D | L | F | A | Pts. | Posn. |
|---|---|---|---|---|---|---|---|---|
| 1892/93 | 30 | 6 | 6 | 18 | 50 | 85 | 18 | 16th[2] |
| 1893/94 | 30 | 6 | 2 | 22 | 36 | 72 | 14 | 16th |

### DIVISION II

| Season | P | W | D | L | F | A | Pts. | Posn. |
|---|---|---|---|---|---|---|---|---|
| 1894/95 | 30 | 15 | 8 | 7 | 78 | 44 | 38 | 3rd[3] |
| 1895/96 | 30 | 15 | 3 | 12 | 66 | 57 | 33 | 6th |
| 1896/97 | 30 | 17 | 5 | 8 | 56 | 34 | 39 | 2nd |
| 1897/98 | 30 | 16 | 6 | 8 | 64 | 35 | 38 | 4th |
| 1898/99 | 34 | 19 | 5 | 10 | 67 | 43 | 43 | 4th[4] |
| 1899/1900 | 34 | 20 | 4 | 10 | 63 | 27 | 44 | 4th |
| 1900/01 | 34 | 14 | 4 | 16 | 42 | 38 | 32 | 10th |
| 1901/02 | 34 | 11 | 6 | 17 | 38 | 53 | 28 | 15th |
| 1902/03 | 34 | 15 | 8 | 11 | 53 | 38 | 38 | 5th |
| 1903/04 | 34 | 20 | 8 | 6 | 65 | 33 | 48 | 3rd |
| 1904/05 | 34 | 24 | 5 | 5 | 81 | 30 | 53 | 3rd |
| 1905/06 | 38 | 28 | 6 | 4 | 90 | 28 | 62 | 2nd[5] |

### DIVISION I

| Season | P | W | D | L | F | A | Pts. | Posn. |
|---|---|---|---|---|---|---|---|---|
| 1906/07 | 38 | 17 | 8 | 18 | 53 | 56 | 42 | 8th |
| 1907/08 | 38 | 23 | 6 | 9 | 81 | 48 | 52 | CHAMPS |
| 1908/09 | 38 | 15 | 7 | 16 | 58 | 68 | 37 | 13th |
| 1909/10 | 38 | 19 | 7 | 12 | 69 | 61 | 45 | 5th |
| 1910/11 | 38 | 22 | 8 | 8 | 72 | 40 | 52 | CHAMPS |
| 1911/12 | 38 | 13 | 11 | 14 | 45 | 60 | 37 | 13th |
| 1912/13 | 38 | 19 | 8 | 11 | 69 | 43 | 46 | 4th |
| 1913/14 | 38 | 15 | 6 | 17 | 52 | 62 | 36 | 14th |
| 1914/15 | 38 | 9 | 12 | 17 | 46 | 62 | 30 | 18th |
| 1919/20 | 42 | 13 | 14 | 15 | 54 | 50 | 40 | 12th[6] |
| 1920/21 | 42 | 15 | 10 | 17 | 64 | 68 | 40 | 13th |
| 1921/22 | 42 | 8 | 12 | 22 | 41 | 73 | 28 | 22nd |

[1] Consisting of 12 clubs.
[2] Consisting of 16 clubs.
[3] Consisting of 16 clubs.
[4] Each Division increased to 18 clubs.
[5] Each Division increased to 20 Clubs.
[6] Each Division increased to 22 clubs.

| | | | | | | | | |
|---|---|---|---|---|---|---|---|---|
| | | | | DIVISION II | | | | |
| 1922/23 | 42 | 17 | 14 | 11 | 51 | 36 | 48 | 4th |
| 1923/24 | 42 | 13 | 14 | 15 | 52 | 44 | 40 | 14th |
| 1924/25 | 42 | 23 | 11 | 8 | 57 | 23 | 57 | 2nd |
| | | | | DIVISION I | | | | |
| 1925/26 | 42 | 19 | 6 | 17 | 66 | 73 | 44 | 9th |
| 1926/27 | 42 | 13 | 14 | 15 | 52 | 64 | 40 | 15th |
| 1927/28 | 42 | 16 | 7 | 19 | 72 | 80 | 39 | 18th |
| 1928/29 | 42 | 14 | 13 | 15 | 66 | 76 | 41 | 12th |
| 1929/30 | 42 | 15 | 8 | 19 | 67 | 88 | 38 | 17th |
| 1930/31 | 42 | 7 | 8 | 27 | 53 | 115 | 22 | 22nd |
| | | | | DIVISION II | | | | |
| 1931/32 | 42 | 17 | 8 | 17 | 71 | 72 | 42 | 12th |
| 1932/33 | 42 | 15 | 13 | 14 | 71 | 68 | 43 | 6th |
| 1933/34 | 42 | 14 | 6 | 22 | 59 | 85 | 34 | 20th |
| 1934/35 | 42 | 23 | 4 | 15 | 76 | 55 | 50 | 5th |
| 1935/36 | 42 | 22 | 12 | 8 | 85 | 43 | 56 | 1st |
| | | | | DIVISION I | | | | |
| 1936/37 | 42 | 10 | 12 | 20 | 55 | 78 | 32 | 21st |
| | | | | DIVISION II | | | | |
| 1937/38 | 42 | 22 | 9 | 11 | 82 | 50 | 53 | 2nd |
| | | | | DIVISION I | | | | |
| 1938/39 | 42 | 11 | 16 | 15 | 57 | 65 | 38 | 14th |
| 1946/47 | 42 | 22 | 12 | 8 | 95 | 54 | 56 | 2nd |
| 1947/48 | 42 | 19 | 14 | 9 | 81 | 48 | 52 | 2nd |
| 1948/49 | 42 | 21 | 11 | 10 | 77 | 44 | 53 | 2nd |
| 1949/50 | 42 | 18 | 14 | 10 | 69 | 44 | 50 | 4th |
| 1950/51 | 42 | 24 | 8 | 10 | 74 | 40 | 56 | 2nd |
| 1951/52 | 42 | 23 | 11 | 8 | 95 | 52 | 57 | CHAMPS |
| 1952/53 | 42 | 18 | 10 | 14 | 69 | 72 | 46 | 8th |
| 1953/54 | 42 | 18 | 12 | 12 | 73 | 58 | 48 | 4th |
| 1954/55 | 42 | 20 | 7 | 15 | 84 | 74 | 47 | 5th |
| 1955/56 | 42 | 25 | 10 | 7 | 83 | 51 | 60 | CHAMPS |
| 1956/57 | 42 | 28 | 8 | 6 | 103 | 54 | 64 | CHAMPS |
| 1957/58 | 42 | 16 | 11 | 15 | 85 | 75 | 43 | 9th |
| 1958/59 | 42 | 24 | 7 | 11 | 103 | 66 | 55 | 2nd |
| 1959/60 | 42 | 19 | 7 | 16 | 102 | 80 | 45 | 7th |
| 1960/61 | 42 | 18 | 9 | 15 | 88 | 76 | 45 | 7th |
| 1961/62 | 42 | 15 | 9 | 18 | 72 | 75 | 39 | 15th |
| 1962/63 | 42 | 12 | 10 | 20 | 67 | 81 | 34 | 19th |
| 1963/64 | 42 | 23 | 7 | 12 | 90 | 62 | 53 | 2nd |
| 1964/65 | 42 | 26 | 9 | 7 | 89 | 39 | 61 | CHAMPS |
| 1965/66 | 42 | 18 | 15 | 9 | 84 | 59 | 51 | 4th |
| 1966/67 | 42 | 24 | 12 | 6 | 84 | 45 | 60 | CHAMPS |
| 1967/68 | 42 | 24 | 8 | 10 | 89 | 55 | 56 | 2nd |
| 1968/69 | 42 | 15 | 12 | 15 | 57 | 53 | 42 | 11th |

| | | | | | | | | |
|---|---|---|---|---|---|---|---|---|
| 1969/70 | 42 | 14 | 17 | 11 | 66 | 61 | 45 | 8th |
| 1970/71 | 42 | 16 | 11 | 15 | 65 | 66 | 43 | 8th |
| 1971/72 | 42 | 19 | 10 | 13 | 69 | 61 | 48 | 8th |
| 1972/73 | 42 | 12 | 13 | 17 | 44 | 60 | 37 | 18th |
| 1973/74 | 42 | 10 | 12 | 20 | 38 | 48 | 32 | 21st |
| | | | | DIVISION II | | | | |
| 1974/75 | 42 | 26 | 9 | 7 | 66 | 30 | 61 | 1st |
| | | | | DIVISION I | | | | |
| 1975/76 | 42 | 23 | 10 | 9 | 68 | 42 | 56 | 3rd |
| 1976/77 | 42 | 18 | 11 | 13 | 71 | 62 | 47 | 6th |
| 1977/78 | 42 | 16 | 10 | 16 | 67 | 63 | 42 | 10th |

# Appendix 3

RECORD IN THE F.A. CHALLENGE CUP

Abbreviations: F. – Final; I.R. – Intermediate Round; M.U. – Manchester United; N.H. – Newton Heath; Q.R. – Qualifying Round; S.F. – Semi-Final.

Except where a neutral ground is involved, the home team is shown first.

| Season ending | Round | Result |
|---|---|---|
| 1890 | 1 | Preston North End 6<br>N.H.1 |
| 1891 | Q.R.1 | N.H.2<br>Higher Walton 0 |
| | Q.R.2 | Bootle 1<br>N.H. 0 |
| 1892 | Q.R.1 | N.H. 5<br>Ardwick 1 |
| | Q.R.2 | N.H. *w.o.*<br>Heywood *scr.* |
| | Q.R.3 | South Shore 0<br>N.H. 2 |
| | Q.R.4 | N.H. 3<br>Blackpool 4 |
| 1893 | 1 | Blackburn Rovers 4<br>N.H. 0 |
| 1894 | 1 | N.H. 4<br>Middl'brough 0 |
| | 2 after extra time | N.H. 0<br>Blackburn Rovers 0 |
| | 2 replay | Blackburn Rovers 5<br>N.H. 1 |
| 1895 | 1 | Stoke 3<br>N.H. 2 |
| 1896 | 1 | N.H. 2<br>Kettering 1 |
| | 2 | N.H. 1<br>Derby Co. 1 |
| | 2 replay | Derby Co. 5<br>N.H. 1 |
| 1897 | Q.R.4 | N.H. 7<br>West Manchester 0 |
| | Q.R.5 | Blackpool 2<br>N.H. 2 |
| | Q.R.5 replay | N.H. 2<br>Blackpool 1 |
| | 1 | N.H. 5<br>Kettering 1 |
| | 2 | N.H. 1<br>Southampton St. Mary 1 |
| | 2 replay | Southampton St. Mary 1<br>N.H. 3 |
| | 3 | Derby Co. 2<br>N.H. 0 |
| 1898 | 1 | N.H. 1<br>Walsall 0 |
| | 2 | N.H. 0<br>Liverpool 0 |
| | 2 replay | Liverpool 2<br>N.H. 1 |
| 1899 | 1 | Tottenham Hotspur 1<br>N.H. 1 |
| | 1 replay | N.H. 3<br>Tottenham Hotspur 5 |
| 1900 | Q.R.1 | N.H. 1<br>South Shore 3 |
| 1901 | 1 | N.H. 0<br>Burnley 0 |

| Season ending | Round | Result |
|---|---|---|
| 1901 | 1<br>replay | Burnley 7<br>N.H. 1 |
| 1902 | I.R. | N.H. 1<br>Lincoln City 2 |
| 1903 | Q.R.3 | M.U. 7<br>Accrington Stanley 0 |
| | Q.R.5[1] | M.U. 4<br>Southport Central 1 |
| | I.R. | M.U. 1<br>Burton United 1 |
| | I.R.[2] replay | M.U. 3<br>Burton United 1 |
| | 1 | Liverpool 1<br>M.U. 2 |
| | 2 | M.U. 1<br>Everton 3 |
| 1904 | I.R. | M.U. 1<br>Small Heath 1 |
| | I.R. replay after extra time | Small Heath 1<br>M.U. 1 |
| | I.R. 2nd replay after extra time[3] | M.U. 1<br>Small Heath 1 |
| | I.R. 3rd replay[4] | M.U. 3<br>Small Heath 1 |
| | 1 | M.U. 3<br>Notts Co. 3 |
| | 1<br>replay | Notts Co. 1<br>M.U. 2 |
| | 2 | M.U. 0<br>Sheffield Wednesday 6 |
| 1905 | I.R. | M.U. 2<br>Fulham 2 |
| | I.R.<br>replay | Fulham 0<br>M.U. 0 |
| | I.R. 2nd<br>replay[5] | Fulham 1<br>M.U. 0 |
| 1906 | 1 | M.U. 7<br>Staple Hill 2 |
| | 2 | M.U. 3<br>Norwich City 0 |
| | 3 | M.U. 5<br>Aston Villa 1 |
| | 4 | M.U. 2<br>Woolwich Arsenal 3 |
| 1907 | 1 | Portsmouth 2<br>M.U. 2 |
| | 1<br>replay | M.U. 1<br>Portsmouth 2 |
| 1908 | 1 | M.U. 3<br>Blackpool 1 |
| | 2 | M.U. 1<br>Chelsea 0 |
| | 3 | Aston Villa 0<br>M.U. 2 |
| | 4 | Fulham 2<br>M.U. 1 |
| 1909 | 1 | M.U. 1<br>Brighton & Hove 0 |
| | 2 | M.U. 1<br>Everton 0 |
| | 3 | M.U. 6<br>Blackburn Rovers 1 |
| | 4[6] | Burnley 1<br>M.U. 0 |
| | 4<br>replay | Burnley 2<br>M.U. 3 |
| | S.F.[3] | M.U. 1<br>Newcastle United 0 |
| | F.[7] | M.U. 1<br>Bristol City 0 |
| 1910 | 1 | Burnley 2<br>M.U. 0 |

[1] Exempt from Q.R.4.
[2] Also at Clayton.
[3] At Bramall Lane, Sheffield.
[4] At Hyde Road, Manchester.
[5] At Villa Park, Birmingham.
[6] Abandoned after 72 minutes.
[7] At Crystal Palace.

| Season ending | Round | Result |
|---|---|---|
| 1911 | 1 | Blackpool 1<br>M.U. 2 |
| | 2 | M.U. 2<br>Aston Villa 1 |
| | 3 | West Ham 2<br>M.U. 1 |
| 1912 | 1 | M.U. 3<br>Huddersfield Town 1 |
| | 2 | Coventry City 1<br>M.U. 5 |
| | 3 | Reading 1<br>M.U. 1 |
| | 3 replay | M.U. 3<br>Reading 0 |
| | 4 | M.U. 1<br>Blackburn Rovers 1 |
| | 4 replay after extra time | Blackburn Rovers 4<br>M.U. 2 |
| 1913 | 1 | M.U. 1<br>Coventry City 1 |
| | 1 replay | Coventry City 1<br>M.U. 2 |
| | 2 | Plymouth Argyle 0<br>M.U. 2 |
| | 3 | Oldham Athletic 0<br>M.U. 0 |
| | 3 replay | M.U. 1<br>Oldham Athletic 2 |
| 1914 | 1 | Swindon Town 1<br>M.U. 0 |
| 1915 | 1 | Sheffield Wednesday 1<br>M.U. 0 |
| 1920 | 1 | Port Vale 1<br>M.U. 2 |
| | 2 | M.U. 1<br>Aston Villa 2 |
| 1921 | 1 | Liverpool 1<br>M.U. 1 |
| | 1 replay | M.U. 1<br>Liverpool 2 |
| 1922 | 1 | M.U. 1<br>Cardiff City 4 |
| 1923 | 1 | Bradford City 1<br>M.U. 1 |
| | 1 replay | M.U. 2<br>Bradford City 0 |
| | 2 | Tottenham Hotspur 4<br>M.U. 0 |
| 1924 | 1 | M.U. 1<br>Plymouth Argyle 0 |
| | 2 | M.U. 0<br>Huddersfield Town 3 |
| 1925 | 1 | Sheffield Wednesday 2<br>M.U. 0 |
| 1926 | 3 | Port Vale 2<br>M.U. 3 |
| | 4 | Tottenham Hotspur 2<br>M.U. 2 |
| | 4 replay | M.U. 2<br>Tottenham Hotspur 0 |
| | 5 | Sunderland 3<br>M.U. 3 |
| | 6 | Fulham 1<br>M.U. 2 |
| | S.F.[1] | Manchester City 3<br>M.U. 0 |
| 1927 | 3 | Reading 1<br>M.U. 1 |
| | 3 replay after extra time | M.U. 2<br>Reading 2 |

[1] At Bramall Lane, Sheffield.

| Season ending | Round | Result |
|---|---|---|
| 1927 | 3 2nd replay[2] | M.U. 1<br>Reading 2 |
| 1928 | 3 | M.U. 7<br>Brentford 1 |
| | 4 | Bury 1<br>M.U. 1 |
| | 4 replay | M.U. 1<br>Bury 0 |
| | 5 | M.U. 1<br>Birmingham 0 |
| | 6 | Blackburn Rovers 2<br>M.U. 0 |
| 1929 | 3 | Port Vale 0<br>M.U. 3 |
| | 4 | M.U. 0<br>Bury 1 |
| 1930 | 3 | M.U. 0<br>Swindon Town 2 |
| 1931 | 3 | Stoke 3<br>M.U. 3 |
| | 3 replay after extra time | M.U. 0<br>Stoke 0 |
| | 3 2nd replay[2] | M.U. 4<br>Stoke 2 |
| | 4 | Grimsby Town 1<br>M.U. 0 |
| 1932 | 3 | Plymouth Argyle 4<br>M.U. 1 |
| 1933 | 3 | M.U. 1<br>Middl'brough 4 |
| 1934 | 3 | M.U. 1<br>Portsmouth 1 |
| | 3 replay | Portsmouth 4<br>M.U. 1 |
| 1935 | 3 | Bristol Rovers 1<br>M.U. 3 |
| | 4 | Nottingham Forest 0<br>M.U. 0 |
| | 4 replay | M.U. 0<br>Nottingham Forest 3 |
| 1936 | 3 | Reading 1<br>M.U. 3 |
| | 4 | Stoke City 0<br>M.U. 0 |
| | 4 replay | M.U. 0<br>Stoke City 2 |
| 1937 | 3 | M.U. 1<br>Reading 0 |
| | 4 | Arsenal 5<br>M.U. 0 |
| 1938 | 3 | M.U. 3<br>Yeovil & Petters 0 |
| | 4 | Barnsley 2<br>M.U. 2 |
| | 4 replay | Barnsley 2<br>M.U. 0 |
| 1939 | 3 | West Bromwich Albion 0<br>M.U. 0 |
| | 3 replay | M.U. 0<br>West Bromwich Albion 5 |
| 1946[3] | 3 | Accrington Stanley 2<br>M.U. 2 |
| | 3 replay | M.U. 5<br>Accrington Stanley 1 |
| | 4 | M.U. 1<br>Preston North End 0 |
| | 4 | Preston North End 3<br>M.U. 1 |
| 1947 | 3 | Bradford 0<br>M.U. 3 |

[1] At Villa Park, Birmingham.
[2] At Anfield, Liverpool.
[3] During this season the competition was determined on aggregate of goals in home and away matches, up to the semi-final.

| Season ending | Round | Result |
|---|---|---|
| 1947 | 4 | M.U. 0<br>Nottingham Forest 2 |
| 1948 | 3 | Aston Villa 4<br>M.U. 6 |
| | 4[1] | M.U. 3<br>Liverpool 0 |
| | 5[2] | M.U. 2<br>Charlton Athletic 0 |
| | 6[3] | M.U. 4<br>Preston North End 1 |
| | S.F.[4] | M.U. 3<br>Derby Co. 1 |
| | F[5] | M.U. 4<br>Blackpool 2 |
| 1949 | 3 | M.U. 6<br>Bournemouth 0 |
| | 4 after extra time | M.U. 1<br>Bradford 1 |
| | 4 replay | Bradford 1<br>M.U. 1 |
| | 4 2nd replay[6] | M.U. 5<br>Bradford 0 |
| | 6 | Hull City 0<br>M.U. 1 |
| | S.F. after extra time[7] | M.U. 1<br>Wolverh'pton Wanderers 1 |
| | S.F. replay[8] | M.U. 0<br>Wolverh'pton Wanderers 1 |
| 1950 | 3 | M.U. 4<br>Weymouth 0 |
| | 4 | Watford 0<br>M.U. 1 |
| | 5 | M.U. 3<br>Portsmouth 3 |
| | 5 replay | Portsmouth 1<br>M.U. 3 |
| | 6 | Chelsea 2<br>M.U. 0 |
| 1951 | 3 | M.U. 4<br>Oldham Athletic 1 |
| | 4 | M.U. 4<br>Leeds United 0 |
| | 5 | M.U. 1<br>Arsenal 0 |
| | 6 | Birmingham City 1<br>M.U. 0 |
| 1952 | 3 | M.U. 0<br>Hull City 2 |
| 1953 | 3 | Millwall 0<br>M.U. 1 |
| | 4 | M.U. 1<br>Walthamstow Avenue 1 |
| | 4 replay | Walthamstow Avenue 2<br>M.U. 5 |
| | 5 | Everton 2<br>M.U. 1 |
| 1954 | 3 | Burnley 5<br>M.U. 3 |
| 1955 | 3 | Reading 1<br>M.U. 1 |
| | 3 replay | M.U. 4<br>Reading 1 |
| | 4 | Manchester City 2<br>M.U. 0 |
| 1956 | 3 | Bristol Rovers 4<br>M.U. 0 |
| 1957 | 3 | Hartlepools United 3<br>M.U. 4 |
| | 4 | Wrexham 0<br>M.U. 5 |
| | 5 | M.U. 1<br>Everton 0 |
| | 6 | Bournemouth 1<br>M.U. 2 |

[1] At Goodison Park, Everton.
[2] At Huddersfield.
[3] At Villa Park, Birmingham.
[4] At Hillsborough, Sheffield.
[5] At Wembley.
[6] At Maine Road, Manchester.
[7] At Hillsborough.
[8] At Goodison Park, Everton.

| Season ending | Round | Result |
|---|---|---|
| 1957 | S.F.[1] | M.U. 2<br>Birmingham City 0 |
| | F[2] | M.U. 1<br>Aston Villa 2 |
| 1958 | 3 | Workington 1<br>M.U. 3 |
| | 4 | M.U. 2<br>Ipswich Town 0 |
| | 5 | M.U. 3<br>Sheffield Wednesday 0 |
| | 6 | West Bromwich Albion 2<br>M.U. 2 |
| | 6 replay | M.U. 1<br>West Bromwich Albion 0 |
| | S.F.[3] | M.U. 2<br>Fulham 2 |
| | S.F.[4] replay | M.U. 5<br>Fulham 3 |
| | F[2] | M.U. 0<br>Bolton Wanderers 2 |
| 1959 | 3 | Norwich City 3<br>M.U. 0 |
| 1960 | 3 | Derby Co. 2<br>M.U. 4 |
| | 4 | Liverpool 1<br>M.U. 3 |
| | 5 | M.U. 0<br>Sheffield Wednesday 1 |
| 1961 | 3 | M.U. 3<br>Middl'brough 0 |
| | 4 | Sheffield Wednesday 1<br>M.U. 1 |
| | 4 replay | M.U. 2<br>Sheffield Wednesday 7 |
| 1962 | 3 | M.U. 2<br>Bolton Wanderers 1 |
| | 4 | M.U. 1<br>Arsenal 0 |
| | 5 | M.U. 0<br>Sheffield Wednesday 0 |
| | 5 replay | Sheffield Wednesday 0<br>M.U. 2 |
| | 6 | Preston North End 0<br>M.U. 0 |
| | 6 replay | M.U. 2<br>Preston North End 1 |
| | S.F.[1] | M.U. 1<br>Tottenham Hotspur 3 |
| 1963 | 3 | M.U. 5<br>Huddersfield Town 0 |
| | 4 | M.U. 1<br>Aston Villa 0 |
| | 5 | M.U. 2<br>Chelsea 1 |
| | 6 | Coventry City 1<br>M.U. 3 |
| | S.F.[3] | M.U. 1<br>Southampton 0 |
| | F[2] | M.U. 3<br>Leicester City 1 |
| 1964 | 3 | Southampton 2<br>M.U. 3 |
| | 4 | M.U. 4<br>Bristol Rovers 1 |
| | 5 | Barnsley 0<br>M.U. 4 |
| | 6 | M.U. 3<br>Sunderland 3 |
| | 6 replay after extra time | Sunderland 2<br>M.U. 2 |

[1] At Hillsborough.
[2] At Wembley.
[3] At Villa Park, Birmingham.
[4] At Highbury.

| Season ending | Round | Result |
|---|---|---|
| 1964 | 6[1] 2nd replay | M.U. 5<br>Sunderland 1 |
| | S.F.[2] | M.U. 1<br>West Ham United 3 |
| 1965 | 3 | M.U. 2<br>Chester 1 |
| | 4 | Stoke City 0<br>M.U. 0 |
| | 4 replay | M.U. 1<br>Stoke City 0 |
| | 5 | M.U. 2<br>Burnley 1 |
| | 6 | Wolverh'pton Wanderers 3<br>M.U. 5 |
| | S.F.[2] | M.U. 0<br>Leeds United 0 |
| | S.F.[3] replay | M.U. 0<br>Leeds United 1 |
| 1966 | 3 | Derby Co. 2<br>M.U. 5 |
| | 4 | M.U. 0<br>Rotherham U. 0 |
| | 4 replay after extra time | Rotherham U. 0<br>M.U. 1 |
| | 5 | Wolverh'pton Wanderers 2<br>M.U. 4 |
| | 6 | Preston North End 1<br>M.U. 1 |
| | 6 replay | M.U. 3<br>Preston North End 1 |
| | S.F.[4] | M.U. 0<br>Everton 1 |
| 1967 | 3 | M.U. 2<br>Stoke City 0 |
| | 4 | M.U. 1<br>Norwich City 2 |
| 1968 | 3 | M.U. 2<br>Tottenham Hotspur 2 |
| | 3 replay | Tottenham Hotspur 1<br>M.U. 0 |
| 1969 | 3 | Exeter City 1<br>M.U. 3 |
| | 4 | M.U. 1<br>Watford 1 |
| | 4 replay | Watford 0<br>M.U. 2 |
| | 5 | Birmingham City 2<br>M.U. 2 |
| | 5 replay | M.U. 6<br>Birmingham City 2 |
| | 6 | M.U. 0<br>Everton 1 |
| 1970 | 3 | Ipswich Town 0<br>M.U. 1 |
| | 4 | M.U. 3<br>Manchester City 0 |
| | 5 | Northampton Town 2<br>M.U. 8 |
| | 6 | Middl'brough 1<br>M.U. 1 |
| | 6 replay | M.U. 2<br>Middl'brough 1 |
| | S.F.[2] | M.U. 0<br>Leeds Utd. 0 |
| | S.F.[5] replay after extra time | M.U. 0<br>Leeds Utd. 0 |
| | S.F.[4] 2nd replay | M.U. 0<br>Leeds United 1 |

1 At Leeds Road, Huddersfield.
2 At Hillsborough.
3 At City Ground, Nottingham.
4 At Burnden Park, Bolton.
5 At Villa Park, Birmingham.

| Season ending | Round | Result |
|---|---|---|
| 1971 | 3 | M.U. 0<br>Middl'brough 0 |
| | 3 replay | Middl'brough 2<br>M.U. 1 |
| 1972 | 3 | Southampton 1<br>M.U. 1 |
| | 3 replay | M.U. 4<br>Southampton 1 |
| | 4 | Preston North End 0<br>M.U. 2 |
| | 5 | M.U. 0<br>Middl'brough 0 |
| | 5 replay | Middl'brough 0<br>M.U. 3 |
| | 6 | M.U. 1<br>Stoke City 1 |
| | 6 replay | Stoke City 2<br>M.U. 1 |
| 1973 | 3 | Wolverh'pton Wanderers 1<br>M.U. 0 |
| 1974 | 3 | M.U. 1<br>Plymouth A. 0 |
| | 4 | M.U. 0<br>Ipswich T. 1 |
| 1975 | 3 | M.U. 0<br>Walsall 0 |
| | 3 replay | Walsall 3<br>M.U. 2 |
| 1976 | 3 | M.U. 2<br>Oxford Utd. 1 |
| | 4 | M.U. 3<br>Peterborough United 1 |
| | 5 | Leicester C. 1<br>M.U. 2 |
| | 6 | M.U. 1<br>Wolverh'pton Wanderers 1 |
| | 6 replay after extra time | Wolverh'pton Wanderers 2<br>M.U. 3 |
| | S.F.[1] | M.U. 2<br>Derby Co. 0 |
| | F[2] | M.U. 0<br>Southampton 1 |
| 1977 | 3 | M.U. 1<br>Walsall 0 |
| | 4 | M.U. 1<br>Queens Park Rangers 0 |
| | 5 | Southampton 2<br>M.U. 2 |
| | 5 replay | M.U. 2<br>Southampton 1 |
| | 6 | M.U. 2<br>Aston Villa 1 |
| | S.F.[1] | M.U. 2<br>Leeds Utd. 1 |
| | F[2] | M.U. 2<br>Liverpool 1 |
| 1978 | 3 | Carlisle Utd. 1<br>M.U. 1 |
| | 3 replay | M.U. 4<br>Carlisle Utd. 2 |
| | 4 | M.U. 1<br>West Brom. Albion 1 |
| | 4 replay after extra time | West Brom. Albion 3<br>M.U. 2 |

[1] At Hillsborough.
[2] At Wembley.

# Appendix 4

## LEAGUE CUP

**1960/61**

| | | |
|---|---|---|
| 1. | Exeter | (A) 1–1 |
| | | (H) 4–1 |
| 2. | Bradford City | (A) 1–2 |

**1966/67**

| | | |
|---|---|---|
| 2. | Blackpool | (A) 1–5 |

**1969/70**

| | | |
|---|---|---|
| 2. | Middlesbrough | (H) 1–0 |
| 3. | Wrexham | (H) 2–0 |
| 4. | Burnley | (A) 0–0 |
| | | (H) 1–0 |
| 5. | Derby County | (A) 0–0 |
| | | (H) 1–0 |
| S.F. | Manchester City | (A) 1–2 |
| | | (H) 2–2 |

**1970/71**

| | | |
|---|---|---|
| 2. | Aldershot | (A) 3–1 |
| 3. | Portsmouth | (H) 1–0 |
| 4. | Chelsea | (H) 2–1 |
| 5. | C. Palace | (H) 4–2 |
| S.F. | A. Villa | (H) 1–1 |
| | | (A) 1–2 |

**1971/72**

| | | |
|---|---|---|
| 2. | Ipswich | (A) 3–1 |
| 3. | Burnley | (H) 1–1 |
| | | (A) 1–0 |
| 4. | Stoke | (H) 1–1 |
| | | (A) 0–0 |
| | | (A) 1–2 |

**1972/73**

| | | |
|---|---|---|
| 2. | Oxford | (A) 2–2 |
| | | (H) 3–1 |
| 3. | Bristol Rovers | (A) 1–1 |
| | | (H) 1–2 |

**1973/74**

| | | |
|---|---|---|
| 2. | Middlesbrough | (H) 0–1 |

**1974/75**

| | | |
|---|---|---|
| 2. | Charlton | (H) 5–1 |
| 3. | Manchester City | (H) 1–0 |
| 4. | Burnley | (H) 3–2 |
| 5. | Middlesbrough | (A) 0–0 |
| | | (H) 3–0 |
| S.F. | Norwich | (H) 2–2 |
| | | (A) 0–1 |

**1975/76**

| | | |
|---|---|---|
| 2. | Brentford | (H) 2–1 |
| 3. | A. Villa | (A) 2–1 |
| 4. | Man. City | (A) 0–4 |

**1976/77**

| | | |
|---|---|---|
| 2. | Tranmere | (H) 5–0 |
| 3. | Sunderland | (H) 2–2 |
| | | (A) 2–2 |
| | | (H) 1–0 |
| 4. | Newcastle | (H) 7–2 |
| 5. | Everton | (H) 0–3 |

**1977/78**

| | | |
|---|---|---|
| 2. | Arsenal | (A) 2–3 |

# Appendix 5

## EUROPE

| YEAR | TEAM | SCORE | SCORERS |
|---|---|---|---|
| 1956/57 *European Cup* | R.S.C. Anderlecht | 2–0 (A) Won<br>10–0 (H) Won | Taylor Viollet<br>Whelan 2 Berry 1<br>Viollet 4 Taylor 3 |
| | Borussia Dortmund | 3–2 (H) Won<br>0–0 (A) Draw | Viollet 2 1 own goal |
| | Athletico Bilbao | 5–3 (A) Lost<br>3–0 (H) Won | Taylor Viollet Whelan<br>Viollet Taylor Berry |
| Semi-Final | Real Madrid | 3–1(A) Lost<br>2–2 (H) Draw | Taylor<br>Taylor Charlton |
| 1957/58 *European Cup* | Shamrock Rovers | 6–0 (A) Won<br>3–2 (H) Won | Whelan 2 Taylor 2<br>Berry Pegg<br>Viollet 2 Pegg |
| | Dukla Prague | 3–0 (H) Won<br>1–0 (A) Lost | Taylor Webster Pegg |
| | Red Star Belgrade | 2–1 (H) Won<br>3–3 (A) Draw | Colman Charlton<br>Charlton 2 Viollet |
| Semi-Final | A.C. Milan | 2–1 (H) Won<br>4–0 (A) Lost | Taylor E. (pen.) Viollet |
| 1963/64 *Cup-Winners' Cup* | Willem II | 1–1 (A) Draw<br>6–1 (H) Won | Herd<br>Law 3 Charlton Chisnall Setters |
| | Spurs | 2–0 (A) Lost<br>4–1 (H) Won | <br>Herd 2 Charlton 2 |
| Quarter-Final | Sporting Lisbon | 4–1 (H) Won<br>5–0 (A) Lost | Law 3 Charlton |
| 1964/65 *Inter-Cities Fairs' Cup* | Djurgardens | 1–1 (A) Draw<br>6–1 (H) Won | Herd<br>Law 3 Charlton 2 Best |
| | Borussia Dortmund | 6–1 (A) Won<br>4–0 (H) Won | Charlton 3 Herd Law Best<br>Charlton 2 Connelly Law |
| | Everton | 1–1 (H) Draw<br>2–1 (A) Won | Connelly<br>Connelly Herd |
| | F.C. Strasbourg | 5–0 (A) Won<br>0–0 (H) Draw | Law 2 Connelly Charlton Herd |
| Semi-Final | Ferencvaros | 3–2 (H) Won<br>1–0 (A) Lost<br>1–1 (A) Lost | Herd 2 Law<br><br>Connelly |

| YEAR | TEAM | SCORE | SCORERS |
|---|---|---|---|
| 1965/66 *European Cup* | Helsinki | 3–2 (A) Won<br>6–0 (H) Won | Connelly Herd Law<br>Connelly 3 Best 2 Charlton |
| | A.S.K. Vorwarts | 2–0 (A) Won<br>3–1 (H) Won | Connelly Law<br>Herd 3 |
| | Benfica | 3–2 (H) Won<br>5–1 (A) Won | Herd Law Foulkes<br>Charlton Connelly Crerand Best 2 |
| Semi-Final | F. K. Partizan | 2–0 (A) Lost<br>1–0 (H) Won | <br>Own goal |
| 1967/68 *European Cup* | Malta Hibs. | 4–0 (H) Won<br>0–0 (A) Draw | Sadler 2 Law 2 |
| | F.K. Sarajevo | 0–0 (A) Draw<br>2–1 (H) Won | <br>Best Aston |
| | Gornik Zabrze | 2–0 (H) Won<br>1–0 (A) Lost | Kidd; (own goal) |
| Semi-Final | Real Madrid | 1–0 (H) Won<br>3–3 (A) Draw | Best<br>Sadler Foulkes; (own goal) |
| Final | Benfica | 4–1 Won (Wembley) | Charlton 2 Best Kidd |
| 1968/69 *European Cup* | Waterford | 3–1 (A) Won<br>7–1 (H) Won | Law 3<br>Law 4 Charlton Burns Stiles |
| | R.S.C. Anderlecht | 3–0 (H) Won<br>3–1 (A) Lost | Law 2 Kidd<br>Sartori |
| | Rapid Vienna | 3–0 (H) Won<br>0–0 (A) Draw | Best 2 Morgan |
| Semi-Final | A.C. Milan | 2–0(A) Lost<br>1–0 (H) Won | <br>Charlton |
| 1968/69 *World Club Championship* | Estudiantes De Plata (South America) | 1–0 (A) Lost<br>1–1 (H) Draw | <br>Morgan |
| 1976/77 *U.E.F.A. Cup* | Ajax | 1–0 (A) Lost<br>2–0 (H) Won | <br>Macari McIlroy |
| | Juventus | 1–0 (H) Won<br>3–0 (A) Lost | Hill |
| 1977/78 *Cup-Winners' Cup* | St. Etienne | 1–1 (A) Draw<br>Played at (Plymouth F.C.)<br>2–0 (H) Won | Hill<br><br>Coppell Pearson |
| | F.C. Porto | 4–0 (A) Lost<br>5–2 (H) Won | <br>Coppell 2 Nicholl (2 own goals) |

# Appendix 6

## CLUB HONOURS

EUROPEAN CHAMPION CLUBS CUP
Winners 1968
Semi-finalists 1957, 1958, 1966, 1969

F.A. CHALLENGE CUP
Winners 1909, 1948, 1963, 1977.
Runners-up 1957, 1958, 1976.
Semi-finalists 1926, 1949, 1962, 1964 1965, 1966, 1970.

F.A. CHARITY SHIELD
1908 Manchester United 4, Queens Park Rangers 0. (This was the first year of this competition, the contestants being the Champions of the Football League and the Southern League. On April 27, 1908, the teams met at Stamford Bridge and the result was a draw 1–1; a replay took place on August 29.)
1911 Manchester United 8, Swindon Town (Southern League Champions) 4.
1949 Arsenal 4, Manchester United 3.
1953 Manchester United 4, Newcastle United 2.
1957 Manchester United 1, Manchester City 0.
1958 Manchester United 4, Aston Villa 0.
1963 Everton 4, Manchester United 0.
1965 Manchester United 2, Liverpool 2. (Shield shared, six months each.)
1967 Manchester United 3, Tottenham Hotspur 3. (Shield shared, six months each.)
1977 Manchester United 0, Liverpool 0. (Shield shared, six months each.)

F.A. YOUTH CHALLENGE CUP
Winners 1953, 1954, 1955, 1956, 1957, 1964.
Semi-finalists 1958, 1959, 1960, 1969, 1970.

LANCASHIRE F.A. YOUTH CUP
Winners 1972, 1975, 1976.
Runners-up 1973, 1978
Semi-finalists 1971.

THE ALLIANCE
Runners-up 1891.

## FOOTBALL LEAGUE

Division I

| | |
|---|---|
| Champions | 1908, 1911, 1952, 1956, 1957, 1965, 1967. |
| Runners-up | 1947, 1948, 1949, 1951, 1959, 1964, 1968. |

Division II

| | |
|---|---|
| Champions | 1936, 1975. |
| Runners-up | 1897, 1906, 1925, 1938. |

## FOOTBALL LEAGUE CUP

Semi-finalists 1969, 1970, 1975.

## CENTRAL LEAGUE

Champions 1913, 1921, 1939, 1947, 1956, 1960.

## LANCASHIRE F.A. SENIOR CUP

Winners 1898, 1913, 1914, 1920, 1929 (jointly with Liverpool), 1938, 1941, 1943, 1946, 1951, 1969.

## MANCHESTER F.A. SENIOR CUP

Winners 1886, 1888, 1889, 1890, 1893, 1902, 1908, 1910, 1912, 1913, 1920, 1924, 1926, 1931, 1934, 1936, 1937, 1939, 1948 1955, 1957, 1959, 1964.

## WORLD CLUB CHAMPIONSHIP (Inter-Continental Cup)

Runners-up 1968.

(V. Estudiantes de la Plata (A) 0–1
(Argentina) (H) 1–1

# Appendix 7

## INDIVIDUAL INTERNATIONAL HONOURS

Key to Abbreviations:
A – Austria; Alb – Albania; Arg – Argentina; Bel – Belgium; Br – Brazil; Bul – Bulgaria; Ch – Chile; Co – Columbia; Cy – Cyprus; Cz – Czechoslovakia; D – Denmark; Ec – Ecuador; Ei – Eire; EG – East Germany; F – France; Fi – Finland; G – Germany (pre-war); Gr – Greece; H – Hungary; Ho – Holland; I – Italy; Ic – Iceland Is – Israel; L – Luxembourg; M – Mexico; Ma – Malta; N – Norway; Ni – Northern Ireland; P – Portugal; Pe – Peru; Pol – Poland; R – Rumania; R of W – Rest of World; S – Scotland; SA – South Africa; Se – Sweden; Sp – Spain; Sw – Switzerland; T – Turkey; U – Uruguay; US – United States of America; USSR – Russia; W – Wales, WG – West Germany; Y – Yugoslavia; Z – Zaire.

ENGLAND

| | |
|---|---|
| Aston, J. | 1949 v. S,W,D,Sw,Se,N,F; 1950 v. S,W,Ni,Ei,I,P, Bel,Ch,US; 1951 v. Ni. |
| Berry, J. J. | 1953 v. Arg,Ch,U; 1956 v. Se. |
| Bradley, J. J. | 1953 v. Arg,Ch,U; 1956 v. Se. |
| Bradley, W. | 1959 v. I,US,M(sub). |
| Byrne, R. W. | 1954 v. S,H,Y,Bel,Sw,U; 1955 v. S,W,Ni,WG,F,Sp, P; 1956 v. S,W,Ni,Br,Se,Fi,WG,D,Sp; 1957 v. S,W, Ni,Y,D(2),Ei(2); 1958 v. W.Ni,F. |
| Charlton, R. | 1958 v. S,P,Y; 1959 v. S.W,Ni, USSR,I,Br,Pe,M,US; 1960 v. W,S,Se,Y,Sp,H; 1961 v. Ni,W,S,L,P,Sp,M,I, A; 1962 v. W,Ni,S,A,Sw,Pe,L,P,H,Arg,Bul,Br; 1963 v. S,F,Br,Cz,EG,Sw; 1964 v. S,W,Ni,R of W,U, P,Ei,Br,Arg,US(sub); 1965 v. Ni,S,Ho; 1966 v. W, Ni,S,A,Sp,WG(2),Y,Fi,N,Pol,U,M,F,Arg,P; 1967 v. Ni,W,S,Cz; 1968 v. W,Ni,S,USSR(2),Sp(2),Se,Y; 1969 v. S,W,Ni,R(2),Bul,M,Br; 1970 v. W,Ni,Ho(2), P,Co,Ec,Cz,R,Br,WG. |
| Chilton, A. | 1951 v. Ni; 1952 v. F. |
| Cockburn, H. | 1947 v. W,Ni,Ei; 1948 v. S,I; 1949 v. S,Ni,D,Sw,Se; 1951 v. Arg,P; 1952 v. F. |
| Connelly, J. M. | 1965 v. H,Y,Se; 1966 v. W,Ni,S,A,N,D,U. |
| Coppell, S. J. | 1978 v. I,WG,Br,W,Ni,S,H. |
| Duckworth, R. | 1910 v. SA. |
| Edwards, D. | 1955 v. S,F,Sp,P; 1956 v. S,Br,Se,Fi,WG; 1957 v. S, Ni,Ei(2),D(2); 1958 v. W,Ni,F. |

Foulkes, W. A. 1955 v. Ni.
Greenhoff, B. 1976 v. W,Ni; 1977 v. Ei,Fi,I,Ho,Ni,W,S,Br,Arg,U; 1978 v. Br,W,Ni,S.(sub),H(sub).
Halse, H. J. 1909 v. A.
Hill, G. A. 1976 v. I; 1977 v. Ei(sub),Fi(sub),L; 1978 v. Sw(sub), L.
Hilditch, C. G. 1920 v. SA(3).
Kidd, B. 1970 v. Ni,Ec(sub).
McGuinness, W. 1959 v. Ni,M.
Mew, J. W. 1921 v. Ni.
Pearson, J. S. 1976 v. W,Ni,S,Br,Fi; 1977 v. Ei,Ho(sub),W,S,Br, Arg,U; 1978 v. I(sub), WG,Ni.
Pearson, S. C. 1948 v. S; 1949 v. S,Ni; 1950 v. Ni,I; 1951 v. P; 1952 v. S,I.
Pegg, D. 1957 v. Ei.
Roberts, C. 1905 v. Ni,W,S.
Rowley, J. F. 1949 v. Sw,Se,F; 1950 v. Ni,I; 1952 v. S.
Sadler, D. 1968 v. Ni,USSR; 1970 v. Ec(sub); 1971 v. EG.
Silcock, J. 1921 v. S,W; 1923 v. Se.
Spence, J. W. 1926 v. Bel; 1927 v. Ni.
Stepney, A. C. 1968 v. Se.
Stiles, N. P. 1965 v. S,H,Y,Se; 1966 v. W,Ni,S,A,Sp,Pol(2), WG(2),N,D,U,M,F,Arg,P; 1967 v. Ni,W,S,Cz; 1968 v. USSR; 1969 v. R; 1970 v. Ni,S.
Taylor, T. 1953 v. Arg,Ch,U; 1954 v. Bel,Sw; 1956 v. S,Br,Se, Fi,WG; 1957 v. Ni,Y(sub),D(2),Ei(2); 1958 v. W, Ni,F.
Viollet, D. S. 1960 v. H; 1962 v. L.
Wall, G. 1907 v. W; 1908 v. Ni; 1909 v. S; 1910 v. W,S; 1912 v. S; 1913 v. Ni.
Wood, R. E. 1955 v. Ni,W; 1956 v. Fi.
Woodcock, W. 1920 v. SA(2).

SCOTLAND

Bell, A. 1912 v. Ni.
Buchan, M. M. 1972 v. W,Y,Cz,Br; 1973 v. D(2),E; 1974 v. WG, Ni,W,N,Br,Y; 1975 v. EG,Sp,P; 1976 v. D,R; 1977 v. Fi,Cz,Ch,Arg,Br; 1978 v. EG,W(sub),Ni
Burns, F. 1970 v. A.
Crerand, P. T. 1964 v. Ni; 1965 v. E,Pol,Fi; 1966 v. Pol.
Delaney, J. 1947 v. E; 1948 v. E,W,Ni.
Forsyth, A. 1973 v. E; 1975 v. Sp,Ni(sub),R,EG; 1976 v. D.
Graham, G. 1973 v. E,W,Ni,Sw(sub),Br(sub).
Holton, J. A. 1973 v. E,W,Ni,Sw,Br; 1974 v. Cz,Wg,Ni,W,E,N,Z, Br,Y; 1975 v. EG.
Houston, S. M. 1976 v. D.
Jordan, J. 1978 v. Bul,Ni,E.

| | |
|---|---|
| Law, D. | 1963 v. W,Ni,E,A,N,Ei,Sp; 1964 v. W,E,N,WG; 1965 v. W,Ni,E,Fi(2),Pol,Sp; 1966 v. Ni,E,Pol; 1967 v. W,E,USSR; 1968 v. Ni; 1969 v. Ni,A,WG; 1972 v. Pe,Ni,W,E,Y,Cz,Br. |
| Macari, L. | 1973 v. E(2),W(sub),Ni(sub); 1975 v. Se,P(sub),W, E(sub),R; 1977 v. Ni(sub),E(sub),Ch,Arg; 1978 v. EG,W,Bul. |
| McBain, N. | 1922 v. E. |
| McQueen, G. | 1978 v. Bul,Ni,W |
| Miller, T. | 1921 v. E,Ni. |
| Morgan, W. | 1972 v. Pe,Y,Cz,Br; 1973 v. D(2),E(2),W,Ni,Sw,Br; 1974 v. Cz(2),WG(2),Ni,Bel(sub),Br,Y. |

WALES

| | |
|---|---|
| Bennion, S. R. | 1926 v. S; 1927 v. S; 1928 v. S,E,Ni; 1929 v. S,E,Ni; 1930 v. S; 1932 v. Ni. |
| Burke, T. | 1887 v. E,S; 1888 v. S. |
| Davies, J. | 1888 v. E,S,Ni; 1889 v. S; 1890 v. E. |
| Davies, R. W. | 1973 v. E,S(sub),Ni. |
| Doughty, J. | 1887 v. S,Ni; 1888 v. E,S,Ni; 1889 v. S; 1890 v. E. |
| Doughty, R. | 1888 v. S,Ni. |
| Jenkyns, C. A. L. | 1897 v. Ni. |
| Jones, T. | 1926 v. Ni; 1927 v. E,Ni; 1930 v. Ni. |
| Meredith, W. H. | 1907 v. E,S,Ni; 1908 v. E,Ni; 1909 v. E,S,Ni; 1910 v. E,S,Ni; 1911 v. E,S,Ni; 1912 v. E,S,Ni; 1913 v. E,S, Ni; 1914 v. E,S,Ni; 1920 v. E,S,Ni. |
| Moore, G. | 1964 v. S,Ni. |
| Owen, G. | 1889 v. S,Ni; 1892 v. E; 1893 v. Ni. |
| Powell, J. | 1887 v. E,S; 1888 v. E,S,Ni. |
| Thomas, H. | 1927 v. E. |
| Warner, J. | 1939 v. F(2) |
| Webster, C. | 1957 v. Cz; 1958 v. H,M,Br. |
| Williams, D. R. | 1929 v. E,S. |

NORTHERN IRELAND

| | |
|---|---|
| Anderson, T. | 1973 v. Cy,E,S,W; 1974 v. Bul,P. |
| Best, G. | 1964 v. W,U; 1965 v. E,Ho(2),S,Sw,Alb; 1966 v. S, E,Alb; 1967 v. E; 1968 v. S; 1969 v. E,S,W,T; 1970 v. S,E,W,USSR; 1971 v. Cy(2),Sp,E,S,W; 1972 v. USSR,Sp; 1973 v. Bul; 1974 v. P. |
| Blanchflower, J. | 1954 v. W; 1955 v. E,S; 1956 v. S,W; 1957 v. S,E,P; 1958 v. S,E,I(2). |
| Breen, T. | 1937 v. W; 1938 v. E,S; 1939 v. W,S. |
| Briggs, W. R. | 1962 v. W. |
| Carey, J. J. | 1947 v. E,S,W; 1948 v. E; 1949 v. E,S,W. |
| Crooks, W. | 1922 v. W. |

| | |
|---|---|
| Gregg, H. | 1958 v. Cz,Arg,WG,F,W; 1959 v. E,W; 1960 v. S,E, W; 1961 v. E,S; 1962 v. S,Gr; 1964 v. S,E. |
| Hamil, M. | 1912 v. E; 1914 v. E,S. |
| Jackson, T. | 1976 v. Se,N,Y; 1977 v. Ho,Bel,WG,E,S,W,Ic. |
| Lyner, D. | 1923 v. E. |
| McCreery, D. | 1976 v. S(sub),E,W; 1977 v. Ho,Bel,Wg,E,S,W,Ic; 1978 v. Ic,Ho,Bel,S,E,W. |
| McGrath, R, C. | 1977 v. Bel,WG,E,S,W,Ic; 1978 v. Ic,Ho,Bel,S,E,W. |
| McIlroy, S. B. | 1972 v. Sp,S(sub); 1974 v. S,E,W; 1975 v. N,Se,Y,E, S,W; 1976 v. Se,N,Y,S,E,W; 1977 v. Ho,Bel,E,S,W, Ic; 1978 v. Ic,Ho,Bel,S,E,W. |
| McMillan, S. | 1963 v. E,S. |
| McMillen, W. S. | 1934 v. E; 1935 v. S; 1937 v. S. |
| Nicholl, J. M. | 1976 v. Is,W(sub); 1977 v. Ho,Bel,E,S,W,Ic; 1978 v. Ic,Ho,Bel,S,E,W. |
| Nicholson, J. J. | 1961 v. S,W; 1962 v. E,W,Gr,Ho; 1963 v. E,S,Pol(2). |

REPUBLIC OF IRELAND

| | |
|---|---|
| Breen, T. | 1937 v. Sw,F. |
| Brennan, S. A. | 1965 v. Sp; 1966 v. Sp,A,Bel; 1967 v. Sp,T,Sp; 1969 v. Cz,D,H; 1970 v. S,Cz,D,H,Pol(sub),WG. |
| Cantwell, N. | 1961 v. S(2); 1962 v. Cz(2),A; 1963 v. Ic(2),S; 1964 v. A,Sp,E; 1965 v. Pol,Sp; 1966 v. Sp(2),A,Bel; 1967 v. Sp,T. |
| Carey, J. J. | 1938 v. N,Cz,Pol; 1939 v. Sw,Pol,H(2),G; 1946 v. P. Sp; 1947 v. E,Sp,P; 1948 v. P,Sp; 1949 v. Sw,Bel,P, Se,Sp; 1950 v. Fi,E,Fi,Se; 1951 v. N,Arg,N; 1953 v. F,A. |
| Carolan, J. | 1960 v. Se,Ch. |
| Daly, G. A. | 1973 v. Pol(sub),N; 1974 v. Br(sub),U(sub); 1975 v. Sw(sub); 1977 v. E,T,F. |
| Dunne, A. P. | 1962 v. A; 1963 v. Ic,S; 1964 v. A,Sp,Pol,N,E; 1965 v. Pol,Sp; 1966 v. Sp(2),A,Bel; 1967 v. Sp,T,Sp; 1969 v. Pol,D,H; 1970 v. H; 1971 v. Se,I,A. |
| Dunne, P. A. G. | 1965 v. Sp; 1966 v. Sp(2),WG; 1967 v. T. |
| Giles, M. J. | 1960 v. Se,Ch; 1961 v. W,N,S(2); 1962 v. Cz(2),A; 1963 v. Ic,S. |
| Givens, D. J. | 1969 v. D,H; 1970 v. S,Cz,D,H. |
| Grimes, A. A. | 1978 v. T,Pol. |
| Martin, M. P. | 1973 v. USSR,Pol,F,N; 1974 v. Pol,Br,U,Ch; 1975 v. USSR,T,Sw,USSR,Sw. |
| Roche, P. J. | 1975 v. USSR,T,Sw,USSR,Sw; 1976 v. T. |
| Whelen, W. | 1956 v Ho; 1957 v. D,E(2). |

F.I.F.A
REST OF THE WORLD

| | |
|---|---|
| Law, D. | 1964 v E. |

REST OF EUROPE

| | |
|---|---|
| Carey, J. J. | 1947 v. GB. |
| Charlton, R. | 1964 v Scandinavia. |
| Law, D. | 1964 v Scandinavia. |

## AMATEUR INTERNATIONALS

ENGLAND

| | |
|---|---|
| Bradbury, J. | 1936 v Ni. |
| Bradley, W. | 1959 v. Ni,Fi,SA,W. |
| Hardman, H. P. | 1908 Olympic Games. |
| Pinner, M. J. | 1961 v Ei,S,F. |
| Walton, J. A. | 1952 v Ni,W,S. |

## 'B' INTERNATIONALS

ENGLAND

| | |
|---|---|
| Berry, J. J. | 1952 v Ho. |
| Byrne, R. W. | 1953 v. S; 1954 v. WG. |
| Cockburn, H. | 1949 v. Ho. |
| Edwards, D. | 1954 v WG,Sw; 1955 v. WG; 1956 v. Sw. |
| Hill, G. A. | 1978 v. WG. |
| Kidd, B. | 1970 v. Co. |
| Pegg, D. | 1956 v. Sw. |
| Rowley, J. F. | 1949 v. Ho. |
| Stiles, N. P. | 1970 v. C,Ec Xl. |
| Taylor, T. | 1956 v. S,Sw. |
| Wood, R. E. | 1954 v. S. |

NORTHERN IRELAND

| | |
|---|---|
| Nicholson, J. | 1960 v. F(2). |
| Shiels, J. | 1960 v. F. |

## UNDER 23 INTERNATIONALS

ENGLAND

| | |
|---|---|
| Aston, J. | 1970 v. W. |
| Charlton, R. | 1959 v. Pol,Cz,F; 1960 v. H,S; 1961 v. I. |
| Chisnall, J. P. | 1964 v. W,WG,S,F. |
| Coppell, S. J. | 1976 v. H. |
| Edwards, D. | 1954 v. I; 1955 v. I,S; 1956 v. S; 1957 v. R,Cz. |
| Edwards, P. | 1970 v. Bul(sub); 1971 v. WG,Se. |
| Foulkes, W. A. | 1955 v. S,I. |
| Gowling, A. | 1972 v. Sw. |
| Greenhoff, B. | 1974 v. Y,F(sub); 1975 v. Cz; 1976 v. H. |
| Hill, G. A. | 1976 v. H. |
| Kidd, B. | 1968 v. W,I,S; 1969 v. Ho,Bel(sub); 1970 v. W, USSR,S; 1971 v. WG,Se. |
| McGuinness, W. | 1959 v. Pol,Cz,F; 1960 v. H. |

| | |
|---|---|
| Pearson, J. S. | 1976 v. H. |
| Pegg, D. | 1956 v. S; 1957 v. S,R. |
| Sadler, D. | 1967 v. S; 1968 v. W; 1969 v. P. |
| Scanlon, A. | 1959 v. P,Cz,F,I,WG. |
| Setters, M. | 1960 v. S,Ho,Eg,Pol,Is. |
| Stiles, N. P. | 1965 v. S,WG,Cz. |
| Whitefoot, G | 1954 v. I. |
| Wood, R. E. | 1954 v. I. |

SCOTLAND

| | |
|---|---|
| Burns, F. | 1968 v. E. |
| Forsyth, A. | 1974 v. W. |
| Holton, J. A. | 1973 v. W. |
| Houston, S. M. | 1975 v. Se,R. |

WALES

| | |
|---|---|
| Griffiths, C. L. | 1974 v. S,E. |
| Moore, G. | 1964 v. E,S,Ni. |
| Morgans, K. | 1958 v. S; 1959 v. S; 1960 v. S. |

NORTHERN IRELAND

| | |
|---|---|
| Briggs, W. R. | 1962 v. W. |
| Nicholson, J. | 1962 v. W; 1963 v. W; 1964 v. W. |

REPUBLIC OF IRELAND

| | |
|---|---|
| Dunne, P. A. G. | 1966 v. F. |
| McEwen, F. | 1966 v. F. |
| O'Brien, R. | 1973 v. F. |

## YOUTH INTERNATIONALS

ENGLAND

| | |
|---|---|
| Bielby, P. A. | 1975 v. Ni(sub). |
| Charlton, R. | 1954 v. Ni. |
| Clayton, G. | 1955 v. Ho. |
| Connaughton, J. P. | 1968 v. Bul,Ho,USSR. |
| Edwards, D. | 1955 v. Ho. |
| Elms, J. B. | 1958 v. Ho,Bel,L,Y. |
| Gaskell, J. D. | 1957 v. Bel,L,W,S,WG,Ni,(IYT); 1958 v. Ho,R; 1959 v. Sp. |
| Hall, A. | 1955 v. S. |
| Hawksworth, A. | 1955 v. W,S,(IYT). |
| Hewitt, R. | 1961 v. S. |
| Holland, E. R. | 1957 v. W,Ho,S,WG,(IYT); 1958 v. Sp. |
| James, S. R. | 1968 v. F,Ei(2),Bul. |
| Jones, E. P. | 1956 v. D,Ho. |
| Kidd, B. | 1967 v. WG,S(2),I,Sp,Y,F,USSR. |
| McGuinness, W. | 1954 v.Ni; 1956 v. D,Ho; 1957 v. H; 1958 v. R. |

| | |
|---|---|
| Morton, R. S. | 1972 v. Sp(sub). |
| Noble, R. | 1964 v. Sp,Pol,Ei,A,P,Sp. |
| Pearson, M. | 1957 v. W,Ho,S,WG,(IYT). |
| Riley, E. | 1971 v. Ni. |
| Ritchie, A. T. | 1978 v. F(2),T,Sp. |
| Rogers, M. | 1978 v. U,H,F,T,Sp,Pol. |
| Sadler, D. | 1963 v. Sw(sub),Sw,USSR; 1964 v. Pol,Ei,A,P,Sp. |
| Smith, B. | 1958 v. Bel,L,Y,W,S; 1959 v. Sp. |
| Smith, R. W. | 1961 v. Ho,WG. |
| Spratt, T. | 1959 v. S,W,EG,I,R. |
| Stiles, N. P. | 1959 v. W,EG. |
| Sutcliffe, P. D. | 1975 v. Sp. |
| Young, E. R. | 1971 v. Sp. |

(IYT) – International Youth Tournament. One cap was presented for entire tournament.

The following have all represented their countries at Youth level, but details are not available.

SCOTLAND – Albiston, A.; Burns, F.; Kelly, J.

WALES – Griffiths, C. L.; Clark, J.; Lucas, J.; Morris, D. M.; Olney, P.A.

NORTHERN IRELAND – McCreery, D.; McKeown, L.I.; Nicholl, J. M.

REPUBLIC OF IRELAND – Carrick, W. E.; Kelly, M. E.

## FOOTBALL LEAGUE

Key to Abbreviations:

SL – Scottish League; IL – Irish League; LI – League of Ireland.

| | |
|---|---|
| Allen, R. | 1951 v. IL; 1952 v. LI. |
| Aston, J. | 1949 v. SL; 1951 v. SL. |
| Beale, R. H. | 1913 v. SL. |
| Berry, J. J. | 1954 v. SL,LI. |
| Bryant, W. | 1897 v. IL. |
| Byrne, R. W. | 1954 v. LI; 1955 v. IL; 1956 v. SL,LI,IL; 1957 v. LI. |
| Charlton, R. | 1961 v. SL; 1962 v. LI,SL,IL; 1964 v. IL; 1965 v. SL; 1966 v. SL; 1968 v. SL. |
| Cockburn, H. | 1951 v. SL; 1952 v. SL. |
| Connelly, J. M. | 1967 v. IL. |
| Duckworth, F. | 1910 v. IL,SL; 1912 v. SL. |
| Edwards, D. | 1955 v. SL,IL; 1957 v. LI,SL. |
| Edwards, P. | 1971 v. IL. |
| Foulkes, W. A. | 1955 v. SL,LI. |
| Halse, H. J. | 1908 v. IL; 1911 v. IL. |
| Hayes, J. V. | 1910 v. SL. |
| Hofton, L. | 1911 v. IL. |
| Kidd, B. | 1970 v. SL. |
| McGuinness, W. | 1959 v. IL. |
| Mew, J. W. | 1921 v. SL. |
| Morris, J. | 1948 v. SL; 1949 v.IL. |

| | |
|---|---|
| Pearson, S. C. | 1952 v. IL. |
| Quixall, A. | 1959 v. SL. |
| Roberts, C. | 1905 v. SL; 1907 v. SL; 1909 v. SL; 1911 v SL. |
| Rowley, J. F. | 1948 v. LI; 1952 v. IL. |
| Sadler, D. | 1971 v. IL; 1972 v. LI. |
| Scanlon, A. | 1960 v. IL. |
| Silcock, J. | 1921 v. SL,IL; 1926 v. SL. |
| Spence, J. W. | 1926 v. IL. |
| Stepney, A. C. | 1968 v. SL; 1970 v. SL. |
| Stiles, N. P. | 1965 v. SL; 1966 v. SL; 1968 v. SL. |
| Sutcliffe, J. W. | 1898 v. SL; 1903 v. SL. |
| Taylor, T. | 1956 v. IL; 1957 v. LI. |
| Viollet, D. S. | 1957 v. LI; 1959 v. LI; 1960 v. LI. |
| Wall, G. | 1909 v. IL; 1910 v. SL; 1912 v. IL. |
| Whalley, A. | 1913 v. IL. |
| Wood, R. E. | 1955 v. LI, IL; 1957 v. IL. |

# Appendix 8

## MISCELLANY

### COLOURS WORN BY MANCHESTER UNITED F.C.

| | |
|---|---|
| Until 1896 | green and gold shirts |
| 1896 – 1902 | white shirts and blue shorts. |
| 1902 – 1923 | red shirts and white shorts. |
| 1923 – 1927 | white shirts with red 'V', white shorts. |
| 1927 – 1934 | red shirts and white shorts. |
| 1934 – | white shirts with cherry hoops, white shorts (latter half of 1933 – 1934). |
| 1934 – | red shirts and white shorts. |

### SOME ATTENDANCE FIGURES

AT CLAYTON

| | | |
|---|---|---|
| September 13, 1902 | League match v. Burton United | c. 20,000 |
| September 5, 1903 | League match v. Bristol City | c. 40,000 |
| March 4, 1906 | F.A. Cup<br>(4th Round) v. Woolwich Arsenal | c. 30,000 |

AT OLD TRAFFORD

| | | |
|---|---|---|
| February 19, 1910 | League match v. Liverpool | c. 50,000 |
| February 4, 1911 | F.A. Cup<br>(2nd Round) v. Aston Villa | 65, 101<br>(£2,464 4 10) |
| April 26, 1911 | F.A. Cup (replayed Final)<br>Bradford City v. Newcastle United | 56,607<br>(£3,487 0 0) |
| March 9, 1912 | F.A. CUP<br>(4th Round) v. Blackburn Rovers | 59,300<br>(£3,114 5 0) |
| October 18, 1919 | League match v. Manchester City | 49,360<br>(£3,039 15 0) |
| February 26, 1920 | League match v. Sunderland | 58,661<br>(£4,823 0 0) |
| January 31, 1920 | F.A. Cup<br>(2nd Round) v. Aston Villa | 48,600<br>(£4,283 9 8) |
| December 26, 1920 | League match v. Aston Villa | 70,504<br>(£4,824 0 0) |

| | | |
|---|---|---|
| March 24, 1923 | F.A. Cup (Semi-Final)<br>Bolton Wanderers v. Sheffield United | 73,000<br>(£7,593 10 0) |
| March 25, 1939 | F.A. Cup (Semi-Final)<br>Wolverhampton Wanderers v.<br>Grimsby Town | 76,962<br>(£8,193 0 0) |

Since the Second World War the attendance capacity has fluctuated between 55,000 and 67,000 until 1977 when Government safety measures limited the gate to 58,500.

## POST-WAR RECORD ATTENDANCES

### AT MAINE ROAD

| | | |
|---|---|---|
| January 1, 1949 | League match v. Arsenal | 82,950 |

### AT OLD TRAFFORD

| | | |
|---|---|---|
| February 22, 1958 | League match v. Nottingham Forest | 66,123 |

## RECORD ATTENDANCES IN AWAY MATCHES

| | | | |
|---|---|---|---|
| February 26, 1949 | F.A. Cup (6th Round) | Hull City | 55,019 |
| April 19, 1952 | Division One | Blackpool | 39,118 |
| January 5, 1957 | F.A. Cup (3rd Round) | Hartlepool | 17,426 |
| January 26, 1957 | F.A. Cup (4th Round) | Wrexham | 34,445 |
| March 2, 1957 | F.A. Cup (6th Round) | Bournemouth | 28,799 |
| October 28, 1967 | Division One | Nottingham Forest | 49,945 |
| February 3, 1969 | F.A. Cup (4th Round) replay | Watford | 34,099 |
| October 8, 1969 | Division One | Southampton | 31,044 |

## AVERAGE ATTENDANCES – POST-WAR

| | | | | | |
|---|---|---|---|---|---|
| 1946 – 47 | 43,615 | 1957 – 58 | 45,583 | 1968 – 69 | 51,121 |
| 1947 – 48 | 53,660 | 1958 – 59 | 53,258 | 1969 – 70 | 51,115 |
| 1948 – 49 | 46,023 | 1959 – 60 | 47,288 | 1970 – 71 | 44,754 |
| 1949 – 50 | 41,455 | 1960 – 61 | 37,807 | 1971 – 72 | 45,999 |
| 1950 – 51 | 37,159 | 1961 – 62 | 33,490 | 1972 – 73 | 48,623 |
| 1951 – 52 | 41,870 | 1962 – 63 | 40,317 | 1973 – 74 | 42,712 |
| 1952 – 53 | 35,737 | 1963 – 64 | 43,753 | 1974 – 75 | 48,388 |
| 1953 – 54 | 33,637 | 1964 – 65 | 45,990 | 1975 – 76 | 54,750 |
| 1954 – 55 | 34,077 | 1965 – 66 | 38,456 | 1976 – 77 | 53,710 |
| 1955 – 56 | 38,880 | 1966 – 67 | 53,984 | 1977 – 78 | 51,938 |
| 1956 – 57 | 45,192 | 1967 – 68 | 57,759 | | |

## RECORD SCORES

### IN LEAGUE MATCHES

October 15, 1892
Newton Heath 10, Wolverhampton Wanderers 1.
March 9, 1895
Newton Heath 14, Walsall 0.
April 3, 1895
Newton Heath 9, Walsall 0.
March 19, 1969
Manchester United 8, Queens Park Rangers 1.

### IN F.A. CUP

1897 (Qualifying Round 4);
Newton Heath 7, West Manchester 0.
November 1, 1902 (Qualifying Round 3)
Manchester United 7, Accrington Stanley 0.
January 13, 1906 (1st Round)
Manchester United 7, Staple Hill 2.
January 14, 1928 (3rd Round)
Manchester United 7, Brentford 1.
February 12, 1949 (5th Round)
Manchester United 8, Yeovil Town 0.
February 7, 1970 (5th Round)
Northampton Town 2, Manchester United 8.

### IN EUROPEAN CUP

September 26, 1956 (Preliminary Round)
Manchester United 10, R.S.C. Anderlecht (Belgium) 0.

## TOP LEAGUE SCORERS OF ALL TIME

| Goals | Player | Season |
|---|---|---|
| 32 – | Dennis Viollet | (1959/60) |
| 30 – | Jack Rowley | (1951/52) |
| | Denis Law | (1963/64) |
| 29 – | Bobby Charlton | (1958/59) |
| 28 – | Denis Law | (1964/66) |
| | George Best | (1967/68) |
| 26 – | Jack Rowley | (1946/47) |
| | Bill Whelan | (1956/57) |
| 25 – | Tommy Taylor | (1955/56) |
| | Sandy Turnbull | (1907/08) |
| 24 – | David Herd | (1965/66) |
| 23 – | Jack Rowley | (1947/48) |
| | Denis Law | (1962/63) |
| | Denis Law | (1966/67) |
| 22 – | Tommy Taylor | (1953/54) |
| | Tommy Taylor | (1956/57) |
| | John Spence | (1927/28) |
| | Stan Pearson | (1951/52) |
| 21 – | Dennis Viollet | (1958/59) |
| | Bobby Charlton | (1960/61) |
| | George Mutch | (1935/36) |

## PLAYERS WHO HAVE SCORED TEN OR MORE GOALS IN A SEASON FOR MANCHESTER UNITED SINCE THE WAR

1946/47 Jack Rowley 26, Stan Pearson 19.
1947/48 Jack Rowley 23, Johnny Morris 18, Stan Pearson 18.
1948/49 Jack Rowley 20, Charlie Mitten 18, Stan Pearson 14.
1949/50 Jack Rowley 20, Charlie Mitten 16, Stan Pearson 15.
1950/51 Stan Pearson 18, John Aston 15, Jack Rowley 14, Johnny Downie 10.
1951/52 Jack Rowley 30, Stan Pearson 22, Johnny Downie 11.
1952/53 Stan Pearson 16, Jack Rowley 11.
1953/54 Tommy Taylor 22, Jackie Blanchflower 13, Jack Rowley 12, Dennis Viollet 11.
1954/55 Tommy Taylor 20, Dennis Viollet 20, Jackie Blanchflower 10.
1955/56 Tommy Taylor 25, Dennis Viollet 20.
1956/57 Billy Whelan 26, Tommy Taylor 22, Dennis Viollet 16, Bobby Charlton 10.
1957/58 Dennis Viollet 17, Tommy Taylor 16, Billy Whelan 12.
1958/59 Bobby Charlton 29, Dennis Viollet 21, Albert Scanlon 16, Warren Bradley 12.
1959/60 Dennis Viollet 32, Bobby Charlton 17, Alex Dawson 15, Albert Quixall 13.
1960/61 Bobby Charlton 21, Alex Dawson 16, Dennis Viollet 15, Albert Quixall 13.
1961/62 David Herd 14, Albert Quixall 11.
1962/63 Denis Law 23, David Herd 19.
1963/64 Denis Law 30, David Herd 20.
1964/65 Denis Law 28, David Herd 20, John Connelly 15, Bobby Charlton 10, George Best 10.
1965/66 David Herd 24, Bobby Charlton 16, Denis Law 15.
1966/67 Denis Law 23, David Herd 16, Bobby Charlton 12, George Best 10.
1967/68 George Best 28, Bobby Charlton 15, Brian Kidd 15, John Aston 10.
1968/69 George Best 19, Denis Law 14.
1969/70 George Best 15, Brian Kidd 12, Bobby Charlton 12.
1970/71 George Best 18, Denis Law 15.
1971/72 George Best 18, Denis Law 13, Brian Kidd 10.
1972/73 —
1973/74 —
1974/75 Stuart Pearson 17, Gerry Daly 11, Lou Macari 11.
1975/76 Stuart Pearson 13, Lou Macari 12, Sammy McIlroy 10.
1976/77 Gordon Hill 22, Stuart Pearson 18, Lou Macari 14, Jimmy Greenhoff 12.
1977/78 Gordon Hill 19, Stuart Pearson 15, Lou Macari 11.

## MAJOR TRANSFERS – POST-WAR

IN

| | | | | |
|---|---|---|---|---|
| 1945 – 46 | J. Delaney | From | Glasgow Celtic | £4,000 |
| 1948 – 49 | J. Downie | ,, | Bradford P.A. | £18,000 |
| | T. Bogan | ,, | Preston N.E. | £5,000 |
| 1949 – 50 | R. Wood | ,, | Darlington | £5,000 |
| 1950 – 51 | R. Allen | ,, | Q.P.R. | £11,000 |
| | H. McShane | ,, | Bolton Wand. | exchange for J. Ball |
| 1951 – 52 | J. Berry | ,, | Birmingham City | £25,000 |
| 1952 – 53 | T. Taylor | ,, | Barnsley | £29,999 |
| 1957 – 58 | H. Gregg | ,, | Doncaster Rovers | £23,500 |
| | E. Taylor | ,, | Blackpool | £8,000 |
| | S. Crowther | ,, | Aston Villa | £18,000 |
| | T. Heron | ,, | Portadown | £5,000 |
| 1958 – 59 | A. Quixall | ,, | Sheffield Wednesday | £45,000 |
| 1959 – 60 | M. Setters | ,, | West Bromwich Albion | £30,000 |
| | A. Dunne | ,, | Shelbourne | £3,500 |
| 1960 – 61 | N. Cantwell | ,, | West Ham United | £22,000 |
| 1961 – 62 | D. Herd | ,, | Arsenal | £35,000 |
| 1962 – 63 | D. Law | ,, | A.C. Torino | £115,000 |
| | P. Crerand | ,, | Glasgow Celtic | £56,000 |
| 1963 – 64 | G. Moore | ,, | Chelsea | £35,000 |
| 1964 – 65 | J. Connelly | ,, | Burnley | £56,000 |
| | P. Dunne | ,, | Shamrock Rovers | £10,000 |
| 1966 – 67 | A. Stepney | ,, | Chelsea | £55,000 |
| 1968 – 69 | W. Morgan | ,, | Burnley | £95,000 |
| 1969 – 70 | I. Ure | ,, | Arsenal | £80,000 |
| 1971 – 72 | M. Buchan | ,, | Aberdeen | £125,000 |
| | I. Storey – Moore | ,, | Nottingham Forest | £200,000 |
| 1972 – 73 | W. Davies | ,, | Manchester City | £65,000 |
| | E. MacDougall | ,, | Bournemouth | £200,000 |
| | T. Anderson | ,, | Portadown | £12,500 |
| | G. Graham | ,, | Arsenal | £120,000 |
| | A. Forsyth | ,, | Partick Thistle | £100,000 |
| | J. Holton | ,, | Shrewsbury Town | £80,000 |
| | M. Martin | ,, | Bohemians | £15,000 |
| | L. Macari | ,, | Glasgow Celtic | £200,000 |
| | G. Daly | ,, | Bohemians | £12,000 |
| | R. O'Brien | ,, | Shelbourne | £15,000 |
| 1973 – 74 | P. Roche | ,, | Shelbourne | £15,000 |
| | S. Houston | ,, | Brentford | £50,000 |
| | J. McCalliog | ,, | Wolves | £60,000 |
| 1974 – 75 | S. Pearson | ,, | Hull City | P. Fletcher plus £170,000 |
| | S. Coppell | ,, | Tranmere Rovers | £40,000 |
| 1975 – 76 | G. Hill | ,, | Millwall | £70,000 |

| | | | | |
|---|---|---|---|---|
| 1976 – 77 | A. Foggon | ,, | Middlesbrough | £25,000 |
| | C. McGrath | ,, | Tottenham Hotspur | £30,000 |
| | J. Greenhoff | ,, | Stoke City | £120,000 |
| | A. Grimes | ,, | Bohemians | £20,000 |
| 1977 – 78 | J. Jordan | ,, | Leeds United | £388,888 |
| | G. McQueen | ,, | Leeds United | £495,000 |

## MAJOR TRANSFERS – POST-WAR

OUT

| | | | | |
|---|---|---|---|---|
| 1948 – 49 | J. Morris | To | Derby County | £25,000 |
| 1951 – 52 | C. Mitten | ,, | Fulham | |
| 1959 – 60 | F. Goodwin | ,, | Leeds United | £15,000 |
| 1960 – 61 | A. Scanlon | ,, | Newcastle United | £18,000 |
| 1961 – 62 | A. Dawson | ,, | Preston N.E. | £18,000 |
| | D. Viollet | ,, | Stoke City | £25,000 |
| 1963 – 64 | J. Giles | ,, | Leeds United | £37,500 |
| | M. Pearson | ,, | Sheffield Wednesday | £22,500 |
| | P. Chisnall | ,, | Liverpool | £30,000 |
| 1964 – 65 | M. Setters | ,, | Stoke City | £30,000 |
| 1966 – 67 | J. Connelly | ,, | Blackburn Rovers | £40,000 |
| 1971 – 72 | N. Stiles | ,, | Middlesbrough | £20,000 |
| | F. Burns | ,, | Southampton | £45,000 |
| | A. Gowling | ,, | Huddersfield Town | £65,000 |
| | J. Aston | ,, | Luton Town | £30,000 |
| 1972 – 73 | C. Sartori | ,, | Bologna | £40,000 |
| | E. MacDougall | ,, | West Ham United | £170,000 |
| | D. Law | ,, | Manchester City | |
| | T. Dunne | ,, | Bolton Wanderers | |
| 1973 – 74 | D. Sadler | ,, | Preston N.E. | £25,000 |
| | J. Rimmer | ,, | Arsenal | £40,000 |
| | R. O'Brien | ,, | Notts County | £40,000 |
| 1974 – 75 | B. Kidd | ,, | Arsenal | £110,000 |
| | T. Anderson | ,, | Swindon Town | £25,000 |
| | J. McCalliog | ,, | Southampton | £45,000 |
| 1975 – 76 | W. Morgan | ,, | Burnley | £32,000 |
| | M. Martin | ,, | West Bromwich Albion | £25,000 |
| 1976 – 77 | A. Foggon | ,, | Sunderland | £30,000 |
| | J. Holton | ,, | Sunderland | £75,000 |
| | G. Daly | ,, | Derby County | £188,888 |
| | G. Hill | ,, | Derby County | £275,000 |

# Index